*The Racial Integration of the
American Armed Forces*

The Racial Integration of the American Armed Forces

Cold War Necessity, Presidential Leadership, and Southern Resistance

Geoffrey W. Jensen

University Press of Kansas

Published by the University Press of Kansas (Lawrence, Kansas 66045), which was organized by the Kansas Board of Regents and is operated and funded by Emporia State University, Fort Hays State University, Kansas State University, Pittsburg State University, the University of Kansas, and Wichita State University.

Library of Congress Cataloging-in-Publication Data

Names: Jensen, Geoffrey W., 1975– author.

Title: The racial integration of the American armed forces : Cold War necessity, presidential leadership, and Southern resistance / Geoffrey W. Jensen.

Description: Lawrence, Kansas : University Press of Kansas, [2023] | Includes bibliographical references and index.

Identifiers: LCCN 2022056005 (print) | LCCN 2022056006 (ebook)
ISBN 9780700635313 (cloth)
ISBN 9780700635290 (paperback)
ISBN 9780700635306 (ebook)

Subjects: LCSH: United States—Armed Forces—Minorities—History—20th century. | United States—Armed Forces—African Americans—History—20thcentury. | Race discrimination—United States—History—20th century. | United States—Race relations—History—20th century.

Classification: LCC UB417 .J46 2023 (print) | LCC UB417 (ebook) | DDC 355.008/0973—dc23/eng/20221123

LC record available at https://lccn.loc.gov/2022056005.
LC ebook record available at https://lccn.loc.gov/2022056006.

British Library Cataloguing-in-Publication Data is available.

Printed in the United States of America

10 9 8 7 6 5 4 3 2 1

The paper used in this publication is acid free and meets the minimum requirements of the American National Standard for Permanence of Paper for Printed Library Materials Z39.48-1992.

In Memoriam

This book is dedicated to my friend and deceased colleague, Robert H. Berlin, the beloved long-serving Executive Director of the Society for Military History, whose kindness, dedication to his students, and love for the historical profession and the field of military history have shaped me profoundly.

Contents

Illustrations

Preface

From the early years of the republic to the Cold War and beyond, African American citizens and civil rights leaders labored tirelessly to ensure that the Black man would have a fair shot at American military service. It was not enough, however, to serve as stevedore or in the motor pool—no, the Black military personnel *needed* to serve in combat. Why would Black men seek war and the terrible, tumultuous, and destructive combat it sowed? They sought it because they were American citizens, even if they were treated and often lived in a second-class manner, who honored the Western notion of being a member of society, an obligation that required military service from its male citizenry during times of peril. Though an intellectual battle has been waged over when this idea—the importance of citizen service to one country—first originated in American history, the fact remains that it did. It was not an idea unique to the citizenry alone. The federal government, if not the military apparatus that served it, which *needed* the voluntary or conscripted service of its citizens to fill the billets and the ranks during times of calamity, expected and counted on it.[1]

For Black Americans, military service was not only a societal requirement as part of a larger civic duty one must honor; it also provided them with a critical opportunity: the chance to use military service, especially in combat, as a means to prove the merits of their race to white America. War after bloody and costly war, even when little racial progress was achieved, the African American community continued to line up to atone for the social and racial crime of being Black in America. Disappointingly, but no less unsurprising, white America ignored the Black sacrificial offering that was continuously being placed before the altar of American society.

The African American community's desire to achieve racial equality in society also motivated them to seek it within the military. Military service has always offered the prospect for the poor or downtrodden an opportunity at a better way of life. African Americans and the leadership recognized this reality; it was partly, along with the desire of serving in combat to racially prove themselves, a justification for military service. But serving in a racially segregated military, while seeking equality outside of it, made little sense. In their quest for racial reform of American society, they reasoned that the racial integration of the armed forces, which presumably meant they would serve equally with whites, would demonstrate not only their toughness on the battlefield but also their ability to work cohesively with white Americans.

For those who have studied the history of African American military service, this strategy for equality and all the wildly oscillating moments that accompanied it, from brutal heartbreaking refusal to change to bitter gradualism to triumphant reform, is well known and timeless, as it originated with the birth of the republic and continues to this very day. During their investigation of this important aspect of the African American experience, scholars have emphasized the importance of the twentieth-century leaders of the growing American civil rights movement, such as W. E. B. Du Bois, Walter White, Whitney Young, Adam Clayton Powell Jr., and A. Philip Randolph, who drove racial reform of the military to the forefront. Though valuable to our understanding of the African American experience, the civil rights movement, and the racial integration of the American military, the historical narrative that developed from this point of view does not adequately explain an important aspect of the story, one that is equally as significant, is dominated by presidential action that occurred during the early decades of the Cold War, and made reform possible.

THE COLD WAR AND PRESIDENTIAL LEADERSHIP

As opposed to past American wars, the Cold War's length and omnipresent nature in society set the stage for the story of the racial integration of the armed forces to unfold. During the nearly thirty years of military racial reform under examination in this book, the *necessity* of World War II, but more important the Cold War, manifested in two intertwined ways that aided and abetted those seeking reform. On the one hand, the racial integration and reform of the military *needed* to occur to protect the nation's image during a largely ideological struggle. In this sense, as Mary Dudziak has observed, racially integrating American society and its military was about parrying the stinging rebukes of communist propaganda mills, overcoming the quips emerging among the various colored populations of the so-called Third World that criticized the deplorable racial situation in the United States, and demonstrating America's moral and ethical superiority as compared to the communist world. On the other hand, it was also about the actual *need* of the Americans, the self-anointed leaders of the free world, to field a fighting force capable of waging the Cold War against communist expansion. This meant that the old standby of the military—racial segregation, which had been repeatedly argued to be the most efficient use of manpower—was obsolete and inefficient. In a global struggle against the communist menace, the American military needed access to a larger manpower pool than a racially segregated one offered.[2]

If Cold War necessity served to set the stage for this drama to unfold, then it needed actors to bring it to life. The most important member of the cast was the president of the United States. No other American, then or now, wielded the constitutional power over the military than that which the commander in chief possesses. This power was not limited to the president's ability to send military personnel into harm's way; it included the ability to control the overall manpower makeup of the armed forces, an influence that the Congress, throughout its history, has largely respected and abided by. So while Congress could control the size of the American military throughout the Cold War, the racial composition of it was largely out of their purview. And, therefore, the president's power in this regard was absolute. In this study, all American presidents examined were aware they had this power. It often came down to whether they wanted to use it or not. If they did use it, there was little Congress or the military could do about it. For the latter, the hierarchical nature of the American military differed greatly from the separation of powers and checks and balances that exist within the civilian realm of the United States. As William Taylor observed, if a president decided to act in the military, their orders were fiat and were not to be rejected.[3]

During the Cold War, American presidents faced intense pressure and scrutiny. The domestic and international expectation was that they would do all that they could and more to thwart communist expansion throughout the world. If there was one commonality for the headliners of the story of the racial integration of the armed forces—whether it was Harry S. Truman, Dwight D. Eisenhower, John F. Kennedy, or Lyndon B. Johnson—it is that they all rely, at one point or another, on the Cold War to provide them domestic and international cover for their racial reform efforts in the military.

They were not, though, equal in their usage of it as a justification for action. The president who did it the most was Harry Truman. When Truman, the president largely responsible for beginning the racial integration and reform of the military, established Executive Order 9981, he tied the issue directly to the fight against global communism. As the first American president in the nation's history to address the National Association for the Advancement of Colored People (NAACP), Truman wed the issues of halting global communism and how the failure to do so impacted negatively American international reputation with the importance of achieving domestic civil rights reform at home. He knew, and admitted as such, that what he asked would be a tall order, but Truman believed during the Cold War that it was a necessary request, one that if achieved would be worthwhile for all:

The way ahead is not easy. We shall need all the wisdom, imagination and courage we can muster. We must and shall guarantee the civil rights of all our citizens. Never before has the need been so urgent for skillful and vigorous action to bring us closer to our ideal.

We can reach the goal. When past difficulties faced our Nation we met the challenge with inspiring charters of human rights-the Declaration of Independence, the Constitution, the Bill of Rights, and the Emancipation Proclamation. . . . With these noble charters to guide us, and with faith in our hearts, we shall make our land a happier home for our people, a symbol of hope for all men, and a rock of security in a troubled world.

Over the years, and to varying degrees, Truman's successors followed his lead and relied on Cold War rhetoric to justify their actions within the military.[4]

LEADING FROM THE TOP

However, for racial integration of the armed forces to be successful, it needed more than just Cold War justification. It required what the presidential historian Jon Meacham has observed is the willingness and ability of the president to lead from the "top." This does not mean that the rationales for presidential leadership were always universal or consistent. Each president was unique and was motivated to action, or nonaction, by personal or political rationales that were unique to each. Tempering presidential power also affected the leader who proceeded this era of reform, President Franklin D. Roosevelt, and the man who came at its end, President Richard M. Nixon. For those presidents that did act, they did so for a wide range of reasons: everything from political gain to morality to pressure from the Black community as well as the domestic and international pressure the Cold War brought upon them.

Leading from the top also did not mean that the president always had to have a burning desire to act or had to be directly involved in any action committed to achieve success, though these certainly helped. Sometimes, all that mattered was that the commander in chief got on board and supported the work of his experts and staff. Though President Dwight D. Eisenhower had experienced a change of heart on the issue of racial integration of the military from his time as Supreme Allied Commander Europe during World War II to that of president of the United States, he was not the era's most stalwart champion of racial reform. Yet the fact he got behind it, regardless the reason, made all the difference during his presidency. A gradualist at heart, Eisenhower was often motivated by the barbs not of communists but of domestic critics who pointed out his administration was failing him on the issue of racial reform in the military. The results of his decision to act are staggering, as he completed the racial integration began by Truman and expanded it to include the racial desegregation of dependent schools on base and the Veterans Administration Hospital system, which ended racial discrimination in its care of veterans. So regardless of why they did it, when presidents committed to action—whether it was Truman, Eisenhower, or Johnson—action could be swift, far-reaching, and impactful.[5]

Throughout this period of reform, presidents were often assisted behind the scenes by teams of dedicated advisers, presidential staffers, and the devoted civilian servants of the War Department and the Department of Defense, who shouldered much of the burden of change. The contributions of these reformers were especially critical, as they often embodied the heart, mind, and soul behind the racial reform of the military. While their drive and desire for change was formidable, they lacked the power of the office of the president to go much farther than achieving low-level change. When staff willingness was present and a push for reform existed, such change was impressive. But when presidential leadership was inconsistent and sometimes absent, as during the so-called Second Reconstruction of the John F. Kennedy administration, that inconstancy trickled down to the leadership of the military. As a result, reforms were humbler and less impactful during Camelot's reign. They were, in a word, gradual.

THE MARTIAL SOUTH

If this is a story about Cold War necessity, presidential protagonists, and diligent foot soldiers who shepherded reform into place, it is also one about segregationists in the South and their conservative allies throughout the country who harbored the greatest trepidation over the racial integration and reform of the military and American society. It is, therefore, also a tale of a desperate Southern resistance against racial reform of the armed forces that echoed aspects of its martial spirit, its adoption of the tenets of the Lost Cause as a social gospel, the distrusting and conspiratorial nature of the region, and the unleashing of a force—nationwide civil rights reform—that they believed was deliberately aimed at ending the Southern way of life.

The South has long identified itself as a region of military spirit and unmatched martial prowess. Southern swagger about its military capabilities owed to its unique nature, John Hope Franklin contended. As Franklin explored the antebellum backdrop of the South before the Civil War, he discovered a mix of several social crosscurrents that converged to pull the region toward a militant identity. Part of that identity owed to its rugged frontier ethos, where whites hunted, fished, and trapped to survive but also feared, whether always necessary or not, war with Native Americans, which fed a personal belief, or perhaps insecurity, demanding that they needed to always be prepared for war. It was also a region that embraced ideas about a boisterous, distinctly Southern form of honor and masculinity, one they were always willing to back up at a moment's notice. In a region full of fighting, dueling, and a hypersensitive view of preserving one's honor, Southern masculinity was not just about protecting the family, especially women of the family, but their own self-dignity and standing in society. Finally, the South believed that slavery, although a necessary evil, was a hard sin for the region to break. Perhaps more vexing to them than the sin of slavery was the idea that outsiders, or "others"—namely, Northern abolitionists—dared to end the "peculiar institution" that lay at the heart of Southern society.[6]

These feelings and others eventually propelled the South into war with the North. Writing a little over two weeks after the Southern attack on Fort Sumter, Sir William Howard Russell, a correspondent for the *London Times*, spoke about the militant identity of the region, devoting considerable space to a description of the slave-planting elite in Charleston, South Carolina:

These gentlemen are well-bred, courteous, and hospitable. A genuine aristocracy, they have time to cultivate their minds to apply themselves to politics and the guidance of public affairs. They travel and read, love field-sports, racing, shooting, hunting, and fishing, are bold horsemen, and good shots. But, after all, their state is a modern Sparta— an aristocracy resting on a helotry, and with nothing else to rest upon. . . . Their whole system rests on slavery, and as such they defend it. They entertain very exaggerated ideas of the military strength of their little community, although one may do full justice to its military spirit.[7]

After its defeat in the Civil War, though the "helotry" of slavery was gone, the idea of the South as a new Sparta remained.

The reason it lived on was thanks to the efforts of the Lost Cause school of Southern history. Born during the era of Southern Redemption and the rise of Jim Crow racial segregation, the Lost Cause school culturally, socially, and historically whitewashed the region of its scandalous past. It provided a convenient out for white Southerners as to the region's culpable responsibility for the perpetuation and expansion of slavery, the responsibility for the initiation of the Civil War, its loss during that same war, a defeat that they considered to be a noble one, and its righteousness maintaining of the Southern way of life, one that celebrated white over Black. Though slavery was dead, the South ensured that the idea of white superiority over Blacks lived on societally, culturally, religiously, and militarily. Furthermore, the Lost Cause school's interpretation of the past guaranteed that Southerners' memory of post–Civil War occupation and Reconstruction never faded.

It also reinforced something that W. J. Cash and other students of the South had discovered about the region. From the time of slavery onward, the American South has seen itself as different, better, and in some regards purer than others. This conspiratorial distrust of others—while Southerners focused on the North in this regard, it would also include those whom they deemed to be liberal, socialist, or communist; the South, then and now, sees little difference in these terms—was reinforced first by the events that unfolded during Reconstruction and, in the twentieth century, by the events of the civil rights movement and the racial integration and reform of the military.[8]

Civil rights reform and other ideas deemed to be too liberal exacerbated the persisting lack of trust among Southerners for all ideas coming from outside its regional milieu. As much as the Cold War provided a good bit of cover for presidents to act, it also afforded opponents of the racial reform of American society a justification to rally around to fight against those efforts. This led to linking racial reform in the military and society to the authoritarian behaviors of the nation's most feared foe: global communism. Akin to the actions of communists in Russia and China who forced reforms on their respective populations, Southerners and conservatives believed that federal reforms that elevated the African American community trampled on their individual rights as American citizens. In a word, they thought they were "communistic."

To be sure, a good bit of red-baiting was used by Southern politicians to stoke fear among their voters as well as to combat racial reform efforts in American society and its military. But the use of anticommunist rhetoric should not overshadow the ongoing fears of the region about the spread of communism. While most feared the red menace, many Southerners obsessed about it and believed that something more egregious and conspiratorial was afoot. For those who felt this way, they believed that the racial integration of the armed forces was part of a larger sinister plot cooked up by a wicked and vile consortium of commies, liberals, and, for some, in anti-Semitic fashion, Jews hell-bent in their desire to subvert the South and the country. This unfounded fear was, as the esteemed political historian Richard Hofstadter observed, an example of the paranoid style of American politics in action, a style that relies on the idea that a "vast and sinister conspiracy, a gigantic and yet subtle machinery of influence [was] set in motion to undermine and destroy a way of life." As Hofstadter further explained:

The paranoid tendency is aroused by a confrontation of opposed interests which are (or are felt to be) totally irreconcilable, and thus by nature not susceptible to the normal political processes of bargain and compromise. The situation becomes worse when the representatives of a particular political interest—perhaps because of the very unrealistic and unrealizable nature of their demands—cannot make themselves felt in the political process. Feeling that they have no access to political bargaining or the making of decisions, they find their original conception of the world of power as omnipotent, sinister, and malicious fully confirmed.

Over the years to come, Southern white politicians, racist white soldiers, and conservative civilians throughout the South and the country labored under the idea that the end was nigh and that they had to fight against conspiratorial communist domination. To do so, some turned to extralegal activity—namely, joining the Ku Klux Klan; others voted for politicians who would defend the existing racial hierarchy of the region and subsequently wrote to them when things were not going their way racially, while others created all-white organizations (such as the White Citizens' Councils) and protested vigorously the racial reform underway in the military and in the country.[9]

To ensure that they were always on top of the alleged wretched activities happening in America, they also consumed a steady diet of the conspiratorial served daily to them from conservative Southern politicians, Southern newspapers, conspiratorial pamphlets, conspiratorial books, and other so-called news outlets. And by taking part in this echo chamber of conspiratorial confirmation, white Southerners believed that what they were doing in fighting against the racial progress underway in the military and American society was the right thing and that it would save themselves, their country, and especially their region and its way of life from certain communist downfall and destruction.

There were also personal interests at stake for some Southerners because of a unique change that occurred in the military during the twentieth century. Once President Woodrow Wilson, a Southerner by birth, had cast the nation's lot with those in Europe seeking to defeat the Triple Alliance during World War I, the United States Army had to work to get itself prepared for war. A war it was not ready for. The Army had spent the better part of three decades waging the Indian Wars, taking part in the tedious job of frontier and shore-line defense, and on occasion was used to end strikes during labor disputes. It had last seen serious action during the Spanish–American War, and it was ill-prepared for conflict with aggressor nations sporting large, conscription-based armies. To get the American military into fighting shape, the federal government built thirty-two new bases across the country; sixteen were in the South. For the military, the Southern installations gave them what they had always wanted: training installations that offered more time to train. The climate in the South appealed to the military because of its warmer weather compared to the North. That did not mean that placing a post in, say, Mississippi did not bring with it difficulties—namely, humidity, heat, and the insects and animals that thrived therein—but it would allow the military the opportunity to train year-round.[10]

But by placing half of the new bases in the South, the military was working toward the consummation of a deeper marriage to the region, one Wilson, through his political actions, which reflected his personal racism and bias on the matter, helped to achieve. During the United Confederate Veterans twenty-seventh reunion in 1917, an event held in the nation's capital that included marching Confederate veterans, among the onlookers cheering them on was Wilson. This was not surprising. He was, after all, a son of the South and was a boy when the Confederacy was defeated, which meant he came of age during the Lost Cause school's rise in Southern culture. As president, Wilson had aided in bringing Jim Crow to the federal government and the armed forces. He would also screen *The Birth of a Nation*, the Ku Klux Klan and white supremacy propaganda film, in the White House. And after celebrating the return of the veterans of the failed Confederacy to Washington, DC, Wilson would travel to Arlington National Cemetery to pay his respects to their war dead at the recently erected Confederate Memorial.[11]

After World War II, the movement of military installations to Dixie only continued. In a very real way this was a boon economically for the South, as it brought jobs, opportunities, industries, and presumably new customers from the bases into the local communities that flanked installations. And to be sure, the arrival of the bases continued to bolster the South's unique military pride and spirit. But it also meant the introduction of large amounts of African American troops who were armed and trained in the intricacies of using such weapons into the region, which for some white Southerners was a terrifying prospect. Slavery may have been vanquished, but the fear of a Black uprising was not. Sometimes white Southerners' worst racial fears turned into reality. In Texas, first in Brownsville and then a decade later in Houston, terrible racial incidents involving white citizens and Black soldiers occurred. Of course, the South conveniently ignored the reasons behind these clashes between the races and instead focused on the clash itself. Perhaps the only thing keeping Southern emotions in check was the fact that their social experiment of Jim Crow racial segregation, an experiment that was supported by much of the leadership of the military, remained the norm.

But once the world wars ended and racial integration of the armed forces unfolded during the Cold War in earnest, the lynchpin of Southern confidence—racial segregation—was removed; Southern fears and concerns, based on old racial stereotypes remaining from slavery, came flooding out. Powered by their distrust of outsiders, adamant that a conspiracy against them was afoot, and fearful of the effect that racial integration of the military would have on the African American community in the South or what would happen when empowered Black soldiers left base, Southerners appealed in a voluminous and desperate fashion to their racial champions in Congress who had fought for decades to maintain Jim Crow in the military. In turn, these political operators dutifully applied pressure throughout the racial integration and reform of the armed forces on presidents, staffs, the War Department, the Department of Defense (after it was established), and all branches of the military.

This, then, is the story of the racial integration of the armed forces, a remarkable reform period that occurred during the Cold War. One that was fought out between two domestic opposition groups who absolutely believed in the essential nature of their cause in the preservation of American society, as they conceived it, against communism.

ORGANIZATIONAL STRUCTURE

The Racial Integration of the American Armed Forces is organized chronologically and follows the story of the racial integration of the armed forces from 1940 to 1970, an astonishing thirty-year period of reform. Chapter 1 sets the stage for the narrative. In general, it traces the history of Black military service to the republic and the development of the concept within the African American community that service in the military was not only beneficial for Blacks but also necessary for their cause of equality. Specifically, African Americans believed that, by serving in the military, ostensibly in combat units, they would be able to prove their racial and societal worth to white America.

Whether white America, let alone white American presidents, always rewarded this sacrifice on the behalf of the Black community was another matter altogether. In particular, the Black community learned to become skeptical of white men of power, who often said one thing during times of war but later betrayed those notions. The most famous example of this was Theodore Roosevelt, who heaped praise on African American military personnel during the Spanish–American War, only later to lie about them and deny them the valor they deserved. Furthermore, Roosevelt was responsible for one of the most controversial moments in all African American military history when he hastily discharged, as opposed to deeply investigating and exploring the racism that underpinned the matter, the entirety of the 25th Infantry Regiment, one of four historic all-Black units, because of his desire to display his authority as commander in chief after the events of the Brownsville Affair.

As the Indian Wars of the West drew to a hasty and tragic end, the United States turned its gaze toward Europe, where turmoil bubbled to the top. Led by the Southerner Wilson, the United States reluctantly entered World War I and equally reluctantly turned toward Black military personnel, who were agitating to join the fight. Their involvement in the war in Europe came with mixed results for African American soldiers. Those who served in the 93rd Division found a semblance of equality and respect, while those who fought in the 92nd Division grappled with racism and rejection and unfairly shouldered the blame for the unit's military shortcomings.

When Black soldiers came home, they were not welcomed with open arms but instead with the noose of Judge Lynch. The lynching and otherwise terroristic abuse of African Americans during the Red Summer of 1919 only highlighted a growing reality for the Black community: military service alone would not guarantee them equality. Still, Black families and their loved ones continued to wager that a life in the military was better than one outside of it, and they doubled down on the idea of military service serving as a bridge to racial equality inside and outside the military.

The remainder of chapter 1 focuses on World War II and the efforts African American civil rights leaders such as A. Philip Randolph made to achieve desegregation of the military. Randolph, though, found his efforts frustrated by the actions and decisions of another Roosevelt: President Franklin D. Roosevelt. Unwilling to put himself in a precarious position with an important voting demographic of the New Deal coalition, the South, let alone to rock the nation as it steamed into international conflict, Roosevelt ducked the problem of racism in the military until Randolph forced the issue. Pressure from Randolph, and from within the White House itself by way of First Lady Eleanor Roosevelt, drove the president to make changes in the military and the larger defense community supporting it. The most impactful action, aside from the creation of all-Black fighting units that fought in the war, was the establishment of Executive Order 8802, which prohibited discrimination within the defense industry. No small measure, Roosevelt's order, though, failed to address the long-term issue of continued racial segregation within the military.

Despite FDR's reluctance to act, the armed forces were forced by events to adapt to the realities of conflict. Namely, they had a Black problem. For example, the United States Navy had a war hero in Dorie Miller that it did not want or wanted to use to attract more African Americans into the service. Meanwhile, the Marine Corps acquiesced and allowed Blacks in the ranks, but it never seriously thought about using them in combat roles.

The most confounding branch of the armed forces on the issue of racial integration might have been the Army, which had among its units the Tuskegee Airmen and the Black Panthers of the 761st, both wildly successful. It had also made news by the temporary and limited racial integration of its fighting forces during the Battle of the Bulge, which halted Adolf Hitler's desperate gamble to reverse the tide of the war in Western Europe. Once the guns fell silent at the conclusion of the war, the Army remained hesitant to integrate its ranks. So it did what it always did: launched a study to explore the idea. Though the results of that study demonstrated positives, Army leadership, including Generals George Marshall and Omar Bradley, decided against proceeding forward with racial integration. Instead, they, along with much of the conservative leadership of the branch, maintained that for the time being the best course of action would be to maintain racial segregation. As for the report and its findings, it was entombed within the files of the Department of the Army, where it would remain out of the hands of those who could use it against the Army's embrace of Jim Crow.

While the Army worked toward maintaining racial segregation, the successor to FDR as president, Harry Truman, faced off against Axis propaganda that targeted America's racism in society and the military. It was a problem, Truman would discover, that would continue during the Cold War.

Chapter 2 begins with the story of Sergeant Isaac Woodard, who was savagely blinded by racist white Southern police officers, and works its way into President Truman's decision to end racial segregation in the military. While a confluence of rationales existed for why Truman should do it—politics, morality, and his adherence to the United States Constitution—the necessity of combating Russian criticism of the American way of life during the Cold War became the most consistent rationale he invoked. Compared to the image that has been painted in recent historical works, Truman proves to be a committed actor in the racial integration of the armed forces. His approach, though, relied heavily on delegating the matter to a specially formed committee, one populated with civil rights advocates, to ensure that racial reform of the military occurred. By the time of the Korean War, Truman's committee had worked with the Navy and United States Air Force (now a separate branch, having replaced the Army's air corps) to achieve significant progress, but it struggled to achieve much movement within the Army and the Marine Corps.

Though Truman's efforts netted great gains, his equality-of-opportunity approach and those of his successors, meant that the racial integration and reform of the military never truly, or willingly, faced racism present within the ranks. Instead, it delt with the symptoms of systemic racism and lack of opportunity that existed—but not racism itself.

Chapter 3 examines how racial integration proceeded during America's first "hot" struggle of the Cold War: Korea. Though the protection of America's international reputation often carried the day during the thirty-year odyssey to racially integrate and reform its military, the physical needs of conflict also played a part as it forced the most unwilling branches of the armed services, the Army and Marine Corps, to finally embrace Truman's order. While both services, and their integration efforts, are covered, most of the analyses revolve around the situation as it unfolded in the Army.

Racial integration did not merit complete acceptance in the Army, and therefore the movement to racially integrate the branch was not widespread or embraced by all within it. Instead, it started gradually, as some American commanders on the ground in Korea began to integrate their forces out of necessity of waging war; it made little sense to these leaders to leave perfectly capable and willing Black men in uniform on the sidelines when they could be used to halt North Korean and Chinese communist aggression. Furthermore, the notion of an American army in Korea, staffed entirely by American personnel, especially when considering the American Eighth Army, was largely not true. The Americans relied on an influx of Korean personnel to be combat operational. Racial integration of the Army in Korea therefore aided the larger effort already underway to ensure there was a capable fighting force to begin with.[12]

Those on the ground in Korea agitating for change found allies back home. Army commanders in the United States who were running training facilities also racially integrated their commands. They did so because of their basic need to make the indoctrination and training process of the military more streamlined and economically efficient. What becomes clear about those leaders, domestically and in Korea, who led the effort to change the Army was that, though some might have held personal reasons for acting, their effort to drive change was never solely about morality but practicality and necessity; in other words, they did it because the needs of the war demanded that they do it.

Neither was the racial integration of the military always carried out in a positive light; thus, racial integration in the Army also took place in Korea because some white commanders questioned the quality and capabilities, based on perceived racial inadequacies, of some all-Black combat units. The prevailing example was the all-Black 24th Infantry Regiment, which famously secured the first American victory at Yechon but later fell to shambles and fled during a clash with communist forces at Battle Mountain (Hill 625). Blame for the unit's downfall was placed solely on its Black personnel as opposed to its white cadre of officers. Shortly after the incident at Battle Mountain, and out of an effort to restore discipline in the unit, a series of hasty military trials were held that centered on the charge of fleeing in the face of the enemy. The punishments proved to be excessive and unfair, as white service personnel charged with similar offenses received far lighter sentences than their Black compatriots in the 24th Regiment.

To investigate the situation, the NAACP, with Truman's blessing, dispatched its top lawyer, Thurgood Marshall, to the Far East. As he probed, Marshall discovered that racism emanated not only within the leadership of the 24th but with the overall commander of American forces, Douglas MacArthur. MacArthur's racial ambivalence and blatant bigotry created a leadership vacuum at the top that slowed the racial integration efforts of those commanders below him who believed that change was necessary to achieve victory.

The problem was ultimately resolved by MacArthur, himself, as he ran afoul of the president and was removed from command. Truman then tabbed a former army paratrooper, Matthew Ridgway, to assume command of American forces. Ridgway, whose morality and personal Christian ethos motivated him to act, accepted the tide of momentum already underway and placed the weight of his command behind the racial integration of the Korean command.

Chapter 3 also focuses on Project Clear, a study launched during the war that gauged the potential of racial integration and remaining resistance to it in the military and society. The researchers of the study discovered that some opposition to racial integration of the military existed throughout the United States but was most concentrated in the American South. In its conclusion, and despite the objections of Southerners, the report considered racial integration of the Army in Korea to be successful. As a result, the Chief of Staff of the Army, General Joseph "Lightning Joe" Collins, who read the report and who was an advocate for reform, ordered the complete racial integration of the Army.

Though General Dwight D. Eisenhower had temporarily integrated troops during the Battle of the Bulge during World War II, he had maintained the belief at the end of his military career that racial segregation of the military offered African Americans the best chance at success. In testimony before Congress, he warned that, if the armed services racially integrated, Blacks, who had not been afforded the same opportunities educationally and socially as whites, would not be able to compete with their white counterparts, which would be detrimental for the Black community.

Though he did not seek to be a hero in the South for his statement, Eisenhower was hailed as such during President Truman's bid to racially integrate the military. Once he occupied the White House in his own right, and with the presence of the Cold War ever-present, however, President Eisenhower did not reverse course. Instead, he continued to carry out racial reform in the military and was goaded by civil rights leaders and the Black press to move even further than his predecessor on the issue. Chapter 4 interprets these developments and discovers that, despite his half-hearted commitment to general civil rights reform, Eisenhower's racial reform accomplishments in the military were staggering: they stretched from the racial integration of on-base dependent schools to the end of segregation in the Veterans Administration Hospital system.

The first half of chapter 5 examines the limited scope of reforms accomplished during the so-called Second Reconstruction of the John F. Kennedy administration. During his short-lived presidency, the New Frontiersman was focused more on waging the Cold War than anything else. On the surface, this might make it appear that Kennedy would become a stalwart advocate for reforming the military. But he instead often demurred. The president became engaged in reforming or redressing racism in the military only when it was necessary to protect America's, and his administration's, democratic image to the rest of the world. As opposed to being a fulcrum for reform, the president instead delegated the issue to those members of his staff more sympathetic to and nuanced in civil rights matters. The golden rule of this arrangement was that any advances they achieved could not impair the president's ability to govern elsewhere. When it did, or if it was perceived that it would, Kennedy halted their efforts.

In the second half of chapter 5, Lyndon Johnson enters the stage. Flawed, egotistical, and insecure, Johnson was simultaneously a political bully and a dovish proponent of civil rights reform. Where Kennedy hesitated to act, Johnson would not. For that matter, neither would Johnson's staff, many of whom were holdovers from Kennedy's administration. Inspired and impowered by Johnson's desire to "put the coon skins on the wall and not just talk and promise and then make big speeches," his staff went to work. This led to many victories for Johnson: the Civil Rights Act of 1964, the Voting Rights Act of 1965, and the Civil Rights Act of 1968. These wins dominate popular understanding of the president's contributions to the quest for African American civil rights, but they often overshadow his impressive gains in the military, which included the racial integration of the National Guard and the end of racially segregated housing off base.[13]

Chapter 6 explores the racial turmoil within the armed forces during the Vietnam War that threatened the unity and effectiveness of the American military. At the root of the problem was the approach that had been taken to achieve racial integration. Racial reform of the military had occurred because of fiat, and though it achieved tremendous benefits for Blacks, the gains depersonalized the scope of the issue. Put simply, the racial integration of the military was treated by some white officers and military personnel just like any other regulation to be followed. As such, the white leadership of the military and its white personnel simply followed the regulations, which meant they never contemplated what it meant to be Black in Vietnam or America.

African Americans continued to join the ranks of the military during the Vietnam War, with many opting for the added pay that came with combat duty; they still saw it as a better way of life for themselves and their families than the alternative. This, along with the continuing systemic racism in the draft and among the draft boards, led to a growing problem for the military: the fact that its Black military personnel disproportionately served in combat units and disproportionately died while in those units as compared to whites. Furthermore, little was done about the racist whites coming into, or who were already present in, the military. And while some whites challenged the flying of the Confederate flag over the hooches of racist personnel, many others did not. The military's leadership also failed to understand African American personnel culturally or socially. Even on the simplest tasks, the military fumbled. Throughout the war, the armed forces failed to consistently provide barbers that could cut African American personnel's hair correctly. To an extent, this racism was sometimes overcome by those whites sympathetic to their fellow Black soldiers, but more often than not it led to the solidification of African Americans against racist whites whom they served with but did not trust.[14]

Perhaps most conspicuous, the white leadership of the military ignored, or did little to mollify, what it labeled the "new breed" of Black soldier who had emerged in the 1960s. Black military personnel of this era proved far less tolerant of the abuse their predecessors had faced. This failure often led to the growth of tremendous distrust in the billets, barracks, and ships of the

American military. But it sometimes also led to violence between white and Black military personnel in the United States and Vietnam.

Working in the background was the Johnson administration, waging a losing war that was sapping the Great Society program and the military alike. In what amounted to the last great surge of racial reform in the military during this period, Johnson launched a controversial social reform program (named "Project 100,000") that intertwined the War on Poverty with Johnson's war in Vietnam. The brainchild of President Johnson, Secretary of Defense Robert S. McNamara, and presidential adviser Daniel Patrick Moynihan, Project 100,000 was an honorable but terribly flawed attempt to go to war with poverty, specifically among the Black community, by enlisting them in the American military. Though criticized then and now by those who felt it was nothing more than an audacious plan to kill off Black youth, Project 100,000 provides the final example of how the influence of the Cold War on the racial transformation of the military reached its troubling zenith, not just rhetorically but in its need for manpower since Korea and prior to and during Vietnam.

Rounding out chapter 6 is a brief examination of Richard Nixon's leadership, the end of Project 100,000, and the embrace of a military and political cure-all for the new president, who desperately wanted to end the war in Southeast Asia and silence his critics on the political left: the end of the draft and the creation of the All-Volunteer Force. Like Kennedy, Nixon was one for political optics; but unlike his predecessor (as when Kennedy, in the eleventh hour of his life and presidency, seemed to evolve on the issue of American racism), Nixon never seemed to care enough to change his mindset. Though Nixon himself was a card-carrying member of the NAACP, he never felt Blacks were good enough and often disparaged them behind closed doors with other white men of power and influence, which included a future president, Ronald Reagan.

The conclusion, read in tandem with the epilogue, examines more recent developments in this long-running story, contending with the power and limits of reform achieved in the name of wartime necessity. It also examines the importance of presidential leadership and the vital role that staffs of chief executives play in ensuring that reform is carried out. Additionally, *The Racial Integration of the American Armed Forces* discusses the obstinance of the South and the role it plays politically—then and now—in shaping the American military. Finally, it contends that further racial reform of the military, unlike yesterday, remains important today as America wrestles with the offspring of the racist demons and sins of its past.

Acknowledgments

From my graduate training at the University of Arkansas to my current post as Associate Professor of History for the College of Arts and Sciences at Embry-Riddle Aeronautical University, Prescott, this work has been a daily part of my life. It is my sincere hope that those who study Southern history, presidential history, race in the military, and War and Society history will find it useful to their efforts. Equally, I hope it is beneficial to students and the layperson who might be interested in this subject. But you must know something up front. Though I am responsible for the information, facts, and opinions that are presented here, I simply could not, and have not, done this alone. It took many contributions from others to bring it to you.

I remain grateful to Randall B. Woods, my doctoral adviser who encouraged me, so many years ago, when I had no idea about what to write about, to pursue first a dissertation and then later a book understanding the racial integration of the armed forces. Equally, I remain grateful to those who served on my dissertation committee, Calvin White and Daniel Sutherland, whose advice, especially the latter, then and in recent years, helped me in my development as a scholar and a professional.

At Embry-Riddle, I was fortunate enough to work under the auspices of leadership dedicated to my growth as a scholar. Here, I think mostly of my time in the College of Security and Intelligence Studies under the guidance of the College's Founding Dean, Philip Jones, and my department chair at the time, Thomas Field, who saw to it that I received funding and, critically, time to think, research, and write, whether it was on sabbatical or during the regular academic year.

I remain grateful to my deceased Embry-Riddle colleague and friend Robert H. Berlin. Bob's dedication to the field of Military History, his enthusiasm for his students, and his energy were infectious. When my wife and I first came to Prescott, we were wayward Southerners far from home. Bob took us in and made us feel welcome. From that point on, he was gracious with his time with me and supportive of my growth. Frankly, it was something I witnessed him do repeatedly every year during the Society for Military History Annual Conference. Bob gave his time to all of us, including myself, who were new in this profession and who were desperately trying to figure out our professional left from our right. I have dedicated this volume in his memory. He was a passionate and caring soul that was taken far too soon and meant so much to so many.

Special thanks also go to Leanne Harworth, reference librarian extraordinaire at the Hazy Library on the campus of Embry-Riddle, Prescott. Her ability to acquire, at almost a moment's notice, the obscure article, journal, or book was impressive to say the least.

I have been blessed to work with Joyce Harrison and Bill Allison at the University Press of Kansas. Their upbeat attitudes, humor, and total confidence in me have enabled me to work in a free and unfettered fashion. During my journey with Joyce and Bill—and those who looked over the manuscript, including William Taylor, who graciously reviewed the work and offered tremendous suggestions; Adrian Lewis, whose insights offered a great deal of further clarity; Jon Howard, whose edits only improved the book; and Kelly Chrisman Jacques, who kept me on schedule—I felt like I was part of a team with a collective mission to produce the best possible work we could. I believe we have done just that.

Whether I was in person or online, that I had access to the documents to begin with owes to the diligent corps of archivists whose mission it is to preserve the echoes of the past. The contents of this book were directly influenced by the following archives and their archivists, whose working knowledge of their holdings and the historical characters involved enriched my efforts: the University of Arkansas Archives, the University of Mississippi Archives, the Mississippi State University Archives, the University of Georgia Archives, Clemson University Archives, the University of Indiana Archives, the United States Military Academy Archives, the US. Army Heritage and Education Center, the Library of Congress, the National Archives and Records Administration, the Abraham Lincoln Presidential Library, the Harry S. Truman Presidential Library, the Dwight D. Eisenhower Presidential Library, the John F. Kennedy Presidential Library, and the Lyndon B. Johnson Presidential Library.

Along these same lines, I received financial assistance over the course of this project from the Harry S. Truman Library Institute, the Lyndon B. Johnson Foundation, and Embry-Riddle. Their generous support enabled me to travel to some of the aforementioned libraries to complete critical research.

Over the years, a handful of colleagues and friends offered good advice and positive uplift as I toiled away on this project. I am particularly indebted to Matt Stith, my good friend and Arkansas alum, for his consistent support of my writing and his willingness, at differing points, to look over aspects of my work. I am equally grateful to Beth Bailey for her time, patience, and the moments where she served as a sounding board for me as I tried to figure out what it was that I was *actually* writing about. Her friendship and guidance over the years, whether it was on this manuscript or my development as a professional, have meant the world to me. I am a better scholar and professional because of her.

Heartfelt thanks go out to my beloved family. My wife, Beth, our daughter, Aurora, and our dog, Oscar, have all provided me, especially during the final leg of this intellectual marathon, with the energy and humor needed to bring it all together. They are my focus; they are my everything, and I remain steadfastly committed to them. This book is as much theirs as it is mine, as they paid the price of missed mornings, nights, and weekends while I was sequestered away researching or writing.

Lastly to my mother, who always believed that when I was motivated, focused, and confident in myself that I would discover whatever it was that I was meant to be. I believe I have. It is my sincere hope that I have made her proud, because I did it in the tradition of our family: hard work, unyielding determination to improve, a little luck, and a lot of humor and love.

—Geoffrey W. Jensen
Prescott, Arizona

The Racial Integration of the
American Armed Forces

A Faustian Bargain: White Presidents, Wartime Necessity, and the Black Pursuit of Civil Rights, 1770 to 1945

On December 8, 1941, one day after the attack on Pearl Harbor, United States Army leaders met with members of the African American press corps to showcase achievements on the racial front. The Army's goal for this long-anticipated conference was to improve relations with the Black press and the larger African American community. This proved a tall order. Over the years, the Black press and its readership questioned the unequal treatment of Black military personnel within the American armed forces. They were cynical for good reason: past treatment of African American soldiers and sailors had been scandalous and wasteful and unequal; Black personnel, it seemed, were second-class.

When considering the backdrop of the attack on Pearl Harbor, Ulysses Lee poignantly observed that emotions were no doubt high for all in the room. Indeed, as the Army and the Black press met, the Japanese attack on the Philippines was already underway. It would have been understandable if the Army's brass canceled the event altogether. But, instead, the Army decided to soldier on as it kicked off the meeting with a speech from its Chief of Staff and the eventual grand architect of Allied victory during the coming war, General George C. Marshall. During his remarks, Marshall highlighted the progress that the Army had made on the race issue. Its achievements included the recent creation of a handful of African American combat outfits, notably the 99th Pursuit Squadron, the beginnings of the famed Tuskegee Airmen, and the 758th Tank Battalion, which was the Army's first all-Black armored unit. Though noteworthy, the Chief of Staff lamented that more needed to be done. This personal aside of sorts by Marshall caught the attention of the Black press, who noted it at the time, and even years later Lee recalled the general's aside in his landmark study of the use of Black military personnel during World War II, *The Employment of Negro Troops*.[1]

Marshall's words were noteworthy for African Americans for a reason. Black Americans, though they lamented the racism of the military, had long believed a career within it, whether it was segregated or not, offered a substantial upgrade from the lack of opportunity many of their race faced outside of it. The leadership of the emerging twentieth-century civil rights community agreed, but they also saw an opportunity to gain something more for their race. They believed that military service, especially combat service during wartime, could help them make their race's case for equitable treatment in American society, which would lead to overturning Jim Crow segregation and usher in era of equality and acceptance between the races.

But those present to hear Marshall or, for that matter, those that read his words in the all-Black newspapers of the era, were not fools. After all, there was a long, terrible, and dramatic history of the thankless use of Black personnel when the nation *needed* them. Regardless of the era or time, once the calamity of the moment was over, the republic that had needed them ultimately failed African Americans horribly when it came to standing by them and doing something about the racism they faced. This sad observation underpins the long history of the employment of Black personnel and the quest to racially integrate the armed forces; it is where this story begins.

THE FUGITIVE SLAVE AND THE SLAVE OWNER

The opening chapter in this sad tale emerges with the American Revolution, specifically the saga of two linked men who never knew each other but who set the stage for the next two hundred and fifty years of American military history. One was a slave, Crispus Attucks, the other a slaveholder-turned-general, George Washington. Attucks had escaped bondage to become a sailor and on one faithful night in the city of Boston transformed from a former slave into a revolutionary patriotic martyr. What motivated this man on a cold night to join with strangers to assault British regulars? The historian Benjamin Quarles believed that Attucks was motivated by his surroundings and the democratic spirit within the air: "It could be said that Attucks was simply an unruly sprit who was looking for trouble. . . . Still, it is hard to believe he could have lived in Boston and not have been influenced by the general feeling against Britain. He must have heard that taxation without representation was tyranny, and perhaps such slogans had given a sense of personal grievance." Heinous though it was, the Boston Massacre of 1770 was not a battle, and therefore Attucks, who supposedly died for American freedom and perhaps for the liberty of his race, never actually served in the American armed forces. But his actions and death during that moment cemented a growing idea within the breast of the African community, one that had been brought to the colonies largely to be slaves: America was theirs, too. Perhaps by fighting for it they, too, would taste freedom.[2]

While Attucks died on the streets of Boston with his fellow patriots, Washington toiled under the awful weight of being the overall commander of a ragtag collection of American forces. Among the many decisions weighing on his brow was whether to use Black soldiers, free or enslaved, against the British, a dilemma that his successors in the military and the presidency would inherit. Much like his successors, Washington had to deal with an often unsympathetic and unhelpful Congress. Though it was no doubt busy coaxing the various states of the new union into motion, the newly established Continental Congress proved to provide the beleaguered Virginian with more obstacles than solutions to the question of using African Americans as soldiers.

When Washington asked the Board of War, the newly minted congressional committee, about whether he could use African American personnel, whether they were slave or free, the committee in short responded that their status mattered little and that he could not use them. The rejection seemed largely to revolve around the idea that they were Black, many were not free, and therefore the Continental Congress did not want its army to become a refuge for those slaves seeking their freedom. Additionally, and with a particular nod to the plantation owners, politicians, and slave owners of the American South, there was a genuine concern and fear about arming slaves. Sixty years earlier in North Carolina, Southern merchants and traders had warned against arming slaves. Their comments would stand the test of time in the South as it reinforced a terrible thought: arming Black men. The merchants cautiously observed that "there must be great caution used [in the military employment of negroes] lest our slaves when armed might become our masters."[3]

The problem was that there were already free Blacks serving within the ranks of the emerging colonial armed forces before Washington had even taken command. Free Blacks were racially integrated during the battles at Lexington and Concord, though they were not a part of the militia. Among those free Blacks fighting at Bunker Hill was Salem Poor, whose conduct and cool demeanor under fire earned him the respect of his white commanding officers and peers. And when the Congress prohibited them from continuing to serve, Washington heard about it from those free Blacks who had already fought for their country, and he felt compelled to try to keep them. In a moment of doing and asking for forgiveness later, Washington began to accept free Blacks into his ranks in late December 1775. The Congress would acquiescence to Washington, but only a little. Shortly after his action, it demanded that only those who had served in the army stationed at Cambridge, where Washington's headquarters was located, be allowed entry, but no one else, especially slaves.[4]

But *the necessity of the moment,* as it would time and again throughout this story, ended up forcing the Americans to do more. Their opposition, the English, in particular Lord Dunmore of Virginia, demonstrated no reservation, personal or political, to dipping into the available African manpower pool before him to fill his ranks and to undercut the efforts of those in rebellion against the Crown. Washington had warned John Hancock, then the president of the Congress, of the possibility of something akin to Dunmore's proclamation occurring and how it could bolster the British. When it happened, African Americans free and slave in Virginia, including three of Washington's slaves, rushed to join the Crown. Dunmore was an "archtraitor to the Rights of Humanity," an enraged Washington declared. Was Washington's bellicose bellyaching about the situation more personal—his loss of slaves to Dunmore's cause certainly hurt his pride and his pocketbook—or strategic concern for his country, an infant nation whose leadership had failed to understand the boon that Africans, free and slave alike, offered them? Regardless of the source of this aggravation, Dunmore's action motivated the Congress to act, and in 1776 it allowed all free Blacks to serve, minus the very young and old. But it also, with a nod to the American South, continued to prohibit the use of slaves.[5]

THE CIVIL WAR

With every American war, except for the Mexican–American War, the reoccurring theme of necessity established during the American Revolution returned. For example, thirty years after the Revolution, Andrew Jackson, though not commander in chief yet, needed and relied on African American soldiers to ward off the British invasion and conquest of New Orleans during the War of 1812. As the nation grew and barreled headlong toward the West, the issue of chattel slavery and its growth continued to fester until the outbreak of the Civil War. During that struggle, Abraham Lincoln and Frederick Douglass represented the continuation of the interlinked story of the needs of white men of power along with the Black man's desire for freedom and equality.

Though his efforts have cemented his image popularly as the Great Emancipator, Lincoln's issuance of the Emancipation Proclamation proved to be more than just a moralistic action designed to free the slaves. It was also a punishing, calculated, and cunning wartime maneuver by a deft commander in chief. In a single gesture, Lincoln, who had rebuffed the idea of using fugitive slaves in the military, changed course and instituted an action that undercut the financial institution, slavery, of America's opposition, the Confederacy, during a time of war. In effect, Lincoln, who had once thought of colonizing emancipated Blacks, decided to weaponize them to help the Union win.[6]

Frederick Douglass did not recoil from weaponizing the Black community; he had embraced it from the start. He simply lacked the executive power to carry out his desires. Still, Douglass had the power of his words when he spoke to white abolitionists, freed people, the president, and those trapped in bondage who might have been fortunate enough to hear or, if they could, read them: "Once let the black man get upon his person the brass letters, 'U.S.,'" Douglass proclaimed, "let him get an eagle on his buttons and a musket on his shoulder and bullets in his pocket, and there is no power on earth which can deny that he has earned the right to citizenship."[7]

Lincoln freeing the slaves, along with the Reconstruction Acts and the Thirteenth, Fourteenth, and Fifteenth Amendments to the Constitution, live on as pillars from which all future civil rights accomplishments are built upon, so, too, would Douglass's words live on as the rationale for Black citizens to serve in the American armed forces. No, Douglass's actions and agitations for Black combatants did not make them or their community believe they were Americans. For free Blacks, that process had likely begun decades earlier with the American Revolution and the ideas of democratic citizenship it brought with it. This was no longer about figuring out if they were American or not but instead about receiving the full benefits of that identity. Therefore, in Douglass's mind, military service was never simply about winning the Civil War; it was about how Blacks bled and sacrificed for that victory and how that justified full societal inclusion in American society.[8]

And so it went, from war to war, starting with Douglass but continuing onward. The belief was fostered annually within the African American community's leadership that if Blacks served in the military, especially doing so in the combat arms where their prowess and triumphs on the battlefield could not be ignored, they would earn a seat at the table in America. At best this was a questionable strategy that relied an awful lot on hope and the good will of the ancestors of those who had once enslaved them; at worst, it was a Faustian bargain that called for the need for war, the generational blood sacrifice of young Black men to fight in those terrible struggles, and the good will and appreciation of white men of power, most notably American presidents, who in the past had largely not budged on the issue of civil rights but who *now* would suddenly become so moved by the African American community's patriotic offering that they would reward it with equality. Whether it was a foolhardy pact with the devil or not, for a desperate, noble, and no less deserving people it was the hand that they chose to play. In reality, it was the only hand they had to play.

A TURN-OF-THE-CENTURY BETRAYAL

For an early-twentieth-century example of how this African American strategy played out, look to the relationship between the Black community and Theodore Roosevelt. The famed Rough Rider had praised African American military personnel while in combat against the Spanish in Cuba: "The Spaniard called them 'Smoked Yankees,' but we found them to be an excellent breed of Yankee. I am sure that I speak the sentiments of men and officers in the assemblage when I say that between you and the other cavalry regiments, there is a tie which we trust will never be broken." Years later, when he was on the campaign trail to become governor of New York, however, Roosevelt shredded that unbreakable bond. First in an article for *Scribner's Magazine*, which became the bedrock for his book *The Rough Riders*, he disparaged the shortcomings and abilities of the very same Black military personnel he had once exalted:

No troops could have *behaved better* than the colored soldiers had *behaved* so far; but they are, of course, peculiarly dependent upon their white officers. Occasionally they produce non-commissioned officers who can take the initiative and accept responsibility precisely like the best class of whites; but this cannot be expected normally, nor is it fair to expect it. With the colored troops there should always be some of their own officers. . . . None of the white regulars or Rough Riders showed the slightest sign of weakening; but under the strain the colored infantrymen (who had none of their officers) began to get a little uneasy and to drift to the rear, either helping wounded men or saying that they wished to find their own regiments. This I could not allow, as it was depleting my line, so I jumped up, and walking a few yards to the rear, drew my revolver, halted the retreating soldiers, and called out to them that I appreciated the gallantry which they had fought and would be sorry to hurt them, but that I should shoot the first man who, on any [pretense], wherever, went to the rear. . . . This was the end of the trouble, for the "smoked Yankees"—as the Spaniards called the colored soldiers—flashed their white teeth at one another, as they broke into broad grins, and I had no more trouble with them, they seeming to accept me as one of their own officers. [emphasis added]

Over a century later, Mark Lee Gardner's study of TR and the Rough Riders and their escapades in Cuba recalled the incident the newly minted governor had so vividly described in his tell-all. It turned out that Roosevelt had lied. The Black soldiers were not shirking their duty or acting cowardly. The display and threat of bravado-laden violence by Roosevelt was hotheaded, cavalier, and overblown. And he knew it because he was set straight by those on the ground who assured him that the men were not retreating. Recognizing his error, the Rough Rider apologized to the wrongly accused and their unit. The matter could have halted there, but it did not. The soon-to-be president's independent and outspoken daughter, Alice Roosevelt, once famously quipped about her father that it was never enough to attend the wedding, he had to be every bride; it was not enough to pay respect for the dead, he had to be every corpse; he always needed to be at the center of everything. Therefore, instead of upholding the praise he had once lavishly laid upon the Black soldiers he had served with, Roosevelt kept up the lie well after the guns of San Juan Heights had fallen silent.[9]

That lie did not go unnoticed within the African American community. In a letter to the editor of the *New York Age*, Presley Holliday, a member of the all-Black 10th Cavalry that had fought alongside Roosevelt and his Rough Riders, responded to the governor's claims about Black soldiers needing to be shepherded along by white commanding officers, let alone the dubious suggestion that they could be cowardly during battle:

In the beginning, I wish to say that from what I saw of Colonel Roosevelt in Cuba, and the impression his frank countenance made upon me, I cannot believe that he made the statement maliciously. . . . But did he know, that of the four officers of connected with two certain troops of the Tenth Cavalry one was killed and three were so seriously wounded as to cause them to be carried from the field, and the command of these two troops fell to the first sergeants, who led them triumphantly to the front?

I could give many other incidents of our men's devotion to duty, of their determination to stay until the death, but what's the use? Colonel Roosevelt has said they shirked, and the reading public will take the Colonel at his word and go on thinking they shirked.

It is telling that Holliday toward the end of his letter resigned himself to the fact that Roosevelt's account would be the one that the audience and history would remember. After all, Holliday was an African American private in the military daring to stand up to one of the heroes of the war who continued to reap favor from Holliday's service in it. What is also illuminating is the personal disappointment Holliday displayed as he chastised Roosevelt for saying what he did. "His statement was uncalled for and uncharitable," Holliday believed, "and considering the moral and physical effect the advance of the Tenth regiment, both at Las Guasimas and San Juan Hill, altogether ungrateful, and has done us an immeasurable lot of harm."[10]

During the campaign of 1900, where Roosevelt served as second fiddle to William McKinley on the Republican presidential ticket, the colonel's past commentary came back to haunt him and the White House ambitions of his party. So Roosevelt altered his story. Instead of admitting that he had misremembered the entire situation or that he had lied about it, he changed the story enough to shift blame from Black personnel to an unnamed white captain:

I had an order to hold a certain position and was supported by the Tenth Cavalry (colored). The position was uncertain and we needed every man available to make the stand. Two or three of the colored soldiers started to the rear in search of water as ordered by their captain. I rebuked the captain for lessening our force, and commanded the men to remain. The statement I made after that, as near as I can remember, was "I have orders to hold this hill and intend to do it. I will shoot any man that gives up this position." This is the whole story in a nutshell.

For some Black voters, Willard Gatewood observed, this was enough, as many felt that Roosevelt's words must have been an error of judgment, not open racism. For others who were more critical, Roosevelt's adjustment of the story and his praising of African American military personnel while on the campaign trail was self-centered malarkey designed to win Black votes. In a letter to the *Cleveland Gazette*, Harry C. Smith, an African American citizen from Cleveland, Ohio, declared that the Rough Rider had "manipulate[d] the race question in a way so as to magnify the name and greatness of himself, or to ingratiate himself into the good feeling of that class that might oppose his promotion [to vice president]."[11]

A couple years later, when he became president of the United States following McKinley's assassination, Roosevelt once again found a way to endear himself with the Black community—only to jeopardize it shortly thereafter. In his first year in office, Roosevelt invited Booker T. Washington, an African American man and noted civil rights leader, to dinner. While the dinner became a highlight for history books, the two men had conferred prior to the engagement and become quite familiar with one another, as they often discussed political matters. During their first meeting, Roosevelt teased the idea of jettisoning the presidential patronage of the past and instead suggested to Washington the idea of picking the best person for the job, regardless of color or political affiliation. In this process, Booker Washington would a play a key role, as he would advise and offer suggestions of officials to the president who were not racist or at the very least open to working with African Americans.

To an extent, this suggestion displayed the president's openness on matters of race, but Roosevelt was cautious in how he carried this out, as he was also thinking about building up a political base in the South for his own run at the White House in 1904.[12]

About a month after their first chat, Roosevelt invited Washington to dine at the White House with the president and his family. Would Roosevelt have invited any other Black man to the White House to dine with him? Unlikely, suggests his biographer, Edmund Morris. There was the political value of having Washington as an adviser while Roosevelt continued building his political standing in the South. That alone might have been enough for Roosevelt, but there was also the "aristocracy of worth" to consider. Roosevelt had a racial bias to him; his actions in Cuba and afterward provided ample evidence of it. Some of his feelings about race also came from his mother, Martha "Mittie" Roosevelt. Mittie Roosevelt was an unrepentant and unreconstructed Georgian who taught her son that most Blacks largely could not cut it in American society, that the right to vote that they were granted by way of the Fifteenth Amendment was a "mistake," and that "altogether [they were] inferior to the whites." Societal worth mattered to his mother, and it mattered to Theodore Roosevelt, and it affected how he viewed people.[13]

Booker T. Washington, though, was not what Roosevelt considered to be average—he was *special*. He had overcome slavery, race, and the difficulties of American life to ascend. The president, a voracious reader, had read Charles Darwin, Jean-Baptiste Lamarck, and Gustave Le Bon, whose theories and ideas cemented in Roosevelt's mind the potential for the societal advancement of the African American people, which neatly matched what his mother had taught him—that only a small few were worthy. Washington, then, was, to the president's eyes, at the vanguard of African American society. As such and much like Harry Truman decades later, Roosevelt had only a passing reservation about what he was doing, a feeling he quickly dismissed. He admitted to Albion Tourgée, a transplanted Ohio Republican who had led the abolitionist cause in North Carolina; "the very fact that I felt a moment's qualm on inviting him [Washington] because of his color made me ashamed of myself." With Roosevelt's brief qualm extinguished, he invited Washington to dinner, which went off without a hitch.[14]

The next day, however, when news of the historic dinner leaked out and made its way into the newspapers, Roosevelt was socially skewered and roasted over an open fire of Southern contempt and outrage. "BOTH POLITICALLY AND SOCIALLY," the *Atlanta Constitution* contended; "PRESIDENT ROOSEVELT PROPOSES TO CODDLE DESCENDANTS OF HAM. [THE] ACTION OF

[THE] PRESIDENT IS ROUNDLY CENSORED." While the *Atlanta Constitution* invoked the Bible, the *Memphis Scimitar* sought a more damning approach to its rebuke: "The most damnable outrage which has ever been perpetuated by any citizen of the United States was committed yesterday by the President when he invited a nigger to dine with him at the White House. . . . He has not [only] inflamed the anger of the Southern people; he has excited their disgust." Other Southern presses feigned sympathy. One put it this way: "Poor Roosevelt! He might now just as well sleep with Booker Washington, for the scent of that coon will follow him to the grave as far as the South is concerned."[15]

Especially grating and galling for the men and women of the white South was the potential for indecent racial mixing, as the president's daughter, Alice—young, white, pretty—was alleged to be in attendance; she was not. If it was not concern over Alice, it was concern over the sexual sanctity of Roosevelt's second wife, Edith. While the Southern press wailed and opined away about the Roosevelt women, one of the region's political leaders offered a frank and threatening assessment of the fallout of the president's actions. South Carolina Senator Ben Tillman declared: "The action of President Roosevelt in entertaining that nigger will necessitate our killing a thousand niggers in the South before they will learn their place."[16]

While Roosevelt weathered the lather of worked-up white Southerners, he received praise from Black citizens, including those from the South, who deemed him "our president." Indeed, the response from the Black community was overwhelmingly positive. An African American citizen from Tennessee believed the dinner was the "greatest step for the race in a generation," while another lauded Roosevelt's dining engagement with Washington "was a masterly stroke of statesmanship—worthy of the best minds this country has produced."[17]

Though the cheers from the African American community no doubt soothed such a wanting soul such as Roosevelt's, the rebuke that he had received equally harmed and hurt him. While attending Yale's bicentennial, an event where both Roosevelt and Washington, along with a handful of other notables, were set to receive honorary degrees, harm both physically and personally were on the president's mind. Prior to the event, the Secret Service counseled against the president's favored activity of exchanging pleasantries with the crowd and also prohibited the two men—Roosevelt and Washington—from sitting with one another. The fear was that their recent dinner and the uproar over it might induce an assassination attempt on the president. Roosevelt heeded their advice, but he began to brood.[18]

Later in the evening, Roosevelt was still brooding about the wound to his pride that came with criticism over his decision to dine with Washington. In that moment, he sought the refuge of counsel. His choice was a curious one: Mark Twain, who had also received an honorary degree along with Roosevelt and Washington. With respect to the president, though, it was questionable if the famed author *respected* the man who held the office. Privately, Twain later lashed out at the president's action as a display of Roosevelt's insatiable desire to be at the center of it all and that he only invited Washington "to advertise himself and make a noise." In the moment, Twain advised Roosevelt that the life of the president differed from that of the ordinary citizen. And therefore, the author surmised, who the president invited to dinner mattered more to some than to others. Though the president was free to do as he pleased, there was a political price to be paid in certain sections of American society—namely, the South—for inviting a Black man to dinner; and in this sense, Twain implied sagely, Roosevelt really was not free at all to do as he pleased.[19]

THE BROWNSVILLE AFFAIR

Colonel Ralph W. Hoyt, commanding officer of the all-Black 25th Infantry Regiment, had warned the War Department that moving the unit, which had fought on the American plains against Native Americans and waged war in Cuba and the Philippines, to Brownsville, Texas, where it would run straight into the buzzsaw of Southern racism, was a mistake: "It is useless to ignore or deny race prejudice which exists in spite of law and justice . . . and I desired as colonel of a most excellent regiment to express my disapproval and to inform and warn the authorities of conditions that are certain to arise from an encampment at Austin with Texas militia." Colonel Hoyt's warning, though, did not prevent the Buffalo Soldiers from heading to Fort Brown, located in the Lone Star State. The truth was that the trouble did not begin when they arrived; it began before they even arrived. A journalist and the man most responsible for the later exoneration of the unit, John D. Weaver, detected that an undercurrent of resentment of their presence—let alone a growing apprehension that the 25th Infantry was going to be a problem—was in the air. A white soldier whose unit was being moved out overhead citizens upset about the decision to bring an all-Black force to Fort Brown. One citizen appeared to be especially enraged and ready to leap into action, the white soldier recalled: "An old gentleman who was there made the remark that the first crooked move they [25th Infantry Regiment] would make they [the people of Brownsville] would annihilate the whole shooting match."[20]

After repeated indignities toward the soldiers ensued, tempers reached a boil when an African American soldier crossed the Rubicon of Southern values by failing to move aside for a white woman to pass. His attacker, a white male named Fred Tate, was a customs inspector who happened to witness the social atrocity and then proceeded to pistol-whip the soldier, Private James Newton. Afterward, Tate, who had allegedly questioned why the soldier had done what he had done, boisterously declared: "Get up and leave, or damn you I will blow your brains out. I'll learn you to get off the sidewalk when you see a party of white ladies standing there." A good bit of intrigue surrounds Private Newton and whether or not he was intoxicated during the incident. At first, the private lied when questioned if he had been drinking—he did have a reputation with some in his unit for drunken behavior—but later admitted to consuming alcohol: "Yes, sir; I drank, but not to an excess, sir." Fortunately for the bloodied Newton, his assailant allowed him to leave and did not attempt to lynch him.[21]

Eight days later, events finally boiled over along the Rio Grande River. An erroneous report disseminated on August 13 claimed a Black soldier had illegally entered a white woman's home and accosted her. This unfounded accusation led to an assault on Fort Brown later that evening by whites from Brownsville. A member of the 25th Infantry, Charles Edward Rudy, recalled hearing an unidentified white voice saying "come out, all you black nigger sons of bitches, and we will kill every one of you." At the end of skirmish, a white bartender was found dead by a stray bullet and a white police officer was badly injured; and though it could not be proven how many Black soldiers were involved, if involved at all, ammo casings and clips from Springfield rifles were found on the ground near Fort Brown, which implied—but did not prove definitively—that someone from the Army was involved in the fracas.[22]

When word got out about the incident, prudence—namely, the president seeking counsel from Secretary of War William Howard Taft—need not apply, as Roosevelt acted on his own merit to remedy the situation. Part of this was because the Brownville Affair, as it became known, occurred while Taft was traveling to Cuba. Since the president could not rely on his defense chief to immediately investigate, and having no desire to wait, Roosevelt turned to the Army's Office of Inspector General to get answers. In less than a week's time, Major Augustus Blocksom of the Inspector General's office sent his preliminary findings to the president. He noted the racism of the area and the town but gave little weight to the idea that local whites caused the incident. Instead, he pinned the blame on a handful of unnamed members of the Black unit. And with his investigation of the incident failing to extract names from the 25th

Infantry, a situation Blocksom viewed as those interviewed covering for their fellow personnel, he suggested to Roosevelt that the entire unit be "discharged from the service."[23]

"By George!," the Rough Rider was reported to have said after examining the information of the case. "The men's guilt is as clear as day!" With said guilt confirmed in his mind, the president saw to it that the unit was relocated to Fort Reno, Oklahoma, to avoid further complications. But he still wanted names. Roosevelt therefore dispatched the Inspector General of the Army, General Ernest A. Garlington, to the Sooner State to try one last time to obtain them. During Garlington's visit, he delivered a message from the president to the men: if they failed to give up the names of those involved, they would all be expelled from the Army. Despite this ominous warning, no one came forward. In a letter to Roosevelt, the Inspector General, mirroring the earlier council of his subordinate, recommended that the president discharge the entire unit. Garlington was aware that this action would likely be unfair to those who had no idea what happened; nonetheless, their unwillingness to speak seamed to form a measure of guilt in his mind, and "since they stood together [in silence] . . . they should stand together when the penalty falls." Roosevelt followed his suggestion and dishonorably discharged the entire unit, which had within its ranks, the biographer Doris Kearns Goodwin noted, Medal of Honor winners and veterans of America's wars of empire, including those who had served with then-Colonel Roosevelt in Cuba.[24]

When Secretary of War Taft returned, he faced a mountain of criticisms and concerns over the president's action. A lover of the law and the system that underpinned it, Taft was not sure that Roosevelt, his longtime friend, was doing the right thing. He encouraged the president to take the time to re-examine the case. "If a rehearing shows that the original conclusion was wrong," Taft cautiously continued, "it presents a dignified way of recalling it; and if it does not, it enforces the original conclusion." Roosevelt refused. When an old enemy within the Grand Old Party, Joseph Foraker, attempted to use the issue to weaken the president's standing in the party, Roosevelt lashed out. The president reminded Foraker, and the rest of Congress, for that matter, that "he was not only acting well within his constitutional rights, but that it was his duty to strip the uniform . . . [off] murders, assassins, cowards and the comrades of murderers." If Congress tried to stop him from discharging these men, he would continue to fight on. One way or another, Roosevelt threatened, the Black men of the 25th Infantry would never again shoulder arms for the Republic.[25]

Roosevelt's decision and punishment, much like his actions in Cuba, were impetuous, hotheaded, cavalier, and completely unnecessary; and just like in Cuba, he backpedaled a little bit. But this time he would do so privately, as he adjusted the parameters of the sanctions that he had levied against the unit. True to his nature, Roosevelt never publicly admitted fault for the damage he had done to one of the most historic African American regiments in the nation's history or the community that loved it so much. Perhaps only as he could, Roosevelt had taken the adulation of the African American community and thrown it all away—again. He had gone from being viewed as a racial deliverer in the image of "our Moses" to that of a political and racial swindler or simply, as some Blacks called him, "our Judas."[26]

In a flyer titled "Roosevelt's Hostility to the Colored People of the United States: The Record of the Discharge of the Colored Soldiers at Brownsville," the African American press took the irascible president to task for his action. "It is becoming more and more apparent to me every day," the editor of the *Washington Bee*, W. Calvin Chase, attested to his audience, "from one official utterance and then another, that President Roosevelt and his advisers are prejudiced against the negro and have no real love for him." For others, they felt that Roosevelt was behaving like a petulant adolescent and not as a rational leader. The *Baltimore Weekly Guide* editorialized that "the method pursued by the President [in dismissing the 25th] is unprecedented and childish," while the *Kentucky Standard* detected a bit of the dictatorial in Roosevelt: "We would scarcely expect the Czar of all the Russias or even Kaiser Wilhelm himself to take so high-handed a method in a matter of this kind."[27]

For the African American community, the bloom was off the rose with Roosevelt. "Certainly the Afro-American cannot but feel that even this idol has been thrown from its pedestal," the *Baltimore Afro-American Ledger* opined. The feelings expressed at the time would only compound over the years for the African American community, as the travesty of Roosevelt's actions was not rectified until 1972 during the presidential administration of another republican: Richard Nixon.[28]

THE HOUSTON RIOT AND WORLD WAR I

African Americans had to wait nearly seventy years to get justice in the Brownsville Affair. They did not have to wait nearly that long to experience the next moment of unfair and outrageous punishment toward an African American military outfit. This time it was the all-Black 24th Infantry Regiment, whose military recorded stretched from the Philippines to the US–Mexico border yet

bore the brunt of racial prejudice in the military. Once again, the incident occurred in Texas, this time in the port city of Houston.

In hindsight, the Houston Riot, or Camp Logan Riot, may not have been
preventable. And the reason for that was the nature of the situation, one where
white racism and the segregationist laws that empowered them reigned supreme. But the Army was going to do all it could to prevent its men from acting violently against the white citizenry of Houston. Upon arriving at Camp
Logan, the Black men of the 24th Regiment discovered that the Army was putting in place strict precautions, such as securing their weapons, to ensure that
a repeat of the Brownsville Affair could not occur. By adhering and appeasing
the cultural norms of the South, though, the Army had failed to learn from
the Brownsville Affair. Instead, by acceding to the needs of one group over the
needs of its own men, it may have ensured that racial violence would occur by
turning its back on the racism that its own men experienced.[29]

While all racial forms of prejudice proved difficult for African American
citizens to bear, for Black Houstonians the ordinance dictating segregated
streetcars proved especially galling. So, too, was it for the Black personnel of
the 24th Regiment, who felt that as defenders of the country they should not be
treated poorly. Racially insulted by the law, the men of the 24th openly defied
it. Further, they challenged anyone to do something about it. "[We] would just
love to see the first son of a bitch that would try to put them off [the streetcar],"
a group of men from the 24th proclaimed. But the Army was not having any
of it. The commander of the unit, Colonel William Newman, did not support
his men, downplaying the indignity to them and Black Houstonians; instead he
cautioned his men to respect the laws, including those pertaining to segregated
streetcar travel, and the customs of the region.[30]

With racism all around them, and with their commanding officer providing
little reassurance or support, the 24th's agitation grew. The stage was set for
mayhem. The Houston Riot began when a Black soldier dared to interfere in
the beating of a Black woman being detained by a white police officer. Once
the member of the 24th got involved, the white officer, Lee Sparks, turned his
scorn to the Black soldier and proceeded to beat him and haul him off to jail.
At this point another member of the unit, an African American military police
officer named Charles W. Baltimore, entered the fracas. Baltimore was off duty
and asked his fellow law enforcement professional about what had happened.
Sparks, likely offended by the presence of a Black police officer questioning
him about the situation, proceeded to assault him, chase him, shoot at him,
and ultimately apprehend him and drag him off to jail as well. Both Black soldiers were ultimately freed when their captain, Haig Shekerjian, a descendant

of Armenian parents, interceded. Shekerjian managed to get the charges, both trumped up, dropped, and charges were actually levied against Sparks, the white officer.[31]

As Bernard Nalty explained, Shekerjian's leadership and actions were notable, but it was too little and far too late for a decorated combat unit of men who had been treated as anything but human by those they swore to protect. It was estimated that at least a hundred men of the 24th marched into Houston seeking revenge for the racism of the area, the heinous actions of Sparks, and the supportive white community. Among them was Charles Baltimore, still seething from the unprovoked beating he had received hours earlier. The men of the 24th came face-to-face with Houston's white police force and a hastily assembled posse. The result was jarring for both the Black and white communities of the nation: sixteen whites, including four policemen, and one white military officer, Captain Joseph Mattes of the Illinois National Guard (who was mistaken for a white police officer), were killed, while the 24th lost four of their own during the skirmish.[32]

As with the Brownsville Riot, punishment was swift and unjust. However, unlike earlier, the Army seemed keen on avoiding the wholesale discharge of the unit. Instead, it charged fifty-four men for their involvement in the riot. Thirty-two faced life in prison for their actions, five were found not guilty, and four received lighter sentences—but they were no less punished, as they were still incarcerated and dishonorably discharged. The remaining thirteen were executed by hanging before Secretary of War Newton Baker or President Woodrow Wilson knew about it or had time to review the situation. Among those hung was Charles Baltimore.[33]

Though even more soldiers would be charged afterward for their involvement, Wilson finally interceded. He did so because Secretary of War Baker advised Wilson to do so as a means to lessen the damage being done with the African American community over the incident. The president's involvement resulted in a handful of sentences being commuted. Still, when all was said and done, six more men of the 24th were hung. Meanwhile, with no one present or powerful enough to check the racism of white Houstonians and officers of the law, such as Lee Sparks, the racism and violent acts of retribution toward Black Houstonians for the riot continued throughout the remainder of the year.[34]

President Wilson was no civil rights saint; he had once screened *The Birth of a Nation*—a propaganda film that served the efforts of the Lost Cause school of history and the Ku Klux Klan more than it did anything else—in the White House and had honored Confederate war dead. Despite these and other racial shortcomings, the president bowed to the growing political pressure from the

Northern Black community and the National Association for the Advancement of Colored People (NAACP) on the issue of allowing Blacks to serve during World War I. This led to the creation of a cantonment that trained Black officers and a handful of all-Black fighting units, including the most successful of the bunch, the 369th Regiment, best known as the Harlem Rattlers, who found tremendous success fighting alongside the French.[35]

Among the Rattlers were Private Henry Johnson and Private Neadom Roberts. During what became know to history as the "Battle of Henry Johnson," the pair repelled a patrol of twenty or more German attackers. For his gallant service to the country, Johnson was promoted to sergeant, awarded the Croix de Guerre from the French, and became a celebrity. But as his star rose, some sought to manipulate him. At the end of his life, one that had brought him great prestige and notoriety, Johnson was broken physically and had little money. He succumbed to myocarditis and died by the age of thirty-two. Decades later, only after substantial lobbying, Johnson would be awarded posthumously the Purple Heart, Distinguished Service Cross, and Congressional Medal of Honor.[36]

Whereas the 369th achieved greatness, the treatment of other all-Black outfits paled in comparison. The woeful tale of the 368th Regiment, a unit of the all-Black 92nd Infantry Division, is revealing. First, members were criminally undertrained. On the one hand, this is not all that surprising, historians have observed. Rushed into war, having to field an army that could rival those of Europe, and with little time to spare, the majority of American forces failed to live up to the training standards of their commander, General John J. "Black Jack" Pershing, who had once commanded African American troops in Cuba. But the 92nd Division's training was particularly bad. The division lacked not only time to train but also the equipment to do it with. The division was short on "[means of] transportation, no heavy machine guns or automatic rifles, no pistols . . . , no one-pounder guns (37mm), no mortars, no grenades, and [had] only one hundred rounds of rifle ammunition for each soldier." Its communications, because of the failure to establish a strong signal battalion in the field, were equally terrible. As for the division's ability to rely on the "King of Battle" (artillery), it, too, was lacking early on, as the artillery brigade was training elsewhere. Once the artillery rejoined the unit, it proved to be a credit, though it would take time to build cohesion.[37]

Other issues plagued the division, such as the way its area of operations, north of Saint Dié, was handed off to it by the French, who did not spend enough time informing their replacements about the situation on the ground. It also contended with the flagrant racism and ineptitude of its own white leadership, who believed the unit could not function or fight without them. These issues combined to lead to a systemic collapse of the 368th Regiment. The unit's struggles, though, do not tell the complete tale of the 92nd Division, as Robert H. Ferrell has claimed. For those inside and outside the armed forces opposing Black military service, however, the image of a flailing and troubled all-Black 92nd Division on the front in Europe proved their biases and became the sine qua non disfavoring Black combat participation in future American wars.[38]

COMING HOME TO RACIAL PERSECUTION

When African American soldiers returned to the States after serving in World War I, they did not find a nation waiting with open arms or delivering on the promise of equality but instead a nation that largely did not value their service. And in the South, they met white posses, with nooses, who were threatened by the powerful image of the Black man in uniform. Sometimes, the murder of a Black solider was even draped in the trappings of a supposedly civilized and law-abiding society. Often, African Americans veterans, such as Sergeant Edgar Caldwell, were lynched, the victims of "legal lynchings." Caldwell was a member of the 24th Infantry Regiment and found himself in a situation eerily similar to his fellow Black soldiers involved in the Houston Riot of 1917. As in Houston, the segregation of white and Black passengers aboard streetcars caused racial angst. On December 13, 1918, Caldwell had caught a ride on a streetcar in Anniston, Alabama—which was just south of Camp McClellan, where the 24th was stationed—headed for Hobson City, the Blacks-only part of Anniston. Though it existed because of racial segregation, Hobson City was a place where an African American, whether civilian or military, could relax and avoid, to the extent possible, the hassles, humiliations, and prejudices of the white racial customs inherent to Southern American towns.[39]

The sergeant's troubles began when he refused to move to the Blacks-only section of the car, which was something James K. Vardaman, Mississippi's seg-regationist senator, feared could happen during the era of World War I. Just months after America had decided to enter that conflict, Vardaman stood on the floor of the Senate and cautioned against the dangers of not only Black military service but also what their return to the Republic would mean. It would be a "disaster," he flatly stated. Those who supported the cause of African American civil rights believed in the power of military service to prove the race's worth. Vardaman recognized it as well. But he was not changing his tune about race in America; he foresaw a problem for the South, its racist cultural norms, and its continued facilitation of Jim Crow—and he planned to stop it. Now, the senator ascertained, the Black soldier, because he had served, would believe "that his political rights must be respected." It was a foolish and dangerous idea, Vardaman thought, as it elevated a race that did not merit equality; it would lead to problems, he believed, and perhaps even violence with whites in the South.[40]

The streetcar's white conductor, Cecil Linten, noticed Caldwell sitting in the whites-only section, and they began to quarrel. Linten accused Caldwell of hopping a ride without paying for it, which the Black sergeant denied. From there the matter escalated to fisticuffs as the conductor, now joined by the white motorman, Kelsie Morrison, assaulted Caldwell. Getting the better of the sergeant, they proceeded to beat him. Caldwell, no doubt fearing for his life, pulled his revolver from its holster and began to fire. At the end of the scuffle, Linten was dead and Morrison wounded. Apprehended by Anniston authorities, Caldwell was hastily sentenced to death for his actions and hanged in July 1919; the only reason for the delay in his punishment was the intervention of the NAACP on his behalf, which sought to but ultimately failed to exonerate him.[41]

Incidents such as Caldwell's became more and more frequent during the Red Summer of 1919, a time when African American civilians and veterans alike faced hostilities and atrocities. Roughly twenty-five anti-Black riots occurred during that summer, from the Midwest to the South to the East Coast. Prepared to meet this challenge were Black military veterans of World War I. No doubt aware that the uniform of the Republic was akin to putting a target on their backs, African American veterans never wavered in their commitment to fight against white prejudice. Nonetheless, they paid a heavy and fatal price for it. In Georgia, Daniel Mack, who had done nothing more than accidently touch a white man while trying to get around him, was assaulted, imprisoned, then removed from jail and nearly beaten to death. In Waxahachie, Texas, Ely Green was beaten for wearing the uniform of the Republic; had it not been for the aide of sympathetic white man, he would have been killed in his hometown for a being a Black American war veteran. To the south of Little Rock, Arkansas, sits Pine Bluff, where a Black soldier was lynched for failing to move out of the way of a white woman. In northwest Arkansas, in the town of Lincoln, Clinton Briggs, an African American veteran, suffered a similar fate for the same offense, as he had not done enough to get out of the way of an approaching white woman.[42]

MORALITY MEETS MILITARY EFFICIENCY

Aware of the long and troubling history of racial prejudice and abuse toward African American military personnel, the Black press had every right to be skeptical of General Marshall's reassurances at the press conference on the day after Pearl Harbor, another white man of power (exceptional power, in his case) in a long line who promised to do more and to do right by Black people. At the beginning of American military involvement in World War II, when patriotism was high, Marshall's words of regret may have carried some weight for the African American pressmen in the room, and their audiences outside of it, who sought to serve out of civic pride and racial ambition. It might have given them hope that the Army's leadership, starting with its top commander, was beginning to come around to the idea that it was no longer a matter whether *if* the branch was going to utilize Black soldiers as combatants against the nation's enemies but rather *when* that would occur. Could his words hint at the possibility of the Army going beyond merely allowing some Blacks to serve in combat roles?[43]

After Marshall spoke at the press conference, it was clear that Blacks would be utilized and, in some measure, see combat. But that was about all the Army and Marshall were willing to do. Any hope, no matter how remote or naïve, that the Army might racially integrate African Americans or support their quest for societal recognition was quashed. Roughly an hour after Marshall concluded his remarks, the Adjutant General of the Army, Colonel Eugene R. Householder, spoke candidly about the racial situation within the Army and the society it sought to protect. Reading from a prepared statement, Householder reaffirmed the Army's long-standing commitment to the philosophy of Jim Crow segregation within the ranks, which mirrored American society, in particular, and where many military reserves resided, as it existed in the South. As far as the Army was concerned, the issue of American racism was not its problem to rectify:

The Army did not create the problem. The Army is made up of individual citizens of the United States who have pronounced views with respect to the Negro just as they have individual ideas with respect to other matters in their daily walk of life. Military orders, fiat, or dicta, will not change their viewpoints. The Army then cannot be made the means of engendering conflict among the mass of people because of a stand with respect to Negroes which is not compatible with the position attained by the Negro in civilian life.

But there was more to Householder's flat rejection of the use of the Army as a sociological weapon against racism. With his mind likely on the events that

had just occurred on Oahu, which served only to reaffirm an old military notion about the perils of racial integration and the Army tackling social issues,
Householder clarified the Army's perspective:

The Army is not a sociological laboratory; to be effective it must be organized and
trained according to the principles which will insure [sic] success. Experiments to meet
the wishes and demands of the champions of every race and creed for the solution of
their problems are a danger to [military] efficiency, discipline and morale and would
result in ultimate defeat.

Note that Householder did not say *right now* the Army is not a sociological
laboratory. His rejection of the Army's use in this manner was not limited
to World War II but to the very premise itself. Neither was the colonel going
rogue as his superior, Marshall, looked on. Both men reflected the Army's conscience and need at that moment. While it faced tremendous pressure from the
political and powerful elites within the African American community to place
more Black men into combat units, the Army also *needed* Black personnel for
the coming war. But it was not going to racially integrate. Instead, it would do
the best it could or was willing to do, out of an effort to offer an olive branch to
a community that the Army needed. To do anything more, the Army and other
branches believed, would be dangerous.[44]

Why was the Army so resistant to racial reform or becoming an advocate of
it? Like any business worth its salt, the Army believed in sticking to the trade
it did best. That trade was warfighting. Everything else—racial issues, gender
discrimination concerns, and, in the years that came long after the guns in
Europe fell silent for the second time in the century, the issue of whether a
gay or lesbian or transgender person could serve openly—all got in the way
of what the Army and the armed forces believed they should be doing. The
historians Sherie Mershon and Steven Schlossman, in their study of the racial
integration of the military, recognized a perennial tactic that the military had
used to justify its opposition to racial reform. The leadership of the armed
forces claimed that reforms of this nature threated the "military efficiency"
of America's fighting forces. The insinuation was that racially intermixing
white and Black military personnel would lead to bedlam, disunion, infight-
ing, and ultimately, as Householder—after all, he had brought up "efficiency"
in his comments—contended, would contribute to the overall "defeat" of the
armed forces. To an extent, there may have been some genuine concern within
the military's leadership that the racial integration of the armed forces could
lead to mayhem. Still, the claim of protecting the "military efficiency" of the
armed forces did not stand up well against the test of past performances of

African American combatants, let alone those to come; ignored the inefficient nature and economic expense of embracing and maintaining a hallmark of the American South, Jim Crow segregation; and became seen more and more for what really was: a convenient excuse to prevent any racial reform from occurring at all.[45]

TO DEFEND DEMOCRACY

Despite the Army's blatant refusal to engage in the pursuit of equal rights for African Americans, civil rights leaders such as W. E. B. Du Bois continued to sell white America on how the disease of racism—most notably by way of lynching, the systematic limiting of African American opportunities for a better education, health care, and general way of life—caused the nation as a whole harm. The plan was to go right at the heart of American democratic idealism. Through the juxtaposition of American racism with the nation's idealism, first during World War I and again during World War II, civil rights advocates illuminated the hypocrisy of a democratic nation that could fight a war to make the world safe for democracy while it simultaneously continued to deny equality not only for a segment of its population but also for a segment that was actively fighting and dying for the nation.[46]

In 1939, *The Crisis*, the journal of the NAACP, published an editorial titled "Defending Democracy." Its author, Roy Wilkins, embraced the domestic potential for racial reform that was being brought about because of the calamitous situation unfolding in Europe:

Not since the World War has so much been said here about fighting for the rights of oppressed minorities, for equality, justice and freedom for the weak and outnumbered, for the privilege of all men to determine their destiny to the extent of their desire and ability. Never before has vicious racialism been so ridiculed and denounced. On the surface it would seem that a new day is in the offing for the disinherited. Colored Americans entertain the hope that this new-found zeal for democracy will find expression in a destruction of the barriers which surround them in this country. After all, democracy, like charity should begin at home.

The editorial also suggested that the prospect for a better tomorrow—one that witnessed the end of lynching, one that restored the voting rights of Black citizens in the American South, and one that ended Jim Crow segregation in all of its most nefarious of forms—could be domestically achieved for the African American community by way of victory in Europe. Furthermore, and as

Jonathan Rosenberg observed, this victory abroad could aid the American civil rights community's longtime pursuit of ending international bigotry toward colored peoples of the world.[47]

While civil rights leadership cultivated this message further, other organs of the African American civil rights apparatus picked up on this theme and ran with it. Famously, the all-Black newspaper the *Pittsburgh Courier* embraced an idea that originated from one of its readers, James G. Thompson. Pointing to the "V for victory" signage appearing across the world, Thompson appealed to Americans to heed his call for a "double victory":

The V for victory signs is being displayed prominently in all so-called democratic countries which are fighting for victory over aggression, slavery and tyranny. If this V sign means that to those now engaged in this great conflict then let we colored Americans adopt the double VV for a double victory. The first V for victory over our enemies from without, the second V for victory over our enemies from within.

. . .

This should not and would not lessen our efforts to bring this conflict to a successful conclusion: but should and would make us stronger to resist these evil forces which threaten us. America could become unified as never before and become truly the home of democracy.

Following Thompson's lead, the *Pittsburgh Courier* launched the "Double V campaign" and called for victory abroad against the forces of fascism and Japanese imperialism while also securing victory against the bigoted forces in America that denied African Americans equality.[48]

Though Black civil rights leadership continued to advocate fighting, and likely dying, to prove Blacks' worth, some leaders were not unaware of the fact that often their sacrifices had ended up in more racial prejudice than racial redemption. Therefore, if a bloodletting were to occur, it had to be for something more this time than just more empty promises from white men of power. Writing in *The Crisis*, Roy Wilkins observed: "Be it said once more that black Americans are loyal Americans; but let there be no mistake about that loyalty. It is loyalty to the democratic idea as enunciated by America and by our British ally; it is not loyalty to many of the practices which have been—and are still—in vogue here and in the British empire." It was time for the nation, Wilkins believed, to pay the bill for the past sacrifices of the Black community. But not just domestically. As he surveyed the era, Wilkins additionally thought that, if the United States sought to lead the world, one that was overwhelmingly colored and not white, it had to give up on Jim Crow. The civil rights leader surmised: "A lily-white navy cannot fight for a free world. A jim crow army cannot fight for a free world. Jim crow strategy, no matter on how grand a scale, cannot build a free world."[49]

ANOTHER ROOSEVELT TAKES THE STAGE

As the Double V campaign unfolded, A. Philip Randolph, the longtime head of the Brotherhood of Sleeping Car Porters, worked to ratchet up political pressure on the federal government to force it to end the gross racism that existed throughout the civilian segregated defense community as well as in the American armed forces. His effort relied on a basic strategy: direct political pressure on the president. While the United States Constitution grants Congress the ability to declare war, it also, in article 2, section 2, gives command over the military to the president. Randolph realized that, to achieve racial change within the armed forces, the best place to start was not with the Congress, a body laden with segregationist Southern Democrats, but instead with the president, Franklin D. Roosevelt, who controlled the manpower requirements of the military. Randolph did not hold a monopoly over this idea, and in the years come civil rights leaders would apply pressure largely on American presidents to institute racial reforms in the armed forces.

In late September 1940, Randolph and a handful of other civil rights leaders met with FDR in the White House. During this meeting, they encouraged the president to end racial segregation in the defense establishment and in the military. Roosevelt politely listened to their requests but responded defensively. He reminded them that the government, and in particular his administration, had made strides on the race issue. As an example, Roosevelt contended that "we are not . . . confining the Negro to the non combat services. We're putting them right in, proportionately, into the combat services. . . . Which is something." While the civil rights leaders agreed that it was "something," it was still only a first step in a much longer journey toward the equality and acceptance that the African American community craved. Challenged by his guests to do more, Roosevelt suggested a cautious, yet no less politically calculated, approach to resolving the issue: "The thing is we've got to work into this. Now, suppose you have a Negro regiment here, and right over here on my right line, would be a white regiment. . . . Now what happens after a while, in case of war? Those people get shifted from one to the other. The thing gets sort of backed into." While Roosevelt's approach reflected good intentions, it was essentially arguing for racial integration by accident or circumstance as opposed to the defining presidential statement striking down Jim Crow that his guests and the larger Black community desired from the commander in chief. Ever the consummate politician, Roosevelt preferred an approach that avoided any political entanglements for himself; things should just sort themselves out on their own. When he did call for direct involvement, Roosevelt's solutions bordered on the racially offensive. For example, on the issue of racial segregation in the Navy and its troubled racist past, Roosevelt, a former assistant secretary of the Navy, joked: "If you could have a Northern ship and Southern ship it would be a different situation . . . but you can't do that." Though it would be easy to confuse this as a joke, the president earnestly discussed with his guests an idea that involved placing all-Black musical bands aboard naval vessels as a way to introduce African American culture to the Navy.[50]

Aside from presidential ruminations—which were largely out of touch with the racial sensitivities of the Black community and offered very few answers on how to solve the conundrum of racial segregation in the defense community and the military—Roosevelt offered little more to his guests. Instead, the civil rights leaders had to begrudgingly accept that, while the president was receptive to their prodding for further change, all that they were going to get from him was a promise that he would consult with his cabinet on the issue.[51]

In a sense, it did not matter whether Roosevelt wanted to act or not. As scholars of politics at the time and the New Deal recognize, the president's inability to commit further was a result of what Ira Katznelson dubbed the "Southern cage." The Southern cage was a political apparatus constructed by Southern segregationists in Congress, sometimes with the aid of conservative Republicans, that contained, restricted, and limited the scope and reach of the New Deal because of the potential disruption and damage it could cause to their region's zeitgeist of white over Black. It should be noted that, while racism existed throughout America, it was ubiquitous in the South, undergirding everything socially, culturally, and economically in the region; it provided the one issue that Southern segregationists could all agree on. For would-be New Dealers and their leader, Roosevelt, who sought to work around these men, they faced tremendous difficulty in doing so if they presented ideas that the Southerners in government felt were controversial.[52]

Roosevelt, the noted biographer William E. Leuchtenburg contended, complicated this predicament even further. The president considered himself a transplanted Southerner. Since the mid-1920s, he spent a great deal of time in and around the recuperating waters of Warm Springs, Georgia; he loved it so much that he built a home there dubbed the "Little White House." Furthermore,

Roosevelt's continued presence in the region and his actions during the Great Depression endeared him to many Southern citizens who began to view the president through a Dixie-colored lens as one of their own.[53]

Local and personal sentiment aside, the political animal within Roosevelt knew he needed Southern Democratic support in Congress or he would achieve little success with his reform-minded policies. This meant, regardless of his own personal feelings, that he had to acknowledge and kowtow to the sociopolitical realties of the region—namely, Jim Crow segregation and the domination of white over Black that it upheld. As Roosevelt told Walter White of the NAACP, who was frustrated over the president's inability to commit to, let alone pass, an antilynching bill through Congress:

> I did not choose the tools with which I must work. . . . Had I been permitted to choose them I would have selected quite different ones. But I've got to get legislation passed by Congress to save America. The Southerners by reason of seniority rule in Congress are chairman or occupy strategic places on most of the Senate and House committees. If I come out for the anti-lynching bill now, they will block every bill I ask Congress to pass to keep America from collapsing. I just can't take that risk.

Though the mechanism of relying on white Southern segregationist and racist support for his administration's policies was morally dubious, it demonstrated the grim political reality that FDR faced. So he went along with it and extracted from this sort of devil's bargain, when he could, some concessions for the Black community. Indeed, FDR, in spite of his pact with the South, gained important victories for the African American community, including: the acceptance of almost a quarter-million African Americans into the Civilian Conservation Corps (CCC); the construction of new Black schools and hospitals throughout the country under the auspices of the Public Works Administration (PWA), including in the South; and several high-level appointments of African American citizens, such as Mary McLeod Bethune, into the federal government.[54]

And though he failed miserably to achieve an antilynching law, Roosevelt earned a measure of appreciation from the Black community for his willingness to decry the extralegal action that he deemed to be nothing more than "murder." He earned further regard from Blacks for his attacks on blatant voter suppression tactics deployed by white racist Southerners seeking to bulldoze the African American vote—namely, their continued use of the poll tax: "The right to vote," Roosevelt began, "must be open to all our citizens irrespective of race, color, or creed—without tax or artificial restriction of any kind. The sooner we get to that basis of political equality, the better it will be for the country as a whole." To that point in the American epoch, excepting Abraham

Lincoln, Roosevelt provided the African American community with a leader, albeit a flawed one, who seemed to understand their plight. Perhaps that was why the Black community continued to vote for Roosevelt, expected more from him, and would eventually be disappointed in him, just as they had been with his famous cousin TR, who had also once demonstrated great potential for them.[55]

Any goodwill generated by Roosevelt's statements to the civil rights leadership who had visited with him in the West Wing were promptly expunged as the civilian and military leadership of the armed forces rebuffed any suggestion that called for engaging in racial reform within the ranks. Now was not the time, General George Marshall contended, foreshadowing Householder's comments a year later, "for critical experiments which would have a highly destructive effect on morale." Roosevelt's secretary of the Navy, Frank Knox, concurred with Marshall and even threatened to resign if he was ordered to racially integrate the Navy and build a two-ocean naval force at the same time. Secretary of War Henry Stimson demonstrated his reluctance to move ahead with racial reform by avoiding meeting with Roosevelt altogether; in his stead, he dispatched his second, Assistant Secretary of War Robert Patterson, to confer with the president.[56]

As civil rights leaders waited to see what would happen next, the situation took an unmitigated turn for the worse for the administration. The White House issued a press release announcing that African Americans would be allowed to serve in all branches of the armed forces, which included training Black pilots, a notable victory for the African American community, but that they would be segregated. Not only did it appear that segregation was here to stay; the White House press secretary, Steve Early, declared in an erroneous statement to the press that Randolph and his civil rights associates who had attended the meeting with Roosevelt supported this decision. After an onslaught of angry letters from Black citizens and scathing editorials from the Black press, the White House rescinded Early's comments. But the damage had already been done within the African American community and its trust in Roosevelt.[57]

In response to what must have felt like a betrayal, Randolph upped the ante. If Roosevelt would not come to terms with African Americans on the issue, then the civil rights leader was going to bring the issue and Black America to the president. With over ten thousand African Americans proposed to be at his side (and more lining up daily to take part), Randolph threatened to launch an all-Black march on Washington under the banner of racial reform of the defense establishment. Sticking to his strategy, Randolph understood the political pressure that such an event would bring to bear on the president. But he also understood that, during World War II, the United States was going to need Black citizens in uniform and in the factories to aid the monumental task of defeating the Axis powers. Thus, as Daniel Kryder suggests, there was more than just the direct pressure of the march on Washington to consider, as it appears that Randolph and others were also following the tenets of "the 'long war' argument." This strategy argued that the needs of the war, in of itself, would force change on a reluctant American society. Certainly, America was going to need Black soldiers, but it was also going to need Black citizens in the defense industry to help make the war machine go. But to get African American citizens in both arenas, concessions would have to be made, and in theory the longer the conflict the more that could be achieved socially, economically, and politically for Black America.[58]

Not all within the African American community agreed with the logic behind this approach then or later. Three years after Randolph threatened to launch the march on Washington, a key component in his "long war" strategy, the noted African American military historian Benjamin Quarles, openly rejected the idea of the benefits of a long war:

Negroes must remember that a long drawn out war will very likely create a national psychosis which would indefinitely delay a solution to the American race problem. War brings many fine examples of heroism and self-sacrifice, especially on the battlefield, but war also breeds misunderstanding, fear and hatred on a global scale. Like the genie in the story we may find it difficult to put back into the bottle some of the forces we have found it necessary to uncork.

Blunt though it was, the historian's warning was sage, as it outlined the potential pitfalls of such an approach. Had it come earlier, it was unlikely it would have stopped Randolph and the tide of those who were determined to raise pressure on the president.[59]

THE STIMSON FACTOR

Prior to Randolph's proposed march, an unofficial way of dealing with racial complaints had existed within the presidential administrations that preceded and that continued during Roosevelt's tenure in office. During the Roosevelt years, this system was largely defined and shaped by the beliefs and actions of Secretary of War Henry Stimson. From his position as chief of the War Department, Stimson sought to mitigate issues coming in from the Black community that could disrupt the administration and the president. Stimson often did so by categorizing them into three groups: "The remediable, about which he was eager to hear, the trivial, rising generally from pride offended by the thoughtless slights of the ordinary white man, and the impossible—those which took no account of a heritage of injustice deeply imbedded in the mores of the nation."[60]

The development of the Stimson system was influenced by the secretary of war's deep reservations over the ability of African Americans to serve as combatants. It also demonstrated his reservations and frustrations with the civil rights tactics of Black leaders during World War II. After World War I, Stimson accepted the idea that Black men were inferior combatants. He did not come to this conclusion on his own. Stimson's judgment on the matter was guided by the white officers who had led Black soldiers into combat and had belabored their alleged shortcomings since the conclusion of the war. These men often used the 92nd Infantry Division and its troubles as a prime example of the Black man's inability to fight. And why would Stimson not listen to them? Stimson had served during World War I in an artillery unit as a colonel, where his interaction with African American personnel was greatly limited. He had no practical experience serving with Black personnel, which would have allowed him to challenge the ideas and beliefs of his racist colleagues. Instead, as secretary of war during the dawn of a new conflict, Stimson embraced their beliefs as fact. He fretted privately in his diary that Black men were simply not yet good enough to be combatants. "[The] poor fellows [Black personnel] had made perfect fools of themselves [in World War I]," a belief that convinced him that white men should not aide them any further until the Black community advanced as a race. To do so would just be a waste of time, he believed. Whenever white leaders and government tried "to lift them a little bit beyond where they can go," Stimson mused, "disaster and confusion follows."[61]

When it came to the ability of Black men to lead, he was equally skeptical and continued to promote the racist beliefs of the military. During his time in the Wilson administration, he recalled the pressure placed on President Wilson to create a camp for training Black officers. This was a mistake, Stimson felt; he believed that "leadership is not embedded in the Negro race yet and to try to make commissioned officers to lead the men into battle is only to work disaster to both." They lacked the intelligence, he argued, to do the job adequately. Because of his concerns, Stimson stuck to the idea of maintaining racial segregation and limiting the number of Black soldiers coming into the ranks.[62]

The secretary of war oscillated between despair, skepticism, and doubt over the Black man's ability to fight to frustration over events, such as Randolph's proposed march on Washington, which seemed in Stimpson's opinion to cause more problems than it solved. An agitated Stimpson believed that African American civil rights leaders were blatantly "using the war emergency to stir unrest and force new [racial] policies for which the Negroes themselves were unprepared." To an extent, he was not completely wrong. While his opinions about their ability to contribute to society were completely misinformed and wrong, he was correct that African American civil rights leaders were deliberately tying the idea of making the world safe for democracy to their own crusade for domestic racial reform. It was the best hand they could play, but it was an action that Stimson just could not accept. Instead, he felt that their strategy was one based in "blind folly." Flummoxed by their behavior, the secretary later argued that "this hot-headed pressure was partly responsible for the rising racial tension which produced such ugly outbreaks at the Detroit [race] riots of June, 1943."[63]

On a passing glance, Stimson's attempt to categorize racial complaints, his questioning of the leadership abilities of Black officers and military personnel generally speaking, and his frustrations with the Black civil rights leadership might reek of the meddling of a bigoted racist who sought to stand in the way of progress. Flawed in his approach and reasoning though he would prove to be, Stimson was more paternalistic toward Blacks—which is equally racist—as opposed to an obdurate and stonyhearted bigot that could see no promise in the African American race or, for example, other racial minority groups such as Japanese Americans.[64] He was a gradualist who saw more the limitations of Black Americans than he did their potential to immediately overcome the supposed flaws of lacking intelligence or courage. That did not mean, however, that he saw no potential in them. As McGeorge Bundy, coauthor of the Stimson biography *On Active Services in Peace and War*, noted, the secretary of war hailed from a Northern abolitionist culture and therefore "believed in full freedom [and] political and economic for all men of all colors." This allowed him to recognize the potential of African Americans as a race while at the same time arguing that they needed more time to grow.[65]

Stimson also believed that neither white bigots nor Black civil rights leaders wanted to truly work with one another. In his opinion, they were twin devils, representative of two different extremes of an issue. One sought to "keep the nigger in his place," the other to uplift the Black man "from complex reality to unattainable Utopia." They were both unrealistic in their demands, dangerous, and problematic for the country. Though he disliked both sides, Stimson defiantly tried to strike an accord between them, a decision that was a fool's errand

and prevented him from addressing what he dubbed "the persistent legacy of the original crime of slavery." But his fears, skepticism, and embrace of racial stereotypes of Black men prevented him from accepting the idea of a world where the two races could coexist in harmony. And therefore Stimson, no matter how much he tried to uphold the racial equality tenets of his upbringing, continued to harbor the belief that the racial integration of the armed forces was a fraught idea doomed to fail: "I hope for heaven's sake they won't mix the white and colored troops together in the same units for then we shall certainly have trouble."[66]

ELEANOR'S INFLUENCE

Prickly and inflexible as he was, Stimpson did not cause FDR to be in his predicament with the Black community. Neither was it Steve Early's fault (entirely, at least). It was Roosevelt's own doing. Years earlier, the president had turned an extraordinarily talented person into his most trusted and gifted adviser. That person was his wife, Eleanor Roosevelt. As the president's eyes and ears on social, political, and economic matters, Eleanor could go places that Franklin could not. She could see things that normally would be out of his sight as either governor or president, and she could hear the stories about what citizens, whether white or Black, faced on a daily basis during the Great Depression and, later, the war. This afforded her a powerful place within his administration. But it also allowed Eleanor to become an important conduit for African American civil rights leaders who sought to bend the ear of the president to their community's dreadful reality.[67]

While Eleanor's power to be a force of change came from within, it was still owed to her husband's ability to trust in her to seek out that which he could not. Famously, the first lady once queried him about how much freedom she had to speak out on social issues. FDR, without hesitation, wittily remarked: "You can say anything you want. I can always say, 'Well that is my wife; I can't do anything about her.'" His remark was not a slight. It was his way to disarm political controversy revolving around her actions. More important, it was FDR's way of supporting her voice. FDR's acceptance of Eleanor's need to be involved, and her recognition that he needed her to be involved where he could not, represented a deep understanding and trust between the two that served as the bedrock of their personal and professional relationship and helped them weather some of the more trying moments of their marriage.[68]

Eleanor's role, then, was to serve as "the more generous, idealistic side of his

[FDR's] own nature, the humanitarian values he himself held but felt unable to act upon in the context of the southern dominated Congress." She was brilliant in this role, as her influence ran the gamut and included the sticky topic of race in the military. It also led to her becoming a legend of sorts. Eleanor once took a joyride with the Tuskegee Airmen, an experience that led to the development of a false myth, J. Todd Moye explained, that gave full credit for the existence of the airmen to Eleanor. What seemed like a harmless overture ran afoul of social and racial taboos of Southern society. But she wanted to back the Black pilots, so she did it anyway. Later, Eleanor was dispatched by her husband's successor, Harry Truman, to achieve a universal declaration of human rights. And even after that, she buried the hatchet with a political rival, John F. Kennedy, yet another presidential admirer of her husband, and worked with him to improve the rights of American women.[69]

For the better part of thirty years, Eleanor Roosevelt became a nonelected fixture in American politics and race and gender relations. But that was yet to come. During the Great Depression, New Deal, and World War II eras, the development and maturity of Eleanor's voice as the first lady, but also as a budding activist on the behalf of the poor, women, and racial minorities, simply made good political sense, as the biographer Doris Kearns Goodwin shrewdly observed. It allowed FDR to maintain the traditional alliance with segregationist Southerners in Congress that Northern Democrats had cultivated for years. Eleanor could in the meantime work with the African American community, which in the not-so-distant future would aid in redefining the party. So in the late 1930s and early 1940s, when civil rights leaders such as Walter White and A. Philip Randolph called upon the White House, it was Eleanor who ensured their message was delivered personally to the president. And it was Eleanor's influence and cachet with her husband that made the meeting between FDR and the civil rights community—which led to Early's gaff and the administration feeling the heat from the Black community—possible.[70]

Though he had tried to placate the civil rights leaders and his wife by meeting with them, the president and his administration had handled their concerns, and the decisions on how to proceed, poorly. With Randolph looking to up the ante, Roosevelt, a master politician, found himself staring down a potential protest march. It became a game of political chicken. Roosevelt blinked first and lost. Though not the complete victory that Randolph and his cohorts sought, they netted vast gains for the African American community—critically, they had done so by way of nonviolent protest, a precursor to the civil rights efforts that would change the country within the next thirty years.

Eleanor Roosevelt—the president's eyes and ears: As Franklin Roosevelt's "eyes and ears," Eleanor Roosevelt provided her husband with the studious observations of a seasoned social and political operative. Her observations shaped his policies while he served as New York's governor and as president. Her ability to go and see where he could not lay at the heart of their tremendous political partnership. Source: 62-53, Franklin D. Roosevelt Presidential Library & Museum.

Beginning with Executive Order 8802, Roosevelt prohibited discrimination, whether racial, religious, or ethnic, in America's wartime defense community. This move on its own provided African Americans with a tremendous economic opportunity, as it afforded some with a chance to gain access to jobs that required more skill, which meant access to more training and as a result would net them better pay. To uphold this mandate, the president created the Fair Employment Practices Commission, charged with investigating cases of discrimination that surfaced within the defense industry. The War Department also named an African American judge, William Hastie, to be its first adviser on Negro affairs. Additionally, the War Department went forward with a plan to establish a Black flying squadron within the Army Air Corps. This all-Black unit was to be stationed and trained in Tuskegee, Alabama, and would be led by Colonel Benjamin O. Davis Jr.; these airmen went on to become one of the most successful and well-known Black outfits of the war. Meanwhile, the Army, which had never had an African American general within its ranks, promoted Benjamin O. Davis Sr. (junior's father), to the rank of brigadier general in 1940.[71]

The promotion of the senior Davis and the elevation of his son to head the nation's first all-Black military flying outfit were glass ceiling–shattering moments for the African American community. For the handful of Black officers already serving in the Army, it brought a small measure of acknowledgement and hope for more opportunities for them to command; it also likely inspired African American civilians to join their ranks. This maneuver, however, did not go unnoticed in the American South, as white Southerners who had expected the Army to maintain a lily-white tone were aghast by the move. "Are you crazy appointing a nigger as General in the U.S. Army?," a dismayed and disgusted West Virginian posed to the president in a letter belittling the decision.[72]

A RACIST NAVY AND ITS BLACK MESSMAN HERO

After the attack on Pearl Harbor and the Army's meeting with the Black press, Roosevelt faced continuing pressure from the African American community—in particular the NAACP—to facilitate the needs of Blacks who wanted to serve in the Navy. Up to that point, the Navy had half-heartedly investigated whether it would or not be feasible to allow Blacks to serve aboard ships as sailors. That it behaved this way ran counter to its long history, one that stretched back to the American Revolution, of allowing African Americans to serve on ships. Instead of embracing this history, a naval board that had been convened

Pearl Harbor hero Dorie Miller—"above and beyond the call of duty": Mess Attendant 2nd Class Doris "Dorie" Miller emerged from the institutional purgatory of the Steward Branch, which kept him and his race systemically belowdecks; he became a hero above and beyond them. But the Navy failed to capitalize on his heroism, preferring instead to maintain Jim Crow segregation throughout the fleet. OWI Poster No. 68., 1943. Source: LC-DIG-ppmsca-408193, Library of Congress.

to investigate upheld the long-standing notion of maintaining the efficiency of the military. It declared: "Enlistment of Negroes for general service would immediately create a situation which would destroy internally the efficiency of the Navy." Unwilling to relent on the issue, Roosevelt directed the newly minted Fair Employment Practices Commission to investigate the matter. The results of its study showed that the branch had used Black sailors effectively in the past and thus the Navy could and should experiment with limited integration of its forces.[73]

Initially, the Navy refused to budge. But then came Pearl Harbor, the needs of a new war, and Messman Doris "Dorie" Miller, who emerged from the racial purgatory of serving below decks in the kitchen as a member of the racially segregated Steward Branch to become a hero for African Americans and the nation. On December 7, 1941, Miller's ship, the USS *West Virginia* was one of eight battleships docked along Pearl Harbor's Battleship Row.

During the attack, the *West Virginia*'s captain, Mervin Sharp Bennion, was badly wounded by a piece of shrapnel from the exploding USS *Tennessee*. Belowdecks, but not out of harm's way, Miller sprang into action. First, he sought out his combat duty assignment; discovering that was impossible because of damage done to the ship, he headed topside to Times Square, the ship's center, to report for duty. From there, Miller was ordered to aide Commander Doir C. Johnson in retrieving the ship's captain from the bridge. During that rescue effort, Miller was also ordered to help load antiaircraft guns to fight off Japanese attackers. Miller did more than that: he manned one of the guns, despite not receiving any training with it, and unleashed fury even as the ship listed to one side. Whether or not he actually shot a plane down is still debated, but more important is the fact that he attempted to do so with no training in the middle of a firefight on a badly damaged ship.[74]

With fire spreading, and his ammunition spent, Miller and others engaged in fighting fires as they sought a way to evacuate the captain. Their efforts, though reflective of their dedication to save the captain, were not enough. As they fought for his and their own survival, Bennion succumbed to his injuries. Shortly afterward, others managed to get off the ship. In the final moments, Miller continued to render aide to his fellow sailors desperate to get off the *West Virginia*. When queried about his experience during the crucible on the *West Virginia*, the African American messman replied: "It must have been on God's strength and mother's blessing" that he survived.[75]

"God's strength and mother's blessing," let alone the patience of both, were going to be needed as the Navy worked to understand the events surrounding what happened on the *West Virginia* and who deserved credit for warding off

Japanese attackers and saving the lives of many shipmates. As the fog cleared and it became apparent that it was Miller, a Black messman, who had taken part in so many heroic actions, the Navy, instead of embracing him, openly rejected him. While the Navy turned away from Miller's heroism, Democratic senator James Michael Mead of New York and Democratic representative John D. Dingell Sr., of Michigan sought to honor him. They both introduced motions to award Miller the Congressional Medal of Honor.[76]

But William Frank Knox—the onetime Rough Rider, political apprentice of Theodore Roosevelt, New Deal critic, and now Franklin Roosevelt's secretary of the Navy—stood in the way. That Knox was an obstacle to Miller receiving his due was not irregular. After the president's meeting with civil rights leaders in the fall of 1940, Knox had threatened to walk out on FDR if Knox was forced to racially integrate the Navy during the war. And it was the secretary of the Navy's opinion, after he journeyed to Hawaii on a fact-finding mission to ascertain exactly what happened on December 7, that the Black messman's actions were not worthy of the Congressional Medal of Honor.[77]

Furthermore, Knox did not keep that opinion to himself; he wrote to the chairman of the Committee on Naval Affairs in the House of Representatives, Carl Vinson of Georgia, a Southern segregationist Democrat, to argue against Miller receiving the nation's highest military honor. The "Swamp Fox"—the nickname Vinson had earned from supporters and critics alike because of the grip he had on the military—had been a mainstay on the House's naval affairs committee since 1917. He was also an opportunist and a racist. Vinson had once attempted, even though he knew it would fail, to revoke the Fifteenth Amendment. Why take on such a Quixotesque endeavor? "[Vinson] knew that [his actions] . . . would impress the people he represented in the rural, racially segregated Tenth District [of Georgia]," the biographer James Cook observed, though Cook would contend that Vinson "never resorted to the vile racial rhetoric used by many Georgia politicians, such as Tom Watson, Gene Talmadge, Herman Talmadge, and Marvin Griffin." That made the Georgian no less of a racist. He was akin to the other Southern segregationist gentlemen of the era, men such as J. William Fulbright of Arkansas and Richard Russell, Vinson's fellow Georgian. Much like them, Vinson did not resort to slurs to peddle out racial discrimination in American society or its military.[78]

Relying on his regional mindset, let along Knox's letter, Vinson never embraced the idea of rewarding Miller. Meanwhile, Knox never yielded in his belief that the messman did not deserve *any* recognition. In the aftermath of Pearl Harbor, fifteen American naval personnel, the majority of them posthumously, received the nation's highest honor. The list included Miller's captain, but not the Black messman who had valiantly attempted to save his life. This did not go unnoticed. Several prominent Americans agitated for him. Republican presidential candidate Wendell Willkie, who had lost the presidential contest of 1940 to FDR, was one; another was the NAACP's Walter White, the venerable civil rights leader who would become a growing voice for racial integration of the armed forces.[79]

As the days after Pearl Harbor turned to months, the Black press, notably the *Pittsburgh Courier*, began to inquire whether or not Miller would be honored. With inquiries, criticisms, and attention rising, Knox finally relented a little. He crafted a letter of commendation but offered little else. It was not enough for the Black community. Soon, activists were selling images of Miller. Though the image quality was not remotely close to what Miller looked like, sale of the images helped lift Miller's family out of poverty and kept his actions in the forefront of African Americans' minds. If the Navy was not going to honor Miller, then it would fall to the commander in chief. Yielding from the pressure emerging within the African American community, and listening to the advice of United States Attorney General Francis Beverly Biddle, Roosevelt on May 11, 1942, awarded Miller the Navy Cross. Sixteen days later, Miller officially received the award where he had earned it. Aboard the aircraft carrier USS *Enterprise*, docked at Pearl Harbor, Admiral Chester Nimitz recognized and awarded the Black messman who had come from below to fight against those from above.[80]

Awarding the Navy Cross to Miller became the basis for an Office of War Information poster, released in 1943, that provided the propaganda arm of the government during the war with ammunition to fight against enemies that were attacking US racial credibility. And it would have made sense for the Navy to capitalize on the Miller moment and drive home the idea to the African American community—a group they had historically relied over the years to fill their ranks when times were lean—that they would have a place in the Navy. Instead, the Navy did just the opposite: it refused to alter course and continued to racially segregate and sequester Blacks into the Steward Branch. That is, until the pressure mounting outside the Navy from civil rights leaders forced the branch to alter course.[81]

On April 7, 1942, almost a month before Miller was honored, Knox declared that the Navy would allow *some* Black sailors to serve outside the Steward Branch. After this shift, African American sailors had the opportunity to become radio and radar specialists; others became gunner's mates, and some even became boatswain's mates. Yet their training reflected the time and the attitude of the Navy and its secretary. It was an experimental exercise, Knox contended, but it was a segregated experience. Not only was their training at Great Lakes Naval Training Station racially segregated; if they completed it, many were disqualified because they lacked the educational abilities to even begin and were assigned to onshore occupations and not onboard racially integrated ships. The racial ostracization of these sailors—Black men with training and the skills to back it up—was representative of one of the most galling moments of naval tokenism.[82]

Any further reform in the Navy would require a change at the top. That change came when Knox died in 1944. Replacing him was James Forrestal, who began the difficult task of opening up the Navy and providing more opportunities for Black servicemen. Under his leadership, he carried out the introduction of African Americans into the officer ranks—a change that Knox had signed off on months before his death—an endeavor that led to the admission of the Golden Thirteen—the first thirteen African American officers in the Navy's history. Though Forrestal sought the further introduction of Blacks within the Navy, his efforts were resisted from the top to the bottom. For example, recruiters—aware of the changing policies within the Navy—largely ignored and deliberately lied to Black recruits and informed them that the only real opportunity for them was in the Steward Branch.[83]

THE BLACK MARINES OF MONTFORD POINT

African Americans seeking the ablution of past racial sins of the Marine Corps would be disappointed and forced instead to accept middling changes. And that is because of the Marine Corps itself. From 1798 onward, the Marines had steadfastly rejected the notion, let alone the thought or suggestion, of African Americans serving in the branch. At one point, the Marines even objected to using Blacks as couriers in Marine headquarters in Washington, DC. During World War II, the most impassioned resistance to the idea of introducing Blacks into the Marine Corps came from its Commandant, Major General Thomas Holcomb, who quipped: "If it were a question of having a Marine Corps of 5,000 whites or 250,000 Negroes, I would rather have the whites." Whether or not change was desired, it was coming; presidential pressure, buoyed by Black civil rights advocates, forced the Marines to evolve.[84]

And though the Marine Corps had historically struggled to keep its ranks adequately staffed, the way its chose to handle the changes being forced upon it was analogous to the Navy's approach; if the branch was forced to admit Blacks, it dutifully did so, but they were not accepted as Marines or men. Once

African American inductees began to arrive for training at Camp Lejeune, they quickly discovered that their training as Marines would be racially segregated, and they were sequestered away from white inductees and trained at Montford Point. It was clear that the Marine Corps had no intention to use these men as frontline combatants; instead, it pushed Black Marines into defensive and support units and, notoriously for those in the African American community who lamented the existence of the Navy's Steward Branch, into the Marine Corps equivalent: the Marines Messman Branch.[85]

Unwanted by the leadership and trained by racist white Marines from the American South, Black applicants in those early graduating classes at Montford Point faced tremendous prejudice. Montford Point Marine Gene Doughty noted that those who trained them "did not concern themselves with turning out an elite bunch of guys. Instead, they would rather see you walk out the door and never come back." Depending on the day or the white Marine in power, treatment of Blacks fluctuated. A paternalistic white Marine, while not directly vicious, was still insulting. Ruben Hines recollected a white paternalistic warrant officer who often referred to the Marines of Montford Point as "you people," a belittling reference that continued the subjugation of the Black race to the white one. In retrospect, the Marine Corps did just enough to placate the wishes of the president but did all it could to make Black men who sought to become one of the service branch feel like they were unwanted and did not belong.[86]

RACIAL SEGREGATION IN ACTION: THE ARMY'S 93RD AND 92ND INFANTRY DIVISIONS

While racial tokenism came to the Navy and the Marines, ridged racial segregation remained the Army's way. There were those within the ranks of the Army's leadership who remained firm in their belief that the Black soldier was incapable of performing in a fashion akin to a white one, and therefore they objected to the inclusion of Black combat units in World War II. They based their feelings on the matter, in part, on the poor performance and struggles of the 92nd Division during World War I. As Ulysses Lee observed in *The Employment of Negro Troops*, "Army planners [and those above them such as Secretary of War Stimson] generally relied upon the testimony of World War I commanders and traditional public attitudes in judging the capabilities of Negroes and in determining possibilities for the use of Negro manpower in time of war." The opinions of the racist white Army leaders included the views of those who had led the 92nd. Their commentary only reaffirmed preexisting negative biases over the potential of Black personnel. These men contended that Black soldiers were intellectually *needy*, which suggested that they were not intelligent enough to think for themselves or morally strong enough—here they meant that Black men lacked courage—to face the emotional rigors of combat. Black soldiers were "absolutely dependent" on their white officer cadre, the commanding officer of the 92nd's 368th Infantry Regiment contended. The commanding officer of the 367th Infantry concurred with his colleague and added: "As fighting troops, the negro must be rated as second-class material, this due primarily to his inferior intelligence and lack of mental and moral qualities." In the minds of these commanders and others within the division, Black soldiers serving during World War II were better suited toting a shovel or a pick, the tools of a common manual laborer, as opposed to the M1 Garand, one of the tools of the trade of the American combat infantry.[87]

The Army's concerns over the future of Black manpower consumed the branch until the outbreak of World War II. There the Army's desire to limit Black involvement met with counterpressure from the civil rights community, which had sought more opportunities for Black men to serve.[88] The result of that confrontation was the maintaining of racial segregation throughout the military; but to acquiesce to the Black community, the president, and the first lady, the Army agreed to the creation of the Tuskegee Airmen and Black armor elements. But it also agreed to the reactivation of the 92nd and 93rd Infantry Divisions. Of the two, the 93rd, was reactivated first (May 15, 1942), with its sister division, the 92nd, coming in the fall (October 15, 1942). To isolate the Black men of the 92nd and 93rd from freely mingling with white communities off base, where problems could arise, the Black soldiers of the 92nd and 93rd trained at Fort Huachuca, located in southeastern Arizona. A product of the Indian Wars, Fort Huachuca provided a safe refuge from local white towns—though, on occasion, Black men of the two divisions ventured off post and explored various parts of Arizona[89]—and maintained strict segregation on post; it also offered a year-round training environment, even if it was a sweltering and dry one.[90]

Of the two divisions, the 93rd Infantry was the first to leave Arizona as it headed to Louisiana—there it traded the dry heat of the Southwest for the humid and stifling heat of the Gulf Coast—where it took part in field training against the 85th Infantry Division. After that, it went back westward and trained in the California desert, preparing to head to war in the South Pacific. Once they arrived in the South Pacific—specifically in areas today known as the Solomon Islands and New Guinea—the 93rd served in a supportive fashion.

Throughout its stay, the division was disparaged and unwanted by white elements of the South Pacific theater of operations. This led to poor treatment of the Black combatants, lackluster instructions given to them by white leadership in the theater, and inadequate time to prepare for missions.[91]

The rejection the men of the unit faced also came from their own officer cadre. "It is known among the troops that many of the white officers who were in command positions do not care to serve with Negro troops. Evidence for this sentiment includes the numerous statements and requests for transfer or reassignment with white troops made by these officers when it was learned that the unit was definitely moving overseas," observed Robert Bennett, a medical officer in the 93rd Infantry Division. As was the case with other Black units facing prejudice, the 93rd's performance would be negatively affected as a result, which only fed concerns, derogatory and racist statements, and rumors that decried the use of African Americans in combat.[92]

A failed operation led by a segment of the 93rd Infantry Division on Bougainville Island would only reaffirm the concerns of racist white officers and enlisted men. Named for the French explorer Louis-Antoine de Bougainville, Bougainville Island is part of the archipelago of the Solomon Islands, though politically it was never a part of the chain, as it was occupied by different states throughout much of its history, starting with the French, then the Germans, then the Australians, and, by the time of 93rd's arrival, the Japanese. Shortly after its arrival on Bougainville Island, the division took part in patrols that aided in blocking the Japanese's ability to utilize trails in the countryside. It was believed that the disruption of these trails would aid the Americans in ridding the island of the Japanese.[93]

On April 7, 1944, Company K of the 93rd Infantry Division's 25th Infantry Regimental Combat Team began what should have been an ordinary and routine mission; however, it turned into a disaster. The Black soldiers were to set up an ambush along a well-traveled Japanese trail, one nestled "nearly two thousand yards into thick undergrowth"; the week prior, it had been utilized by "nearly a hundred [retreating] Japanese foot soldiers." The men of Company K knew about the trail and the effort it was going to take to get to it, but they did not know about its recent use as determined by a Company K recon team. This oversight led to the Black men of Company K walking unexpectedly into an ambush laid by retreating Japanese forces.[94]

The good news for the men of Company K was that, although the Japanese had the Black soldiers contained on three sides, they could not surround them. As Black soldiers explained to Army investigators afterward, the Japanese had positioned themselves in a "horseshoe shape," which offered the besieged unit a chance to fall back. The bad news, though, was that the confusion and bed-lam of the moment made falling back, let alone hearing the call to do so, prob-lematic. Compounding this confusion were the Japanese, who were shouting military commands in English at their opposition. It became difficult for the men of Company K to determine where to fire or to decipher who they were shooting at as they kept hearing the Japanese shouting commands at them. The very thick brush greatly aided the Japanese, but it equally hampered the ability of Company K to maneuver and regroup. And therefore those Black soldiers who were the deepest in held out as long as they could, but ultimately they be-gan to fall back, which opened up the other segments of the unit to increased pressure. The situation ended only after William Crutcher, a forward observer attached to the 25th Infantry Regimental Combat Team, called for a risky artil-lery strike that resulted in a little over twenty-five rounds being dropped on the Japanese. Crutcher's barrage bought Company K time to regroup. At the end of the battle, Company K lost twenty men to wounds, while seventeen others, including Lieutenant Oscar Davenport, a Black officer who valiantly led his men while riding the wave of conundrum and confusion surrounding him, perished.[95]

Afterward, blame and accusations abounded in the unit and outside of it for what had happened. Black members of the unit pinned the blame on its white leadership, who they believed had failed to prepare them or lead them properly during the ambush. At one point, the white inspector general, who had been charged with the investigation of Company K, claimed that some of the blame resided with the Black noncommissioned officers. In time, though, the men of the 93rd were ultimately exonerated, but the image of them as untrustworthy lived on. Therefore, what mattered most was not the truth but instead the ru-mors that emerged that claimed otherwise. Some of these rumors even falsely asserted that the unit had fled in the face of the enemy and that this supposed act of cowardice resulted in several white casualties.[96]

These false claims did not remain locked to the islands of the South Pacific. Some reached back to Washington and made their way to Secretary of War Henry Stimson. Stimson, who had repeatedly expressed his doubts about the ability of Black men to lead, found more grist for his concerns in the rumors swarming out of the South Pacific about Company K. "I do not believe," Stim-son surmised after hearing about the ill-fated mission of Company K, "they [Black soldiers] can be turned into really effective combat troops without all officers being white." Years later, General George Marshall, the grand architect of the Allied effort during the war, agreed with the secretary of war's general view of the Black man's ability to lead or fight. Marshall even went as far as falsely stating during an interview that "the men of the Ninety-third wouldn't fight… [we] couldn't get them out of the caves to fight."[97]

The disparagement of the 93rd did not go unchecked. Walter White, who in the years to come would play a critical role during the racial integration of the armed forces, got involved. After spending time with the 93rd Infantry Division, White wrote to President Roosevelt about the situation. He informed the president that, shortly after the ambush of Company K, the 93rd had been largely divided up and relegated to manual labor tasks. White felt this was a mistake and unfair. White requested that the Army take them out of the rear and put them back into the fight. Meanwhile, he recommended the War Department halt the practice of rotating competent white and Black officers out of the unit (an issue the men of the 93rd had informed him was occurring), that it continue the practice of getting rid of white leaders that disdained serving with Black personnel, and that Black officers—as a way to show support to the men of the division—should be assigned to the white-dominated headquarters branch of the 93rd Infantry Division. White also thought it critically important that the War Department probe the overall racial leadership of the Southwest Pacific theater's commanding officer, General Douglas MacArthur. As he surmised to Roosevelt: "Statements have been made to me by responsible persons that MacArthur is at least partly responsible for the failure to train properly and utilize the Ninety-third Division in combat."[98]

Though MacArthur would claim he was not a racist—a matter that is discussed to a greater extent in chapter three—and that race had nothing to do with what was happening in his command, his actions said otherwise. When White sought an audience with the general about the 93rd Infantry Division, the response to him was that MacArthur was too busy planning the campaign to retake the Philippines. A similar situation occurred during the Korean War, when Thurgood Marshall sought to investigate the incrimination of African American personnel accused of largely shirking their duties; instead of welcoming the NAACP's lead attorney, MacArthur sought to have him blacklisted from the theater. Therefore, MacArthur did not respond to Walter White; he instead responded to a white man of superiority, General George Marshall.[99]

In his conversation with Marshall, MacArthur echoed the ideas originating from the South Pacific that other white units were better in just about every facet than the 93rd outside of "motor maintenance." Though White voiced concerns over the 93rd being reassigned to labor tasks, MacArthur responded that it was not unheard of, as other units had to do so as well. That did not mean that the 93rd would remain in that capacity. MacArthur informed Marshall that the 93rd was heading soon to Morotai Island to be a part of the fight against the Japanese. As for the replacement of dedicated and seasoned white leaders out of the unit, MacArthur noted that was a requirement and a burden that all units faced in the theater, as a shortage of experienced officers persisted.[100]

It was at this point that the pleasantries ceased. MacArthur shifted from the defensive to the offensive, and he informed Marshall that the notion of race being a problem in his command was not possible. "The violent opinions and unfounded statements of Mister White would seem to mark him as a trouble-maker and a menace to the war effort." In a historical vacuum, MacArthur's statement alone meant very little but, combined with his actions during the Korean War, helped to establish a pattern with the man when it came to his objection to outsiders commenting about his command and his abilities as a leader—especially when it came to racial matters. Indeed, when MacArthur finally agreed to meet with White, in a move that was nothing more than a cal-culated effort to put out a political fire, the general claimed: "Any man who says that another man's fighting ability can be measured by color is wrong." And perhaps to an extent he somewhat believed this, as MacArthur had led Filipino troops during his youth. As will be demonstrated later, however, MacArthur never treated Black soldiers under his command like the Filipinos he had once paternalistically led as a younger officer.[101]

The fact of that matter was that MacArthur never seemed to have respected African Americans at all, which was why he never championed or attempted to lead on the issue of racial reform within the ranks. This did not make him unique but instead *ordinary*. For a man such as MacArthur, who often claimed to be anything but ordinary, this is telling. Instead of leading, MacArthur tended to follow the racist sentiment of the Army and segments of American society of the era. If he had respected the African American community or one of its most important leaders during the war, MacArthur would have been more forthcoming to White about the *actual* role that the 93rd Infantry Divi-sion would play on Morotai Island. In a sense, the general had not lied to the leader of the NAACP. The 93rd was going to Morotai Island, and it would join the fight, but largely as an occupation force as compared to being a part of the invasion. It was there to clean up the remaining Japanese holdouts and to hold the island.[102]

During warfare, combatants sometimes gain a measure of respect for their opposition. But if MacArthur had any respect for Walter White, it would have shown. He would have studied the man and would have come to know some-thing about him to give himself a better opportunity to thwart White's barbs and charges. But MacArthur never respected White. If he had, he would have known that White, who was pale-skinned in appearance, was no less Black in racial identity. According to Francis Ellis, a member of the 93rd who was privy to the meeting that took place between MacArthur and White, the general at the end of their meeting queried the leader of the NAACP over "why he was so interested in these niggers anyway?" White then promptly informed MacArthur that he was Black.[103] Stunned, MacArthur, Ellis recalled, "turned and left the division headquarters without saying another word."[104]

If MacArthur had cared at all, he would have lauded the fact that, outside the incidents surrounding Company K, the men of the 93rd who operated in his theater of the war had carried themselves in a respectable and noteworthy fashion. During a patrol on Morotai Island, the men of the 93rd apprehended Colonel Muisu Ouichi, who was "the highest-ranking Japanese prisoner of war in the Pacific war." But he paid little mind to their accomplishments because MacArthur did not care; he cared only about keeping White from snooping around his theater of operations. Lastly, MacArthur did not do anything about the continued proliferation of rumors inside and outside the Pacific theater about the 93rd.[105]

If MacArthur's actions in the Pacific theater presaged his later ones in Korea, then so, too, did the actions of General Edward "Ned" Almond, the commanding officer of the 92nd Division. Almond biographer Michael E. Lynch noted that "alongside his positive traits [which included courage, leadership, dedication, and efficiency] and considerable achievements lurked the distasteful beliefs of a fervent racist and right-wing political zealot." A graduate of the Virginia Military Institute (VMI), Ned Almond was a product of his region and the Jim Crow segregation that it had created. Jim Crow was not seen as a problem but as a necessary evil to give a downtrodden race—Black Americans—a chance at some measure of success as opposed to cruelly forcing them to compete with white America. And the Supreme Court had reaffirmed this thinking in 1896 with the *Plessy* ruling, which promised "separate but equal" but instead did more to relegate the Black community to the status of second-class citizens than anything else. Almond's racism was the Southern social norm of a paternalistic white man. Then he joined the racist, white-led Army.[106]

By the time that Almond was a junior officer in the Army, the Americans had already concluded the Philippine–American War and therefore had taken up what the English poet Rudyard Kipling deemed "the White Man's Burden":

Take up the White Man's burden—
Send forth the best ye breed—
Go bind your sons to exile

To serve your captives' need;
To wait in heavy harness,
On fluttered folk and wild—
Your new-caught, sullen peoples,
Half-devil and half-child.

It was the age of Social Darwinism and "scientific racism," both of which contended that whites, because of their intrinsic abilities, biological makeup, and
racial characteristics, were at the top of the global racial heap. These ideas did
not simply ooze from the back alleys and byways of intellectual American society; they were taught in the mainstream to all whites, including those in the
military. And once this was accepted as the societal intellectual gospel, those
whites who followed it strove to maintain not only the global racial dominance
of the United States but also its racial purity. From the most virulent racists and
supremacists to those who were more paternalistic, racist whites in the United
States worked to limit nonwhite immigration into the country. And they did
so with spectacular success. For instance, the National Origins Act of 1924
greatly limited the number of Asian immigrants coming into the country and
remained law until the 1960s.[107]

Almond was no stranger to the white man's burden; he was the embodi-
ment of it. And he demonstrated his dedication to it when he penned the article "Training for Citizenship" for *Infantry Journal*. His article was written not
only to help his own country in its development and improvement of white
America; it was composed in a fashion that would also help the white American mission in the Philippines.[108] By embracing Christianity, patriotism, civ-
ics, military service—Almond placed particular importance on the concept of
Universal Military Training for citizens—and basic hygiene to improve their
health, white Americans could, in turn, teach these concepts benevolently to
the Filipinos. Still, it was unlikely given the static beliefs associated with the
racist pseudo-sciences of the era—essentially that upward racial mobility in
the pantheon of races was not possible—that those white officers, including
Almond, who served in the Philippines thought that they could racially reform
the Filipinos. At best, they might have believed they could alleviate *some* of the
supposed racial failings of the Filipinos. So, if they believed that they really
could not change things, why did Almond and other whites bother to try to
do it? Likely, in Almond and his compatriots' minds, this was part of the white
man's burden—the realization that, no matter how earnest their efforts, they
could never lift up those to be like themselves if those individuals lacked the
racial ability to do so; but that did not mean you did not try. Instead, it meant

that, if you were to fail, you were to fail in a noble fashion, one befitting of the superiority of your race. To riff off a line from William Shakespeare's *Henry IV, Part II*, for racist white America, it seemed, uneasy was the head that wore the crown of global racial supremacy.[109]

The white racial burden also influenced the Army when it came to the selection of its commanding officers over Black divisions. Operating under a warped racial philosophy, Army leadership, from Marshall down, believed that Black soldiers needed the best white commanders they could get and that, moreover, this leadership largely needed to come from the South because of the long history and familiarity of Southern white men with the African American community. The idea that this philosophy was flawed never seemed to emerge. It was just accepted that Southern whites knew how to "handle Negroes" better than Northerners because their forebearers had done so during slavery. For this reason, along with his qualifications, Almond, a Virginian, was a natural choice to lead the 92nd Infantry Division.[110]

From the start, Ned Almond faced three obstacles that hampered his ability to succeed: the Army and its racist policies toward Black personnel; the racist environment of the communities surrounding the installations where his division trained; and his own racism, which allowed him to accept both the Army's and communities' prejudices toward his men. During World War I, the 92nd had formed and trained in a segregated fashion and separated from one another. Indeed, the 92nd was spread across seven bases, a practice at the time that some individuals within the War Department thought was a mistake. It was a mistake, but the War Department would repeat the same mistake during World War II. Almond's version of the 92nd Division was fragmented and trained at four different camps: Fort McClellan, Alabama; Camp Atterbury, Indiana; Camp Breckinridge, Kentucky; and Camp Robinson, which was located just outside Little Rock, Arkansas.[111]

As it had with Almond's appointment, the Army turned to a Southerner, someone who had already commanded Black soldiers, as his second: General John E. Wood. Returning from Liberia, Wood had made a name for himself because of the quality and performance of his Black soldiers in Africa. The combination of two "Marshall men"—they both owed their status in the Army to some degree to Marshall's patronage—did not always mix, though. They sometimes clashed because each man thought he knew how to train the division the best. Where they did agree was in their racist opinion of Black military personnel. Edward Rowny, who had served with General Wood in Liberia and would serve again with him in the 92nd, believed him to be fair-minded and paternalistic toward his Black soldiers, but he also wholeheartedly supported the Jim Crow racial segregation of the era.[112]

Though their racial zeitgeist aligned, this was Ned Almond's division, and he would run it as he saw fit. This meant that the 92nd Infantry Division would never challenge the societal norms or customs of the region it was training in. And in a maneuver that followed the larger beliefs of the Army at the time, he reminded his subordinates continuously that racial segregation was in fact fiat: "The existence of these laws and customs is a fact. The personnel of this division must avoid any activity or conduct that will interfere with military training or with the discipline of the command." Echoing Householder's comments earlier in the war, Almond declared: "It is not our function to attempt to alter the existing order. The problem is social, not military." The job was not racial reform, Almond felt; it was warfighting.[113]

Though he was not going to lead a revolution, Almond seemed willing to give the Black men of the 93rd Infantry Division a fair shake. But could he really? And if he did, how long would it last? His upbringing in a racially segregated Virginia, his attendance at VMI, where Thomas "Stonewall" Jackson was venerated like a God and his famous epitaph "You may be whatever you resolve to be" was worshiped like scripture (Almond repeatedly referenced the quote throughout his life), and his social maturation in an Army that embodied the racism of the era as opposed to challenging it likely made this difficult if not impossible for him. While an assessment of Almond and his command has already been conducted elsewhere, a telling example of his leadership and the treatment of his men emerges when briefly examining the 92nd's performance while in Italy.[114]

To start their involvement in the war on a good footing, Almond dispatched the best he had: the 370th Regimental Combat Team, known by those within the 92nd Infantry Division as "Sherman's Raiders"—they were named after their leader, Colonel Raymond Sherman. In early fighting in Italy, including its fair share of patrol duties, the unit performed well. It was, like so many new units of the war, inexperienced and made mistakes, but it recovered and learned from them. As the 370th worked to make a name for itself, the rest of the 92nd Infantry Division arrived in Italy. Shortly after its arrival, the ranks were bolstered by a new unit, the 366th Infantry Regiment.[115]

The 366th Infantry Regiment was an all-Black unit that had historical ties to the 92nd Infantry Division but had been activated and trained separate from the division. Furthermore, it was unique in that its officer cadre was entirely Black. To begin with, Ned Almond's racism made him a problematic leader of

Black men, but to now have him assume authority over a unit staffed entirely with Black officers compounded that problem. It was a challenge to the racial standard of white over Black that he had known since being a child and to the racist education he had learned from American society and during his service in the Army. It was also a matter of belonging for Almond. The 366th did not belong to him. Almond may have been a racist, but he did feel a measure of pride in the 92nd, which he built from the ground up. He was not involved with the creation of the 366th, and therefore he had no emotional or shared experiences with it. If anything, its existence challenged the racist notion that Black men needed white men to teach them and lead them. It therefore challenged the notion that it needed Almond, a white Southerner who believed himself to be capable, because of his heritage, to lead Black men, who he did not feel could lead themselves, into glory.[116]

From the moment he welcomed the 366th to the 92nd Infantry Division, it was clear that Almond did not want them. Parts of his speech were in fact confrontational. "*Your* Negro newspapers have seen fit to cause *you* to be brought over here, [and] now I'm going to see that *you* suffer *your* share of the casualties [emphasis added]," Almond informed them. This was not a speech that could be used to build esprit de corps among the men. It was a speech designed to inform them he did not want them or need them. Almond's loathing of the 366th Infantry Regiment did not go unnoticed. His own Black soldiers felt that Almond did not want the 366th Infantry Regiment around, which had to have made them question their own worth to the man.[117]

To acquiesce to the Army's wishes that the unit join the 92nd Infantry Division, Almond made a series of decisions that wrecked the 366th's cohesion. Though it was normal practice at the time, he split up the men of the regiment and spread them throughout his command. This included the Black officer corps of the 366th, a talented and educated group who worked well with one another. Instead of treating the regiment's Black commanding officer, Colonel Howard D. Queen, with a measure of respect, Almond refused to accept him as an equal. For that matter, the general took little stock in Queen's observations or requests. Prior to joining the 92nd, the 366th had largely guarded air bases. Shifting from a secondary and supportive role to that of mainline fighting would take time. And time was what Queen felt he needed to get the unit into fighting shape. To get them there, he called for three months of remedial infantry training. This did not happen. The needs of the war demanded that the men get in the line sooner than later. They received some basic marksmanship training, and the Black officers of the unit received about three weeks of leadership training, but that was largely it. Mentally and physically exhausted by the situation, Queen was out within two weeks of joining Almond's command staff. Queen's departure from the regiment was ominous and a foreboding sign for those Black men who had served under him.[118]

The troubles for the 366th—and, for that matter, the 92nd—were just beginning. Almond planned to launch a Christmas strike against German forces. The attack was designed to coincide with a larger Fifth Army offensive to capture Bologna, but Almond was forced to call off the attack when intelligence reports confirmed that to the western flank of his position was a large German presence. Understanding the situation did not favor him or his forces, Almond began the process of pulling back, but the Germans beat him to the punch, launched an assault, and overwhelmed the withdrawing 366th. While the men of regiment fought for their lives, Almond and the 92nd proved unable to aide them. The cost for this failure was high; only eighteen of the seventy men trapped by the Germans made it back to the 92nd.[119]

Within the tragedy of this moment an act of heroic sacrifice emerged. Lieutenant John Fox, an African American forward observer of the 366th Infantry Regiment, assisted by his radio man, gave their lives by maintaining their post and directing artillery strikes against advancing German soldiers, which included calling for fire on his own position. According to Michael Child's gripping investigation of Black Medal of Honor winners, Fox during the precious few remaining minutes of his life exclaimed to Fire Direction Control: "Yes, damn it. [I know what I am asking.] Fire it. Give 'em Hell!" When the smoke cleared, John Fox and those with him had died, but so too had roughly 100 German combatants.[120]

No commanding officer wishes to lose men. But heroic death can be inspirational. Honoring the fallen through the recommendation of awards can spur onward those weighed down by the burdens of war. At the very least, it can show that they matter. For Black soldiers during World War II, mattering as a race, as fellow human beings, and knowing that their sacrifices were appreciated were critical to maintaining morale. There is power in such a gesture, but that was not going to happen in Ned Almond's division. An effort had been launched by General William Colbern, who commanded the 92nd's artillery, to award the Distinguished Service Cross to Fox. His recommendation was quickly squashed. Somehow, some way, Colbern's recommendation was lost. Michael E. Lynch contends that it was likely that Almond stopped it. Almond could not stomach celebrating a loss. And he abhorred the thought of giving the Black man any equal footing with that of the white man, even if the Black man in question was deserving of the nation's second-highest military honor. As with so many Black veterans of past American wars, Fox would not posthumously receive any recognition until years after his sacrifice. Not until the early 1980s, when he received the Distinguished Service Cross, would he receive the recognition he deserved. Fifteen years later, it was upgraded to the Congressional Medal of Honor. It came over fifty years too late.[121]

Likely embarrassed that an element of his division, one he had not wanted in the first place, could not hold the line, and rocked by personal tragedy within his family—his son-in-law had died in action, and his own son had been wounded and would eventually perish—Ned Almond was under tremendous professional and personal strain. The situation would not improve for him or the men he commanded. Almond schemed to launch an offensive, Operation Fourth Term—a nod to FDR's presidential victory in November 1944. His offensive called for a coastal assault that would begin in February 1945 and take the fight to aspects of the German military; more important, it would support the Allies' larger coastal offensive toward Massa. During the first two days of the offensive, the advance of the 92nd went slowly, but it gained roughly 800 yards of enemy ground at the cost of ten officers and 206 enlisted soldiers; another forty-two suffered noncombat-related injuries. Conducting an operation of this type produced men separated from their units that were trying to get back to them. There were those trying to get back to their units and then there were stragglers—those who were not trying to get back to their units or, if they were, took their time doing so. Thus, the term "straggler" is often seen in a negative light. It was believed that there were 121 stragglers during the first day of fighting; the majority—110—came from the 3rd Battalion of the 366th Infantry Regiment. Though they had done their part on the first day of the offensive, the fact that the 366th—the very same unit that Almond did not want and, in his opinion, had already failed him once—had the most stragglers likely galled him.[122]

The second day of Operation Fourth Term proved to be problematic, as the 92nd could not advance any further and suffered nearly the same number of casualties as it had on the first day. On this day, the 92nd lost fifteen officers and 183 enlisted men and also suffered another fifty-eight noncombat injuries. Not only were stragglers again a problem—this time there were ninety-two—but some Black soldiers from the 371st Infantry Regiment who were unwilling to continue the fight had deliberately injured themselves. As the second day drew to a close, Almond, whose pride was on the line, appealed to his superiors, who were considering scrapping the endeavor, for another crack at the opposition. His wish was granted, but the results only worsened for the 92nd. By the end of the third day, the 92nd lost an additional ten officers and 137 enlisted. Stragglers were still a problem for the 92nd. The unit suffering the problem the most was again the 366th. On that day, 260 men of the 366th had decided they wanted no further part of Almond's ill-fated offensive. With little to show for their efforts, Almond's offensive was called off.[123]

What happened to the 366th, a unit that had done well before joining Almond? At times during Operation Fourth Term it had carried its fair share of the load, but as the offensive went on it only seemed to get worse. It must be remembered that, shortly after joining the 92nd Infantry Division, the men of the 366th felt unwelcomed by Almond. And though it was not an unheard of practice, he then split it up within the rest of his command, a decision that broke up the cohesiveness and experience of the 366th's command staff. Then its commanding officer, Colonel Queen, who had asked for and was largely denied more time and training to prepare his men for infantry duty, left the unit under physical and mental duress. During its first action, it was overrun because it was in position to launch an attack but was quickly beaten back by a larger German force. It was at the right place but at the wrong time. And despite that, it still fought to hold the line. As it broke, a war hero from the 366th emerged in the form of Lieutenant John Fox, who gave everything—including his life—to stop the advance of the Germans. At the time, he never received any recognition for his valor. And by the time he did, the war was long over.[124]

Unappreciated and unwanted, and likely not ready to continue combat operations, the 366th still performed admirably on the first day of Operation Fourth Term, but it came with a cost. Major Willis D. Polk, the commanding officer of the 3rd Battalion of the 366th Infantry Regiment, perished in the fighting. While Polk was replaced with a capable officer, the 3rd Battalion of the 366th Infantry Regiment struggled at times until the very end of the offensive, when the number of stragglers coming from its ranks rendered the unit combat-ineffective. In hindsight, it is clear that the racism of its overall commander, Almond; its reallocation throughout the 92nd; a lack of infantry preparedness from the start; the loss of leadership at the regimental and battalion levels; and a feeling of little appreciation, along with a failure to establish a esprit de corps, let alone organizational pride, coupled with the punishing blows landed by its German opposition—it had the most casualties (347) and the most stragglers (630)—took an exhausting toll on the 366th, one that it failed to recover from.[125]

Shortly after the offensive's failure, Almond wanted to know why the 366th, and the entire 92nd, struggled. Under the leadership of General Wood, a board was selected to examine the division from front to back. It was determined that the units that had struggled the most were within the infantry. And there were several reasons for failure, as Almond and many throughout his command argued. There was a level of inconsistency within the officer ranks, the belief being that a weak leader could undermine the talents of others. That inconsistency could explain why early in battles the units of the 93rd did well but weakened and, in the case of the 366th on the third day of Operation Fourth Term, fell apart. While some of this certainly was attributable to the lack of consistent leadership, and what Almond thought was a general lack of confidence among the men, the strength of the opposition certainly had something to do with why the 92nd struggled as well. But instead of focusing on the difficulty of the fight, Almond instead returned to his favorite ax to grind: the 366th. Part of the reason the 92nd failed was because the Army ordered him to take on the 366th, which was a problematic unit from the start.[126]

In the end, Almond, who had promised to be fair to all his men, jettisoned that idea so that he could blame them for the failure of the 92nd Infantry Division. He informed the overall commander of the Fifth Army, General Mark Clark, that the reason the division failed was not because Almond or his white leadership or the struggles of the 366th; instead it failed because of all the Black soldiers of the division:

In my opinion the failure of this operation [Operation Fourth Term] is due almost entirely to the unreliability of the infantry units as shown by their repeated withdrawals in the face of enemy fire and small, though determined, hostile counterattacks; the withdrawals, by our infantry, take the form of panics, or disorderly retirements with little heed to command and leadership, particularly the weak leadership in the platoon echelons. Little if any determined offensive spirit to meet the enemy at close quarters existed in most of the infantry units.

The board's report matched Almond's commentary to Clark. In general, they agreed that, while some Blacks in American society—here they cited "the Dr. Carvers, Booker T. Washingtons, [and] Marian Andersons of the Negro Race"—had shown great potential, they were the exception to the rule. And instead of owning the failure of the 92nd Division, the white leadership of the division—with Almond leading the way—passed the buck by declaring that all the Black soldiers of the division were cowardly, stupid, and weak and that their collective failure served, once again, as a painful reminder of why Blacks should not be used as combatants.[127]

RACIAL INTEGRATION DURING THE BATTLE OF THE BULGE

Just prior to Almond's division falling to pieces in Italy, which led to renewed questions about the viability of Black combatants, the demands of the

European theater begged for the introduction of more combatants, whether white or Black. Hitler's counteroffensive in the West during the winter of 1944/45 plunged German forces fifty miles behind Allied lines, exposing the manpower inadequacies that had plagued the Allies in Europe since the summer of 1944. To meet this manpower challenge, the Ground Forces Replacement Command reassigned enlisted soldiers from other specialties to serve as combat infantry. But this move fell short of the Allies' needs, as shortages only continued to grow. And that was because, prior to the Battle of the Bulge, the Allies were already roughly 23,000 men short of what was needed. After the beginning of Hitler's campaign in the Ardennes, the situation became only more dire. Now, *every* available soldier who could fight and wanted a chance to do so was needed to plug the line.[128]

Lieutenant General John C. H. Lee, commanding officer of the Service of Supply in the European theater, had been doing his part by dispatching enlisted soldiers under his command for retraining. Early on, he was sending only white soldiers, but the racism of the armed forces—which had relegated most Black soldiers to support roles—had inadvertently placed Lee in a tremendous position of opportunity. As the commander of a largely support group, he had the most African American soldiers under his command in the entire theater. This meant that he had an abundance of something the supreme commander of the Allied forces, General Dwight D. Eisenhower, needed at that very moment: men. As the Battle of the Bulge unfolded and the need for more personnel became pressing, Lee convinced Eisenhower to expand the call for volunteers to include African American soldiers under his command. Ike agreed, and a plan was drawn up to introduce hastily trained African American reinforcement forces into the fight. Shortly thereafter, Eisenhower released a formal call for volunteers:

The Supreme Commander desires to destroy the enemy forces and end hostilities in this theater without delay. Every available weapon at our disposal must be brought to bear upon the enemy. To this end the Theater Commander has directed the Communications Zone Commander to make the greatest possible use of limited service men within service units and to survey our entire organization in an effort to produce able bodied men for the front lines. . . . This opportunity to volunteer will be extended to all soldiers without regard to color or race, but preference will normally be given to individuals who have had some basic training in Infantry.

Though a groundbreaking moment for advocates of racial inclusion, Eisenhower's action was not true racial integration of the Army. Instead, it was something more akin to what Roosevelt had suggested years before: the creation of partially integrated battalions that consisted off all-white platoons operating near all-Black ones that during the ferocity of combat would invariably intermix; this provided Black military personnel the opportunity to prove themselves, repeatedly, to white comrades-in-arms.[129]

As the war in Europe wound down, the Army decided to investigate the temporary racial integration of its forces. The Army's findings were captured in ETO-82. Overwhelmingly, this report demonstrated that, after whites overcame reservations and anxieties about serving with Black personnel, they quickly found them to be equals as combatants. As a white platoon sergeant from South Carolina admitted:

When I heard about it [racial integration] I said I'd be damned if I'd wear the same shoulder patch they did. After that first day when we saw how they fought I changed my mind. They're just like any of the other boys to us.

His comments were seconded by a first sergeant from Alabama who confessed:

I didn't want them myself at first. Now I have more trust in them. I used to think they would be yellow in combat, but I have seen them work.

Seeking a deeper understanding on the matter, ETO-82 also solicited the opinions of 1,710 noncommissioned whites who were not involved with the partially integrated companies that fought at the Bulge. The results were telling. The more isolated that white personnel were from Black soldiers, the less they trusted and were willing to work with them. Two questions from the survey dispatched to these men highlight this reality. The first question asked: "Some Army divisions have companies which include Negro and white platoons. How would you feel about it if your outfit was set up something like that?" Unsurprisingly, given the racial segregation of the era, 62 percent of whites from the all-white companies stated that they "would dislike it very much." A follow-up question posed: "In general, do you think it is a good idea or a poor idea to have the same company in a combat outfit include Negro platoons and white platoons?" Only 18 percent of the all-white companies agreed that it was a "very good idea," let alone a "fairly good idea."[130]

As the Army's highest ranking officers digested ETO-82's findings, two camps formed on what to make of it and what to do about racial segregation going forward. One group was led by General Benjamin O. Davis Sr., the nation's first African American general, and General F. H. Osborn, commander of the Information and Education Division. They felt that the information should be released to the American public, as it proved that racial integration, at least within the ranks of the Army, worked. In stark opposition was a second group, which included General Brehon B. Somervell, the head of the Army Service Forces, and General Omar Bradley, the "soldier's general." Somervell worried that releasing the report would turn it into a political football that would empower integration-minded groups, such as the NAACP, to push for further integration and reform within the military. To do so at the end of the war would also muddy the waters about what the armed forces should be doing, which was, he believed, concluding the war; he also warned that it could be politically dangerous for the Army to get involved in race matters, as it would likely insult Southern racial conservatives in Congress. Somervell, who questioned the science behind the study, was also unsure the report proved anything.[131]

The larger objection, though, came from a man intimate with the fighting on the ground in Europe and especially during the Battle of the Bulge: Omar Bradley. Born and raised in a part of Missouri known as "Little Dixie," Bradley once contended "I was not a racist," but questions remain to this day. Bradley's biographer, Steven Ossad, observed as much when he noted that, "like his fellow Missourian, Harry Truman, he may well have harbored the racial prejudices that were typical of the time for people of his background and milieu." Though he was no card-carrying member of the Ku Klux Klan or some other nascent white supremacist outfit, Bradley, much like many of those involved in the long story of the racial integration of the armed forces, was undeniably a gradualist, sometimes a borderline obstructionist. When it came to the proof in the pudding provided in World War II Europe by recently racially integrated fighting forces, Bradley callously rejected that it proved anything and systematically dismantled the idea that what happened at the Bulge demonstrated that racial integration worked. Instead, he contended that the African American volunteers who fought alongside whites were unusual because they displayed courage and cunning. The general contended that the Black volunteers of the battle exhibited greater motivation and intelligence than that of the typical Black soldier. Conveniently, the general never explained what the average or typical Black soldier looked and performed like. Moreover, Bradley's suggestion that there was a difference hints at his possible acceptance of the long-standing racist stereotypes of African Americans that emerged during American slavery that argued Black slaves were lazy, stupid, and cowardly—a belief that stubbornly persisted into the twentieth century and throughout both world wars. When he was not denigrating Black veterans of the Battle of the Bulge, he took shots at their opponents, claiming that the racially integrated fighting force that was fielded by the Army faced off against a demoralized, defeated, and disorganized German opposition.[132]

Certainly, the German forces that locked horns with the Allied forces were desperate, but were they as bad as Bradley contended? Or had Bradley and others misread the tea leaves of the war? It seems the latter was the case; when writing about the Bulge, Ossad observed in his biography of Bradley:

From his first undeniable realization late in the evening of 18 December [1944] that the Germans had achieved total strategic surprise, and until the US First Army was returned to his command a month later, Bradley was off balance, frustrated, and defensive. In the counsels of power he was a secondary player during the greatest and most contentious land battle America ever fought. The Battle of the Bulge was a stunning reversal of fortune for the constantly feuding Allied field commanders, an operational loss of momentum complicating the end-game in Europe, a blow to the prestige of the 12th Army Group, and the professional nadir of Omar Bradley's career. At terrible cost, the US First Army was taken completely by surprise and barely managed to stop the last powerful gasp of a skillful, dangerous, and undefeated enemy.

But this was not the way Bradley described the enemy facing racially integrated forces. He might as well have just called the Germans that the racially mixed forces engaged "hacks." According to Bradley, they were not a worthy opponent to measure the effectiveness of racial integration, let alone one that should be used to justify changing the racial composition of the Army.[133]

THE GILLEM BOARD

To avoid any public controversy over the findings of ETO-82, General George Marshall, the Army Chief of Staff, sided with Somervell's and Bradley's opposition to releasing its findings and instead buried it. Marshall did believe, however, that further investigation into the matter was warranted. This led to the creation of a four-man board led by Lieutenant General Alvan C. Gillem Jr. By the winter of 1946, the Gillem Board, as it became known, delivered to the leadership of the Army its recommendations. In a sense, the board wrapped itself in the spirit of the Constitution—Blacks had the constitutional right to serve—and the rhetoric of military efficiency—any changes should be gradual —as it called for greater Black inclusion. First, the board believed that the Army needed to get serious about recruiting more qualified African American soldiers during peacetime. The goal here was twofold: the Gillem Board sought more qualified Black personnel who displayed the necessary traits to become good leaders, while also seeking to purge those already in the ranks who lacked these abilities. This meant setting a cap on the number of African American soldiers inducted into the Army, which the Gillem Board set at 10 percent of the force, mirroring the African American to white population in the United States. Coinciding with this suggestion, the board focused on the Army's need to provide more opportunities for its Black officers. One way to achieve this was to continue the gradual introduction of Black soldiers with those of whites by doing what it had done during the Battle of Bulge—namely, deploying all Black units (with Black officers in charge of them) within larger white elements. This would allow for more command opportunities for Black officers, even if it was still in a quasi-segregated environment. Furthermore, those African American officers deemed to be specialists or highly skilled within their respective fields should be utilized in staffing positions, "regardless of race," throughout the Army. The board also called for the indoctrination of the Army's leadership on the issue and the formation of a racial advisory group to ride herd over the process of racial reform within the Army and work with lower-level groups to carry out this mission.[134]

The Gillem Board's middle-of-the-road approach, which did not call for the immediate or complete racial integration of the Army, held sway and became official policy through the dissemination of Circular No. 124 in April 1946. Though not true racial integration, the solutions the board provided proved enough to placate the conservative elements—though many white officers objected to outpacing society on the issue—within the Army, and also provided a degree of acceptance among the African American community and the small minority of white and Black officers and personnel who sought greater movement. Assistant Secretary of War Howard C. Petersen summarized the situation in 1946 to members of the Black press:

Basically, I think we all understand that there can be no single magic solution to the Army's problems in the racial field. The problem must be viewed, as the Board has done, as one of bringing about a continuing and progressive development. The important thing is that the objective should be agreed upon and that the initial steps should constitute a firm foundation for further progress.

Much like Marshall's comments to the Black press at the onset of the war, Petersen's words seemed to offer a measure of hope that racial integration was still a likely outcome. But just as before, any optimism surrounding the promise for further change was diminished by the reality of the Army's actions.[135]

The reason further change was not achieved within the Army was because of the efforts of the conservative leadership majority within it, which dug in its heels and waged war against racial progress. It began with the efforts of the Army's assistant chief of staff for personnel, General Willard Paul, who aided

those within the branch's leadership who disapproved of these moves by scut-
tling efforts to create the proposed racial advisory group tasked with directing change within the Army. With the potential of the advisory group snuffed
out from the inside, it seemed to Black military personnel within the ranks,
and those who criticized the Army from the outside, that the Army's stubborn
embrace of efficiency above all, most often played out by its employment of
Jim Crow segregation, had won out once again. This belief was compounded
by the fact that the utilization of Black officers remained as limited as it had
always been, which in of itself was a reminder of the power Jim Crow held
over the ranks. Indeed, General Paul, facing increasing pressure from Assistant Secretary of War Petersen to uphold the Gillem Board's findings, warned
commanders about threatening the precarious balance between the Army and
the local populations surrounding military facilities who might be offended by
racial changes within the branch. This, along with the natural fallout from the
end of a conflict, led to the exodus of talented and experienced Black officers,
noncommissioned officers (NCOs), and enlisted men.[136]

CONCLUSION

Established in 1940, the Orientation Branch served as the educational arm of
the Army. It provided troops with information on various subjects, including
the "origins and issues of the war." Out of this desire to educate the manpower
of the Army, *Army Talks*, a pamphlet-type publication that ran from 1944 until the conclusion of the war, emerged. Issues covered a range of topics, from
understanding the dynamics of World War II foreign policy to how to keep
a fox hole nice and tidy. *Army Talk* #70, though, was different. In this issue,
the Army addressed racial prejudice during the war. First, it identified what a
prejudice was: "A prejudice is an opinion or emotional feeling which isn't based
on fact or on reason. It is an attitude in a closed mind." Prejudice was also, the
circular warned, a tool of the enemy:

Enemy attempts to cause confusion in the U.S. through the spread of racial doctrines
have made it particularly necessary that there be frank and objective discussion of this
subject during the present War. The doctrine of 'Aryan' superiority has become one
of the dominant factors in the present world struggle. Hitler has made this doctrine
the 'reason' for untold aggression and devastation. . . . Likewise on the other side of
the world . . . the Japanese have been trying to demonstrate their inherent superiority. . . . The magic of race prejudice, the Japanese discovered, had performed miracles

in Europe. It had enabled the Nazis to get away with murder. If Hitler could seize Germany and disrupt Europe with the help of race hate, the Japanese saw no reason why they couldn't do the same thing in Asia.

Even more troubling, "race hate" was being used against the United States, it declared, to divide it: "About a week after Pearl Harbor, the Japanese were broadcasting: 'How can America be fighting for racial equality when it does not exist in America?'" In Germany, Nazi propaganda minister Joseph Goebbels predicted to a colleague: "Nothing will be easier than to produce a bloody revolution in America. No other country has so many social and racial tensions. We shall be able to play on many strings there."[137]

Army Talk #70, however, sought to push back against those who used race hate to divide the country: "Any American who 'plays on these strings' by spreading prejudices against minorities—Catholics, Jews, Negroes, foreign-born, and others—is, whether he knows it or not, playing the Axis game." Along with this rebuttal, the pamphlet provided a series of talking points and additional material so officers and soldiers could discuss the debilitating and nation-dividing potential of prejudice among personnel.[138]

While the educational wing of the Army sought to go to war with racism, the main body of the Army struggled to get into gear, as the unwillingness to carry out the Gillem Board's recommendations highlights. But, the Army's sister branches—the Navy, the Marine Corps, and the soon-to-be-created Air Force—also struggled to change. That the military proved reluctant to do more was not surprising to Karl Gunnar Myrdal, the famed Swedish economist, sociologist, and author of *An American Dilemma: The Negro Problem and Modern Democracy*. He contended: "American white officers cannot be expected to be much better than others [white civilians]; the over-representation of Southerners among officers with peacetime training tends to make those in the higher ranks particularly conservative, on the average, in respect to race relations." He would concede that "they have a huge job on their hands. However wrong they may be in believing a change in race relations to be a matter of secondary or no importance, it is understandable why they believe it." Still, Myrdal, with a comment that was emblematic of the logic behind *Army Talk* #70 and that recognized the growing problem American racism was going to have on the country's international efforts during the dawning Cold War, believed that the military, and its Southern-dominated leadership, was making a critical mistake in the war of international public opinion: "To advertise bad American race relations by maintaining them in [the] armed forces sent overseas is, under present circumstances, highly detrimental to American interests."[139]

If it was becoming clear that American racism damaged the nation internally, as *Army Talk* #70 suggested, and abroad, as noted by Myrdal, what was it going to take to make change happen and stick within the republic and its armed forces? Seeking to answer that question, historians have tended to focus on the rise in civil rights activity that came with the end of World War II and carried on throughout the 1950s and 1960s. While African American civil rights leaders played a crucial role, their efforts alone were not enough. They understood the importance of the issue to their community and to the United States image abroad, but they lacked the power, outside of pressure tactics, to do anything about it. What was needed was presidential leadership and action, which was slow in coming during World War II.

Despite his accomplishments for the Black community, Franklin Roosevelt moved on the issue of race in the military only because he had to. He could no more ignore his wife's urgings for him to act than he could the political fallout that would come from the African American community if he did not do so. But Roosevelt also could not ignore the suffocating grip that Southern politicians had on Congress. It was not worth the risk to the New Deal, he had once informed Walter White, but he might have well said it was not worth the risk to *himself* and the New Deal. When he acted to reform the military, Roosevelt did so in a limited and measured fashion; he was just politically unwilling and unable to go any further. Though it demonstrated a great moral failing on his part, it was understandable, though no less frustrating, why he did not do more.[140]

After Roosevelt's death, the man most responsible for racial reform and change in the military, Harry S. Truman, assumed the mantle of the presidency. But his early months in office did not offer those who sought the ouster of Jim Crow from the military much hope. Truman, however, was not ambivalent on the matter. Even at this early juncture, the Missourian understood full well the damaging power American racism had on the republic's wartime fortunes. In fact, Truman knew it before he became president. Then–Vice President Truman, a month before destiny shoved him onto the world's stage as America's new president, observed: "Evil doctrines of discrimination frequently imported from gangster nations plague certain areas in America. Racial and religious intolerance is being preached and practiced here by agents of our enemies, as well as by innocent victims of their propaganda. With relentless determination, our deadly opponents still seek to apply the ancient doctrine of 'divide and rule' in their drive for world domination." Though he was talking about the Axis during World War II, Truman was just scratching the surface of a much larger American dilemma: how continuing racism undercut its potential as leader of the free world. For real and lasting change to occur in the American armed forces and, for that matter, in American society, there needed to be leaders—such as Truman, though others would follow suit to varying degrees—who understood the danger American racism posed to the Republic and who would be willing to undertake the political risks necessary to carry out the reforms needed to address it. But to carry out racial reform in the military, American presidents, beginning with Truman, needed an overarching justification for doing so. Political pressure from the Black community was not enough; neither were personal feelings or desires on the matter. What was needed was the omnipresent nature of a global conflict with more destructive potential than the world wars combined. What presidents needed to get the racial reform job done in the military was the threat of the Cold War.[141]

CHAPTER 2

"It Was Good Trouble, It Was Necessary Trouble": Truman and Reform

In the winter of 1946, after completing a fifteen-month stint in the South Pacific and receiving his honorable discharge from the United States Army, Sergeant Isaac Woodard was preparing to leave the military behind. He climbed aboard a bus at Camp Gordon, Georgia, bound for Winnsboro, South Carolina. Once in South Carolina, the veteran was to meet up with his wife, who he had not seen since the inception of the war. From there, they were to journey together back home to the Bronx in New York City, where he planned to visit his parents.[1]

After a while on the road, the white bus driver, Alton Blackwell, made a brief stop just outside of Atlanta, Georgia. During the stop, Woodard asked if it would be okay if he quickly went in and used the restroom. Apparently, the request proved too much for the white bus driver, who bellowed back at the Black veteran: "Hell, no. God damn it, go back and sit down. I ain't got time to wait." Insulted, Woodard gave the bus driver a piece of his mind. "God damn it, talk to me like I am talking to you. I am a man just like you." After this brief and heated exchange, Blackwell begrudgingly allowed Woodard the chance to relieve himself. Having returned from the restroom, Woodard, thinking the matter was over, settled back into his seat and prepared for the long road ahead.[2]

Thirty minutes later, Blackwell stopped the bus in the town of Batesburg, South Carolina, and abruptly got off.[3] While Woodard thought nothing of the stop, Blackwell—apparently still smarting over their earlier altercation—had stopped the bus for a reason: he sought racial redemption. He approached the Batesburg chief of police, Lynwood Lanier Shull, and claimed that Woodard and a white soldier had been drinking during the trip and were "drunk and disorderly."[4] Instead of calling both soldiers off the bus, though, Blackwell called only for Woodard, claiming someone wanted to see him. That someone was Shull, who promptly arrested the Black veteran. During his arrest, the Black sergeant denied that he had been drinking or that he had caused any problems.

Instead of hearing him out, Shull physically assaulted him with a blackjack (a short club). A battered Woodard was then led by the police chief toward the town's jail, while his deputy Elliot Long searched the bus for the supposedly intoxicated white soldier, which, curiously, neither he nor Blackwell could find.[5]

As Shull led Woodard toward the jail, the police chief asked if he had been discharged from the military. Woodard responded with a simple "yes." The shortness of the answer—one that apparently did not fulfill the Southern racial deferment required of Black citizens toward their white counterparts, let alone an officer of the law in Batesburg—enraged Shull. He hit Woodard again with the blackjack. This time, though, Woodard had had enough and began to fight back. The incident hastily concluded when Deputy Long arrived on the scene and drew his gun on Woodard. Outmanned and outgunned, Woodard stopped quarreling with Shull. But Shull was not through with Woodard. Having been racially humiliated by the veteran, Shull responded by proceeding to beat Woodward so savagely that he permanently blinded the Black veteran. Following this heinous incident was a mockery of a trial, with a clumsy attempt to frame Woodard by offering him alcohol while under arrest, which the veteran wisely refused, and the unceremonious dumping off of the blinded veteran at the Veteran's Hospital in Columbia, South Carolina, where he remained for the next two months recovering from his injuries. Though Sergeant Woodard would eventually be reunited with his wife, he would never be able to see her again.[6]

The famous actor and radio personality Orson Welles, noted for his 1938 "War of the Worlds" radio broadcast and 1941 film *Citizen Kane*, heard about the Woodard incident and was so moved that he told the sad tale to his listening audience. Knowing just the surface-level details of the case, and thus unaware of who had blinded Woodard, he referred on the air to the guilty party as "Officer X." Officer X was, Welles surmised, "just another white man with a stick who wanted to teach a negro boy a lesson, to show a negro boy where he belonged, in the darkness." And in Welles's mind, the incident was a stain on the democratic promise of American society. But for Welles, true to his nature and style, it was not enough to just read the facts; he needed to imprint in his audience's mind the savage imagery of a Southern white officer beating and blinding a Black war veteran so as to shock them into consciousness about American racism and, perhaps, their own complacence in it all:

Wash your hands, Officer X, wash them well. Scrub and scour, you won't blot out the blood of a blinded war veteran. Nor yet the color of your own skin; your own skin.

You'll never, never, never change it. Wash your hands, Officer X, wash a lifetime, you'll never wash away that [leprous] lack of pigment. The guilty pallor of the white man. We invite you to luxuriate in secrecy, it will be brief. Go on, suckle your anonymous moment, while it lasts, you're going to be uncovered. We will blast out your name. We'll give the world your given name, Officer X; yes, and your so-called Christian name, its going to rise out of the filthy deep like the dead thing it is.

Welles's coverage and commentary on the incident over the course of five episodes thundered over the American Broadcasting Company's airwaves and created a firestorm of public opinion around the Woodard case, which aided the NAACP in bringing the affair to the nation's and the world's attention.[7]

It also garnered a great deal of animosity from the town of Aiken, South Carolina, which Welles erroneously attributed as the place the crime took place. The mistake was not deliberate, as Welles's knowledge of the events largely came from Woodard's affidavit, in which the Black veteran incorrectly stated where his assault occurred. Whether accident or not, with its name besmirched, the town demanded an apology, prevented the showing of a film that the radio personality starred in, lynched a dummy of Welles in effigy, and sued him for $2 million. The libel suit against Welles targeted ABC, the parent company behind the *Orson Welles Commentaries* radio series, so much so that its leadership demanded that from now on that he provide the producers his scripts before going on air. If Welles failed to do so, ABC planned to fire him. Welles refused, and Welles's *Commentaries* series was abruptly canceled.[8]

American civil rights history remembers Harry S. Truman as an essential player in the eventual passage of the twentieth century's greatest civil rights advancements under the Lyndon B. Johnson administration: the 1964 Civil Rights Act, 1965 Voting Rights Act, and 1968 Civil Rights Act. Back in the winter of 1946, however, the potential of "The Man of Independence" to become a civil rights forefather, let alone a crusader for that cause in his own time, of the Great Society's later contributions to the civil rights struggle was not abundantly clear. The White House, though, has a way of providing opportunities for its occupants to take powerful stands for or against causes that shape the future of the Republic.

During that same winter, Truman received a delegation from the National Emergency Committee Against Mob Violence, a group that included Walter White, the head of the NAACP, representatives from the American Federation of Labor (AFL) and the Congress of Industrial Organizations (CIO), along with various religious organizations. They were there to tell the president that, even though World War II had been a war about race and preserving democracy over fascism, hate and division, something Truman had fought against, were still present in American society and were targeting African American citizens and soldiers alike.[9]

THE BATTLE OF BAMBER BRIDGE, 1943

As sad as it was that they had examples of racial prejudice to share with the president, what was even more distressing for the civil rights leaders was that they had *so many tales* available to tell. Where should they start? They could have started with the war itself and the racial prejudice African American personnel faced. Indeed, they could have told Truman about the Battle of Bamber Bridge, which occurred on June 24–25, 1943.

It started, like so many fights in the military do, in a bar, in this case an English pub in Lancashire, England, just north of Liverpool. White soldiers went to bars; so did Black soldiers. All things considered, they likely went for the same reasons: they were looking to blow off a little steam, or perhaps they were seeking the accompaniment of English women—interracial mixing was not as taboo as in America. If they found their efforts to gain female companionship to be lacking, perhaps they ended up just drinking the night away with the locals. On this night, though, as it wore on and as the liquor took effect, tensions rose inside the pub. Someone must have felt the situation was getting a bit too raucous, because as the night became the early morning, the American military police (MPs), who were predominantly white, showed up. But why did they show up? Was this about keeping the peace? Was it about ensuring that Black soldiers did not cause problems with locals? Or was it because white soldiers feared that African American men sought the company of white English women? The historian Bernard Nalty believed it was about the women. The mostly white MPs felt it was their duty to impose Jim Crow racial segregation in the Queen's England, especially if interracial sex might occur, and it seemed they would use whatever excuse they could conjure up to enforce this standard.[10]

On this early morning, the rationale that the white MPs gave for harassing African American soldiers was the need to confirm that they were in proper uniform. The issue of maintaining uniform protocol, though important during regular service hours, was a fool's errand to attempt to police after hours, especially in a pub or similar setting. Neither was the issue of policing a soldier out of uniform in this type of situation an issue limited to Black GIs, as white GIs likely struggled to maintain proper military decorum while engaging in similar activity.[11]

But the focus was not on white GI's whose uniforms were likely not at their best, but instead it appears the white MPs were looking for an excuse to remind their Black comrades-in-arms of their social place. And the white MPs discovered some of the African American personnel in the pub were in fact out of uniform. Among them was Private Eugene Nunn, who the MPs sought to apprehend, but white Englishmen, military and civilian, came to the aid of him and his Black comrades. With the numbers siding with the opposition, a white MP drew his pistol, but cooler heads prevailed as a Black soldier talked him into putting it away. The MPs then left. But their retreat was only a tactical retreat; they planned to return.[12]

When they returned their numbers had grown. There would be no peaceful resolution to the matter as the white MPs threated the Black soldiers with batons. This increased tension brought about by the white MPs led to a fight breaking out in the pub and into the street. It ended, but again only temporarily, when the white MPs opened fire on the Black soldiers and wounded two. Those Black soldiers who were unharmed relayed the events that occurred to the rest of their company, which resulted in a series of pitched skirmish engagements against the military police, who now brought to bear against the Black soldiers and their unit an armed car toting a machine gun. After setting up roadblocks and other choke points to prevent the white MPs from advancing, some Black soldiers commandeered vehicles and shot indiscriminately at whites in general. This continued until the African American soldiers surrendered their weapons.[13]

This was not a race riot, though it is often couched in those terms; it was another battle in the long-running racial war of white versus Black. And like all battles, it came with a price, one that led to five American soldiers—three Black, two white—being wounded, while two white MPs were sent to the hospital after being severely beaten. As in Brownsville and Houston, the trials that came afterward were swift and the punishment was harsh. Originally, the majority of those involved were to be dishonorably discharged and sent to jail for varying lengths. But, unlike in Brownsville and Houston, further investigation into the matter resulted in immediate adjustments being made to the sentences of the Black personnel. In the end, the men were allowed to stay in the military after serving a thirteen-month sentence.[14]

LYNCHING BLACK VETERANS

Though it is unclear if Walter White ever discussed the situation that had oc-curred in Lancashire, England, he certainly discussed the lynching of African Americans in Louisiana and Georgia. One of the stories he told Truman was that of Maceo Snipes.

Snipes had to have seen the sign, how could anyone miss it? During the 1946 Georgia primaries, someone, likely a white person, had taken it upon themselves to place a sign on a Black church that read: "The first nigger to vote will never vote again." Maceo Snipes had served in the Army during World War II. After his service, Snipes returned to his native Georgia, where political upheaval was already underway. In 1946, the federal judiciary had ended the practice of whites-only primaries, which meant that, for the first time since Reconstruction, African Americans could vote in the state's primary. In Geor-gia, as was the case in the rest of the South, that meant voting for a Democratic candidate.[15]

The 1946 Democratic primary included a controversial moment in Geor-gia's political history. The longtime favored son of Georgia, Eugene Talmadge, sought to return to the pinnacle of state power, the governorship. He squared off against James V. Carmichael. Talmadge would defeat Carmichael and go on and win the 1946 Georgia gubernatorial race, but he died before he could take office, which setup a controversial moment in Georgia's political history known as the "Three Governors controversy."[16]

After deliberating with himself about the potential trouble it could bring him (the Ku Klux Klan had warned the Black community not to take part in the election), and likely after seeing that pejorative and prejudiced sign hang-ing outside a Black church reminding him of his place in a racist society, Snipes cast a vote in the 1946 primary, the only African American to do so in his county. It would be his last. Within three days, the World War II veteran was dead. Snipes was the victim of white lynching and the Jim Crow racial segrega-tion of the state that treated him as substandard and inhuman. The bloodlust did not end with Snipes, White informed Truman. The civil rights leader then proceeded to tell the president about an incident that occurred five days after Snipes succumbed to his wounds. On July 25, 1946, four African Americans, including two males (one being a veteran of World War II) and two females (one entering her third trimester of pregnancy), were abducted, beaten, and murdered in what became known as the "Ford lynchings."[17]

Of all these terrible examples, which, according to White's recollection, af-fected the president, the one that may have been the final straw for Truman was the sad tale of Sergeant Isaac Woodard. After White had completed telling the tale of Woodard and his blindness, a startled and shaken Truman exclaimed: "My God! I had no idea it was as terrible as that! We've got to do something!" This was not a hyperbolic statement designed to placate the intimate gathering of civil rights leaders; Truman was truly appalled by what he had heard, and he meant to rectify it. A day later, the troubled president observed in a memo to Attorney General Tom Clark:

I had as callers yesterday some members of the National Association for the Advancement of Colored People and they told me about an incident which happened in South Carolina where a negro Sergeant, who had been discharged from the Army just three hours, was taken off the bus and not only seriously beaten but his eyes deliberately put out, and that the Mayor of the town had bragged about committing this outrage.

Shortly thereafter, Truman encouraged, and supported, Clark's federal prosecution of Shull. But privately, the president wondered if that would be enough. Instead of punting on the fiery political issue, which his predecessor, Franklin D. Roosevelt, had largely done, he thought over the possibility of doing something more about the civil rights dilemma facing the nation. As he told Clark: "I have been very much alarmed at the increased racial feeling all over the country and I am wondering if it wouldn't be well to appoint a commission to analyze the situation and have a remedy to present to the next Congress-something similar to the Wickersham Commission on Prohibition."[18]

While Truman's vision of a new civil rights commission slowly began to take shape, the Department of Justice (DOJ) and the Federal Bureau of Investigation (FBI) pursued the prosecution of Shull for the next three months. Throughout that endeavor, they weathered tremendous criticism from law enforcement officials in South Carolina who viewed the involvement of the DOJ and FBI as prime examples of "federal meddling" in a "states' rights" matter. Though Clark and company tried to achieve some measure of justice for Woodard, the effort was doomed before it even started. When it came time to field a jury for the case, the trial's location in Columbia, South Carolina, proved foretelling. An all-white body was selected from the capital city of the state, a group that heard the case and that deliberated for thirty minutes before it promptly and defiantly acquitted Shull.[19]

"IT WAS GOOD TROUBLE, IT WAS NECESSARY TROUBLE"

Decades after the failed attempt to prosecute Shull for his crimes against Woodard, the renowned civil rights leader and the long-standing congressman from

Georgia's 5th District, John Lewis, reflected over Truman's actions in the civil rights arena: "As president of the United States of America, Harry S. Truman got in trouble. It was good trouble, it was necessary trouble. He got in the way. It was necessary for him to get in the way on the question of civil rights." The thing was that Truman did not have to do it. Why was it "necessary" for Truman, a Southerner, to act on an issue that his predecessor feared to address?[20]

Part of the answer lies with the fact that he first got involved because Woodard was a soldier. Black or not, his service mattered to Harry Truman. Though they never met, it gave them a commonality. During World War I, Captain Harry S. Truman served in the Missouri National Guard and thus was a member of the American Expeditionary Forces that fought in Europe. As with others who served, his experience during the baptism of fire on the Western Front affected him on various issues, such as loss of life, which also engrained in him the value of serving one's country.

While he had not served with any Black veterans, the future president of the United States appreciated those who had served, regardless of their race, because he could empathize with them as a former soldier about the price they had to pay. In short, Truman understood and shared in carrying the soldier's burden of war. A fellow veteran, regardless of his color, who was blinded so heinously struck a nerve with the soldier inside of the president. And it only angered him further when he heard about more stories involving Black veterans who were assaulted by racist whites. Truman once noted: "My very stomach turned over when I learned that Negro soldiers, just back from overseas, were being dumped out of army trucks in Mississippi and beaten. Whatever my inclinations as a native of Missouri might have been, as President I know this is bad. I shall fight to end evils like this." But if Truman were to tackle civil rights reform, he would have to contend with the terrific conundrum that was his racist upbringing in Missouri.[21]

Harry Truman had been born in Lamar, Missouri, but was raised in Independence, just east of Kansas City. During the Civil War, his family had been pro-Union but anti-Lincoln; he was therefore reared by his parents, most notably his mother, Martha Ellen Young Truman, his community, his school, and his spouse, Bess Truman, in the racist norms of the region. There can be no doubt that Truman was very much a work in progress on racial sensitivity, especially when one reads some of his most racist comments. During his courtship with Bess, a young Truman surmised:

I think one man is just as good as another so long as he's honest and decent and not a nigger or a Chinaman. Uncle Will says that the Lord made a white man from dust[,] a nigger from mud, then He threw up what was left and it came down a China Man. He does hate Chinese and Japs. So do I. It is a race prejudice I guess. But I am strongly of the opinion that negros ought to be in Africa, yellow men in Asia[,] and white men In Europe and America.

Later, as president, Truman still proved capable of acting in a prejudicial way. During a private moment, he lashed out over New York congressman, and one of the few Black men in Congress at the time, Adam Clayton Powell Jr.'s rebuke of the first lady's attendance of a Daughters of the American Revolution (DAR) event. The DAR had rejected the admittance of the congressmen's wife, the talented Trinidadian-born jazz pianist, actress, and civil rights advocate Hazell Scott. After Powell's comments, the president angrily fumed "look up that 'damn nigger preacher' and kick him around." By "kicking him around," Truman meant politically isolating him from executive access, and then he promptly barred Powell from any social functions at the White House.[22]

Despite his most heinous racist moments and his family's steady embrace of the Lost Cause school of Southern history, Truman evolved on the issue of race. Part of that evolution was owed to his military service. But it also came from his commitment to the nation. In a remarkable way, his belief in the Constitution and the Bill of Rights superseded the racial zeitgeist of Independence and the Southern pacing and way of life it emulated. His biographers have demonstrated that Truman's first foray into the morass of American racism came years before the Woodard incident or his comments during World War II as vice president; they occurred during his stint as a senator from Missouri.[23]

While stumping on the campaign trail in Sedalia, Missouri, Senator Truman declared that he believed "in the brotherhood of man, not merely the brotherhood of white men but the brotherhood of all men before the law." "I believe," he explained, "in the Constitution and the Declaration of Independence. In giving the Negroes the rights which are theirs we are only acting in accord with our own ideals of a true democracy." Once reelected, Truman kept his word as he investigated incidents of racial prejudice toward African American soldiers at Fort Leavenworth, Kansas, railed against the poll tax that disfranchised Black voters, and battled against the murderous extralegal act of lynching, a hallmark of domestic terrorist organizations such as the Ku Klux Klan.[24]

Political survival also played a role in Truman's decision to pursue civil rights reform. Black voters had been an important part of FDR's New Deal political coalition. Starting in 1936, FDR could start counting on winning a majority of the Black vote in his successive bids to win reelection, but that did not mean that the Democratic Party had cornered the market on African American patronage. And with the name "Roosevelt" not appearing on the ticket for the first time since 1932, Truman was going to have to do some work to garner, gain, and solidify the Black community's trust in him. Competing for that trust was former vice president Henry Wallace, who was far more progressive on the race issue at this point than Truman. If Truman was successful in swaying Black voters toward his wing of the party, he would earn the chance on the national stage to compete against the Republican nominee, Thomas Dewey, a candidate who also recognized the importance of catering to the Black vote.[25]

A TIME FOR ACTION

When it came time to do something about civil rights, Truman was savvy enough to realize that the nature of mid-1940s politics would likely prevent him achieving many, if any, legislative victories. Much like Roosevelt before him, Truman faced stiff resistance against any civil rights reform proposals from Southern segregationists serving in the "Do Nothing Congress." If he truly desired change, Truman would have to do it on his own. So he did. On December 5, 1946, Truman issued Executive Order 9808 establishing the President's Committee on Civil Rights (PCCR).

When Truman met with the PCCR for the first time, American lawlessness was on his mind, just like that which Woodard, Snipes, and the victims of the Ford lynching had faced. He therefore wanted to avoid a continuation of America's extralegal past and present: "I want our Bill of Rights implemented in fact. We have been trying to do this for 150 years. We are making progress, but we are not making progress fast enough. This country could very easily be faced with a situation similar to the one with which it was faced in 1922." The extralegal activity of the 1920s that Truman was referring to was the reemergence of the Ku Klux Klan. The second iteration of the Klan encompassed millions of protestant middle-class white men, who singled out groups, including African Americans, Catholics, Jews, and elites, that they believed were behind all the world's problems. Through various terrorist tactics, including violence and intimidation, the Klan plagued and bullied various rural areas across the country, including the hometown of Harry S. Truman.[26]

During the years of Klan influence in Missouri, a younger Harry Truman, just back from the war, was running for the position of Jackson County judge. Here a moment of what the biographer David McCullough believed was "naïveté" by the president enters the historical record. Truman had been convinced during the race by a friend to join the Klan. The friend, Edgar Hindle, claimed it would be "good politics" to do so. As McCullough explained, the Klan of 1922 had not yet fully earned the reputation it would later garner. Reluctantly, Truman went along with the process. During his meeting with a Klan official, who expected a $10 fee and a commitment from Truman that he would not employ any Catholics, Truman halted the process immediately. Not being able to work with who he wanted, especially Catholics, was a nonstarter for Truman, who had commanded Irish Catholics during the war.[27]

Truman's flirtation with the Klan was over, but the white supremacist group was not done with him yet. It paid close attention to the candidacy of the war veteran and deemed Truman unfriendly to their political zeitgeist because of his rejection of them and support of Catholics. Namely, the Klan fretted over his affiliation with a couple of Roman Catholic and Democratic political bosses that Klan members referred to cryptically by the first names "Tom and Joe." It was likely that "Tom and Joe" were really one man, Thomas Joseph Pendergast, who was the long-running political boss of the Democratic machine operating out of Kansas City.[28]

The entire episode with the Klan taught the future president a lesson, according to the author Michael Gardner, about the unchecked power and influence that ultra–white nationalist groups such as the Klan wielded against political opponents, let alone those who did not meet with the requirements for inclusion in white society. Over twenty years later, when a much older Truman spoke before his committee tasked with investigating American racism, he did so from a personal perspective on the matter. For Truman, a line could be drawn from the Klan activity of the 1920s to the brutal beating of Woodard. In his opinion, both moments were part of a visceral assault on American rights and the Constitution. Borrowing a line from the Atlantic Charter, he informed his committee that fear was prohibiting the American promise for some:

Freedom From Fear is more fully realized in our country than in any other on the face of the earth. Yet all parts of our population are not equally free from fear. . . . In some places, from time to time, the local enforcement of law and order has broken down, and individuals—sometimes ex-servicemen, even women—have been killed, maimed or intimidated.

This would no longer stand. It was the duty of the federal government, Truman believed, to protect all American citizens' civil rights, especially from those "who take the law into their own hands and inflict summary punishment and wreak personal vengeance."[29]

President Truman speaking at the feet of the Great Emancipator: President Harry S. Truman becomes the first American president to deliver an address before the NAACP about the state of American racial relations. Lincoln Memorial, Washington, DC, June 29, 1947. Source: 73-2563. Harry S. Truman Library and Museum.

Prior to becoming the first American president to address the NAACP on June 29, 1947, it was clear that Truman, the biographer Alonzo Hamby observed, was in a reflective mood about his past and his upbringing. On the eve of one of the most monumental moments of his presidency, he wrote a letter to his sister Mary Jane, who, outside of his mother, he was closest to. In it, Truman admitted: "I've got to make a speech to the Society for the Advancement of Colored People tomorrow and I wish I didn't have to make it. . . . Mamma won't like what I say because I wind up quoting old Abe." It was a moment of old ideas and feelings clashing with new ones. To say it another way: Truman was human. His lamentation and consternation was the stuff of a man contending with his past as he did battle with an evil he saw in his present. It was not the racism or inexperience of his youth that carried the day; instead it was his matured humanity. "But I believe what I say and I'm hopeful we may implement it," a contemplative Truman informed his sister.[30]

When speaking with the Truman biographer Jonathan Daniels year later,

Mary Jane bristled at the notion that her brother, whether or not he had spoken before the NAACP, was for racial equality. "Harry isn't anymore in favor of nigger equality than I am," she quipped. Given his past racist statements on the matter, it was understandable why she believed her brother had not changed. But Mary Jane was wrong; she was speaking about an iteration of Truman that no longer existed. Something had been stirred in him since the Woodard incident that melded with his beliefs in the power of the Constitution and the Bill of Rights, something he could not simply whisk away or politic away. And indeed, from the moment he met with White and others and learned of the abuses facing African Americans—in particular war veterans—to the moment he created his committee on civil rights, to the day when he became the first of his office to speak before the NAACP, Truman had remained consistent in his message. He had the Justice Department go after Shull because he had violated Woodard's rights as an American citizen, but the act itself was equally damning in Truman's mind, as it continued a pattern of terror and racial retribution toward Blacks that was akin to the night rides of the omnipresent Klan of the late nineteenth and early twentieth centuries in America. None of it was legal, and none of it was right.[31]

When he spoke before the NAACP, which was held at the Lincoln Memorial in Washington, DC, he continued this line of reasoning and his remedy for it: "The extension of civil rights today means, not protection of the people against the Government," Truman explained, "but protection of the people by the Government." For this to happen, he argued that "we must make the Federal Government a friendly, vigilant defender of the rights and equalities of all Americans." Roosevelt, who Truman channeled during his speech as much as he would Lincoln, had used the power of the government to wage war against the Great Depression and the creeping and dastardly nature of international fascism that threatened the country. Truman was going to use that same power to wage war on the domestic threat that racial oppression represented to the Constitution and the American way of life.[32]

In addition to carving out an expanded role for the federal government, Truman also provided an international justification for action in the struggle for civil rights reform, one that would appear again and again with increasing frequency over the coming years. At the feet of Lincoln, flanked by civil rights leaders and before the crowd of white and Black faces, he linked civil rights reform in America to its larger battle against global communism:

The support of desperate populations of battle-ravaged countries must be won for the free way of life. We must have them as allies in our continuing struggle for the peaceful solution of the world's problems. Freedom is not an easy lesson to teach, nor an easy cause to sell, to peoples beset by every kind of privation. They may surrender to the false security offered so temptingly by totalitarian regimes unless we can prove the superiority of democracy. Our case for democracy should be as strong as we can make it. It should rest on practical evidence that we have been able to put our own house in order.

If the United States did not demonstrate the superiority of its democratic way of life, which for Truman meant embracing civil rights reforms that would uplift African Americans from their status as second-class citizens, those European and Asian nations recovering from the onslaught of World War II might succumb to communist propaganda and subversion that argued America and its pursuit of equality for all was a fraud.[33]

For Truman and his advisers, they also had to worry about the so-called Third World. The Truman administration realized, as those that succeeded him also realized, that the Soviet Union had repeatedly used American racial injustice to appeal to the nonwhite nations of the Third World, which represented, for both powers, the unharnessed potential of the Cold War periphery. In a speech before the Fair Employment Practice Committee, Secretary of State Dean Acheson remarked that "the existence of discrimination against minority groups in this country has an adverse effect upon our relations with other countries. We are reminded over and over by some foreign newspapers and spokesman, that our treatment of various minorities leaves much to be desired." Acheson continued: "I think it is quite obvious . . . that the existence of discriminations against minority groups in the United States is a handicap in our relations with other countries." Civil rights reform was important, Truman and his staff believed, but it was not solely about the domestic welfare of the nation, or elevating the African American community, or avenging the racist wrongs faced by Black veterans such as Woodard. It was also about winning the Cold War. It was what the most powerful nation in the world seeking that victory should do. Or as Truman succinctly put it to Jonathan Daniels during an interview for his biography of the president, *The Man of Independence*: "The Top Dog in a world which is over half colored out to clean his own house."[34]

TO SECURE THESE RIGHTS

Formed from a group of white and Black citizens that sought to racially reform America, the PCCR responded enthusiastically to the president's call for action by producing *To Secure These Rights: The Report of the President's Committee on Civil Rights.* The report was both a comprehensive examination of America's racist past and a primer for federal action against the rampant discrimination toward minorities that occurred, and was still occurring, in the nation. In its report, the PCCR outlined four basic rights that it believed all Americans possessed: these included "the right to safety and security of the person," "the right of citizenship and its privileges," "the right to freedom of conscience and expression," and "the right to equality of opportunity." Using these rights as a baseline for it findings, the PCCR uncovered and highlighted several aspects of American society that had proved to be racist in its actions. In the committee's estimation, one governmental institution stood out above the rest for its racist ways: the American military. Throughout its history, the PCCR contended, the American armed forces had endeavored to exclude African Americans at every turn. From attempting to prohibit the use of Black soldiers in combat to its adoption of Jim Crow segregation to within the ranks, the American military had not only demeaned the Black community and its soldiers by affixing a "badge of inferiority" to them but also wasted an asset for defense.[35]

During its inquiry into America's racist past, the PCCR met with several prominent civil rights leaders to discuss the matter of racism in American society. Among them was Walter White of the NAACP. White spoke at great length on the topic of American racism and how it threatened democratic principles. He also suggested to the committee that American racism opened the door for communist subversion of the nation:

Hitler is presumably dead, but his spirit lives in America today, at times, I believe as viciously as during the heyday of the Nazi Party in Germany.

We have seen the rise of bigotry since the close of the war, the denial of the right to protection of the laws and the denial of the right to earn a living to various segments of our population, which in my opinion is one of the surest ways of bringing Communism into the United States; namely, the denial of human rights and civil rights here in our country.

We have seen vicious anti-Semitism, an in the recent Lilienthal hearings and debate in the United States Senate. We have seen it in the smearing of Jewish and other displaced persons in Germany. We have seen it in recent lynchings and in the cold-blooded blinding of a Negro veteran recently discharged from the Army, by police officers in Batesburg, S.C.

White offered a long list of areas, including the American armed forces, where reform needed to take place. As head of the NAACP, but also as a war correspondent, his thoughts on racism in the military during the war and beyond carried significant weight. He surmised that racial segregation in the military hurt the morale of white and Black soldiers alike, but even more damaging was "the harm that was done to our national reputation by our presumably going out to fight a war against the racial theories of Adolf Hitler when we carried overseas two armies, one white and one black, with hatred and bitterness between them even as were fighting a war presumably for the preservation of the democratic process." To help ward off the dangerous threat that racism presented to American democracy, and to prove to the world the United States was a true champion of democratic values, the nation's military, as with much of the republic, had to change.[36]

White was hinting at the potential of the military to be a reform agent, an idea that was also formulating within the PCCR. Words and opinions are fine and well; proof that the military could serve in this way and that it would work were something else completely. They discovered the proof they needed when they uncovered ETO-82, the World War II report that Marshall had buried because of its explosive potential years earlier. In it, the committee discovered that the military *had already* served during World War II as a sociological laboratory—an accomplishment that proceeded Jackie Robinson's historic bid to racially integrate Major League Baseball by three years—where racial integration was tested and proved successful. As the PCCR digested ETO-82, it became clear that the military had failed to capitalize on what was learned during the war, which was that the armed forces were a sociological laboratory that had already achieved incredible results between the races. Racial integration worked. In *To Secure These Rights*, the PCCR observed:

During the last war we and our allies, with varying but undeniable success, found that the military services can be used to educate citizens on a broad range of social and political problems. The war experiences brought to our attention a laboratory in which we may prove that the majority and minorities of our population can train and work and fight side by side in cooperation and harmony. We should not hesitate to take full advantage of this opportunity.

The problem was that the momentum created during the war toward racial cohesiveness was never given the chance to blossom or grow after the guns fell silent in Europe and in the Pacific, the committee reasoned. And although the military had made inroads that remained in place afterward, a deliberate unwillingness to go further pervaded throughout the leadership of the armed forces. This reluctance to move further on the issue, the PCCR felt, prevented the nation from wielding the armed forces as a tremendous weapon against racism.[37]

The PCCR offered several justifications for why reform in American society, and the military, should occur. In one sense, racial reform was necessary for moral reasons. Allowing white racism against Blacks to continue unabated eroded the core democratic values of the nation and denied a segment of the population the very liberty and equality that were at the nexus of the Constitution. Economically, it was foolish to treat African Americans as second-class citizens. The continuation of this practice meant that the buying power of the Black community would remain miniscule. In a world of economic competition, the PCCR reasoned, it was best to harness the spending power of all Americans. Finally, and relevant to the affairs of the world at the time, the failure to racially integrate African Americans into mainstream society harmed the nation in its fight against communism:

We cannot escape the fact that our civil rights record has been an issue in world politics. The world's press and radio are full of [examples of] it. . . . Those with competing philosophies have stressed—and are shamelessly distorting—our shortcomings. They have not only tried to create hostility toward us among specific nations, races, and religious groups. They have tried to prove our democracy an empty fraud, and our nation a consistent oppressor of underprivileged people.

Racial integration of American society and the military, the PCCR advocated, was about the preservation of American values from the forces that threatened them, whether domestic (racism) or foreign (communism). To carry out these changes, the PCCR suggested to the president a series of legislative reforms that could address the issue. Among them was the committee's suggestion to racially integrate the armed services.[38]

Truman accepted the report and used it as the basis of his address to Congress on civil rights. His address covered issues of discrimination toward African Americans, Japanese Americans, concerns of racist treatment in the Panama Canal Zone, and more and attempted to fuse the rights of minority groups within the United States facing the stinging rebuke of racism with those of the nation's original immigrants. Like the first European immigrants, African Americans had come to the United States in search of freedom, opportunity, and equality. The fact of the matter, though, was that African slaves did not come to America of their own accord. This omission was likely deliberate, as the president was trying to sell a message, one that essentially argued that Africans, who became African Americans, were here and they—as did the other groups he discussed in his message—deserved fair and equitable treatment alongside the white majority of the nation.[39]

To make his case, he relied on the timeless tenets established by the

Declaration of Independence and later the Constitution and Bill of Rights, which the president believed protected the rights of all Americans. Indeed, in the 1940s, Truman observed "the American people enjoy more freedom and opportunity than ever before." There remained a glaring problem, however: racial prejudice. The issue of racial prejudice, the president acknowledged, prevented all Americans from reaping the benefits of the freedom and equality afforded by the Constitution. The issue could no longer be ignored. And as Truman contended in his speech, it was time for the republic to look at itself in the mirror: "The protection of civil rights begins with the mutual respect for the rights of others which all of us should practice in our daily lives."[40]

Truman had always felt that lasting civil rights reform would come only when the American people personally committed themselves to change. But that did not mean he had to wait to do something about the persisting racism present in the country. During his civil rights address, Truman declared that it was time for local, state, and national governments to live up to their responsibilities as the guardians of the rights that had been robbed from racial minority groups. In this process, the federal government, which had a "clear duty" to protect the rights of its citizens, had to play a special leadership role. Following the recommendations of the PCCR, Truman placed the lion's share of responsibility for civil rights reform on Congress. He requested the enactment of laws that ended lynching, protected the rights of voters, protected interstate transportation, created a permanent Fair Employments Practice Commission, established commissions in Congress and the Department of Justice that focused solely on civil rights issues, created "a permanent Commission on Civil Rights" to advise the president on civil rights matters, and much more.[41]

Truman's plan for civil rights reform was both audacious and politically dangerous, as it attempted to introduce societal changes to the nation that the white majority had not called for or seemed to desire. That he did this during the 1948 presidential campaign was politically and socially remarkable, but it was also calculated. To be sure, he would reap tremendous voting benefits from the Black community for his stance, but he also genuinely believed that the changes were necessary for the good of the nation both domestically and internationally.

To bring his message home to the American people, he again tied the matter to the Cold War:

We know that our democracy is not perfect. But we do know that it offers freer, happier life to our people than any totalitarian nation has ever offered. If we wish to inspire the peoples of the world whose freedom is in jeopardy, if we wish to restore hope to those who have already lost their civil liberties, if we wish to fulfill the promise that is ours, we must correct the remaining imperfections in our practice of democracy. We know the way. We need only the will.

While morality and the promise of the Constitution were important, those rationales were not going to sell or unite all people throughout the republic. But taking a cue from the PCCR, the president focused on the perceived monolithic threat of global communism emerging from Moscow as a means to unite much of the country to get behind racial reform in order to win the Cold War.[42]

THE SECOND RED SCARE

As the Truman administration gravitated toward racially integrating the military and society in general, the growing paranoia among Americans that their way of life was being subverted, better known as the "Second Red Scare," intensified. Political committees such as the House Un-American Activities Committee (HUAC) only made matters worse. HUAC charged that the forces of international communism had already seeped into just about every facet of American life; from academia to politics to education to the silver screen, no area had been spared from its insidiousness grasp. As a result, HUAC launched a holy war to purify the soul of America and its institutions. Often, it simply made matters worse. Instead of combating the fear communism instilled in some Americans, it spread it.

Much of this fear-mongering was politically and socially intentional. For some, it transformed their careers. Red-baiting pols such as Senator Joseph McCarthy, Republican of Wisconsin, grew to become tremendously powerful pundits for a petrified population that hung on their harangues, which often claimed to know the true dirt of the situation. For others, the fear of communist spread and subversion provided a powerful political foil against one's enemies or ideas that seemed to socially or culturally go too far. This will prove to be the case especially for racial reform in American society and its military.

With witch hunts growing throughout the nation daily, and with his administration and party being called "soft" on communism, Truman responded by issuing an executive order that launched a loyalty investigation of the federal government. His investigation uncovered close to 400 members of the government who were potentially communist sympathizers; another 2,500 officials within the federal bureaucracy resigned because of the hyper-charged nature of the era or fear of being branded as communist, whether or not they really were. But instead of containing the fear, this only fueled it.[43]

AND THE MIND OF THE SOUTH

Writing on the verge of World War II about the lasting effects of the Civil War and Reconstruction on the American South, W. J. Cash observed:

Reconstruction not only did all the things I have just set down, but in the same process, as we need to observe specifically, it also complicated the South's old terrified truculence toward new ideas from the outside. . . . And so here, by an extension which would have been inevitable in any people and which was doubly inevitable in this one with its habitual incapacity for distinctions, was a propensity to see in every notion coming out of the North a menace and an abomination; to view every idea originated by the Yankee or bearing the stamp of his acceptance as containing hidden with itself the old implacable will to coerce and destroy; to repudiate him intellectually as passionately as he was repudiated politically.

This long-running distrust of Yankee or Northern involvement ultimately broadened to include ideas considered to be liberal. In this sense, civil rights reforms during the twentieth century were viewed by Southerners as a continued assault on their way of life.[44]

At the heart of this vestigial distrust of the North and its reformers was the South's continued racist and paranoid, fear-based, and quack-science belief that African Americans, in particular African American males, were substandard, lustful, ignorant, lazy, and unfit to be *their* societal equals. This belief, which was as old as slavery, continued to get new life long after slavery's demise. For the defeated white citizens of the Southern Confederacy, the ascendancy of the African American community was a reality that they refused to accept. So they didn't.

During Reconstruction, they waged legal and extralegal warfare against it, leading to the murder, beating, and gross intimidation of Blacks, and any whites, who supported Blacks' newfound freedoms and equality. After that era, white Southerners engaged in the "Redemption" of the region, terrorized and ran off the reformers, launched Jim Crow segregation, and reaffirmed white over Black. From that effort emerged the Lost Cause narrative, which practitioners used to fabricate an alternative history of slavery, the Civil War, and Reconstruction. It romanticized chattel slavery and submitted that Blacks wanted to be slaves all along. The Lost Cause narrative also lionized the South's political and military defenders to the point of deifying and erecting statues to them while also fabricating an entirely false mythos for their involvement in the Civil War—namely, that it was a righteous struggle between advocates of states' right opposed to the vicious tyranny of a repressive federal government. Ultimately they blamed the whole bloody affair on liberal meddlers from the North—which is why Southerners often called it the "War of Northern Aggression"—as opposed to any wrongdoing of their own. When it came to explaining their defeat, Lost Cause advocates concocted a justification that intertwined unfair play with the gallant stand of a people destined to lose but who decided to fight on anyway.[45]

The propaganda and fear-driven nature of the Second Red Scare dovetailed with the preexisting Southern distrust and resentment of the North and Northern reformers, and therefore Southerners continued to blame their racial problems on their pesky Northern rivals. While a good bit of red-baiting naturally came out of all this, the South, as Jeff Woods noted, was also experiencing its own unique regionally focused red scare within the confines of the larger one engulfing the nation.

Some Southerners truly believed that a coalition—communist, liberal, Jewish, and African American—existed that sought to eradicate the Southern way of life. The betrayal of a Southern son, Truman, further fed their natural inclination to distrust, to spite, and to be paranoid of all things Yankee. As a result, throughout the president's pursuit of civil rights reform, Southern segregationist Democrats at the state and federal levels lashed out. Buoyed by their largely prosegregation voting bases, Southern segregationist politicians used anticommunist red-baiting rhetoric against Truman and his policies. After all, the *Nashville Banner*, a Tennessee-based newspaper, claimed, some of his policies "originated in the left wing of imported politics."[46]

As the Cold War and Second Red Scare went on, Southern attacks against Truman and his policies became more visceral. A willing advocate of all things visceral, and a well-known red-baiter and anti–civil rights advocate in his own right, was John Elliot Rankin, Democratic representative from Mississippi and a prominent and powerful member of HUAC. For Southern segregationist politicians such as Rankin, the haunting specter of red insurrection served as a useful instrument to combat racial integration, whether it be in the civilian or military realm. Rankin's reputation was well known in Washington and beyond. In an article for *Liberty* magazine, the journalist Stan Frank observed that "Southern liberals join Progressive Northerners in denouncing him as the No. 1 bigot, hatemonger, and native-born Fascist in America." So caustic was

Rankin that he was dubbed "the most dangerous man in public life." Along with other conservative Republicans and Democrats, Rankin seized on the nation's growing anxiety over the expansion of communism to attack liberals, Jews, Blacks, and any other group that threatened the white racial status quo that dominated Southern life. After Truman announced his civil rights initiative, the representative from Mississippi pounced on the measures, calling them "damnable, communistic, unconstitutional, anti-American and anti-southern."[47]

When Rankin's slanderous and vitriolic words proved inadequate to move the president on the issue, Southern segregationists conspired to send a sterner rebuke, one that threatened to vote down the European Recovery Program, better known as the "Marshall Plan." The Marshall Plan proposed to uplift war-torn Europe from the ashes and wreckage of World War II so that it might once again resume its important role as a trading partner with the United States while also serving as a Cold War buffer against Russia. It would seem, however, that the martial and militaristic spirit of the region trumped the self-serving nature of its politicians to wage war on anything remotely considered communist. And therefore, though the threat to hold up the Marshall Plan was made, Southern Democrats did not have the stomach or political courage necessary to vote against such a popular anticommunist measure.[48]

While that effort to stop Truman died on the vine, Southern segregationist governors stepped up to the plate to take their swings at the president. Dispatching a five-man committee to the White House, a group headed by South Carolina governor J. Strom Thurmond, a military veteran, segregationist, and rising star in the Southern wing of the Democratic Party and conservative politics in general, they hoped to persuade the president to alter his stance. But they failed. The administration remained rigid and refused to move on the issue.[49]

Those Southerners frustrated and flummoxed by Truman's intransigence believed the only way forward was to isolate the president in a way that would force him to comply with their segregationist beliefs. Their strategy was simple: they were going to cripple Truman's election bid. Those who embraced this strategy defected from the party of Jefferson and formed the States' Rights Democratic Party, known as the "Dixiecrats." Through the candidacy of Strom Thurmond, the Dixiecrats hoped to split the Democratic vote, which would hinder Truman's election chances, while at the same time preventing the election of the Republican civil rights advocate, Thomas Dewey. With no clear-cut winner, the House of Representatives would decide the fate of the election. The Dixiecrats believed that a solid South would prohibit either candidate from

getting a clear majority. This would either force Truman or Dewey to abandon his civil rights agenda or lead to the rise of a new candidate that all parties—preferably, for the South, one that put forth a watered-down civil rights
agenda—could agree upon. And the plan had some political merit, as four
months after the release of *To Secure These Rights*, Truman's approval rating
among Southerners had plummeted to 35 percent. In fact, the Southern political backlash against his reform efforts was so potent that the president deliberately remained silent on the issue until the conclusion of the Democratic
National Convention in July 1948.[50]

THE ORDERS

During the summer of 1948, one month before the president announced his
executive order racially integrating the armed forces, new developments in the
Cold War fanned the flames of anticommunist paranoia in the South and the
nation at large. On June 24, West German citizens and their Allied protectors
awoke to discover their access to the jointly occupied capital city of Berlin was
blocked off by Soviet occupation forces. Compounding this already dangerous
and unexpected standoff was the city's geographical location within the Sovi-
ets' tightly controlled eastern occupation zone. In response, the United States
and its allies launched a humanitarian airlift lasting ten months that sustained
those trapped behind the iron curtain. To protect the Berlin Airlift, Truman
rattled the atomic saber, as he openly announced that he had provided England
with B-29 bombers armed with atomic weapons.[51]

Almost two weeks after he had accepted his party's nomination to run for
the presidency and with the drama of the Berlin Airlift unfolding, Truman
found himself in an unenviable position. A large contingent of his political
party had bolted to become Dixiecrats, with many of them being directly responsible for bogging down his civil rights agenda in Congress. Additionally,
he was facing pressure from the longtime civil rights crusader and dogged
advocate of racial integration of the military A. Phillip Randolph, head of the
Brotherhood of Sleeping Car Porters.[52]

A seasoned civil rights crusader, Randolph was no stranger to presidential
promises. Having tangled with Franklin Roosevelt, he was especially nuanced
in their potential duplicity. Truman's proposed Universal Military Training
(UMT) initiative, however, intrigued Randolph, as it offered a new means to
carry out the goal of racial integration of the military.[53]

War was expensive, and the way that the United States had been waging it was inefficient, argued the War department planners agitating for UMT. It was also foolhardy, they believed, to continue to operate on the historical American notion that the magnificent seas blanketing the flanks of the United States would continue to protect the nation. Pearl Harbor was example enough of how technological advancement could easily penetrate the supposed security the oceans supplied. And then there was the fact that America had been quite fortunate in its involvement in the world wars; it was allowed to bide its time and prepare for war as opposed to being pressed into it from the onset. There was no guarantee that the Americans would be allowed to continue to enjoy this advantage into the future. The enemy, as historian William Taylor later observed, was going to adapt and come after the Americans from the jump.[54]

UMT sought to overcome these issues. Designed to establish a pipeline of ready and able young men for military service, UMT required all men aged eighteen to twenty to perform a year's worth of military training. Instead of creating another leviathan like the American military of World War II, these men would serve in a smaller and more professional military force for the next war. But there was no logical, let alone moral reason, Randolph felt, that this new force needed to be limited to white men or that it should be racially segregated. To do so would be foolish and prevent the Americans from reaping the best talent available throughout the Republic. Understanding this, Randolph sought to have those in Congress sympathetic to his and the Black community's cause attach an antisegregation provision to the UMT bill. But an old dilemma returned. The South controlled the purse strings of the military, which meant that Southern congressmen posed a grave threat to UMT and the funding of the armed forces at large. It would be unwise, the Army reasoned, to do anything that offended them. Because of this, the Army objected to the inclusion of an antisegregation clause as part of the bill. Not only did Randolph's gambit fail; UMT failed to pass at all.[55]

The failure of UMT's passage into law did not deter the disappointed, but no less focused, Randolph. During World War II, Randolph had to raise the prospect of peaceful civil disobedience to achieve reform. With UMT out of the picture, perhaps the same strategy would work on Truman? During a March meeting with Truman, Randolph warned the president: "Negroes are in no mood to shoulder a gun for democracy abroad so long as they are denied democracy here at home." "In particular," he counseled Truman, "they resent the idea of fighting or being drafted into another Jim Crow army."[56]

With the pressure mounting from Randolph, and with his civil rights agenda dead on arrival in Congress, Clark Clifford, the president's chief adviser, gleaned that the only way forward for the president on civil rights reform, particularly for the federal government and the military, was by way of executive orders. Once Truman agreed to Clifford's suggestion, the matter was delegated to Phileo Nash, the Special Assistant to President for Minority Affairs and a civil rights advocate in his own right who had championed for racial integration of the armed forces. The result of Nash's handiwork: two unique but conjoined executive orders (9980 and 9981), which Truman issued on July 26, 1948.[57]

The first, Executive Order 9980, targeted the social behavior of the federal government by revamping its staffing and hiring practices. The federal bureaucracy would now follow a formula that focused on the abilities and attributes of job applicants. Ostensibly, human resource decisions within the federal government would not be made based on an applicant's skin color or religious affiliation. Truman placed responsibility for the success of this program on his cabinet members, who were required to designate civil rights officers within their respective departments. Working with the cabinet was the newly minted Fair Employment Board (FEB). Consisting of seven members, the FEB was charged with overseeing the staffing decisions of the various branches of the government. If the FEB found a grievance, it could force the executive of that department to make a change. Executives who dragged their feet on an issue potentially faced the wrath of the president, as a direct channel of communication existed between Truman and the board.[58]

Though it had always controlled the purse strings of the military, Congress had historically respected the president's authority over it. As a result, the president, in consultation with civilian and military leaders, set manpower guidelines for the armed forces. Had the president not had the constitutional authority to do so, or had Congress sought to curtail the president's powers over the military, it would have been unlikely that Truman would have achieved such a drastic reform. But it did exist, and the president, as would some of his successors, took advantage of it. The second of the two orders, Executive Order 9981, effectively began the process of racial integration of the American military:

It is hereby declared to be the policy of the President that there shall be equality of treatment and opportunity for all persons in the armed services without regard to race, color, religion or national origin. This policy shall be put into effect as rapidly as possible, having due regard to the time required to effectuate any necessary changes without impairing efficiency or morale.

On the one hand, it seemed that the armed forces of the nation, now matching the behavior of its revamped government, would be racially integrated. On the other hand, the order gave Truman a political out, as he did not clearly state that the military would be racially integrated or when it would happen. The move was certainly politically savvy, as it worked to gain the votes of moderate white Democrats and African Americans alike. It also created a firestorm of controversy for Truman with the Black community. In an editorial in the venerated African American newspaper the *Pittsburgh Courier*, the vagueness of the executive order was severely criticized. "Of the score of American nations the United States is the only one that persists in the wrong-headed and unnecessary policy of racial segregation in its armed forces, yet it is this country which assumes the leadership in carrying democracy to others." The editorial mused, no doubt with an eye toward Truman's order, that "the time has long passed for half-way measures."[59]

Another reason for Truman's vagueness was the problem of implementation. Prior to the release of the executive order, Secretary of Defense James Forrestal attempted to convince Clifford to prevent the inclusion of any wording in the order that would establish a timetable for racial integration. Forrestal reasoned that the universal desegregation of the armed forces was a nonsequential undertaking, as the various branches of the military operated largely independently. What worked in the Navy, for example, would not work in the Army, and vice versa. Forrestal's rational for prudence of action was genuinely motivated. He did not want to slow or stop the process before it had begun; instead he thought it best to racially integrate pragmatically. Listening to the secretary of defense's suggestion and believing that it was better to leave the issue to the various heads of the armed forces, Clifford agreed with Forrestal and prevented the inclusion of a deadline in the order.[60]

Despite the vague phrasing of the order and the concerns it created in the Black community, Truman wanted racial desegregation to go forward. Three days after issuing the order, a reporter asked Truman: "Mr. President . . . does your advocacy of equality of treatment and opportunity in the Armed Forces envision eventually the end of segregation?" The president, a man raised in the shadow of Southern racism, answered, "Yes." He also wanted accountability on the issue. To obtain it, he created the President's Committee on Equality of Treatment and Opportunity in the Armed Services. Nicknamed after its chair, Charles Fahy, the Fahy Committee would investigate the armed services to flesh out activities and behaviors that prevented the implementation of Executive Order 9981. If the Fahy Committee discovered something, however, it did not have the power to remedy the situation. Instead, it was up to the secretary of defense and the respective heads of the armed forces to resolve any grievances or policy shortcomings.[61]

DIXIE'S RESPONSE

Executive Order 9981 resonated with the report of a cannon shot across the bow of Southern society. Out of the conflagration and commotion that erupted afterward, Southern segregationists—often by tapping old regional fears and anxieties over federal intrusion into the South—returned fire against the president and his order. Democratic congressman A. Leonard Allen of Louisiana called the president's decision to racially integrate the armed forces a "wound to the south" and predicted that it would "greatly increase [racial] tension, strife and turmoil . . . [and] diminish the efficiency of our armed services." Allen's Democratic colleague from Louisiana, Overton Brooks, believed that "at a time when the world looks to us for strength and courage," the integration of the armed forces was a foolish prospect, as it would only "cripple and impair" the services. The always contemptuous John Rankin of Mississippi, who had been against the president's civil rights efforts all along, considered Truman's decision to integrate the armed forces "one of the greatest blunders that could possibly have been made at this time. If we get into another conflict, it would do more to cripple our national defense than anything else that has taken place since Pearl Harbor." Lacking the scorched-earth nature of Rankin's discourse, Ed Gossett, a Texas Democratic representative, simply bemoaned that "the President has again surrendered to the Reds and radicals."[62]

Disgusted, disparaged, and disappointed, Southern political actors viewed the president's encroachment on the civil liberties of white Southerners to be a bridge too far, an example of heinous executive overreach worthy of a legislative response. That response came from one of South's brightest political sons, Senator Richard B. Russell, Democrat from Georgia.

A constant on the Senate Armed Services Committee, Russell was an avid defender of American military might throughout the twentieth century, but he was also a segregationist and a racist. He was not a visceral and guttural ideologue of, say, Rankin's stature, and Russell did not often engage in cockamamie conspiracy theories or voracious rants about race. He was a refined member of the Southern gentry elite, a gentleman's racist who understood the machinations of politics far better than the average overly passionate bigot.

Russell embraced the Southern notion, built on a faulty foundation, that Blacks were substandard, but as a cunning political operator he more gathered that his constituents, those who controlled his political fate, also *believed* Blacks were not worthy of equality in society or its armed forces. Despite his own feelings, which frankly meshed with those whom he represented, Russell was smart enough to realize that he had better stand firm with the rest of the South against racial integration. As Forrestal sarcastically observed in his personal diary: "The motivation for Senator Russell's amendment [against racial integration] extends from the fact that he is up for re-election this year and he must therefore be clearly and strongly on record against the spirit of the President's Civil Rights message."[63]

Russell entered the debate over racial integration of the military by labeling Truman's executive orders as nothing more than the "Articles of Unconditional Surrender by the present occupant of the White House to the Negroes A. Phillip Randolph and Grant Reynolds and their Civil Disobedience Campaign." The amendment that Forrestal referenced in his personal diary made its initial appearance during the summer of 1948 and returned in the summer of 1950, when Russell, flanked by Senator Burnet R. Maybank, Democrat from South Carolina, proposed an amendment to the Selective Service Act that allowed new recruits in the military the right to choose whether they served in integrated or segregated units.[64]

The press pounced on the amendment as nothing more than an attempt to perpetuate segregation in the military, which was exactly what Russell was attempting to do. The senator from Georgia remained coy about the whole thing. He argued that his act was not racial segregation at all. Instead, Russell felt that it afforded recruits, white or Black, "freedom of choice." In this way, he presented his actions as those of a man seeking to defend the rights and social sensitivities, regardless of race, of the citizenry. In addition to supposedly protecting the rights of citizens, Russell viewed his actions as the preservation of the armed forces from what he believed would be the demoralizing and debilitating effects of racial integration. After all, the Southerner contended, "the morale and health of the men is sure to be adversely affected" by racial desegregation. Russell was not content with making simple arguments rooted in individual rights and national security, however. He willingly dipped into a cherry-picked, and highly questionable, justification of the quasi–social scientific belief that Blacks were substandard, untrustworthy, and lustful creatures compared to whites. Focusing on Black criminal and sexual behavior during World War II, he informed Congress:

The official figures of the War department during the last war show that the percentage of crime in Negro organizations was approximately twice that of white units. The official reports of the United States Public Health Service show that of the first 2,000,000 selectees examined in World War II the prevalent rate for syphilis among whites males was 17.4 percent per 1,000, but among nonwhite males it was 252.3 percent per 1,000. In the age group 20 to 25 years the prevalent rate of syphilis among nonwhite males was 19 times greater than among white males.

Afterward, Russell, who admitted to having many Black acquaintances, lamented that "it is painful to the point of nausea" to have to use these damning statistics against them. That it pained the senator from Georgia personally to use this information remains highly dubious. He deliberately dredged up long-standing racial stereotypes of Blacks—using questionable data to do so—to reinforce a Southern point of view about the racial composition of the military, one shared by several of its leaders, which was that racial integration jeopardized the effectiveness of the armed forces in its global struggle with communism because it would introduce untrustworthy criminals and sexual deviants into the ranks. Despite his attempt to paint a wide image of the African American community, Russell's efforts failed to pass. Shortly thereafter, the threat of a potential Southern filibuster as a form of reprisal to Truman's civil rights actions also failed to materialize.[65]

The cacophony of calamity emanating from the South was not limited to Southern politicians; it also originated from angry and fearful white Southerners who wrote to their representatives condemning the president's reform agenda, including the racial integration and reform of the military. In several letters, Southerners voiced displeasure to political leadership by making references to the Civil War, Reconstruction, and the unwanted intrusion of Northerners or liberal outsiders into their region's affairs. Other letters made even wilder unsubstantiated and conspiratorial claims. For them, civil rights reform efforts in the military and American society became synonymous with a communist conspiracy to subvert the nation. There was no limit to the lengths that some Southern white citizens, and white citizens from elsewhere, were prepared to go to ascertain who was really behind all of it.

Some believed that the conspiracy was not just communist but the work of Jews, who were behind a Jewish-controlled, big-government endeavor to penetrate and betray the sanctity of the nation, specifically the American South. For instance, in a letter to Senator J. William Fulbright of Arkansas—over the years, Fulbright received many letters from constituents who confused his position on the Senate Foreign Relations Committee with that of the Senate Armed Forces Committee—Mary Ethel Haldane Kindle, a transplanted Arkansan living in New York City, contended that Jews, Catholics, and communists had conspired together to attack the South. Why the South? "The South," she observed, "is the one solid, substantial American, decent Protestant section of the country left." One of the ways that leftist provocateurs in American society attacked it, Kindle ascertained, was through civil rights reform, and "communist front organizations and Jews (do you realize that their philosophy is essentially communistic?) are the motivating forces behind this anti-discrimination etc." Phil Poston of Silver Springs, Maryland, all but seconded Kindle's comments by demanding that Fulbright take action against this "Communistic effort disguised as the so-called Civil Rights Program in their plan to enslave the South and to take the first step in Russia's insidious plan to "Divide and Conquer."[66]

Truman also received several letters from citizens, predominately in the South, who opposed his actions. After writing to Fulbright, Poston, a former major during World War I, then penned a letter to the president. In it, he gravely warned Truman of the impending civil war that would no doubt occur if he continued forward with his civil rights agenda. "I believe I am correct in assuring you that the so-called Civil Rights program, if enacted into law, will be defied and defeated in the Southern States at what-ever cost in life and treasure necessary to defend that which is more dear and vital than life itself." B. E. Thomas of West Virginia reminded Truman of the racial status quo of the region when she observed: "In the world, the negro has got arrogant, overbearing, and who is the cause of it, a few mistaken people, and gov[ernment]," to which she added "you have a great responsibility on your shoulders and you should put the negro in his place and keep him there, and should quit appeasing Russia." Y. F. Stewart of Kansas City, Missouri, a stone's throw from Truman's hometown of Independence, brought Christian faith—a refrain that would continue to be chanted over the years to come—into the issue: "I do not believe that God ever intended that negroes and white people be as one, even animals cling to their kind."[67]

Sometimes the criticisms the president received came from more personal sources, such as old acquaintances and friends. One such letter came from Truman's friend Ernie Roberts of the Faultless Starch Company in Kansas City, Missouri. As opposed to a cordial letter seeking to catch up with Truman, Roberts admonished the president for his stand on civil rights. Roberts reminded the president that he was a Southerner, and therefore if Truman wanted to survive politically, he needed to embrace the gospel of Jim Crow. Instead of letting the president handle the issue of civil rights reform for the Black community, Roberts suggested: "Harry, let us let the South take care of the Niggers, which they have done, and if the Niggers do not like the Southern treatment,

let them come to Mrs. Roosevelt." Getting to the heart of the matter, he continued: "Harry, you are a Southerner and a D—good one so [listen]. . . . I can see,
you do not talk domestic problems over with Bess," but if "you put equal rights
in Independence and Bess will not live with you, will you Bess[?]"[68]

While Roberts's advice was bigoted and personal, as it brought the first lady
into the issue, it fit with the political and racial climate of the time. It was advice, however, that Truman just could not take. The president responded: "I
am going to send you a copy of the report of my Commission on Civil Rights
and then if you still have that antebellum proslavery outlook, I'll be thoroughly
disappointed in you." "The main difficulty with the South," the president continued, "is that they are living eighty years behind the times and the sooner
they come out of it the better it will be for the country and themselves." He
concluded his letter by reminding Roberts of that which he often stated but
truly believed: "I am not asking for social equality, because no such thing exists, but I am asking for equality of opportunity for all human beings and, as
long as I stay here, I am going to continue that fight."[69]

THE GENERALS CHIME IN

While Truman promised to keep up the fight, Southerners discovered allies
to their anti-integration mission within the leadership of the military. The research of Sherie Mershon and Steven Schlossman has demonstrated that, over
the years, the leadership of the armed forces had concocted numerous reasons for maintaining racial segregation of personnel, rationales that focused
on maintaining the role of the military as the defender of the republic while
also being wary of the political ramifications—especially considering that the
domination of Southern segregationists in key defense funding positions had
changed little since the era of Franklin D. Roosevelt—that could occur by
launching a civil rights reform program within its ranks. These concerns fit
neatly within their greater belief that racial integration or civil rights reforms
would threaten the "military efficiency" of the armed forces.[70]

A notable defense of segregation before Truman's order was issued came
from General Dwight D. Eisenhower. Though Ike had himself temporarily racially integrated American fighting forces in Europe during the Battle
of the Bulge, in testimony before the recently established Senate Armed Services Committee in 1948 he defended the military's embrace of segregation by
suggesting that it worked as a policy because it thwarted the inherent racism
of the nation. The former supreme commander contended that, through the

separation of the races, white and Black alike could develop in a way that utilized the natural gifts and talents of both.[71]

This idea that segregation was a positive boon and could lead to positive developments for Black soldiers was not an idea that was exclusive to Eisenhower. A common belief among some American military leaders of the era was that racial integration would deny African Americans, who had poorer educational backgrounds than whites on average, a chance at social advancement. The racial segregation of the military, they asserted in a paternalistic but no less racist way, maintained the necessary racial barriers to exist that allowed Blacks to solely compete with other African Americans. Racial desegregation would end this advantageous situation for those Blacks with stronger educational backgrounds; and of course, leaning back on the efficiency dogma that the military continued to champion, it would also disrupt the harmony of the armed forces. Through education and time, Eisenhower mused, African Americans could overcome their social and educational disadvantages. Until then, racial desegregation of the military was an unwise move, as Eisenhower informed the Senate: "If you make a complete amalgamation, what you are going to have is in every company the Negro is going to be relegated to the minor jobs, and he is never going to get his promotion to such grades as technical sergeant, master sergeant, and so on, because the competition is too tough."[72]

During Eisenhower's testimony before the Senate, the general did pause to reflect on his own past views on the matter: "I do not by any means hold out for this extreme segregation as I said when I first joined the Army 38 years ago." He also reflected on the future and believed that through the evolution of American society racism would no longer constrain the nation or its military. However, it would not come, in his opinion, through federal fiat. "It will disappear," Eisenhower ascertained, "through mutual respect, and so on. But I do believe that if we attempt merely by passing a lot of laws to force someone to like someone else, we are just going to get into trouble." Though he was evolving, his comments served as grist for the Southern segregationist mill and attacks on Truman's actions.[73]

Another dissenting voice came from the man who replaced Eisenhower as Chief of Staff of the Army, General Omar Bradley. From the Battle of the Bulge onward, Bradley waged a counteroffensive against racial reform that prevented the possibility of what he referred to as the "instant integration" of the Army. In 1945, he had downplayed the role Black volunteers played during the Battle of the Bulge, which ran counter to the findings of ETO-82 and later *To Secure These Rights*. Bradley had also worried about the morale of a racially integrated fighting force. With no enemy to destroy, and no war to be waged, would the cohesion achieved on the battlefield between white and Black remain? Or would racial animosity sweep in and cause disruption? Bradley seemed to believe the latter.[74]

While he was not convinced of the necessity for racial integration, Bradley did not want to totally rid the Army of Black soldiers either. Instead, he called for a lighter form of racial segregation: the use of Black forces in combat should continue, but only in a way that relied heavily on racial segregation. For instance, he suggested in 1945 to then–Chief of Staff General George C. Marshall that African American rifle companies should be segregated within white regiments, a prospect that he believed would help avoid racial conflict.[75]

After the release of Executive Order 9981, Bradley continued his efforts to stymie the racial integration of the armed forces. During an inspection visit at Fort Knox, Kentucky, Bradley, who claimed to be oblivious to Truman's executive order racially integrating the military, announced that no changes would be made to the racial policy of the military until the nation changed its attitudes on the issue of race. After Bradley was informed that the president had in fact signed an executive order on the matter, the general quickly backpedaled and apologized in a letter to Truman. In that letter, the chief of staff attempted to get out of the hot water he found himself in by explaining his gaff, which in reality was a defense of the position of the Army on racial integration: "While I do believe it would be hazardous for us to employ the Army deliberately as an instrument of social reform, I do likewise believe the Army must be kept fully apace of the substantial progress being made by the civilian community." Bradley's explanation fit with the conventional thinking of the Army, which had relied on this thought process as a justification for maintaining a racially segregated fighting force since the conclusion of the Civil War. In sum, civilian society, not the Army, would dictate when it was time for change. In a 1954 interview with Lee Nichols, during a period when the Army was almost completely integrated, Bradley reiterated his position, as he feared "pushing it [racial integration of the military] before people were ready to accept it."[76]

In *A General's Life*, Bradley further elaborated upon his deliberate efforts to slow the racial integration of the armed forces by claiming that most of the military hailed from Dixie. To integrate would disrupt that key recruiting base. Allowing the armed forces, let alone his beloved Army, to lead the way on racial integration, Bradley felt, was akin to placing the cart before the horse. Worse, pushing racial reform before it was accepted would shake the armed forces and the communities near its installations, many of which resided in the American South, to the core. Bradley also reminded readers in his autobiography that the politics of the era mattered. Strong and powerful Southern men in congress, the general observed, controlled the purse strings of the military; to move against racial segregation could be fatal to the budget of the sword and shield.[77]

Bradley's comments about the executive order did not faze Truman, though he would have to engage in a good bit of damage control because of them. Upon receiving the Franklin D. Roosevelt Memorial Brotherhood Medal from the Interdenominational Ministers Alliance, an award given to those who demonstrated Roosevelt's commitment to human rights, Truman reaffirmed his pledge, just days before the 1948 election, to civil rights: "Eventually, we are going to have an America in which freedom and opportunity are the same for everyone. There is only one way to accomplish that great purpose, and that is to keep working for it and never take a backward step. . . . For my part, I intend to keep moving toward this goal [civil rights reform] with every ounce of strength and determination that I have." Once Truman made this statement, he moved on from the incident and never looked back. But Walter White and A. A. Heist, head of the American Civil Liberties Union, found the Bradley's statements concerning. It "is another illustration," White explained, "of how men who have been isolated in the Army for many years are unable to understand or even be aware of the growth of enlightened public opinion." Meanwhile, Heist worried about the deeper ramifications that could result from Bradley's off-the-cuff comments. In essence, he worried that a sense of doubt could creep into the collective mind of the Black community on the eve of a presidential election that would question Truman's true intentions behind the order.[78]

While such concerns were valid, a greater threat to the racial integration of the armed forces surfaced. Southern segregations seized Bradley's and Eisenhower's statements and used them to support their stand against racial integration of the military. Senators Russell and Maybank, for instance, used Eisenhower's and Bradley's statements while they advocated for "freedom of choice" for military recruits. In many ways, Bradley became a quasi–folk hero in the South for his stance against the actions of a forsaken and fallen son, Truman. Democratic congressmen Joseph Bryson of South Carolina celebrated the Army's top general "for his courage in continuing the policy of General Eisenhower on segregation." The *Fort Worth Star Telegram* hailed Bradley's comments as "realistic and courageous" and observed that efforts to institute civil rights reform and end racial segregation should "be deplored because they are violative of the free individual's right to choose his own associates and companions." Chiming in as well was the *Montgomery Advertiser*, which believed that Bradley "has given the back of his hand to Truman's military rights proposal." The chief of staff's candor "rates a national salute," the *Jackson Clarion-Ledger* victoriously declared.[79]

THE FAHY COMMITTEE

During the summer and fall of 1948, Truman weathered the political intensity hurled at him from his own party. But the president had to deal with the loss of four Southern states that defected to back the Dixiecrat candidate, Thurmond, and defeated the challenge presented by the civil rights–minded Republican candidate, Dewey, to win the election. Working quietly in the background of the 1948 election was the Fahy Committee. With seven members, including two prominent African Americans—Lester Granger, head of the National Urban League, and John H. Sengstacke, patriarch of the *Chicago Defender*—the Fahy Committee embarked on its goal of bringing the armed forces in line with the president's executive order.[80]

As an advisory and compliance body, the Fahy Committee operated with little power of its own. A head-on assault against the military's segregationist policies and its practitioners would net little, as it could not force change. Another constriction on its ability to act was the president. Although highly supportive of the committee's work, Truman was not going to "knock somebody's ears down" over racial integration unless it was necessary. Instead, the president seemed to hope that the committee and the military would be able to work out the situation. Within these tight confines, the Fahy Committee adopted a strategy that sought to convince the military to reform based on the moralistic and practical benefits of change.[81]

The Fahy Committee quickly discovered, however, that the newly created Department of Defense, which was designed to maintain a layer of civilian control over the military, would be an obstacle to its efforts. The first secretary of defense, James Forrestal had the unenviable task of establishing and protecting the power and integrity of his position for himself and his successors while at the same time cudgeling and cajoling the various personalities and egos of the military to get them in line with his policies. The Fahy Committee's arrival presented an unwanted intrusion into his affairs. To curtail the committee's influence in his department's affairs, Forrestal set Thomas R. Reid, head of the Personnel Policy Board, to work on a plan that racially integrated the armed forces by July 1950.[82]

Forrestal, however, never had a chance to approve it. Being the first secretary of defense put tremendous pressure on him. The defense chief had made his job even more difficult by creating enemies within the administration when he openly opposed the creation of the state of Israel. Though he was not alone in his dissent, as Secretary of State George C. Marshall also disagreed with the move, the difference was that Marshall carried far more political and military cachet than the lifelong public servant Forrestal did. Party loyalists also openly questioned what they considered to be his lackluster effort on behalf of Truman during the 1948 presidential campaign. On occasion, even Truman questioned Forrestal's ability to do the job, as the president felt the secretary of defense was too hesitant, unsure of himself, and not prepared for the task at hand. Under the combined weight of criticism and pressure, Forrestal suffered a mental breakdown that hastened the end of his tenure in the office. Taking the high road, Truman made his defense chief's exodus look like a resignation. The president awarded Forrestal the Distinguished Service Medal, gave him a pat on the back, and then quietly and quickly removed him. Tragically, a month and a half later, James Forrestal committed suicide. Forrestal's untimely death also impacted the racial integration of the armed forces. With no firm hand on the tiller at the Department of Defense, the armed forces, ostensibly because they had not played a role in its development, shot down Reid's plan for racial integration by July 1950.[83]

The new secretary of defense, Louis Johnson, supported his predecessor's determination to protect the sanctity of the office. But any similarity between the two men ended there. Rather than being overwhelmed by the office, Johnson embraced it. For the new defense chief, he viewed the job as a stepping-stone to bigger and better political positions. As Johnson settled into his new role, Reid returned to work on a new plan for racial integration. To placate the armed forces, Reid removed the original target date for integration, which had been set for July 1950. Though there was no formal deadline for compliance, the new plan required the military to submit its individual plans for racial integration by May 1, 1949. Johnson approved of the idea because it protected his autonomy, prevented the Fahy Committee from making any recommendations that challenged the authority of his office, and gave him an issue—racial integration—that he could use to further his own career.[84]

AIMING HIGH: THE AIR FORCE AND RACIAL REFORM

While Johnson schemed to protect his office and political future, the Fahy Committee discovered a willing ally supporting racial reform in the military in Secretary of the Air Force W. Stuart Symington. During World War II, Symington had served as head of Emerson Electric, and in that position he racially integrated its operations. Abandoning racial segregation made sense to Symington; a war was on, he had orders to fill, and he needed all able-bodied workers.[85]

His upbringing also played a role in the decision. Like many families, Symington's was complex. Part of his family owed their lineage to the stars and bars of the failed Southern Confederacy, but his mother, who raised him in the Northeast, chose to embrace African Americans. Additionally, as a young man working for his uncle, Symington cut his teeth in the world working side by side with Black workers. These experiences codified in his mind that not only was racial segregation morally abhorrent; it was equally as wasteful. Reflecting on his growth in this regard, Symington observed: "What determined me many years ago was a quotation from Bernard Shaw in [Gunnar] Myrdal's book, *American Dilemma*, which went something like this—'First the American white man makes the negro clean his shoes, then criticizes him for being a bootblack.'" "All Americans should have their chance," Symington asserted, and that was coming from a man whose "grandfathers were in the Confederate Army." Symington's thoughts were not bluster. Assistant Secretary of the Air Force Eugene Zuckert recalled of his boss: "With Symington, it was principle first, efficiency second." Two years prior to the implementation of Executive Order 9981 and the arrival of the Fahy Committee at his doorstep, Symington had worked energetically with Air Force leadership to hammer out a plan to racially integrate that branch.[86]

When the Fahy Committee met with Air Force leadership, Symington presented his plan for racial integration, which was already underway. Symington's plan called for the slow but steady racial integration of the service. Under the plan, the Air Force no longer took into consideration race when administering promotions, training, or job assignments. Furthermore, the Air Force combined all African American airmen into two pools of talent: skilled and unskilled. Skilled African American airmen gradually moved into white units that had open slots. Unskilled Black airmen remained in segregated units until a similar unskilled position opened in a white unit. While the Fahy Committee offered some minor suggestions, which the Air Force willingly made, it largely approved of the plan. On May 11, 1949, with Johnson's blessing, the Air Force officially began to racially integrate, but in reality it had been doing so all along.[87]

The prospect of racially integrating the Air Force meant running afoul of

Southern politicians and their constituents who fretted over challenging and changing the racial environment around Southern air bases. The *Pittsburgh Courier* reported that some Southern politicians had vowed to fight against the integration of Southern Air Force bases by threatening to cut funding. Without batting an eye, the Symington-led Air Force declared that the policy of racial integration, originating with the president's order, "will be followed straight down the line." Southern fears were soon realized as racial integration on base spilled over into the local community. At Maxwell Air Force Base, located near Montgomery, Alabama, Black airmen sought to integrate the Montgomery City Bus Line. Believing they acted in accord with the president's executive order, they attempted on two separate occasions to force the bus company to comply with racial integration. Both attempts failed, however, as the bus company was not part of the federal government and therefore was not under the purview of Truman's order. Six years later the issue resurfaced, but this time it was not servicemen challenging racial segregation on Montgomery buses but Rosa Parks.[88]

The Air Force's plan also required the end of all-Black units, including the famed 332nd Fighter Wing. During World War II, the 332nd was comprised the 99th, 100th, 301st, and 302nd Fighter Squadrons. Known collectively as the "Tuskegee Airmen," these men had dared to fly for a nation that for the better part of its history turned its back on them. The deactivation of this pioneering and wildly successful force meant the end of an era. The 332nd was important not only because of its lineage but also because it provided command opportunities for African American officers. Others worried that the decommissioning of the 332nd was a harbinger of a racial purge of Black airmen from the service. Although the scenario of a forced exodus of African Americans from the Air Force was understandable considering the racism present in the armed services, it failed to materialize. Those Black airmen who remained in the service took advantage of the racial inclusiveness of the branch to enroll in integrated training programs and development schools to better themselves. That said, the Air Force did discharge 20 percent of its African American personnel, which caused a measure of consternation within the Black community. To ease any remaining concerns over potential racial chicanery within the branch, the African American press, specifically the *Pittsburg Courier*, investigated the matter and found that the Air Force had acted fairly in discharging these men.[89]

To be sure, there were more than a few difficulties during the journey toward racial integration in the Air Force. Southern white officers and enlisted men pleaded with Air Force leadership that reducing the proximity between the races was a dangerous idea. In their minds, one wrong look, poorly uttered phrase, or some other social misstep could end in a racial brawl. To counter these concerns, the Air Force relied on its policies and procedures and high-ranking officers and their subordinates to carry out the transition from racial segregation to integration. The methodology was clear: when the Air Force put reforms into place, they were unified and structured. The officers behind racial integration utilized orders and military discipline to force compliance; racist white officers and enlisted men who stood in the way of integration faced disciplinary action or discharge from the service. In 1950, the Fahy Committee checked in on the Air Force's progress and came away impressed, as few problems existed between the races.[90]

For all the rapid achievements, racial issues persisted in the Air Force and carried on for decades. African Americans throughout the military found that, once the bugle had sounded and the workday ended, the military did little to ease their existence off base in the racist communities that excluded and belittled them. In particular, Black personnel struggled to find suitable housing close to the base. Often, they settled for housing in some of the most impoverished areas of towns or in the next town over.

The experience of Charles E. McGee, a member of the Tuskegee Airmen and noted pilot, was illustrative. Stationed in Salina, Kansas, during the early months of racial integration of the branch, McGee quickly discovered that racial segregation off base, especially in housing, remained the norm. Because of the lack of available housing on base, and the racial segregation and racism off base, he was unable to move his family with him to Kansas. Later, after relocating to California, McGee again encountered the off-base racism that plagued all African American personnel as he continued to struggle to find housing for his family. Through the help of a friendly white man, McGee finally managed to acquire housing, but that housing was a considerable distance from the base.[91]

Though McGee found his professional life within the confines of the integrated Air Force to be acceptable, he was socially isolated from those whites whom he commanded. In the early days of racial integration, whites begrudgingly accepted Blacks among their ranks. It seemed that whites tolerated and treated African American personnel in a professional manner only because to do anything else could jeopardize their careers. For instance, at Salina, McGee discovered that, even though some white men under his command respected him, as they knew he was a decorated combat veteran, they never embraced him as a comrade or as a social equal.[92]

ROUGH RACIAL WATERS FOR THE NAVY

While the Air Force moved forward on integration, the other branches followed suit at their own unique, sometimes meandering, pace. The Navy—which would clash with the Air Force over the future of strategic bombing and carrier-based aviation during the so-called Revolt of the Admirals, which occurred during the racial integration of the armed forces—was no stranger to the employment of African Americans. During the colonial era, when American ambitions, let alone "Americanism," were born, free Blacks and slaves served on naval vessels because the Navy needed them. And it made sense why they were needed. Naval travel was arduous, unpredictable with the weather, and lonely, so much so that some free white sailors deserted their vessels, which provided Black colonials and slaves seeking opportunities and escape from the racial purgatory of the mainland, let alone the peculiar institution itself, a chance to serve in the navies of the United States, whether Continental, colonial, or privateer. As the Revolutionary War unfolded and George Washington's dilemma over whether to use Blacks in the armies of the emerging Republic raged on, the situation proved different on the high seas. The historian Jack Foner observed that the colonial trend of employing free Blacks and slaves continued and that they discharged their duties well and were even present when the father of the Navy, John Paul Jones, and his *Bonhomme Richard* clashed with the HMS *Serapis* in 1779.[93]

After the Revolutionary War, the new nation passed in 1792 a law that pivoted hard toward the creation of an armed forces that championed white military personnel, ages eighteen to forty-five, over those of differing colors. While a few standouts among the states emerged, most viewed this as an outright prohibition against Black military service. While the Army and the Marine Corps toed the line with this new law, the Navy did not. And the reason they did not was necessity. It remained difficult for the Navy to attract an appropriate number of white sailors to serve on their ships, so when it could not, it turned to African Americans.[94]

It was not as if the Navy had not wrestled with the idea of racial integration. Within its confines existed the Special Programs Unit (SPU), which was tasked to examine and study the use of African American naval personnel. In time, the SPU became the engine behind racial change within the Navy. The SPU, though, needed a cause to help make reform palatable or necessary. The necessity of the moment, World War II, provided it. But it also needed a leader dedicated to the issue to lead reform in the Navy. Indeed, the desire to promote racial integration onboard naval vessels required a certain level of institutional "want-to" among the Navy's leadership. Under the guidance of Frank Knox, that want-to was largely nonexistent. When Knox unexpectedly died and James Forrestal assumed the office, the new leader met the necessity of the moment.[95]

The difference in leadership was immediate. During the closing moments of World War II, a racial incident occurred onboard a Navy vessel involving African American soldiers of the US Army returning Stateside for demobilization. Shortly after hearing about the incident, Secretary Forrestal released a memorandum reminding all commanding officers and personnel in the Navy that "no differentiation shall be made because of race or color. This applies also to authorized personnel of all the armed services of this country aboard navy ships or at navy station and activities." The SPU now found itself in a position where it was working in tandem, and not against, the secretary of the Navy, which so often seemed to be the case under Knox. The result was the beginning of experimenting with racial integration of the Navy.[96]

It started first with the racial integration of twenty-five auxiliary (support) ships with the total compliment of African Americans onboard not to exceed 10 percent. The 10 percent ceiling seemed to keep, in the minds of reformers, concerns about conflict between the races emerging to a minimum. Largely, these ships were to operate completely integrated, but one caveat did emerge: sleeping quarters. Though racial integration was the rule of the day, captains of the ships had the ability to segregate sleeping quarters if they deemed it necessary. Though they were deterred from doing so, some did segregate their crews. Of the twenty-five ships, only one gave an unfavorable evaluation. After digesting the findings of the reports submitted about the experiment and with no major problems present, the Navy decided to integrate all its auxiliary vessels. It also began racially integrating its basic training courses and other advanced training facilities. These reforms did not stay isolated to American naval vessels or domestic ports of call but also applied to the Navy's ports of call throughout the world. As compared other branches after World War II, Forrestal and the Navy had embraced the notion, even if only gradually, that racial integration made it a more efficient fighting force.[97]

While the Fahy Committee recognized the gains the Navy had made, it wondered why the Navy still struggled to attract African Americans into the service or why it had so few Black officers amid its officer ranks. The Fahy Committee ultimately came to believe that the Navy had been too reticent to change during the end of Forrestal's tenure (by 1947, Forrestal had left the Navy to become the first secretary of defense), and therefore this reluctance to go further left several remaining problems in place that adversely affected its ability to recruit from the Black community. The most prominent issues plaguing the Navy were the continued existence of the racially segregated Steward Branch and the lack of Black officers.[98]

During the attack on Pearl Harbor, the Steward Branch had produced a war hero, Messman Doris "Dorie" Miller. While inspirational, Miller's experience was an outlier. The fact that he was limited to the Steward Branch was not. Though the Navy claimed that the Steward Branch—a services-based organization within the larger branch—was open to all races, its staffing practices transformed it into a notorious dumping ground for racial minority service personnel. In 1948, 62 percent of all African American naval personnel were in the Steward Branch. While it purportedly offered an opportunity for its members at a better way of life, service as a steward was largely demeaning in nature. The uniforms they donned were deliberately different and designed to set themselves apart from the rest of the Navy. Even higher ranks held within the branch were lessened; for example a chief steward, the highest rank one could achieve, carried no authority in the general Navy even with seamen of a lower rank.[99]

Systemic racism in the Navy's entrance requirements also played a part in racial composition. After World War II, the Navy raised its general entrance requirements, but it refused to adjust the low entrance requirements of the Steward Branch. The Navy defended the change by contending that the technological nature of the service demanded the induction of educated seamen who could handle the challenges these technologies presented. In this sense, they contended it was not about race but about educational ability. Furthermore, the decision to keep the entrance requirements of the Steward Branch low was defended in a racist and paternalistic fashion by naval leadership, who in their own way were mirroring the ideological framework of Eisenhower and other Army generals on the need to maintain segregation of the ranks; they contended that they were doing a favor to those undereducated whites and Blacks who wanted to join the general service of the Navy but could not qualify to do so by offering them a chance to join the Steward Branch. From there, the Navy reminded its critics, stewards who had earned the proper qualifications could transfer out of the branch and into the general service. Lastly, naval leadership argued that there was a positive outcome that emerged from their method of staffing the Steward Branch: retention rates. Stewards, the Navy noted, had some of the highest reenlistment rates among all naval personnel.[100]

Though the Navy had come a good way on the journey toward racial integration, it was stonewalling. And the Fahy Committee knew it. The Fahy Committee responded to the Navy's defense of maintaining the segregation present in the Steward Branch by observing that the technologically driven Air Force did not have the same problems as the Navy did when recruiting unskilled African Americans. And it did not, the committee noted, have the same problem of offering African Americans an opportunity at advancement. Though the Navy offered the option to transfer out of the Steward Branch, most stewards did not have the education and skills to do so; furthermore, the Navy never seriously attempted to grant them a means of gaining the experience necessary to matriculate out of the branch. Instead, if you were African American and in the Steward Branch, you found yourself in a service that had limited advancement opportunities, prevented you from gaining the technical skills necessary to seek employment in the civilian world, let alone the general service of the Navy, and little to no means to gain the experience necessary to transfer out of the career purgatory you found yourself in.[101]

To rectify this deleterious situation in the Steward Branch and the issue of a lack of Black officers, the Fahy Committee suggested that the Navy go to the African American community and sell it on the Navy's commitment to the president's goal of racial integration. Dutifully, if not begrudgingly, the Navy met this requirement by sending active-duty and reserve African American officers and petty officers into the Black community, where they could serve as walking, talking, breathing proof of the Navy's commitment to change and that an opportunity to serve outside the Steward Branch existed. Meanwhile, Black naval officers were also to spearhead a plan within the Navy to recruit African Americans into officer candidate programs such as the Naval Reserve Officers Training Corps (NROTC). With an eye toward improving the image of the Steward Branch within the Black community, the Navy, amid a good bit of grumbling from within, granted chief stewards the rank and pay of chief petty officer.[102]

Any change to the Navy would not come from within but instead came by way of the Department of Defense, which in 1951 instituted a new aptitude test for the armed forces. This new test sought to eliminate the factor of race and instead focused on the individual qualifications of the applicant. To strike a balance in the new test, the Department of Defense installed a quota system that demanded the services fill their ranks with recruits of all aptitude levels. While designed with the entire armed forces in mind, this new system increased the number of African Americans, primarily those from impoverished and poorly educated backgrounds, into the Navy.[103]

Even with these reforms in place, the Navy still struggled to attract African American recruits. And rightfully so, as Black citizens believed that nothing had really changed in the branch. While the number of African Americans in the Steward Branch declined significantly by 1953, they still represented the majority (51.7 percent) of the Navy's Black population. To make matters worse, while naval bases had integrated as it applied to servicemen, civilian workers employed by those facilities continued to face racial segregation, which only reaffirmed in the minds of Black naval personnel, potential Black recruits, and the Black community that the Navy was not serious about racial integration.[104]

For instance, in a telegram to President Truman during the summer of 1952, Walter White lamented the horrid conditions facing African American workers at the Charleston and Norfolk naval bases. Seeking clarity on how racial segregation toward Black civilian workers could continue after the issuance of Executive Order 9981, the NAACP reached out to the Department of the Navy directly. In response to the NAACP's inquiry, Rear Admiral W. McI. Hague, chief of industrial relations, admitted that segregation existed for Black civilian workers "at water coolers, rest rooms and in the cafeterias" on base because they did not fall under the jurisdiction of Executive Order 9981. The order applied only to service personnel, not civilians employed by the base. Instead of working to halt this practice, the Navy stood firmly in the corner of Jim Crow segregation. The justification for this stance came from OIR Notice CP 75, which ordered naval personnel to follow the local social and racial norms of the communities surrounding naval institutions on the issue of race. The only exception was if the commander of a base believed he could institute racial integration of civilian employees without trouble from the locals. The Navy's concession to the omnipresent nature of Jim Crow racism in the south ensured that African American civilian employees on base would continue to suffer racial indignities for the foreseeable future and, as a byproduct, that Blacks would continue to view the Navy in a negative light.[105]

BRINGING UP THE REAR: THE ARMY AND THE MARINE CORPS

The Fahy Committee's efforts to encourage racial integration in the Air Force and the Navy proved much easier than its attempts to work with the Army and the Marine Corps on the issue. Clinging to the racist science and sentiment of the past, Army leadership continued to advocate, from Secretary of the Army Kenneth Royall on down, that their own form of sociological experimentation, a racially segregated Army, offered the best way to uphold the military efficiency of the service, while also invoking the common defense of segregationists that essentially contended that a "separate but equal" Army provided an excellent opportunity for African American soldiers to achieve advancement by competing with their own race.[106]

While Royall understood and appreciated that racial integration would ease monetary and administrative burdens, he clung to the rationale of Householder and others that "the Army is not an instrument for social evolution." "It is not," Royall emphatically believed, "the Army's job either to favor or to impede social doctrines, no matter how progressive they may be." And therefore the Army should not change or serve as a catalyst for change. The Chief of Staff of the Army and hero of the segregationist South, Omar Bradley, heartily agreed. "Why ruin a good thing?" "I believe that the Negro soldier, in general, considers his lot, from his viewpoint, a good one," the general remarked before the Fahy Committee. À la Eisenhower's rationale, Bradley believed that, once the competitive advantage racial segregation provided disappeared, undereducated Black soldiers would have to compete with whites who had a higher education. The result, in his mind, would be disastrous to the morale and prosperity of Black personnel.[107]

The Fahy Committee moved swiftly to debunk and counter the Army's racist argument for racial segregation. To achieve this, it had to show that a racially segregated Army was not efficient and that segregation did not provide African Americans with an equal opportunity for advancement. A natural starting point for the committee was the flawed staffing and induction practices of the Army, which had sought to maintain a tight cap on the number of Black soldiers inducted into the service. A product of the Gillem Report, the number of Blacks serving in the Army had been capped at 10 percent of the total population. In a sense, this would prevent the overrepresentation of African American soldiers in a fashion that was disproportionate to their population, which meant that they were not potentially fighting or dying in a ratio that was out of step with other segments of the American population. But it also greatly reduced the number of educated and qualified African Americans available to enter the service. Instead of working to rectify or improve the quality of personnel entering or remaining in the branch, the Army focused on retaining those African Americans already among their ranks. This meant that most of the available Black talent already in the Army remained in largely unskilled or semiskilled positions.[108]

Compounding the problem further, the Army operated a racially exclusive training program. Various slots or positions existed that filled specific needs: armorer, electrician, and communications specialist among others. To gain the training necessary for these positions, a soldier was required to attend a specialized training school. White soldiers in the Army could choose from 530 different specialized training classes. African American soldiers, though, only had 179 courses to choose from. Equally problematic, if a Black soldier was accepted into an advanced training course, there was no guarantee upon his graduation that he would find a Black unit to go to, as racial segregation limited the number of Black units with slots available. Equally perplexing, the Fahy Committee discovered that there were some white units that had slots that were open, but because of the nature of racial segregation, African American soldiers were prohibited from applying to them.[109]

The Fahy Committee wondered: How was what the Army was doing efficient? Though flummoxed by the Army's rationale and justifications for a wasteful approach to conducting its affairs, the committee understood that the Army was not going to have a racial epiphany overnight and rectify every dilemma that remained. So instead of trying to force a dramatic change, the committee unveiled in May 1949 a set of proposals to initiate gradual change within the Army. The proposals proved unwelcome. For almost a year, a political battle between the Fahy Committee, Secretary of Defense Louis Johnson, and the leadership of the United States Army took place. During this struggle, the Army submitted to Johnson a plan that made promises to reform without providing clarification on how it would do so. Secretary Johnson, eager to begin the process, gave the thumbs-up and announced the plan to the press without consulting with the Fahy Committee. Frustrated, the committee enlisted the aid of the president. Though Truman had once quipped that he did not want to have to get involved, it did not mean that he would not do so. He informed the media that the Army's plan was in the preliminary stages of development and that the Fahy Committee would review it.[110]

The committee's risky political gambit to involve the president paid off, as the two sides hammered out an agreement that removed the 10 percent quota restriction, ensured more educated and qualified African Americans could join, and allowed Black soldiers to transfer into white units that needed their skills. It was not perfect, as the Army managed to secure a loophole that allowed it to return to the 10 percent quota restriction threshold if a racial imbalance occurred, but it was a step forward for those Blacks in, and who desired to join, the service. Though change was coming to the Army, its lackluster advancement on the issue in comparison to the Air Force and even the Navy was not enough for some in the African American community. A Black newspaper, the *Minneapolis Spokesman*, believed that the changes achieved were superficial at best and blamed a "prejudiced southern officer element" within the Army for standing in the way of racial progress and reform.[111]

Although located within the Department of the Navy, the Marine Corps followed its own unapologetic and uncompromising path on the racial composition of its forces. So much so that the Marine Corps proved to be the most reluctant of all the active-duty elements of the armed forces regarding racial integration and reform. During World War II, the Marine Corps had begun integrating its forces reluctantly in a limited way. But that was because it had been ordered and pressured to do so. Left to its own affairs, the Marine Corps would not have integrated. As far as the Marine Corps was concerned, the limited integration that it had achieved was as far as it was willing to go. Much like its brethren throughout the armed forces, the leadership of the Marine Corps believed that the racial integration of the service was akin to transforming it into a social laboratory, one that jeopardized its primary purpose as a tool of national defense.

It maintained this obstinate attitude despite criticisms from the Fahy Committee. Much like the Navy, the Fahy Committee was perplexed over the lack of African American interest in joining the Marine Corps, as well as by the dismal number of Black officers within the Corps. During an interview with Brigadier General Ray Albert Robinson, the Marine officer continuously articulated his belief that the Marine Corps did not have a racial problem in its officer program or its training at places such as Camp Lejeune. But as the Fahy Committee's questions became more pointed, Robinson's claim proved to be questionable. It was disclosed during the meeting that the active-duty component of the Marine Corps had one African American officer out of the 7,200 Marines serving as an officer. The Reserves had four Black officers. Hardly the stuff of an institution that treated everyone equally in the pursuit of becoming a Marine Officer.[112]

As for the lone active-duty officer, Second Lieutenant John Earl Rudder, he resigned one month after Robinson's interview. On his way out of the Corps, Rudder took the high road and put the blame squarely on himself. Rudder claimed he had gained in "recent weeks" religious convictions that prevented him from continuing in good stead as a Marine, and he admitted to struggling academically during his training. While this may have been true, something did not add up. Rudder was a graduate of Purdue University, where he earned his commission from the NROTC to become a Marine officer. He had also served as an enlisted Marine in the Pacific theater during World War II. Rudder, therefore, was not lacking in ability or talent or knowledge of what life in the Marines was like; what he was lacking was support. Rudder left the Marine Corps because of the racial atmosphere within it, which proved, in his words, to result in him receiving "unsympathetic treatment." It started the moment he arrived in Quantico, when the base commandant, Lieutenant General Lemuel Shepherd, stated, "Rudder, you will make a good Marine officer if you stay in your place." One might consider this, out of historical context, to be the standard advice given to any young officer by their superior. Essentially, keep your head down, shut up, and listen and learn. But this was not just any era or statement; it was a common racial euphemism toward the Marine Corps' only Black active-duty officer that was akin to telling Rudder not to be "uppity" and question any racial prejudice that he may witness.[113]

Other issues emerged as well that reaffirmed that no racial punches would be pulled during his training. Often, racial jokes, referring to a Black male as a "darky," popped up from time to time. Though offensive jokes existed in a largely male-dominated realm such as the military, that did not make them any less *offensive*. But it was not simply a matter of the joke's existence; it was who was telling them that made all the difference. Sometimes, the jokes were told by his instructors at Quantico; other times it was his commanding officers and even chaplains.[114]

Two different views about race and the Marine Corps emerged, but which was accurate? Both. From General Robinson's perspective, which was also the perspective of the Marine Corps, the branch had evolved some on race. In 1949, the Marine Corps began to launch subtle changes, but they largely had little to do with Executive Order 9981. Instead, it turned out that racial segregation was costly, not only in the waste of talented Marines segregated away because of the color of their skins but also in how much it economically cost to do it. To redress this and justify its actions for doing so, and as General Robinson noted to the Fahy Committee, the Marine Corps, which prided itself on being different and elite, borrowed from the Army's playbook on race. During questioning, Robinson observed to the committee:

When we started the program [racial integration]—I know, for I was here in Washington at the time—I went over and asked the Army if they'd let us read their files [and discover their approach] on it and I read everything I could on it and I came to the conclusion that insofar as tactical units, service units and really, combat units were concerned, that the system the Army had adopted [racial segregation of units by color] was the most efficient and the best one for people performing the type of duty the Army and our combat units were performing

As a result, Marine training programs, including basic training, racially integrated in a fashion that mimicked the Army. But was also the result of the persisting belief that the best use of white and Black Marines was that of racial segregation. And at the same time, that was why John Rudder could legitimately claim that he did not feel targeted or under pressure to leave the Corps but also to admit freely that he felt had been racially ostracized by his fellow white Marines. To say it simply, the Marine Corps did the bare minimum and did so only for economic reasons, not moralistic ones. It was not going to bend over backward to make Blacks feel welcome within.[115]

CONCLUSION

Truman has received a great deal of criticism for his actions at the end of World War II, the Cold War, and for the larger issue of civil rights. On this last issue, though, some historians have especially questioned Truman's dedication to the cause of racial justice. In her influential study *Eyes Off the Prize*, Carol Anderson appreciated aspects of Truman's historical accomplishments as far as civil rights were concerned but still opined:

Truman's efforts did not even come close to what needed to be done. Instead, it becomes evident that he often engaged in the politics of symbolic equality—executive orders issued with little or no funding to finance the endeavor; powerless commissions created to once again study "the Negro problem" and give an aura of action; and directives issued from on high with no enforcement mechanism and no serious repercussions for noncompliance.

Years later, Christine Knauer, in a provocative historical investigation of the role that African Americans played in establishing a place for their race in the American military, wrote:

President Truman's position on civil rights and racial equality of blacks was ambivalent and his actions often lagged behind his words. While his civil rights rhetoric increasingly broke new ground and, according to historian John Hope Franklin, managed to create an atmosphere of change that could support the betterment of race relations, it did not result in decisive and far-reaching actions on behalf of black civil rights. Fearful of losing Southern support and splitting the Democratic Party, Truman remained cautious.

Regarding the latter criticism, it was true that Truman was wary of the political cost in the American South of his actions. And yet despite those risks he never felt obligated to completely kowtow to the Southern wing of his party, while his predecessor, Roosevelt, did. If Truman had, Strom Thurmond and the Dixiecrat revolt would never have materialized or threatened his election bid. But as we now know, Truman would not toe the line as Roosevelt had.

The Missourian's caution-be-damned approach to civil rights reform cost him four states in the 1948 election that followed Thurmond and his Dixiecrats. Further, it fractured the Democratic Party, with the final break occurring during Lyndon B. Johnson's presidency, whose achievements and actions as president, along with the party's growing alignment with the African American population, promptly ended unwavering Southern support for the party of Jefferson.[116]

The larger criticism leveled by Anderson deserves a bit more scrutiny. Her claim that Truman was no more than a purveyor of "symbolic equality" might have some merit if the criticism is solely geared toward the Universal Declaration of Human Rights or if the focus is solely on Truman's actions in the civilian civil rights arena. Ideologically, the Universal Declaration of Human Rights was a grand statement, but practically it had really no teeth or enforcement mechanism behind it. It is also true that Harry Truman failed to achieve any real traction with his Fair Deal program, specifically regarding his proposed civil rights package. Still, Truman's actions built the foundation for what was to come. So he did not achieve monumental civil rights reform within civilian society during his presidency, but Lyndon Johnson did, and he credited the efforts of his fellow Southerner, Truman, who largely paved the way for it.[117]

Where Anderson's comment on Truman misses the mark is in the military realm. While Truman stumbled in the civilian arena on civil rights, he exerted the powerful influence of his office more effectively in the armed forces. Consider this: apart from Abraham Lincoln, civil rights achievements in the American armed forces from the nineteenth century to the Cold War could be viewed as nothing more than tokenism or, as Anderson put it, exercises in "symbolic equality." Then why were Truman's actions, especially in the military, different? When one boils away the politics of the 1948 election, the president's contentious struggle with his Southern heritage and upbringing, and the failure of the civil rights portion of the Fair Deal program to stay afloat, we are left with two linked realities. First, Truman acted to racially integrate the military despite the costs personally and politically to him; second, he did it during a time of war: the Cold War. History does not occur in a vacuum. Neither did Truman's actions. His decision to move forward with racial desegregation of the military was political and foreign policy–driven; and for Truman, a World War I combat veteran, it was simply the right thing to do for Black men and their families who had served the country. His decision to act altered the racial composition of the American military fundamentally, began the process of allowing greater opportunities for African American military personnel within the ranks, and ultimately aided the dependents of those same soldiers.

What about his supposed ambivalence? Just as his predecessor, Abraham Lincoln, had, Truman had his own limits to civil rights reform. In *Freedom to Serve*, Jon E. Taylor highlighted why Truman remained committed to civil rights reform but could no longer agree with what he was seeing in the decades following his presidency:

He [Truman] had witnessed the civil rights movement of the 1960s and he was very uncomfortable at what he saw, but he had not changed his views on civil rights—they stayed the same. What had changed was the civil rights movement. The movement had pushed beyond Truman's view of civil rights, which in his mind only included "equal opportunity" and not social equality. In 1960 he was asked to comment on the sit-ins that were underway at lunch counters across the United States to protest segregation and he responded that they were Communist inspired. Dr. Martin Luther King responded back to the former president and described his remarks as "unfortunate" and that sit-ins served to "dramatize the indignities and injustices that Negroes are facing." There were limits to Truman's approach on civil rights. He was willing to use the power of the executive branch to address civil rights, but he grew increasingly uncomfortable when African Americans took the lead.

Anyone who grapples with Harry Truman and his resolve for racial reform is better off avoiding the notion that he was simply just a hawker of "symbolic equality"; instead, more complexly, and as Taylor noted, he was a champion of civil rights reform if it fell within his worldview and social limitations as a Caucasian male raised in the shadow of Dixie who was living in an ever-changing racial world, one that was leaving him behind. These faults should not be expunged from the record, and therefore we should not lionize Truman either. When the civil rights movement passed him and left him flat-footed in the 1960s, the former president struggled to understand that as a white male his view of what was needed no longer matched the reality of the moment for the Black community—not because the movement was wrong but because Truman could not see beyond his own limitations and ideas about where racial reform should go.[118]

As the nascent years of racial integration of the armed forces faded into the recent past for Truman and his administration, the Army and the Marine Corps defiantly refused to change. But they would eventually come around and racially integrate. Their justification for doing so was not based on morality, the pressures of the Fahy Committee, or the president, though Truman would continue to play a role. It was the necessity for manpower caused by America's involvement in the Korean War, which ultimately drove the reluctant Army and Marine Corps toward compliance.

CHAPTER 3

Born out of the Necessity of War: The Korean War and Reform

Six months prior to the unexpected communist invasion of South Korea in June 1950 and the onset of the Korean War, civil rights activists and Southern segregationists in the House of Representatives squared off over continued racial segregation in the Army and the Marine Corps. The man at the center of this latest clash, who had introduced a resolution on the House floor that sought to investigate the vestiges of racial segregation in the military, was Representative Jacob Javits, a progressive Republican from New York.

Having returned from Europe recently, and keenly aware of the importance of the United States maintaining a positive international image, Javits informed his colleagues that Europe and the world were watching. "I was impressed," he admitted to his colleagues in the House, "by the questions of people in all walks of life about our race relations policies and about segregation and discrimination in employment, housing, and education, and in the armed serves." European interest in the social affairs of the United States was not fleeting. During the Cold War, the ideological confrontation between Western-style democracy and Soviet communism resonated with the citizens of Western Europe, who resided on the front lines of the struggle. It was a dangerous gambit, Javits believed, to fail to address the issue, as it unnecessarily risked alienating the loyalty of Western Europeans who might be susceptible to Cold War propaganda designed to drive a wedge between them and the United States. "The communist propagandists in Western Germany and Western Europe," Javits observed, "seek to build up the alleged evils [such as American racism] and to magnify them, but there is enough [truth] to them to damage us seriously in the Cold War."[1]

Winning European hearts and minds through civil rights reform was not Javits's only aim, however. Two other populations concerned the congressman as well: Africa and Asia. "With communist China as a propaganda base," he proclaimed, "segregation and discrimination on grounds of race, creed, or color in the United States can be used to win tens of millions to the communist cause." For Javits and others, the matter was clear: it was not just an issue of African American rights and dignity. Continued racial discrimination in the United States had a negative impact that on the nation's international image and threatened its ability to combat the expansion of global communism. For these reasons, it was time to ferret out racial segregation in American society and all the service branches.[2]

Months later, Javits call for action was supported by another New Yorker, Congressman Adam Clayton Powell Jr. Though he never served in the military, the African American Democrat from Harlem spent the better part of the 1940s and 1950s building a reputation as a dogged civil rights advocate and a pursuer of meaningful racial reform in the armed forces. One month prior to the Korean War, and no doubt thinking about racial segregation remaining in the Army and Marine Corps, he directly wed his cause for racial integration to the greater global dilemma of the Cold War. "We cannot wage a Cold War much less a hot one with a Jim Crow Army," he mused. Building on the momentum generated by the Fahy Committee and convinced that the military intended to drag its feet on the implementation of racial integration, Powell submitted an amendment to the Selective Service Act of 1948 that prohibited "against discrimination and segregation" in the military. Under the new language, "no person inducted pursuant to the provisions of this act shall be discriminated against or segregated because of race, creed, or color." With that in mind, it was time for action. "Now in peacetime," Powell reasoned, "I ask that we here will do that which at least we owe to the citizens of this nation, to our conscience and to the world, give men the right to serve side by side with their fellow citizens in all branches of our services."[3]

Though Jacob Javits supported his fellow New Yorker's amendment, he submitted his own amendment to the Selective Service Act. The intent of the two amendments—upholding the end of racial discrimination in the armed forces—were the same, but the language differed markedly. Whereas Powell's amendment was more direct, Javits's amendment offered a more nuanced approach to rectifying the issue: "The obligation and privileges of serving in the armed forces and the reserve components thereof shall be without discrimination in selection or service, or segregation on account of race, creed, color, or national origin." Why the alternative statement? Javits hinted that "my substitute may satisfy some Members who wish to stay within the pattern of the act's declarations." While he played coy about it, Javits was likely thinking about the racial sensitivities of Southern members of the House, whose votes he would need to get his amendment passed. A more direct and confrontational statement, such as Powell's, might be a poison pill for some Southern segregationists. But a more tempered declaration from Javits, a white Jewish man, might help the medicine go down. Regardless of which version passed, Javits understood implicitly that each moment the Congress squandered by failing to address racial discrimination in the armed forces only compounded America's negative image abroad. "Mr. Chairman there is no argument we give the Communist propagandists calumniating the United States on the radio and the platform daily from behind the iron curtain and in most countries, which is better grist for their mill than segregation in our armed forces."[4]

Throughout the spring and summer of 1950, the noted red-baiter and devoted champion of the anticommunist HUAC, John E. Rankin of Mississippi, had heard enough about civil rights reform in the country and its military. During an April debate over the 1951 general appropriations bill, whereby a civil rights amendment for Washington, DC, was submitted, the Southern Democrat pounced and unleashed a verbal tirade, stating "it is really an amendment to persecute white Americans in the District of Columbia, using the Negro as a smokescreen to carry out a communist program." Unrelenting in his offensive against those elements in Washington he perceived to be subversive, anti-American, and red, Rankin compared the District amendment to the lunacy, in his thinking, of issuing Executive Order 9981:

But the craziest step that I have ever known to be taken in a civilized country was the Executive order wiping out segregation in our armed forces. That was the greatest victory Stalin has won since Yalta. It did more to cripple our national defense than anything else that has ever been done in all the history of this Government. How much longer, I ask you Members of the House, are you going to tolerate these communistic movements that threaten the very life of the Nation?

When it came to the Powell and Javits amendments, Rankin maintained the rationale that "this is nothing in the world but a Communist amendment, and that the ones who are pushing it are not trying to help the people they represent. It is nothing in the world," the Mississippian concluded, "but a Communist movement to try to disturb the Armed Forces of America."[5]

While Rankin ranted over what he believed was the downfall of the nation and its military, a fellow Democratic segregationist, Representative Charles E. Bennett of Florida, offered a controversial solution to the matter. Assuming that the Powell and Javits amendments were defeated, Bennett suggested an alternative stating that "no order for or against segregation in the armed services shall be effective until the Joint Chiefs of Staff have determined that such order is in the best interest of the national defense." While he claimed the contrary, Bennett's amendment suggested circumventing the power of the presidency, as it subsumed the commander in chief's orders to the review of the Joint Chiefs of Staff. Another segregationist and staple on the House Committee on Armed Services, Carl Vinson of Georgia, questioned the constitutionality of Bennett's amendment. Rankin, eager to defend his colleague from Florida's audacious plan, observed that "the gentleman [Bennett] is not questioning the right of the Chief Executive, the gentleman is looking out for the interests of his country and welfare of the Nation." The result of this melodrama of amendments and alternative amendments was that they were all defeated and that the Army and Marnie Corps remained racially segregated heading into the Korean War.[6]

On June 25, 1950, Kim Il-sung, the communist leader of the Democratic People's Republic of Korea, ordered the North Korean army to cross the 38th parallel. His goal was simple: the complete and utter eradication of the democratic government of South Korea and the reunification of the Korean Peninsula. Though they both expressed reservations prior to the action—reservations alleviated by Truman's efforts to cut the budget and Secretary of State Dean Acheson's Press Club speech, which left the peoples of Taiwan and South Korea unprotected—the Soviet Union and Chinese Communist Party supported Kim Il-sung's bold action. Meanwhile, as North Koreans raced southward, leaving destruction in their wake, Truman and Acheson backpedaled on their previous stances toward Taiwan; the president dispatched the US Seventh Fleet to defend it and Korea, as he secured approval from the United Nations (UN) to send a US-dominated "peacekeeping force" to the troubled and divided nation. To lead these men into Cold War combat, Truman tapped General Douglas MacArthur, who at that time was overseeing the occupation of Japan, for the job. When MacArthur arrived in the war-torn nation, he found himself in charge of a largely racially segregated and unprepared fighting force.[7]

From the start, though, the Korean War was not going to be conducted like prior American wars. The Korean War was the first hot war of the Cold War, but it was also the first limited war of the nuclear age. North Korea and South Korea were aligned, respectively, with the Soviet Union and the United States, the preeminent Cold War powers of the era. This meant that, once hostilities began on the Korean Peninsula, there was a real possibility of not only involvement with superpower allies but also a puncher's chance that events could dramatically expand from a regional conflict to a global war. Truman knew and understood the potential for this to occur. In concert with congressional leadership, it was decided that the United States would not declare war but instead that the executive branch would launch what became known as a "police action." When queried by a member of the press over what the United States was doing in Korea, Truman agreed it was akin to a police action that targeted "bandits" and would be quick; the Korean War was anything but quick and exposed several issues with the postwar American military, including persisting manpower problems.[8] Nonetheless, Truman's police action had two intertwined goals: avoid a third world war, and liberate—unless it threatened the first goal—South Korea.[9]

RACIAL INTEGRATION OF THE ARMY

When Harry Truman began to speak more openly about civil rights, including his efforts to racially integrate the armed forces, he did so surrounded by the ideological trappings of the Cold War. By linking the two causes—Cold War victory over communism and civil rights reform—he had the opportunity to achieve a modicum of success on the latter by waging ideological battle on the former. But it turned out that the Cold War could also deliver civil rights success to the president and the cause in another fashion, one less about ideology and more about the practicality of waging war. Put simply, waging the Cold War required the constant need for American military manpower to defeat the scourge of global communism.

From the onset of the Korean War, it became clear that the necessity of victory on the peninsula, and in the larger sense against global communism, undermined all remaining efforts within and outside the Army to keep it segregated. With the removal of the old racial quota of 10 percent, a result of Executive Order 9981 and the continued prodding of the Fahy Committee, African American enlistments skyrocketed. Prior to the quota's removal in March 1950, African American enlistments in the Army hovered around 8.2 percent of all new Army recruits. After its removal, one month later, enlistments rose to 22 percent, and by the summer of 1950 African American recruits made up 25 percent. Whether or not it wanted to, the Army was becoming more diverse. But racial integration proceeded at a slow pace. Instead of embracing the growing ranks of African Americans, the Army cautiously decided against distributing new Black recruits into white units and instead overstaffed existing all-Black ones. As the Army struggled to come to grips with this problem, post commanders—in what amounted to a grassroots movement stateside in places such as Fort Ord, California, and Fort Jackson, South Carolina—went against the Army's leadership and integrated training facilities on their own accord.[10]

In the case of Fort Jackson, the post could ill afford to wait for the Army brass to act. Responsible for training personnel from eleven different states, including a large contingent of African American soldiers, the leadership of the post recognized they lacked the resources (buildings, billets, and money) necessary to maintain the Army's tradition of racial segregation. So they abandoned the practice wholesale. While they could no longer afford to racially segregate, their decision to integrate did come with a cost. Racially integrating a military post in the first state to secede from the Union brought with it heavy criticism, including from a favorite son of the state and military veteran, Governor Strom Thurmond. Prior to Fort Jackson's integration, and amid a tough Senate primary battle against Senator Olin D. Johnston, the erstwhile Dixiecrat Thurmond used the issue of racial integration of the armed forces to rail against his opponent:

As Governor and commander of the South Carolina National Guard I protested to [Secretary of Defense] Louis Johnson and we are maintaining our segregation policy in the national guard in this state. If I had been in the Senate you would have heard from me when that order came down and never would I have remained silent. I would have taken my stand with General Omar Bradley, and General Dwight Eisenhower, and General George Marshall and I would have opposed this move to break down segregation and done something about it. But not your junior Senator [Johnston]. He remained as silent as the tomb.

As Thurmond thundered at Johnston on the campaign trail, a South Carolina judge, A. G. Kennedy, wrote a scathing letter to Secretary of Defense Johnson decrying the action, ridiculing Truman for what was happening on the post. He proclaimed: "I would not blame any white man forced to train, eat, sleep, and be mixed with negroes while sick to burn the cantonment buildings [and] shoot the insolent negro officers and non-commissioned officers." Thurmond and Kennedy's comments notwithstanding, it appeared that the economic practicality of racial integration, combined with the growing amount of African American enlistees and the need for manpower in Korea, overrode their concerns.[11]

Over time, the leadership of the state—including Thurmond, who had lost his Senate bid—proved to offer little resistance to Fort Jackson's racial desegregation. After all, there was money to consider. In the past, South Carolina politicians had sought to protect the base from closure because of the economic fallout that would occur to its citizens and to them politically. And because of that fallout, and even though they loathed what was happening, they did not dare challenge the racial desegregation of the facility, but off base the local communities did very little to embrace the Black soldiers in their midst. Along with Fort Ord, Fort Jackson became an example for other Army installations throughout the country. Within a year, all Army training installations followed their lead and racially integrated.[12]

Beginning in the summer of 1950 and continuing into the next year, the Americans were faced with a particular problem that had to be resolved. There really wasn't an American Army in Korea. As the Korean War specialist Sheila Miyoshi Jager observed, "calling the [American] Eighth Army a 'US Army' was a significant misnomer by the summer of 1951. More appropriate would have been the 'UN Army in Korea' since less than half of its half-million men were Americans." The Americans required an influx of Korean personnel—most notably the infusion of the Republic of Korea's army into the US Army by way of a program known as Korean Augmentation to the United States Army—to even field an army. For that matter, the South Korean military also provided manpower aide to the French, Dutch, and Belgians.[13]

Operating under these type of manpower conditions, where you needed any and all personnel that you could find, helped motivate white American commanders on the battlefield to racially integrate their forces. They would take this step despite the remaining concerns that many in the Army still had over the ability of Black men to fight let alone coexist with whites. For example, the 9th Infantry Regiment of the Eighth Army's 2nd Infantry Division began to accept African American soldiers into previously all-white combat units. Facing questions about the possible problems that could come with racial integration, a white commander in the 9th Infantry Regiment stated flatly: "So what? They are good fighting men. I need men." Any trepidation over the abilities of a racially integrated fighting force quickly disappeared as the 9th exceeded expectations on the battlefields of the Korean Peninsula. While Southern segregationists within and outside government continued to fight against this change, it was becoming difficult to ignore that racial integration, as units such as the 9th demonstrated, worked.[14]

THE TALENTED OR TROUBLED 24TH?

While necessity and the economic cost of racial segregation drove racial integration, it did not drive out racism from the Army. In the past, white commanders justified racial segregation because they believed that the intermingling of the races jeopardized the morale and efficiency of a unit. Maintaining racial segregation avoided destroying, in their minds, the camaraderie of a white unit, and as military leaders such as Eisenhower had noted in the past, it gave

Blacks an opportunity to achieve social mobility within a Black unit. During the Korean War, however, some white commanders now believed that racial integration of the Army could make up for the perceived racial shortcomings of Blacks. An example of this paradigm shift that turned on their head past beliefs on why racial segregation was a good thing emerges when examining the experience of the all-Black 24th Infantry Regiment.

In the early months of the war, the all-Black 24th Regiment posted an inconsistent record. At times, its soldiers proved to be excellent warriors, as they aided in securing the first American victory of the war at Yechon. Indeed, back in the States, the regiment received tremendous praise for its role and involvement in that victory. Articles in the *Washington Star*, the *St. Louis Post-Dispatch*, and other newspapers detailed the heroics and sacrifices of the unit as it was defeating communism in Korea and communist propaganda throughout the world:

Valiant American Negro troops fighting under the United Nations flag in Korea are helping to win more than strategic hilltops in the struggle with communism. In the opinion of Washington psychological warfare experts they are also helping to win the battle against Communist propaganda. They are dramatic proof that the war to smash Red aggression in Korea is not a "white man's war."

After Yechon, though, the 24th Regiment's reputation as a fighting force fell into serious question. The most damning moment for the beleaguered unit occurred at Battle Mountain (Hill 625). According to several controversial accounts from those on the ground, members of the all-Black regiment fled in the face of enemy hostility. While some claimed the stories of the mass exodus of the unit were true, others—including those who had served with it or later studied the history of the regiment—vehemently denied it. For the latter, they felt that the 24th Regiment had suffered the same deleterious effects from the rapid demobilization that occurred after World War II and Truman's efforts to balance the budget that had afflicted the entire American military. The result was the exodus of talented and capable soldiers of both races. Therefore, part of the problem with the 24th Regiment was that its veteran core was long gone before the North Koreans rampaged over the 38th parallel.[15]

While the rapid demobilization and fiscal maneuvers of Truman played a part, a larger menace plagued the outfit: substandard and racist white officers. Even though the Army had believed it needed to place capable white officers over Black soldiers, and to be sure, some white officers of the regiment showed concern, provided unbiased leadership to Black soldiers, and were talented, they proved to be the minority. For years, white officers in the Army had heard false and scurrilous stories about the inherent flaws of African American troops, whether it was intellectual limitations, lustfulness, or cowardice. Because of these long-standing racial stereotypes, some white officers avoided serving with Blacks because they worried that it would tarnish their own careers.[16]

Unwanted by more capable white leaders, Black soldiers in general often found themselves commanded by less than capable white men—the 24th Regiment was no exception. Compounding the problem, it was not uncommon that a militarily incompetent white officer within a Black unit received a promotion over a more qualified and capable Black one. Infusing the unit with racist and underperforming white leadership only confirmed the suspicions among the unit's Black NCOs and enlisted soldiers that their regiment was nothing more than a dumping ground for worthless white officers. As a result, and in hindsight, it was hardly surprising that the white leadership of the 24th Regiment lost the respect and trust of its soldiers. The comments of Curtis Morrow, a member of the unit, summed up the frustration of Black soldiers who went to Korea to fight communism but ended up fighting a war against American racism at the same time:

We heard all the bullshit about fighting the spread of communism to protect our land of liberty. What the hell did we know about communism? Not a motherfuckin' thing. What had the commies ever done to us black people (that is, before we came to Korea)? . . . Have the communists ever enslaved our people? Have they ever raped our women? Have they ever castrated and hanged our fathers, grandfathers, uncles, or cousins? Hell, blacks couldn't even vote in certain parts of the country we were here fighting and dying for. . . . And to top it all, any one of the [white] officers calling the shots here could be the very one that put a rope around one of our necks next year some place in the States (America) and just for kicks. Or they may quite possibly be the ones to deny us the very rights that we are here fighting for the South Koreans to enjoy. Or, they may just conveniently look the other way. How can they wonder why we don't trust them? Would they trust us if they were in our place?

It seems that the white racist leadership of the 24th Regiment sapped the morale of the unit long before it even arrived in Korea, let alone struggled at Battle Mountain, a stark contrast to the belief that the unit lacked courage under fire. Nonetheless, the image of the outfit remained tarnished as rumors about its actions at Hill 625 spread throughout the Korean command. The result was that Black and white soldiers alike in Korea viewed one of the oldest and most storied African American units in American military history as the "Bugout Brigade" or the "Runnin' 24th."[17]

Because of an inability to field a consistent fighting force, the commanding officer of the 25th Division, Eight Army, Major General William Kean, called for disbanding the 24th Regiment because he considered it "untrustworthy" and believed that it risked "the United Nations war effort in Korea." That did not mean, however, that Kean 100 percent blamed the Black soldiers of the unit for the problem. For that matter, General Kean, William Perry, Inspector General of Eighth Army, and Edwin A. Zundel, Inspector General of the United States Far East Command, and other white commanders blamed racial segregation for the woes facing African American units. To their way of thinking, the solution was the racial integration of all-Black units.[18]

MARSHALL V. MACARTHUR

Prior to pursuing racial integration for the 24th Regiment and other Black units, General Kean sought to restore its discipline by making an example out any African American soldiers who had allegedly failed to live up to their duties. In response to their subsequent experience in the military's criminal justice system, Black soldiers from the troubled unit wrote letters to the NAACP and the African American press informing them about the unfair treatment they had received while on trial. General MacArthur, Commander-in-Chief United Nations Command, responded to the NAACP's inquiries with the following:

Not the slightest evidence exists here of discrimination as alleged. As I think you know in this command there is no slightest bias of its various members because of race, color or other distinguishing characteristics. Every soldier in this command is measured on a completely uniform basis with the sole criteria his efficiency and his character. Nevertheless, on receipt of your message I at once ordered the Inspector General to make thorough investigation of your charges and will be glad to have you forward here any evidence in your possession bearing upon the matter.

In any individual trial a soldier can obtain special counsel to defend him if he so desires. In such individual trial there would be of course no objection to Thurgood Marshall representing the accused and coming to this command for such purpose. You understand of course that courts martial are convened by the Major Subordinate Commander in Korea and the hearings are conducted there.

As had been the case during World War II, MacArthur was squaring off against a civil rights leader. And as he had done before, the general underestimated the tenacity of his opposition. Skeptical of MacArthur's response to the charges that Black soldiers of the 24th Regiment had leveled against the Army, interested overall in the situation they faced on the front lines, and willing to take up MacArthur on his offer, the NAACP dispatched Thurgood Marshall to Japan, where the Far East Command was headquartered, and to Korea.[19]

From the onset of his fact-finding mission, Marshall encountered stiff resistance from the Army's leadership in the theater—namely, MacArthur. It seemed that the general, despite his dubious offer, *really* did not want the Black civil rights lawyer in his theater of operations. Out of an effort to stymie Marshall, MacArthur contacted the Federal Bureau of Investigation and asked it to probe Marshall's background for any negative information that the general could use against him. According to the FBI, the NAACP's lead attorney had loose ties to a few communist organizations. While his association with these groups were superficial at best, they proved good enough for MacArthur. Using the FBI's investigation of Marshall as justification, MacArthur denied the trip. Outraged, Walter White, who had tangled with MacArthur before, contacted President Truman, who also was no stranger to MacArthur's antics. The general's actions agitated the commander in chief to no end. Marshall later reminisced that, after Truman heard about MacArthur's intransigence, he exclaimed: "Who's running this damned show?" The president overruled his malcontent general and granted Marshall unfettered passage to East Asia.[20]

After completing his investigation, Marshall blamed the 24th Regiment's problems on the unit's low morale. He concluded that its morale problems stemmed from the racism of the regiment's white leadership and from the psychological effect of serving in a racially segregated Army. Understanding the cause, Marshall expressed concern about the punishment. Through a careful examination of Army court records, he uncovered some troubling statistics about the trials of these men. According to Marshall, the thirty-two Black soldiers charged with "cowardice" faced longer and stiffer sentences than two white soldiers charged with the same offense.[21] The speed of the trials also proved problematic and alarming. Black soldiers receiving life in prison often had the shortest trials, with several running under an hour. This statistic surprised even the seasoned Marshall: "I have seen many miscarriages of justice in my capacity as head of the NAACP legal department. But even in Mississippi a Negro will get a trial longer than 42 minutes, if he is fortunate enough to be brought to trial."[22]

Troubled by his findings, Marshall presented them to MacArthur, who was uninterested in the lawyer's discoveries. Irked, Marshall noted that there were no African Americans within the Far East Command or among the general's security forces. The general defiantly retorted that no African American soldier had distinguished himself enough to be a member of his command or special guard. Marshall doubted the claim: "Well, I just talked to a Negro yesterday, a sergeant who has killed more people with a rifle than anybody in history, and he's not qualified?" MacArthur demurred. By this point in the conversation, and as detected by the biographer Juan Williams, Marshall had grown tired of MacArthur and his racist excuses. And the Black lawyer sought to confront MacArthur about it.[23]

Instead of continuing with the overall issue of racism within the general's command, Marshall shifted the discussion to the previous day, when a military band was playing on the parade grounds adjacent to MacArthur's office. Receptive to this change in topic, MacArthur remarked, "Yes, wasn't that wonderful?" Marshall then responded that he noticed that the band lacked a Black musician. But before MacArthur could retort, the NAACP attorney pounced: "Now, General, just between you and me, goddamnit, don't you tell me that there is no Negro that can play a horn." In a world where Dizzy Gillespie and Louis Armstrong were making their bones as jazz trumpeters, Marshall knew better. After returning from East Asia, Marshall toured the country, informing his audiences of the unfair treatment that the African American soldiers of the 24th Regiment had faced.[24]

IT STARTS AT THE TOP

Through his investigation into the Army's criminal justice system and during his exchange with MacArthur, Thurgood Marshall, a future justice of the US Supreme Court, was stating the obvious: leadership flows from the top to the bottom. Thus, if racism—whether blatant bigotry or systemic subtlety—existed at the top of the command structure, it would most certainly sink all the way to the bottom of it. In his opinion, the same conclusion that Walter White had come to during World War II, it was MacArthur's responsibility to address the issue. Yet the Commander-in-Chief United Nations Command never addressed the problem. He was as "biased as any person I've run across," Marshall recalled. But was MacArthur a racist? According to the work of the biographer Geoffrey Perret, the general was anything but a racist, as he had always treated his Filipino soldiers, and the Japanese he governed, with respect. To an extent, MacArthur had taken after his father, Arthur MacArthur, in this manner. Still, Arthur MacArthur had lorded over the Philippines during the turn of the century, an era of social Darwinism when Asians, specifically the Japanese, were seen as honorary whites. It was possible that his son inherited this view of the Japanese and a sense of paternalism over Filipinos. At best, though, this was racial elitism and not a reflection of a man who embraced either group as equals.[25]

Nonetheless, MacArthur never seemed to share even these views when considering the racial significance of African American personnel or their impact on the Cold War. During the early stages of the war, the *Chicago Defender* called for the immediate drafting or promotion of a Black officer to the rank of general to assist MacArthur in East Asia. The war in Korea was not one waged solely with bullets, the African American newspaper believed; it was also waged with ideological propaganda. "The Reds in North Korea are using racial propaganda as effectively as they are using Russian tanks, planes, and other weapons of war. This race-hate propaganda is costing American lives just as surely as bullets and bombs." The *Defender* suggested promoting to the rank of general either Colonel James Robinson or Colonel Benjamin O. Davis Jr., the latter of Tuskegee Airmen fame. If neither of these men would suffice, the paper supported drafting Ralph Bunche, the well-known and respected African American foreign diplomat who had helped secure peace in the Middle East. MacArthur, though, never seriously considered this proposition.[26]

Ever prideful and supremely self-confident in his abilities as a commander, MacArthur never wanted anything to do with outsiders who suggested to him how to handle problems of racial discrimination in his command or how to fight red propaganda. The first lady of Black journalism, Ethel L. Payne, keenly observed that MacArthur "had no tolerance of criticism and the writer who dared to criticize him knew before he put his pen to paper that he was writing his own ticket of banishment from the Far East." While the general lorded as a quasi-emperor over Japan and conducted the war in Korea akin to a warlord, the matter of racial discrimination and segregation failed to gain his attention. Payne informed her readers: "One of the main reasons for the continued persistence of segregated units in the Far East, particularly Japan[,] is the blatant ignorance of the problem by Douglas MacArthur." This problem originating from the highest-ranking officer in the Far East led to a systemic situation that aided in the continued segregation of troops. According to Payne, the general willfully looked the other way: the problem of racism in the East "was not discovered, in fact, it never existed [as far as MacArthur was concerned] and any attempts to question policies were aborted before they got aborning."[27]

FADING AWAY

Putting racial insensitivity and arrogant self-aggrandizement aside for the moment, there can be no doubt that MacArthur was a daring leader. The Inchon landing proved that point; it altered the course of the war. After this spectacular reversal of fortune, the North Korean army was driven back across the 38th parallel. At this point in the war, the objective of preserving South Korean independence had been achieved. Then the Americans complicated things. The United States sought stability in Korea through the establishment of a unified and democratic Republic of Korea. But to do so would go past the original and limited UN resolution that had called only for preserving South Korean independence. Out of an effort to sidestep the security council, where the Soviet Union would likely veto their plan, the Americans introduced a resolution into the UN General Assembly that sought to stabilize Korea by way of the creation of a "unified democratic Korea." Meanwhile, MacArthur was authorized by Truman and the Joint Chiefs of Staff to proceed into North Korea for the sole purpose of eradication of the North Korean army, which was seen as a necessary step toward achieving the unity of the peninsula. Thus, MacArthur crossed over the 38th and into the North, but not because he had decided to do so (he was eager to do it); he was ordered to do it. However, there was a catch to MacArthur's orders: if Chinese or Russians forces entered the fray or threatened to do so, he must cease any and all preparations to cross the parallel. Furthermore, if MacArthur did go over the line, his forces were not to breach "the Manchurian or USSR borders of Korea." Apparently, Truman had recognized the warning signs in the air. In October 1950, Zhou Enlai, the foreign minister of China, warned that the Chinese were prepared to strike back at the Americans for "expand[ing] the war." To ensure his commander understood this was a possibility, Truman traveled to Wake Island and met with a less-than-enthused MacArthur on October 15. Four days later, China made good on its threat as its forces stealthily crossed the Yalu River and descended into North Korea. On October 25, Chinese forces attacked and began to brutally repel UN forces. Although MacArthur had defiantly promised to Truman victory by Christmas, the Chinese drove his forces back below the 38th parallel.[28]

Once the disappointment of stalemate along the parallel line had set in, the Truman administration returned to the notion of preserving an independent South Korea and not expanding the war. Frustrated and openly disgusted with this decision, MacArthur stopped listening to Washington and continued to propagate his own strategy for the war. Internationally, he threatened to use atomic weapons against the flow of Chinese troops and equipment crossing the border into Korea. Domestically, MacArthur went behind the commander in chief's back and sent a letter to the Republican House Minority Leader, Joseph Martin, who had requested MacArthur's views on the Truman administration's handling of the war. The letter was a direct appeal from the beleaguered and frustrated general to the American people to follow his course of action in Korea, a course of action that would have turned China, by way of Taiwan, into a second front in the war and was predicated on the total destruction of communism in East Asia. The president considered MacArthur's actions a clear display of "insubordination" and informed the head of the Joint Chiefs of Staff, Omar Bradley (who did not trust MacArthur at this point in the war but was also against the public removal of the general), "the son of a bitch isn't going to resign on me, I want him fired."[29]

Though the Missourian would have his pound of flesh, the American Caesar, as the biographer William Manchester aptly dubbed MacArthur, returned home to a hero's welcome. At the height of his popularity and political power, MacArthur went before a joint session of Congress and declared to the members: "Old soldiers never die. They just fade away." MacArthur did not, however, just fade off into the void. Instead, he left in a petulant and childish rage because he had an ax to grind with Truman. Because of this, the general remained in the headlines. Throughout his testimony before Congress on the conduct of the war, MacArthur belabored the war strategy of the administration. In one noted exchange, the retired general bellowed: "The inertia that exists! There is no policy—there is nothing, I tell you—no plan, or anything!" For MacArthur, war against the communists was an all-or-nothing gambit— victory or defeat.[30] There was no room for what he viewed as the endless warfare that he associated with the strategy of limited warfare.[31]

When he was not attacking the strategic capabilities of the Truman administration, the retired general was behaving in a political manner, perhaps eyeing a presidential run. In the past, MacArthur had sought the nomination for the Republican Party, and he would do so again in 1952. But if he sought the presidency, he would have to defend to the Black community his inactivity on racial issues during his career.

In an interview with the *Pittsburgh Courier*, MacArthur flatly denied that he was a racist and instead invoked his expertise in the matter of racial affairs: "I know and understand the needs of colored peoples throughout the world . . . perhaps more than any living American." It was not his fault, the general contended, that racially segregated units existed in Korea; the blame, he believed, belonged with the federal government, which meant that MacArthur blamed the administration and the president for the racial calamity in the Far East. As the general noted: "I did not ask for men by race. I did not ask for Negro nor for white men. I asked Washington for 'men.' I accepted what Washington sent me." MacArthur had made the best of the situation, he believed, and continued to promote his record: "I don't believe that any theatre commander in American war history accepted and integrated the number of Negro troops that I did." This last claim is worthy of brief historical retort: it was dubious, self-serving, and wrong. The initiative for racial reform came originally from the commanders on the ground desperate for manpower and not from MacArthur, who could never grasp the issue.[32]

On the troubling issue of harsh punishments and speedy trials of African American soldiers under his command in Korea, MacArthur backpedaled: "I was unaware of the prevalency of these courts-martial as far as race is concerned until they were called to my attention." Once he was aware of the situation, the general "ordered a complete investigation." However, according to MacArthur, "the report I asked for had not reached me when I left Tokyo." Though he readily admitted "that these courts-martial may have been excessive," he was not entirely forthcoming with the *Pittsburgh Courier* about his knowledge on the subject. After all, the general had received a report on the situation from a capable and reliable source, Thurgood Marshall, and before he left the Pacific. In MacArthur's summation, he failed to mention that fact and instead offered up, weakly: "During the early days of the Korean campaign, morale of all troops was low."[33]

"OLD IRON TITS" TAKES COMMAND

In December 1950, the commander of the Eighth Army, General Walton Walker, died, the victim of a motor vehicle incident in the field. His replacement was no stranger to the battlefield: General Matthew Ridgway. A veteran of World War II, he had served with the All-American Division (the 82nd Airborne); he earned the moniker "Old Iron Tits" from his paratroopers because it appeared that he famously carried two grenades on his jump harness. The truth was that the supposed second grenade was no explosive at all—it was a first aid kit. But the myth of Old Iron Tits, largely because of his unyielding resolve, persisted.[34]

After he assumed command of the Eighth Army, the former paratrooper discovered that it lacked esprit de corps: "It was clear to me that our troops had lost confidence. I could sense it the moment I came into a command post. I could read it in their eyes, in their walk. I could read it in the faces of their leaders, from sergeants right on up to the top." Desperate to rejuvenate the morale of the Eighth Army, Ridgway embraced the opinion of his subordinate officers, such as General William B. Kean, and supported immediate racial integration. While concerns over the fighting ability of the Eighth Army influenced him, Ridgway had never personally supported racial segregation. For moral and religious reasons, Ridgway objected to the practice: "It had always seemed to me both un-American and un-Christian for free [Black] citizens to be taught to downgrade themselves this way, as if they were unfit to associate with their fellows or to accept leadership themselves."[35]

After breathing new life into the now racially integrating Eighth Army, Ridgway found himself tabbed for an even bigger job. With MacArthur out, Truman turned to the former paratrooper, who's efforts had succeeded in driving North Korean and Chinese forces back above the 38th parallel, to assume command of all UN forces. It was a unique moment for Ridgway and one that highlighted a key difference between himself and the man he replaced. Ridgway believed racial segregation of the military and racism in general was a problem. He believed this morally, religiously, democratically, and militarily.[36]

As for the impact of racism on a unit militarily, Ridgway directly addressed the topic in his book *The Korean War*. As he discussed the power of racism to derail a unit, Ridgway expressed his belief that racial integration was necessary to restore the will to fight in the Eighth Army and in those all-Black units within it. It was important to Ridgway (And also to Kean) that "each soldier stands proudly on his own feet, knowing himself to be as good as the next fellow and better than the enemy." Where Ridgway saw a problem, MacArthur never saw anything worth worrying about. And by not acknowledging it or addressing it, MacArthur allowed racism to continue unabated.[37]

One of MacArthur's chief lieutenants, General Edward Mallory Almond, serves as a prominent example of the lack of leadership MacArthur demonstrated on the matter. Ned Almond's racism continuously led to the misuse of Black personnel within X Corps, which he commanded. A Virginia Military Institution alum who worshiped VMI's most favored son, Thomas "Stonewall" Jackson, and was a devoted racial segregationist Southerner, Almond flat-out refused to utilize African American troops, believing them to be inherently substandard—a belief he developed during World War II as the commanding officer of the 92nd Infantry Division, which led him to blame all of the woes of his command on his Black soldiers. He even objected to African Americans winning battlefield honors, going so far as to reject the recommendation of Ridgway to award the Silver Star to Captain Forest Walker for his heroics during fighting at Wonju—he had also taken a similar action during World War II when he halted the attempt to award Lieutenant John Fox, who valiantly tried to hold off a German advance on his position, the Distinguished Service Cross.[38]

As opposed to MacArthur and others who ascribed to racist ideology, Ridgway knew that racial integration of his forces offered him positive benefits because he had seen it firsthand with his rejuvenated Eighth Army. Now as the overall commander of the war and the Far East Command, he decide to implement racial integration throughout all areas under his purview. He presented his superiors in Washington with a plan for the complete racial integration of his forces in Korea and the Far East Command. In July 1951, Ridgway was given the green light by the Army to proceed forward. To ensure that racial integration went smoothly, Ridgway limited the amount of African American soldiers in a combat unit to no more than 12 percent of the total population. The Eighth Army's African American population hovered around 17.6 percent. He strived, as did all American commanders in the conflict, to balance the racial population out of concerns over racial animosity and the impact it could have on overall combat effectiveness. In his quest for balance and efficiency, Ridgway controversially sought the power to make race a determining factor in the process of filling openings within the Eighth Army. Though his intentions were geared toward balance and efficiency and not racism, the Army quickly shot down this idea, but it also promised to take steps to slow down the flow of African Americans moving into Ridgway's forces. Less than a year later, Ridgway completed the racial integration of the Eighth Army and the Far East Command.[39]

PROJECT CLEAR: A STORY OF FACTS OVER FICTION

Prior to the Korean War and the racial integration that ensued, Army commanders were surveyed on their opinions of the potential racial consolidation of white and Black forces within the service. The investigation and surveying of opinions were conducted by a group known as the "Chamberlain Board," which consisted of senior branch officers selected by Secretary of the Army Gordon Gray to investigate the issue. The board issued two findings; the first came five months before the start of the Korean War. In that report, the board leaned heavily on the combat experiences of 322 Army leaders to assert that racial integration would be a disaster. These men "vigorously opposed amalgamation [of whites and Blacks] and strongly urged the retention of segregation," as it provided for the best possible use of these men and upheld the "combat effectiveness" of the Army. The second report came in spring 1951, after racial integration had been proven successful. But the leadership of the Chamberlain Board suggested that, even though progress had been achieved, that the Army's best possible future would be one that maintained racial segregation.[40]

While the board's member and its twin reports carried weight, the feelings among some of the Army's leadership on the subject were still evolving. As opposed to accepting any lingering doubts about the reports, Army brass ordered a deeper investigation into the matter, the caveat being that this time an outside group, funded by the military, would conduct the research. The result was the commissioning of a group of social scientists from Johns Hopkins University to study the racial desegregation of the nation's largest fighting force. Code-named "Project Clear," these researchers were to determine the most effective way to utilize African American soldiers within the branch, whether it be racial segregation or integration. The genius of their work was published as *The Utilization of Negro Manpower in the Army: A 1951 Study*.[41]

The first conclusion that Project Clear researchers reached was that racial segregation was not efficient: "*The continued existence of racial segregation limits the effectiveness of the Army.* It results in the concentration of low-scoring [African American] personnel, which, in turn, intensifies problems of leadership, training, and command." Project Clear researchers observed that race and racism likely played a part,: "White officers commanding all-Negro units tend to attribute their problems to race; white officers commanding integrated units tend to regard their problems as military."[42]

Believing that racial integration was more beneficial than Jim Crow segregation, the researchers turned to age-old Army concerns over the use of Black military personnel. For instance, did the presence of African American soldiers in a white outfit positively or negatively affect the combat efficiency of the unit? Was the use of Blacks in combat overall the best way to utilize them? To address these questions, Project Clear researchers examined the issues of morale, teamwork, and fighting spirit within racially integrated units.

Over the years, Southerners, within and outside the military, as well as those in the military sympathetic to the Southern way of life, erected a series of barriers that protected the Jim Crow Army from racial integration. One of the traditional defenses against racial integration was that the introduction of Black soldiers into white units would sap the morale of those units. Southern segregationists contended that the prospect of racial desegregation would demoralize white soldiers because they would have to serve with Black soldiers, who they viewed as lesser beings socially and culturally. When investigating the morale of racially integrated units, 95 percent of white officers and 89 percent of white enlisted men believed that racial integration did not negatively affect morale. Chaos, disruption, and racial strife—the hallmarks of a lack of teamwork—segregationists contended, would be the result if the Army racially desegregated. But they were wrong. Eighty-nine percent of white officers and 63 percent of white enlisted men who had served in racially integrated units felt that teamwork within a racially integrated unit paralleled that of all-white outfits.[43]

As far as tenacity or fighting spirit in combat, 84 percent of white officers believed that the combat tenacity of a racially integrated unit was as good as that of a white one. While the results proved positive, a level of racial doubt in the ability of Black soldiers remained among some white enlisted men, as only 58 percent believed that a racially integrated unit performed as well as a white one. Equally noteworthy, only 51 percent of white officers and enlisted men believed that Black soldiers were as good as whites in combat.[44]

While concerns among some white personnel persisted, racial desegregation of the Army encouraged African American soldiers to perform at a higher level, and as a result the attitudes of some of their Caucasian colleagues changed. As one Black soldier succinctly put it: "The Negro feels like he is letting his race down if he is thrown in with a bunch of whites and proves to be the ass end of everything that goes on." At first, it seems, racial competition spurred recently integrated African American soldiers to be the best they could be for their race. But then a curious development occurred: the bond of camaraderie began to form between white and Black soldiers. Instead of being all one could be for one's race, an African American soldier mused, "he begins to see the fellows [white and Black] getting along in the Army and begins to say to himself, it would be so goddam nice if it could be like that all over." "You begin to forget about being colored and want to make your company or battalion the best outfit of the post."[45]

The camaraderie emerging in Korea was not a one-way street. And though it was slow-going for some, it was developing in some Southern whites as well. During an enemy firefight in Korea, a white soldier from the American South, who remained noncommittal to the racial integration of his unit, noted that two Black soldiers showed remarkable poise and courage in the face of enemy hostility: "One of them stayed on a hill the [Chinese] were taking so that we'd all be sure [to] get off OK. We don't forget things like that." Meanwhile, he recalled, "the other [Black] boy helped white boys off that were wounded." While the white solder's comments were not a wholehearted embrace of change, it was not an absolute rejection of it either. More than anything, it demonstrated what racial reformers had believed all along: if whites could witness firsthand the success and courage of Black soldiers on the battlefield, a great many of the old racial stereotypes would wither away and die because they had been proved to be false.[46]

Although researchers had addressed the primary concerns of the Army, its all-white leadership still expressed reservations over racial integration. Leaders continued to echo the fears of Omar Bradley years prior, worried about what would happen when the lynchpin for integration—military necessity— ended. In addition, they worried about how the American people, especially Southerners, would respond to the change. Military installations dotted the American heartland, but following World War II a disproportionate amount of them resided in Dixie. With Dixie on their mind and the investigation of racial integration in Korea completed, the Army dispatched Project Clear researchers stateside to continue their work.[47]

During the domestic portion of their research, Project Clear researchers noticed that their stateside findings mirrored those discovered in Korea. First-hand experience, it seemed, often led to positive reactions from white soldiers about serving with African American soldiers. Regardless of the region a white solider hailed from, North or South, if he had not served with a Black soldier he often supported the status quo of racial segregation. For example, Project Clear researchers discovered that, in all-white segregated units, 56 percent of Northern whites and 79 percent of Southern whites believed that Black soldiers should remain in segregated all-Black battalions. If a white soldier had practical experience working and training with African Americans, though, the answer was quite different. In examining white recruits participating in racially integrated basic training, the survey found that 56 percent of Northern whites and 36 percent of Southern whites believed that Black soldiers should serve where they are needed and not segregated based solely by their race.[48]

THE SOUTH AND . . .

Project Clear researchers recognized that racism permeated throughout the Republic. Letters coming into Senator Richard Russell of Georgia, a fixture on the Senate Armed Forces Committee, attested to that fact. One such letter came from Nellie Baker, who was "raised above the Mason-Dixon" but planned to return to Georgia, where her husband and she had once lived. She confided to Russell:

My Husband M/SGT Lambert Baker . . . has been in the United States Army for over 24 years. Now he has always loved the Army & planned [to serve] for 30 years. But he has

had to change his mind. As you no doubt know before W.W. II the Army had segregation, but since then the segregation has been fouled up, in other words, there is none.
Now that is alright for all the nigger troops who in the most part want to live with the
white people, but it makes it rough on the white boys, who don't like eating, sleeping,
and in general living with colored people. In fact I think it is an insult to a white mans
dignity and his intelligence.

Project Clear researchers focused their attention on one region over the rest:
the South. They believed that, if the racial integration of the armed forces were
to continue, any trouble that emerged would largely not come from the North
but from the South; it represented the region with the most military installations and a sizeable population wed to military service. But it was also a matter of pure common sense. The South was the inheritor of the legacy of the
Confederacy and slavery; it was the home of the Lost Cause and Jim Crow. If
there was going to be trouble racially integrating the armed forces, it would
occur there.[49]

Why did the South matter so much to the racial integration of the Army?
Throughout history, the South contributed a large contingent to the manpower
needs of a nation often at war. And why should it not? It was built to do so. With
all its bluster and pomp, with all the self-exalting and self-anointing about its
ability to produce leaders and soldiers of immeasurable comparison, it would
be more startling if the South sent very few of its sons, brothers, and fathers
to war. The South viewed military service as part of its identity. Historians,
from John Hope Franklin to Ed Ayers and many more, have wrestled with the
ideological makeup of the region, which of course included contending with
its self-inflated martial spirit.[50]

It was an image that was not entirely false, but it certainly embellished a
good bit about regional prowess. It was made of myth, the pursuit of manhood, a desire to protect women from African American men, and the fear
and hatred of all those who threatened the South. Nonetheless, other regions
seemed to believe in it as well, so much so that the military's leadership often
constructed military racial policy in a fashion that adhered to the social norms
of the region—specifically Jim Crow segregation.

For instance, during World War I, Army leaders, including General John J.
Pershing, who had once commanded Black soldiers in his own right, worried
about Black men fraternizing too much with white officers, whether American, English, or French, and, critically for some white Southerners, with white
French women. This example, from a war waged almost forty years earlier, is
illustrative as the concerns Pershing fretted over challenging Southern white

racial societal norms. The feeling for Pershing and others at the time was that to challenge these norms would shatter the delicate balance in place within the armed forces, which racial segregation had allowed to exist. It was best to try and keep African Americans in their place "while over there."[51]

. . . SERVING WITH BLACKS

Two wars later, and with more military installations dotting the Southern countryside, many Southerners continued to object to the racial desegregation of the military. As George T. Laney of Macon, Georgia, wondered to the ever-sympathetic Russell:

Why does this government destroy the moral[e] and pride of its white men by put-ting them in the same outfit as a bunch of half savage worthless niggers. . . . Many a young [white] soldier is getting mental breakdowns because of his having to stomach the nigger all the time in an equal basis. In the final analysis the burden of victory is on the white man, the burden of everything else is on him so why weaken, humble and humiliate the white boys putting them in the ranks with negroes. It is an apauling situ-ation. A very sick prematurely aged young soldier back from Korea told me today that the hell of it would not be so bad if there were not so many niggers to contend with. He said he would rather die than go back into an outfit with niggers in it. It does something to a white man. It destroys something in him. It takes something vital out of him to put him on a plane with the niggers that everyone knows that ever had any thing to do with him how unreliable he is, how irresponsible he is. . . . The nigger is to[o] close to the jungle to fully fit into the whitemans pattern. White men resent him violently, hehas [sic] no place with the young white men of this country.

It had been long argued that it was dangerous to racially integrate because of the cost to military efficiency that would result, but even Laney's blatantly rac-ist feelings offer a bit more nuance on the matter. He believed, and others of his racist sort would agree, that the true lunacy of the issue was not solely the risk of impairing the military; instead, it was the *damage* done to Southern white men's psyches to be on an equal footing with Black men.[52]

A fellow Georgian, J. T. Beverley Jr., concurred and lamented how this af-fected the mental well-being of young white Southern soldiers raised in the shadow of Jim Crow. His son was one of those white soldiers who was trau-matized by having to be physically *near* Black soldiers: "You know it is hard for a southern boy to get used to sleeping and eating with Negroes and my son tells me that he even had a colored gentlemen of the Harry S. Truman variety

sleeping in the buck above him. He says that the odor in the barracks is terrific."
He wondered out loud to Russell: "I am wondering why they [the Army] mix
the races down in our part of the Country."[53]

For other Southerners, such as Reverend George T. Beasley of Gadsden,
Alabama, it was not just a matter of mental well-being or physical proximity or
any social calamity that arose because of racial integration; the action, in and
of itself, was an affront to the Lord. "Unmistakably, Sir, the advocates of anti-
segregation [in the armed forces and elsewhere] for negroes are placed and
condemned by this portion of God's Pure and mighty Word: '*Without natural
affection*, despisers of those that are good, Traitors, Heady, High-minded, lov-
ers of pleasures more than God. Having a form of godliness, but denying the
Power thereof: FROM SUCH TURN AWAY.'" All of it, the racial integration
and reform of the military, in the end, claimed Walter McClenny of Cairo,
Georgia, was going to cost the Army the loyalty of the South and, as Beasley
had observed, its God-fearing Christian young white men.[54]

... DANCING IN AN INTEGRATED FASHION

If the presence alone of African American personnel in a desegregated fashion
was not troubling enough for some Southern whites, the idea of racially integrating social activities on base, such as dancing or swimming with whites—
specifically white women—was a harbinger of the End of Days. Just the thought
of whites and Blacks dancing together in the same place, let alone whether or
not they were doing so together, conjured up in racist white Southern minds
the ideas of the sexual domination of white women by overbearing and sexually lustful Black men. This pervading fear of some Southern white men, and
some women, had many justification. For Southern whites, interracial sex between Black men and white women challenged the prevailing racial hierarchy
of the region. If allowed to occur, it created a quasi-equality between the two
races. Worse, whites worried that interracial intercourse weakened their rich
Anglo-Saxon bloodlines that lay at the heart of their racial supremacy, a feeling
supported by the erroneous beliefs of the Lost Cause school.[55]

During an on-base dance at the Officers Club at Camp Breckinridge, Kentucky, Rose Hepp, the spouse of a white soldier, danced with a friend of their
family, a Black second lieutenant named George Dunnings. Though her husband had danced with Dunnings's wife, a Black woman, earlier in the evening,
nothing was said then. But the moment a Black man set foot on the dance
floor with Mrs. Hepp on a Southern installation, things were different. A white

colonel motioned for Hepp's husband to come over to him and then began to berate him before the entire gathering over the matter. Though Mr. Hepp pleaded with the colonel that Dunnings was a fellow officer in a racially integrated Army, his disgusted superior threatened to ban Mr. Hepp from the Officers Club. He then added further insult and fuel to a tense and terse situation, exclaiming: "We don't allow colored and white to dance together." After the incident, Mrs. Hepp, understandably, fretted that her action of simply dancing with a Black man, who was a family friend and a fellow officer, would jeopardize her husband's career. The incident did not remain localized; as Mrs. Hepp, who was very concerned not only for her husband but also their Black friends, penned a letter to the commander in chief, President Harry S. Truman, detailing to him the entirety of the event.[56]

Truman's response to the event remains unknown, but when Project Clear researchers discussed the issue of segregated dancing on posts in the South, where Jim Crow overruled Executive Order 9981; they noted an uncannily similar story in their official report. Their example came from a post they dubbed, anonymously, "Post A":

A white officer and his wife and a Negro officer and his wife together attended a function at the officer's club. During the course of the evening, the couples exchanged dance partners and entered the dance floor, whereupon the general sent a senior officer to tap one or both of the couples on the shoulder and ask them to be seated. Shortly thereafter the white officer was transferred to a different regiment on the same post, and the Negro officer was shipped overseas. The incident was widely discussed on the post and its handling was criticized even by officers who disapproved of mixed dancing.

If this event was indeed the same one at Camp Breckinridge that Mrs. Hepp described to Truman—the available evidence suggests that it likely was—then her forebodings proved correct: her spouse and their Black family friends paid the price for adhering to the president's desegregation order. Even if it was not the same event, the impact of the anonymous story ultimately led to African American officers on "Post A" feeling apprehensive about attending any integrated social functions. As one Black lieutenant on "Post A" put it: "Since that time the colored officers don't go to the officers' club for hardly anything, and certainly not for social affairs."[57]

In comparison to the North, the situation in the South involving racially integrated dances was deplorable; but that did not mean the reality above the Mason-Dixon line was a racial utopia either. Project Clear researchers surmised that "at Northern installations integration at dances is the general rule. The policy has been, generally, to invite white and Negro girls and to encourage joint rather than mixed dancing." But they also recognized that racism still persisted to a degree.[58]

What emerged on Northern installations was a quasi-integrated dance, something akin to the racial integration of platoons during the Battle of the Bulge years earlier; but unlike in Europe, the couples ultimately did not mix. Why didn't they? At play seemed to be "informal pressures"—the establishment of unwritten rules between the races about when and where intermingling was socially permissible—that existed and that prevented racial integration from being embraced fully during dances on military bases in the North. As a white sergeant major at a Northern installation recalled: "Black and white don't usually mix socially, but we had a company dance at which there were colored couples and everybody had a wonderful time." The reason that everyone enjoyed themselves, he believed, was because "there was no mixed dancing" because "none of the colored boys would have tried that." Such so-called informal pressures, and perhaps grassroots knowledge based on an example—the story of the Hepps, for instance—of what could happen if you did do so prevented African American soldiers from daring to challenge the situation and dance with white women, even if it was a friendly exchange of partners between couples, and even if it was on a Northern installation where racial harmony was likely to be perceived to be better than in the South.[59]

. . . SWIMMING TOGETHER

The other contentious issue on Southern posts involved the racial integration of swimming facilities. Some Southern whites thought swimming together was just as sexually suggestive and socially explosive as dancing, and the quandary of how to integrate racial swimming facilities in the South led to Southern base commanders canoodling with the old standby of the region: Jim Crow. For example, a Southern white commander explained to Project Clear researchers that he had embraced racial segregation out of an effort to prevent any problems between white and Black soldiers and their families: "Since the post was reactivated a year ago, we have spent an enormous amount of money to fix up a really nice colored beach. It is not as large as the white beach, but in many ways it is much nicer." Thus, the solution was not new, it defied Truman's order, and it was not particularly cost-efficient, as it required the construction of separate swimming facilities.[60]

While some military bases could afford to do this, most could not. Short on funds needed to build additional pools or spruce up existing racially segregated beaches, Southern base commanders segregated existing swimming facilities. If they had multiple pools already, one would be operated as a Blacks-only pool, while another would be for whites. If that option was not practical or possible, then base leadership would practice a limited form of racial integration of existing facilities with one notable exception: no women would be allowed. One officer noted: "They swim together [white and Black soldiers]. I would say at least 50 percent of the people using the pools are colored. When we set up the policy of letting colored swim, about two years ago, we specified no dependents. That way there would be no girls around in bathing suits, so there would be no trouble." But it was not just the commanders of the base attempting to keep the racial peace; white military personnel on Southern bases also used informal pressures to maintain the racial segregation of on-base facilities, including pools integrated by base leadership.[61]

Over time it became more apparent that it was simply not economically feasible to maintain the practice of racial segregation, and so the pools integrated. And in some instances, the result of this change was positive (or so that was how it was reported to Project Clear researchers). On an unidentified Southern installation, a general observed to Project Clear researchers "that there were about 60 percent white swimming with about 40 percent colored. The surprising thing was that among the white there were about 40 white girls. I said to myself, 'Now I've seen everything.'" One thing worth noting was that the majority swimming were whites, which could have been the result of informal pressures and the reality that the installation resided within the American South. Still, it was a more racially integrated experience then much of what the region's African American population had experienced.[62]

THE NEXT STEP

Project Clear researchers agreed that racial integration was moving forward at a logical pace, and the Army decided to take the next logical step: the complete racial integration of all its bases throughout the world. The decision to move forward with racial integration was aided by an inside agitator for racial reform: the Army Chief of Staff, General "Lightning" Joe Collins.

Prior to his deployment in World War II, Collins had served as the chief of staff for VII Corps. In that capacity, he experienced firsthand the negative impact of racial segregation on the Army and its Black personnel. While training in southwestern Arkansas, the general dealt with an incident involving an all-Black Illinois National Guard unit. Members of the outfit had allegedly

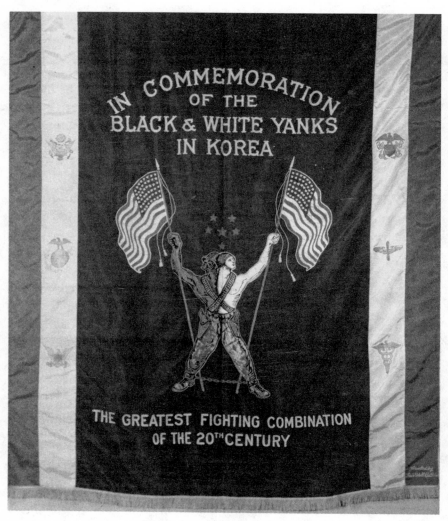

"In Commemoration of the Black & White Yanks in Korea—The Greatest Fighting Combination of the 20th Century": This handcrafted flag celebrated the role that racial integration of the armed forces played in securing peace during the Korean War. Source: 71-2530. Harry S. Truman Library and Museum.

harassed a couple of white women and a handful of state troopers. Word of this racial slight to the white race spread fast in the Piney Woods region. A group of white Arkansans, who had armed themselves with guns and gusto, proved bound and determined to restore the racial balance and the honor of their kinsmen. In part because of his Southern heritage (Collins was a native of New Orleans), he managed to calm down the sensibilities of the excited

Southerners and prevented a potential showdown between two heavily armed camps. "Lightning" Joe, though, never forgot the incident and relied on it to justify his support for racial integration.[63]

In December 1951, General Collins issued a directive that completed the racial integration of the United States Army. It took time, however, for that directive to take hold in Europe. Since the end of World War II, American soldiers in Europe maintained the tradition of Jim Crow racial segregation. As the number of troops increased exponentially in Europe during the early throes of the Cold War, Army leadership on the continent refused to adjust their stance on the issue, as they argued it risked and would no doubt upend the military efficiency that racial segregation purportedly afforded them. The successful results emerging from the Korean theater did little to change their minds. In an attempt to breach this ideological inflexibility, the Army sent Dr. Eli Ginzberg, a noted adviser and Columbia professor, across the Atlantic to change the minds of the Army's leadership in Europe. But Ginzberg met with an impenetrable wall of racial resistance and disbelief among European commanders, rendering his efforts to convince them otherwise to be futile. Unrelenting, Army leadership stateside, especially "Lightning" Joe, ordered the European Command, under the leadership of General Thomas C. Handy, to racially integrate all its forces anyway.[64]

INTEGRATION OF THE MARINE CORPS

General O. P. Smith of the Marine Corps had fought at Peleliu and Okinawa; he knew carnage when he saw it. During the Korean War, he commanded the 1st Marine Division, which was attached to General Ned Almond's X Corps, United States Army. In a sense, both were company men when it came to the issue of racial integration. However, where Almond's Southern sensitives and stonyhearted bigotry prevented him from changing, O. P. Smith, to borrow from his most famous quote, was about to start advancing in a new direction. Historian Jeremy Maxwell noted that Almond was livid about the changes occurring within his command, but the ever-professional and efficient Smith had little regard for Almond's concerns; like many Marine leaders, Smith thought little of Almond as a commander.[65]

Racial integration for O. P. Smith and the Marine Corps was about one thing: winning. Wars are fueled by blood and treasure, and the Marines were short on the former. Instead of waiting for recently recruited and trained white Marines to get up to speed, Smith used the African American Marines among his ranks. Once allowed to fight, they did not disappoint and performed their duties in an exemplary fashion, which earned them a level of respect among their white comrades-in-arms. An African American Marine, Thomas Cork, a light machine gunner, who fought at Inchon and at Chosin Reservoir, noted that, as the savagery of the war unfolded, he "never heard another word about calling me any kind of names. I became a Marine like the rest of them. And that made me feel good." Firefighting Leatherneck turned infantrymen Johnnie Givian recalled a similar experience: "Racism didn't show up then; nobody ever talked about it, it was almost forgotten. I was the only black at one time there in our regiment of people, that's 300 some people." Black Marines, albeit in limited numbers, also took to the air to combat communism. The First African American Marine commissioned as a pilot, Frank E. Petersen Jr. fought in Korea and later became the first of his race to reach the rank of general in the Marine Corps. The defeat of segregation in the Marine Corps at the time, whether on the ground or in the air, was like that of the Army. The need of the moment drove it, but once some segregationists witnessed firsthand the military capabilities of African American Marines, their former beliefs and concerns about inadequacies on the battlefield quickly faded, and they accepted the change.[66]

While combat performance was enough for some white Marines, others refused to change. They believed that the Marine Corps was an all-white organization with no room for minorities. Recognizing they could not stop the advancement of racial integration, prosegregation Marines resisted. Through the manipulation of Marine Corps policy, some commanding officers prevented the transfer or acceptance of African American NCOs into their units. Relying on age-old racist philosophies, they justified their actions by claiming that racial integration damaged the combat effectiveness of their commands. Some even manipulated the manpower distribution system to prevent the introduction of enlisted Black Marines into their units. The Marine Corps also kept African Americans out of high-profile duty stations, such as embassy duty. By the end of the Korean War, racial integration had finally come to the Marines, but true equality of opportunity and acceptance for Black Marines had not.[67]

A RELUCTANT STALEMATE

Much like the way the war in Korea ended, so, too, did the efforts of some Southern segregationists in their war against racial integration—with bitter stalemate and a reluctant acceptance of the new status quo. Though they loathed the concept of racial integration, Southern congressmen allowed it in the armed forces to continue, as it proved to be effective and strengthened the overall defense of the nation. Senator Richard Russell, who had actively fought against racial integration, even proved willing to acquiesce to reform. The Georgian confidentially informed Assistant Secretary of Defense James Evans: "I won't help him [Secretary of Defense Robert Lovett] integrate, but I won't hinder him either—and neither will anyone else." Had Russell gone soft on racial segregation? No. The senator from Georgia instead faced a great paradox. He had always advocated for a powerful military, but if Russell were to challenge the racial integration of the Army or the Marine Corps, after it had proven to work, he ran the terrible risk of weakening both during the Cold War. It was a dilemma he would have to face again during the Vietnam War—but that was yet to come. With his mind fully on the present, the Southern segregationist from Georgia, an avid cold warrior, broke bread with the devil he knew—racial integration—to vanquish the devil he feared: global communism.[68]

TRUMAN'S LAST HURRAH

Harry Truman had loved history since boyhood. His time in the presidency did not sway his deep and abiding affection for the subject. But President Truman, lover of history or not, was not an academic. History's lessons were important to him, but not so that he could try to reclaim a past era to understand it further. Instead, history taught him how to be a good citizen, the importance of dedication and duty to one's country, the mistakes that had been made, and how to learn from them. It effectively helped him become the leader he would become. These lessons and more were not just for Truman; they were for every American. But, Truman reasoned, those lessons were often learned hard. "I've wondered why the next generation can't profit from the generation before but they never did until they get knocked in the head by experience," Truman confided to his biographer, Merle Miller.[69]

History and perhaps time were not on Harry Truman's mind as the Korean War settled into an uneasy stalemate along the 38th parallel, while his presidency rapidly drew closer to its end. When it came to the end of his presidency, Truman was directly responsible. He had supported the creation of the Hoover Commission and its mandate to reform the administration of the federal government, which led that body to recommend passing the Twenty-Second

Amendment to the Constitution, which prevented future presidents from serving more than two terms, a reaction to FDR's four-term dynasty of sorts. Because of the nature of his presidency, Truman had assumed the office after FDR's death in 1945 and won on his own accord in 1948. Truman's situation did not run afoul of the Twenty-Second Amendment, and he could have run in 1952. But he didn't. When he sat down to do the political calculus of his standing with the American people, Truman realized that his popularity was in the dumpster. At the beginning of the year, the president had a 22 percent approval rating. Unpopular with the people and with Dwight D. Eisenhower throwing his hat into the ring, Truman's decision not to run was guided partly by this electability calculus in 1952.[70]

There was more, however, to Truman's decision than whether or not he could win. It had to do with history, tradition, and his keen desire to preserve both. Like many American leaders then, and even today, the example of the Roman general Cincinnatus and his service to a troubled empire remained ubiquitous. George Washington mimicked it during his own presidency and by doing so began the unofficial tradition of American presidents serving two terms in office. Only one—Roosevelt—had broken with tradition.[71]

Truman felt no burning desire to follow his predecessor across the political Rubicon. Quite to the contrary. He rebuked FDR for his actions and warned future generations about the dangerous allure of power that came from occupying the most powerful office in the world. "There is a lure in power," Truman cautioned. "It can get into a man's blood just as gambling and lust for money have been known to do." The United States was a democratic republic, Truman reminded all who would listen. If he were to break with tradition again, it could lead America—as with Rome—down the road of ruin. As the president observed: "When Rome forgot Cincinnatus its downfall began." For Harry Truman, it was time for the Republic to return to the exalted example of Cincinnatus.[72]

Though his approval rating was sinking and his days in office were dwindling, Truman had not lost the stomach to continue racial reform of the military. An incident late in his presidency illustrates his continuing dedication to the matter. In his Pulitzer Prize–winning biography *Truman*, David McCullough recounts the story of when Truman learned that Korean War veteran Sergeant John Rice had been rejected burial in a military cemetery in Sioux City, Iowa, because he happened to be a Winnebago Indian. It was an indignity of a sort that likely reminded Truman to some degree of the racial mistreatment of Black soldiers such as Isaac Woodard years earlier. It could not or would not stand. So incensed was the Man from Independence that he saw to it personally that Rice was entombed in Arlington National Cemetery with full honors and that his family was flown to the funeral at no cost to them.[73]

BUT WHAT OF THE CHILDREN?

A remaining quandary for the Truman administration was the question of what to do about the children of minority personnel, whose parents served in a racially integrated armed forces, while they studied under Jim Crow while on the base. The administration's efforts to redress this situation would not be easily achieved, as dismayed and fearful Southern citizens continued to rail against the advancement of civil rights in the military and the liberal communist-fueled conspiracy they believed was behind it all.

The political warriors of the South found willing accomplices to their cause in the right-wing fringe media of the era, which added to the anticommunist recipe formulating among those who were complaining against racial integration, tinged with the conspiratorial and the anti-Semitic. "'Integration' is destroying U.S. Army," blared the bold headline of the right-wing conspiratorial newspaper the *American Nationalist*. The heavily anti-Semitic piece attacked what it viewed as a Jewish- and communist-orchestrated conspiracy to undermine the fabric of the United States. "Only a propagandist—or a dullard—would argue," the piece exclaimed, "that the customs and tradition which our forefathers have followed since the establishment of Jamestown have all of a sudden become 'un-American.'" In what amounted to a manipulation of past African American military accomplishments, the mental capabilities of Black soldiers, questions of their loyalty under fire, and the impact of racial integration on American military morale, the newspaper sought to eradicate what it coined as the "compulsory mongrelization" of the American armed forces and American society as a whole.[74]

To stir racist sentiment among its readership further, the article also included pictures of Black soldiers and white women interacting with one another. Readers of conspiratorial newspapers understood the role that Truman or his high-level advisers played—but what about others? Who *was really behind* it all? Who were the *real* foot soldiers of the Jews and the communists? The *American Nationalist* was happy to provide names, whether substantiated or not, for a rabid audience desperate for answers and someone to blame. According to the conspiratorial newspaper, one of the main conspirators behind the "mongrelization" of the American armed forces was a foreign-born Jewish woman named Anna Rosenberg.[75]

THE FIRST OF HER GENDER

Intelligent, magnetic, and politically savvy, Rosenberg became entrenched in the democratic system in New York during the Great Depression, which aided in her education in the ways of the New Deal and endeared her in the eyes of many powerful men, including Franklin D. Roosevelt. During A. Philip Randolph's proposed march on Washington to protest racial segregation in the armed forces, FDR turned to Rosenberg for advice on how to proceed. Over time, her stature grew in Washington, and it netted her regard from presidents of both political parties; Dwight D. Eisenhower and Harry S. Truman awarded Rosenberg for her service during World War II with the Medal of Freedom and the Medal of Merit, respectively.[76]

After the conclusion of World War II, Secretary of Defense George C. Marshall, who was equally impressed with Rosenberg, made her the first female to serve as the assistant secretary of defense for manpower and personnel. In the years to come that office became synonymous with civil rights reform in the military. And because of this recognition, those who occupied the office became targets for conservative fringe element groups and citizens who embraced the views they propagated.[77]

But before she faced the fire of the conspiratorial press, Rosenberg had to face the heat from Congress. During her Senate confirmation process, the committee received letters from men and women who protested the appointment, whether it was because she was a woman, inexperienced, or the fact that she was a foreign-born Jew, which led to concerns about her loyalty to the position. Baltimore resident Joseph J. Philbin put it flatly to Truman: "For the love of the gentle Jesus Christ and long-suffering people of these United States, can't you find in all this broad land of ours a native American, wholly loyal and above all possible criticism, who can fill this or any other position in the government?" When it came to congressional opinion, noted red-baiters such as John Rankin of Mississippi lined up to hurl insults and accusations at Rosenberg. In a rant that mixed gender discrimination and anti-Semitic ideology with the fear of communist infiltration in American society, Rankin decried the idea of the "little Yiddish woman from Austria-Hungary" becoming the assistant secretary of defense for manpower and personnel. In Rankin's opinion, the selection of Rosenberg was blasphemous, highly questionable, and flat-out reeked of communist subversion: "The American people are aroused and indignant that this exalted position, one of the most powerful in the world, should be turned over to a foreign-born individual whose record for association with Communist organizations shows that she is unfit to occupy such a

Assistant Secretary of Defense Anna Rosenberg—a civilian-military trailblazer: Avid New Dealer and favored target of conspiratorial ultra-right wing media, Anna M. Rosenberg became the first female assistant secretary of defense for manpower and personnel. To her right is General George C. Marshall. November 15, 1950. Source: 97-1860. Harry S. Truman Library and Museum.

place of responsibility." Once she survived the baptism of fire that came with her confirmation hearings, Rosenberg's next step was to facilitate the needs of her boss George Marshall and tackle his pet project: manpower reform.[78]

The grand architect of Allied victory during World War II, Marshall had actively sought an improvement to the American method of accruing manpower based on his experiences having to build a warfighting machine. He found a willing ally in his quest in President Harry Truman, who had proposed the Universal Military Training program. During his attempt to make UMT a reality, Marshall backed off any and all agendas that might irritate the Southern members, specifically Richard Russell, on the Senate Armed Services Committee. Still, as the battle for manpower improvement unfolded, so, too, did the battle for racial integration of the armed forces. Ultimately, both were achieved to varying degrees: Truman achieved, as we have seen, Executive Order 9981, which was cemented with the blood sacrifice provided by the Korean conflict, while Marshall achieved modest reform through the Selective Service Act.[79]

Working diligently on the manpower problem was Rosenberg, who leveraged her skills as an organizer and negotiator to aid in remedying the military's archaic set of induction examinations. In the past, each branch had conducted its own series of tests and induction exams. Afterward, and thanks to the work of Rosenberg and others, the armed forces started conducting a uniform exam that not only aided in reforming the problems of the past but also addressed remaining racist practices, which resulted in the further enlistment of African American personnel in the years to come.[80]

RACIAL INTEGRATION OF ON-BASE SCHOOLS, PART 1

Though the achievement of the Selective Service Act was a step in the right direction, a racist holdover remained: the education of minority school children in a racially segregated environment on racially integrated military bases. In particular, the Army had to repeatedly weather criticism from civil rights advocates about the racial segregation of its on-base schools. In a world where Executive Order 9981 existed, the Army reasoned that the matter of dependent education was out of their hands. Although schools resided on federal property, they were under the jurisdiction of state agencies and not the Army. In effect, the Army—adhering to the local racial customs of the communities surrounding its installations—retreated on the matter.[81]

A critic of the Army's defense of racial segregation was Senator Hubert H. Humphrey of Minnesota. While in graduate school in Louisiana, Humphrey experienced firsthand the deplorable nature of racial segregation and remarked that he "was dismayed by . . . the white, neatly painted houses of the whites, the unpainted shacks of the blacks; the stately homes on manicured lawns in the white sections, the open sewage ditches in black neighborhoods . . . [and] the WHITE and COLORED signs for drinking fountains and toilets[.] I found them both ridiculous and offensive." Convinced that he could and should do more, Humphrey spent the rest of his life fighting against racial segregation within and outside the military and the society it sought to protect.[82]

The senator from Minnesota found the Army's excuse for maintaining segregation in on-base schools ridiculous. He scoffed at the Army's claim that its stance complied with the guidelines of Public Law 874, a law that Humphrey had helped push through Congress. A product of World War II, Public Law 874 provided financial support for schools that resided on federal property; the law importantly also aided schools that did not reside on federal property but contained enough federal dependents to warrant federal support. Conservative Republicans and Southern segregationists in Congress worried this legislation could remove control of schools away from the community and deliver it into the hands of the federal government; they feared it would likely use the law to racially integrate institutions. In order to protect the sovereignty of the states when it came to educational matters, the federal government allowed schools supported by federal funds to follow state guidelines.[83]

As far as Humphrey was concerned, though, this did not mean that Public Law 874 supported racial segregation or that the Army did not have a say in the matter. In a letter to Rosenberg, who was involved in the issue, Humphrey warned that the Army's stance created the possibility of a gross manipulation of a state entity directing the affairs of a federal one. As he put it: "If this is allowed to stand unchallenged, there is no limit to the possibilities for other local invasions and we may shortly be confronted with a situation in which the commanding officer of a post would be subordinate to a local mayor or city council in administering other regulations." Agreeing with Humphrey, Rosenberg brought the matter to the attention of US Commissioner of Education Earl J. McGrath. In a letter to McGrath, Rosenberg declared that "this practice is unsatisfactory and is violative not only of the policy of the Department of Defense but also contravenes the policy set forth by the President." The policy she was alluding to was Executive Order 9981, which had unleashed a wave of civil rights reform throughout the military.[84]

Five days later, on January 15, 1953, McGrath sent a letter to Rosenberg explaining the intricacies of Public Law 874 and that, "in all but three instances," on-base schools practiced racial integration. In McGrath's estimation, that matter was out of his hands, as the ultimate authority for these decisions were base commanders who had a better grip on the local customs of the communities surrounding military installations. Though McGrath pledged his willingness to support Rosenberg's call for sweeping change in policy, the sands of the hourglass of the Truman administration had run out. Within a matter of days, President-elect Dwight D. Eisenhower was slated to be sworn in. Those minority children still facing racial prejudice in schools on base would have to wait.[85]

CONCLUSION

In the October 1953 issue of *The Crisis*, Colonel George C. Reinhart observed that "communist propaganda has won more victories in the battle for men's minds by capitalizing on the color of their skins." As a result, "hostility to the white man threatens the Far East, India, The Moslem [*sic*] World, and Africa." Undeniably, it had been "the 'color' question," he alleged, that "helped the communists win China and spurred their troops to fight in Korea." Still, the United States had an important weapon against the slander of communist propaganda:

Elimination of racial segregation in our armed forces is the best possible proof of American democracy in action. In German casernes, French and English billets, white and colored soldiers of the United States Army share quarters without regard to race; stand formations with mixed races, but identical uniforms, in the same squad. United Nations' troops and observers returning from Korea can attest there was no color line in foxholes, nor in the rest camps either, of the 8th U.S. Army.

Whether or not he meant to do so, Reinhart's comments were setting a triumphant tone in the narrative emerging over the racial integration of the armed forces. It would continue. A year later, in 1954, Lee Nichols's *Breakthrough on the Color Front* became the first published work to examine the racial integration of the armed forces. A larger and more nuanced examination, it marched to a triumphant beat. In that work, Nichols felt that "by knocking down its racial barriers, the military had shown it could be done; that Negroes and whites, despite a long history of sharp separation and frequently deep-seated antagonism, would work, live and play together with little or no concern once they got used to the idea." He was only partially correct.[86]

When thinking back over the long-term historical ramifications of racial integration of the military on American society, it cannot be denied that it aided in the larger struggle for equality achieved by the civil rights movement and those who supported it within the federal government. But it also should not be ignored that this watershed moment for the African American community occurred in an inauspicious fashion and was more focused on dealing with a different ideological demon—global communism—and not Jim Crow segregation and its bedfellow, American racism.

That it continued and expanded from Korea onward was not because all in the military, including commanders, desired to drive a stake into the heart of fallacious and phony racial stereotypes that degraded Black citizens—specifically Black men—as ignorant, cowardly, and sexually decadent individuals. Rather, it filled the physical necessity of waging war against communism. Therefore, while many white commanders racially desegregated their forces out of good intentions, the fact remained that the reason the military turned to African American military personnel in the Army and the Marine

Corps was not because they wanted them or perhaps initially considered them equals; it was because they needed them. In a sense, it sped up a process that had already been underway since Truman's executive order had been issued. And it did expose the fallacy of the manmade artificial barrier placed within the military that denied Blacks a chance to serve with whites out of a fear of total disarray being the result. But without a common enemy, the unthinkable—racial integration—would not have been possible or, at least for some, desired. While Truman talked often about equality of opportunity, the only opportunity on the table was the opportunity to win. The racial integration of the armed forces that had taken place up to that point failed to end racism in the ranks or the country because it was not designed to do so. But unlike World War II, where for a time partial integration took hold, racial integration of the armed forces persisted and, under the newly elected president, Dwight D. Eisenhower, expanded in unforeseen ways The reason for that was because it had been successful, the Black community would not allow it to retract, and the Cold War was still raging.

CHAPTER 4

The Frustration of the Middle Way: Eisenhower and Reform

Long before Jackie Robinson was staring down National League pitching and winning a World Series and Most Valuable Player honors with the Brooklyn Dodgers, he was an officer in the United States Army. Going from corporal to second lieutenant in the Army during World War II, and as a Black man on top of that, was no easy feat. But Jackie Robinson, as he would always do, proved his doubters wrong. A great deal of his success, of course, was a result of his work ethic. But it also helped that he knew boxing's world heavyweight champion, a fellow athlete-turned-soldier, Joe Lewis. With Lewis's support and the earnest efforts of Judge William H. Hastie, Secretary of War Henry Stimson's able and active civilian aide for Negro affairs, Robinson went to Officer Candidate School and earned his commission as a lieutenant.[1]

Commissioned officer or not, Robinson faced, as did all Black soldiers, the racism within and outside the military. For instance, while serving in Fort Riley, Kansas, Black soldiers, including the former UCLA standout Robinson, were prohibited from utilizing the post exchange, or PX. While the average Black soldier's complaints about the situation was likely ignored, Robinson's complaints garnered a bit more attention. And the reason for that was because he mattered to the white officer command of the post. The commanders at Fort Riley valued Jackie for his athletic abilities on the football gridiron, and he had already been conscripted to play for the post's team. Jackie sought to capitalize on that need to garner change for all. In a tit-for-tat moment, Robinson threated not to play if things did not racially improve; unwilling to compromise, the leadership of the post said they would force him to play. While Robinson agreed they had that power, it did not mean he would perform at the level befitting his All-American status. Ultimately, the problem of Robinson playing or not was rectified when he was transferred to Camp Hood (later Fort Hood), Texas, to serve with the 761st All-Tank Battalion, the famed Black Panthers.[2]

Within his unit, Robinson found himself among kindred spirits working toward a greater cause. Though the men of the 761st had found some sort of

Jackie Robinson—US Army tanker, baseball slugger, civil rights champion:
Throughout his pursuit of racial equality, Jack "Jackie" Robinson proved willing
to stare down racism within the military, within Major League Baseball, and
with those presidents of the United States who were not doing enough to rectify
it. Source: Jackie Robinson in his Brooklyn Dodgers Uniform, 1950. Record
Group 306: Records of the U.S. Information Agency, 1900–2003, Master File
Photographs of U.S. and Foreign Personalities, World Events, and American
Economic, Social, and Cultural Life, ca. 1953–ca. 1994. National Archives and
Records Administration, Washington, D.C.

respect on post, they still encountered racist whites in the local community. In particular, white bus drivers in the South exerted a great deal of power over Black soldiers and citizens. This was certainly the case with Sergeant Isaac Woodard after the war as it would be for Jackie Robinson during it. In the heat of the summer, on July 6, 1944, Jackie Robinson boarded a bus and sat in the whites-only section next to the wife of a fellow Black Panther tanker, Virginia Jones. Both were African Americans, but Jones could pass for white; Robinson could not, and it is unlikely that he would have tried to do so. When the bus driver yelled for Robinson to get to the back of the bus, the Black officer refused. Upon arrival at Robinson's destination, the argument continued and got more agitated. The Black officer recalled:

The bus driver asked me for my identification card. I refused. . . . He then went to the Dispatcher and told him something. What he told him I don't know. He then comes back and tells the people [those gathering as the argument became more heated] that this nigger is making trouble. I told the driver to stop f—in with me, so he gets the rest of the men around there and starts blowing his top and someone calls the MP's.

After the arrival of the MPs, Robinson was arrested. Furthermore, he ran afoul of the commander of the military police, Captain Gerald M. Bear, who felt disrespected by Robinson and charged him with Article of War No. 63 and No. 64, the first pertaining to the disrespectful actions of a subordinate toward a superior officer, the latter disobeying of a direct order from a superior officer. Jackie was ultimately acquitted of all charges against him, but his career in the Army was ending: nursing a long-running ankle injury, Robinson had sought and received a medical discharge. His Army career, short-lived though it was, was now behind him. But fate and sheer talent would deliver Jackie onto an equally large stage.[3]

Years later, and now recently retired after being the first of his race to integrate Major League Baseball, Robinson turned to civil rights activism. In the fall of 1957, he wrote to a man he had long admired and supported: President Dwight D. Eisenhower. This letter, though, was no bit of fan mail. It was a calling-on-the-carpet moment for Ike, as Robinson was disturbed by the president's request for patience during the Little Rock Crisis. Robinson observed: "It is easy for those who haven't felt the evils of prejudiced society to urge it [patience], but for those of us who as Americans have patiently waited all these years for the rights supposedly guaranteed us under our Constitution, it is not an easy task." Now was not the time for patience, the former member of the 761st All-Black Tank Battalion declared, but a time for action: "A mere statement that you don't like violence is not enough," Robinson told Eisenhower;

instead, he believed that the president would reap tremendous praise and benefit if he acted. Looking toward the Cold War horizon, Robinson felt that "people the world over would hail you if you made a statement that would clearly put your office behind the efforts for civil rights." Lastly and poignantly, he contended that the president's failure to act had damaged American prestige abroad, as the Soviet propaganda machine was spewing out one incendiary story after another that ripped and teared away at the Republic's credibility on the issue. Robinson reminded the president "you see what the Communist nations are doing with the material we have given them." And it was true. The communists were continuing to use America's civil rights shortcomings to discredit the nation in the eyes of allies and nonwhite Third World nations on the Cold War periphery—and Eisenhower knew it.[4]

Robinson's correspondence and criticism of the president highlight a general feeling about the Eisenhower era—bitter disappointment at the time and afterward. It has often been described as an era disturbingly devoid of presidential leadership and action regarding civil rights reform. The most damning criticism came from a celebrated Eisenhower biographer, Stephen E. Ambrose.[5] In Ambrose's words:

In civil rights, as in civil liberties, Eisenhower was not a reluctant leader—he was no leader at all. He just wished the problems would go away. . . . With regard to civil rights, an area in which the depth of commitment by the American people was considerably less than the commitment to civil liberties, Eisenhower's refusal to lead was almost criminal. Who can say what might have been accomplished in dealing with this most permanent of problems had President Eisenhower joined Chief Justice Warren in enthusiastically supporting racial equality and justice? But he did not; and by putting the problem off, by leaving it to his successors, he just made it worse.

In the civil rights arena outside the military, there can be no doubt that Ambrose's analysis of the president has some measure of merit, as it highlighted his reluctance to act on one of the most quintessential issues of the time.[6]

Considering Eisenhower's background, however, it would have been surprising if he had done something. Abilene, Kansas, was a predominantly all-white community, offering little interaction with African Americans. In 1873, Henry O. Flipper entered West Point, integrating that fabled institution, and four years later he became its first Black graduate. From 1873 to 1922, it graduated a total of three Black cadets. When Eisenhower attended (1911–1915), however, there were no African Americans in attendance.[7]

From the racially segregated backdrop of West Point to service in the racially segregated Army, Eisenhower was weaned on the racism of the twentieth-century military. Over the length of his career, Eisenhower served in various racially segregated duty stations throughout the country, most notably in the American South, and the world. And when he did spend time with African American personnel, it was a greatly limited experience. The lone example of his command experience with Black soldiers came as a punishment. The biographer Jean Edward Smith noted: "Eisenhower himself had briefly served as executive officer of the 2⁴th Infantry at Fort Benning in the 1920s. The assignment had been a punitive one inflicted by the chief of infantry, and Ike quickly managed a transfer." Instead of embracing the men he had been assigned to lead, Eisenhower retreated, likely out of a fear of what longtime service with a Black unit, often deemed a punishment by white officers, would look like in a racially segregated service branch.[8]

EISENHOWER THE GRADUALIST

Decades later, though, General Eisenhower was in a desperate situation and forced to make the choice whether or not to use African American soldiers for combat. During the Battle of Bulge, he chose to use them. But he did this in a limited and temporary fashion because Eisenhower and the Army *needed* them, not because he had a scorching desire to rectify the inefficiency that racial segregation brought about or because he personally felt that it was morally wrong. He simply needed them.[9]

After the war, Eisenhower was questioned by members of the Senate Armed Services Committee about his experience with racial integration. His response was revealing. The general admitted that his feelings over the racial integration of the armed forces were evolving, but Eisenhower felt that the best course for the military was segregation. To defend his belief, the general outlined a gradualist point of view to the committee: "I believe that the human race may finally grow up to the point where it [race relations] will not be a problem. It will disappear through education, through mutual respect, and so on. But I do believe that if we attempt merely by passing a lot of laws to force someone to like someone else, we are just going to get into trouble."[10]

As president, Eisenhower maintained unapologetic gradualism. Furthermore, his social activities reinforced his stance. Eisenhower often vacationed at Augusta National Golf Club in Georgia, where he encountered all the beauty and splendor of America's beloved course, while at the same time receiving a heaping dose of the virulent racism that still pervaded the South. Duffers often swap stories, tall tales, and jokes, which sometimes contained racial themes. Although no hack by any stretch, Bobby Jones spun a racist story or two for the president when they golfed together. When Eisenhower returned from his Augusta sojourns, he often retold these stories to friends and colleagues.[11]

A pattern developed as Eisenhower's consistent interaction with the Southern way of life, both as a soldier and a president, engrained in him sympathy for the white South. Prior to the *Brown* decision, Eisenhower pleaded to Chief Justice Earl Warren about the South and racial integration: "These are not bad people." the president of the United States insisted, "all they are concerned about is to see that their sweet little girls are not required to sit in school alongside some big overgrown Negroes." Ike's aside, which hinted at the long-running fear of the sexual nature of Black men, with Warren had little effect.[12]

The *Brown* verdict provided the president an opportunity to get out in front of the situation and lead the nation. After the Supreme Court rendered its verdict and outlawed racial segregation, the president weakly promised to comply with the order yet offered to do little more. Instead of seeking out an alternative viewpoint, Eisenhower retreated into his own personal and social echo chamber, a decision that reinforced his gradualist feelings. He reached out to longtime friend, segregationist, and South Carolina governor, Jimmy Byrnes. After discussing the matter with Byrnes, the president informed his administration that forced racial integration by way of laws and overt government action would cause a white backlash against African American Southerners. The result would be costly and likely lead to the destruction of the Southern education system and the loss of what little civil rights gains had been achieved. Ike's fear of a pending social calamity was so great that he even worried that "we could have another civil war on our hands." Conflict did come as Southern congressmen and senators signed the Southern Manifesto in 1956, decrying the *Brown* decision and launching a political and legal assault against it.[13]

While Southerners in Congress raged, the events that unfolded in Little Rock, Arkansas, confirmed Byrnes's warnings and Eisenhower's deepest fears about government intervention into social affairs. Located in the heart of the state capital, Little Rock Central High School had traditionally been an all-white institution. In early September 1957, however, that changed when nine African American students attempted to attend classes. This presented a political conundrum for the governor of Arkansas, Orval Faubus. Casting his lot with his segregationist constituents, Faubus decided against integration and quickly dispatched the Arkansas National Guard to the school to put a halt to the situation. After a brief struggle in the federal courts, which he lost, Faubus was forced to remove the guardsmen from the school. With the military removed from the equation, the students again attempted to enter. This time they met an angry mob. Once inside, the safety of the nine Black students came into question as some members of the crowd outside threatened to kill the students after they left the premises. In order to bring a semblance of sanity to the situation and to protect the children, the Little Rock Police Department escorted them from the school.[14]

With tensions rising, the mayor of the beleaguered city, Woodrow Wilson Mann, appealed to the president for help. Although loathe to become involved, Eisenhower, who had failed to reach an agreement with Faubus behind the scenes and was feeling stinging criticism coming from the communist press overseas, reluctantly ordered in the 101st Airborne. The following day, protected by the US Army and the now-federalized Arkansas National Guard, the Little Rock Nine, as they were now known, entered the school. What should have been a great victory for civil rights and equality of opportunity quickly turned hollow; the following year, Governor Faubus closed all public high schools in the capital city as opposed to letting racial integration march forward.[15]

EISENHOWER THE ACTIVIST?

The narrative on Eisenhower that is provided above only tells part of the tale, but in so doing it offers an incomplete picture of him as a civil rights actor. A counterthesis attempts to clarify the story. In *A Matter of Justice*, David Nichols contends that Eisenhower, although he was a gradualist, deliberately and actively set about addressing civil rights failings within the armed forces. Whether on purpose or by happenstance, Nichols's thesis borrows heavily from the work of Fred Greenstein. To rebuff those historians and political scientists who had initially viewed Eisenhower as more of a placeholder than a decisive force as president, Greenstein wrote *The Hidden-Hand Presidency*. This work transformed Eisenhower from what appeared to be a rather nonactive leader into a cunning and manipulative president in firm control of his administration. Often using his administration as a shield, Eisenhower acted in a subversive fashion to retain a sense of power without suffering the negative press that coincided with failure or shortcomings. The president behind the scenes saw to it that Mohammad Mossadegh in Iran and Jacobo Arbenz in Guatemala, both of whom were believed to be associated with communists, were removed from power.[16]

While Eisenhower acted in the background, it was his administration, especially his cabinet, that often absorbed the punishment for his actions. As Herbert Brownell, Eisenhower's attorney general, observed:

At times, his [Eisenhower's] techniques of delegation put us on the proverbial limb. Other cabinet members and I became the point men identified with and responsible for policies that were actually the president's. As he once told Jim Hagerty, [the press secretary of the Eisenhower administration,] who had to face a hostile press with some bit of unwelcome news, "Better you, Jim, than me." Eisenhower's reluctance to associate himself with difficult policy decisions sometimes made it a little harder for us to do our jobs.

Eisenhower's hidden-hand manipulation did not always work for him, as his failed attempt to jettison Richard Nixon from the 1956 presidential ticket demonstrated. Never really sold on Nixon as a trustworthy partner in governance, the president attempted in 1956 to persuade his vice president that it would be better for him politically to abandon the ticket and instead serve as a department secretary. The plan, of course, failed; Nixon remained popular within the party, particularly its stridently anticommunist constituency. While it did not always work, Eisenhower continued to utilize hidden-hand tactics throughout his presidency. This included efforts to continue racial integration of the armed forces.[17]

PRESIDENTIAL MOTIVATORS

It was Eisenhower's predecessor, Harry Truman, who had placed the armed forces on the path toward racial integration. Though Eisenhower may have had some doubts years before on the viability of racial integration, the time to countermand the order had passed. By the time he had assumed the office, the armed forces had been racially integrating the ranks for almost five years. While detractors remained, it was unlikely that Eisenhower would have risked undoing something that was working. And as historians have noted, the prospect of racially reforming the military gave American presidents a valuable piece of counterpropaganda to use against Russia's barbs about the Republic's racial dilemma. Therefore, though Eisenhower remained concerned about how the white South would react to this development, the fact remained that the action of racial integration of the military and federal government was already underway; that was the law of the land, and he would not fight it. Instead, Eisenhower expanded it.[18]

But Eisenhower never would have done so had he not believed that he could.

Compared to his conservative handling of the Little Rock Crisis, the president believed that *he had the power and the responsibility* to end racial discrimination within the federal government. He had once observed: "I feel that my oath of office, as well as my own convictions, requires me to eliminate discrimination within the definite areas of Federal responsibility." This was not a matter solely of political manipulation designed to appeal to African Americans or liberal voters, though it certainly played a part; instead, it reflected what the biographer Michael Korda believed was Eisenhower's "sense of justice and his determination to avoid empty gestures." Of course, a key component of the federal government was the military. While running for president, Eisenhower promised to finish integrating the armed forces. And as president, he more than kept his word.[19]

Outside of his personal belief that he could act, the president was also influenced and prodded into action by the pugnacious efforts of Congressmen Adam Clayton Powell Jr. Whether it concerned the right of African American soldiers to volunteer to serve within the segregated ranks of the military police in Fort Bliss, Texas, or some other remaining bulwark of racial exclusion, Powell remained a stalwart champion of racial integration. As far as the president and his notable intransigence on the issue, Powell became something of an Eisenhower whisperer. As the biographer Charles Hamilton has noted, the congressmen from Harlem had manipulating the former general down to a science. Instead of overtly going after Eisenhower, Powell would rail against his administration for failing to live up to the president's civil rights wishes. In this manner, the congressman was challenging Eisenhower's inaction without challenging the president directly. What gave Powell's pressure tactics teeth was Eisenhower's recognition of the growing power of the African American vote.[20]

During the early to mid-1950s, some African Americans, disillusioned with Democratic segregationists, returned to the party of Lincoln. As Jackie Robinson's letter to Eisenhower during the Little Rock desegregation crisis demonstrated, the president had gained a following within the African American community. When the president acted on civil rights issues, he likely did so partially because of Powell's actions—but also for political reasons. Eisenhower's choice to make this commitment paid dividends, as he was reelected to the presidency with 39 percent of the Black vote in 1956, which remains the highwater mark for the Republican Party.[21]

And as with Harry Truman, Eisenhower had to deal with the Cold War and the persistent threat of communist expansion. Throughout his tenure, the president sought out different methods to coalesce the American people against communism. One such method was religion. According to William Inbolden, the president viewed the Cold War as both a spiritual and a moral struggle. Before his election to office, Eisenhower told the columnist Drew Person: "The more intimately I become familiar with the desperate difficulties that abound in the world today[,] the more convinced I am that the solutions must be firmly base in spiritual and moral values."[22] Speaking in a language that linked Judeo-Christian beliefs with the foundation of the Republic, Eisenhower often differentiated the United States from the Soviet Union on religious grounds. This resonated with an American population that had turned toward religion after the stress of World War II, the Korean War, and the persistent possibility of nuclear annihilation. From his conversion to the Presbyterian Church to his decision to brand "In God We Trust" on the nation's currency, Eisenhower repeatedly found ways to remind the American people of the religious nature of their nation's heritage and its struggle against its enemies.[23]

Eisenhower used Judeo-Christian morality when speaking about his feelings about civil rights and reform. During the Little Rock Crisis, he called, as he often did, for "patience and tolerance, consideration":

I personally believe, as I have told you so many times, I personally believe this problem is never going to be solved without patience and tolerance, consideration. We just simply cannot solve it completely just by fiat or law and force. This is a deeper human problem than that.

The South has lived for 56 years under a social order that was approved by the Supreme Court, and specifically with respect to education, the theory of separate but equal facilities. Now they are asked suddenly to consider that whole system unconstitutional and, naturally, this causes difficulties.

Now, with respect to the Little Rock situation, it seems to improve daily. *I most devoutly hope and pray* that we soon can be confident enough of the situation that we can remove all Federal force, and I hope that all future steps in this will be accomplished in a spirit of real conciliation, and it does remain with us as a very *urgent problem.* [Emphasis added]

Prayer was to be the way forward as opposed to further federal action on a matter that had tried the patience of the African American community in perpetuity while frustrating American foreign policy leaders who had to fend off communist propaganda slander based on America's abysmal civil rights record.[24]

To his credit, albeit with far less frequency than his use of religion, Eisenhower tried to use civil rights reform as a congealing force for America against the menacing infiltration of the world by communist actors. In his first State of the Union address, Eisenhower declared: "Civil and social rights form a central part of the heritage we are striving to defend on all fronts and with all our strength." When he was reluctantly compelled to racially integrate Little Rock Central High School, Eisenhower was quick to point out to the American people:

At a time when we face grave situations abroad because of the hatred that Communism bears toward a system of government based on human rights, it would be difficult to exaggerate the harm that is being done to the prestige and influence, and indeed to the safety, of our nation and the world.

Our enemies are gloating over this incident and using it everywhere to misrepresent our whole nation. We are portrayed as a violator of those standards of conduct which the peoples of the world united to proclaim in the Charter of the United Nations. There they affirmed "faith in fundamental human rights" and "in the dignity and worth of the human person" and they did so "without distinction as to race, sex, language or religion."

To an extent, he believed that domestic reform played a role in strengthening the nation's image abroad in its clash with its Marxian rival, but he did not consistently apply the rationale in the same manner as his predecessor.[25]

THE MIDDLE WAY AND REFORM

Eisenhower's approach to achieve change in the civil rights area frustrated many who wanted him to follow Truman's lead and risk condemnation to act. To do so, however, would have gone too far out of ideological step with Eisenhower's political beliefs. Eisenhower was no political charlatan or a "chameleon in plaid" in the Roosevelt vein; he had limits. Eisenhower truly believed that the correct path was one that traveled right "down the middle of the road between the unfettered power of concentrated wealth . . . and the unbridled power of statism or partisan interests." He felt that his path of moderation would prevent internal conflicts between segments of American society, and that was why he had campaigned in 1952 on his belief in the "Middle Way."[26]

Though he sought to mollify the political left and right, he exasperated both. Certainly, the prospect of Eisenhower enthralled conservatives who desperately sought to end what they believed to be the tyrannous reign of FDR's politics, in which he and Congress empowered the federal government to get involved in all manners of American life. But his actions or inactions frustrated those same conservatives, as he did not completely torpedo the remaining aspects of the New Deal like they hoped he would. He likewise flummoxed those on his political left who had voted for him, when Eisenhower expressed his concern over creating a "paternalistic government" that if left unchecked would "gradually destroy, by suffocation in the immediate advantage of subsidy, the will of a people to maintain a high degree of individual responsibility." And in that regard, Eisenhower viewed Truman's Fair Deal program as nothing more than an attempt to mollify segments of the population, whether it be African Americans or labor, at the expense of others. This was not the way to harmony; it was the path to division and conflict, the old general believed.[27]

When it came to civil rights, Eisenhower followed his own path, one built on moderation. Better for the nation to mature and reform on its own on the issue, the president would always advocate, than for Eisenhower to dictate reform to the masses. That was why, during his first State of the Union address, he asked the American people to rededicate themselves to "these values and virtues" and embrace the challenge of civil rights reform as opposed to the government solving the problem for them. But he also assured the American people that he would act where he believed he could: "I propose to use whatever authority exists in the office of the President to end segregation in the District of Columbia, including the Federal Government, and any segregation in the Armed Forces."[28]

A CRUSADER FOR COMMUNISM

Eisenhower's commitment to end racial segregation in Washington, DC, and finish the racial integration of the armed forces caught the attention of those in the civil rights community, but it also attracted the condemnation of those aligned on the radical right of American politics. This meant that there was a real political cost for Eisenhower's actions, one that would not go away and that would eventually encompass other members of his administration. But, as with Truman, the first victim was the president. The attacks against Eisenhower bore the same traits of those that assailed Harry Truman or, more recently, Anna Rosenberg; they were baseless, racist, wholly conspiratorial, and anti-Semitic. According to the author of a letter originating from Philadelphia, and that was widely distributed throughout Manchester County, General Eisenhower was a part of larger conspiracy against America:

General Eisenhower is the "Kike's Ike" And the "JEWS FRONT." He was hand picked and sponsored by the American Jewish Congress, And The Zionist International Jewish World Organization. He is also a "Racial Swine-ologist." During the War under his Military Command and Orders White Girls were used exclusively in Europe and Africa in all the U.S.O.'s and Cafés under M.P. Guards to Dance with and entertain and Date Negroes. That's the "Kike's Ike" Version of Romeo & Juliet.

The author, going by the moniker "A Factician," claimed that "all the Negro Organizations and all the JEW Organizations and all The Communist Organizations are openly supporting Eisenhower" and that his actions that posed a grave threat to the Republic. In another propaganda piece, this time by Eustace Mullins, a known white supremacist, anti-Semite, and conspiracy theorist, titled "IMPEACH EISENHOWER!," provided a laundry list of rationales, all of which were false, to justify the immediate removal of the president.[29] Perhaps the most heinous of Mullins's accusations alleged that "Eisenhower must also be held responsible for the Negro troops in his command who herded three thousand white girls into a tunnel near Dresden and systematically raped them while their Jewish officers cheered them and reportedly took mobbing pictures of the scene which were shown before Jewish fraternal organizations in New York City." The age-old fear of racial mixing had apparently not left; neither had fears of communist subversion, as the author claimed that Eisenhower's actions on the behalf of Stalin should not be known as a "Crusade in Europe" but instead a "Crusade for Communism."[30]

RACIAL INTEGRATION OF ON-BASE SCHOOLS, PART 2

As Eisenhower became a target for ultraconservative and conspiratorial media outlets, the issue of on-base education returned. During a presidential news conference, Alice A. Dunnigan, a member of the Associated Negro Press, noted that several Army installations, including some in Texas, Oklahoma, and Virginia, had failed to integrate on-base schools. How, she posed to the president, could Eisenhower reconcile this with his desire to end racial segregation in the armed forces? The president admitted that he was unaware of the situation. In the immediate, Eisenhower dispatched Jim Hagerty, his press secretary, to check on the issue. But Eisenhower did not leave it at that:

I will say this—I repeat it, I have said it again and again: wherever Federal funds are expended for anything, I do not see how any American can justify—legally, or logically, or morally—a discrimination in the expenditure of those funds as among our citizens. All are taxed to provide those funds. If there is any benefit to be derived from them, I think they must all share, regardless of such inconsequential factors as race and religion.

When Eisenhower made his comments, he did so without any knowledge on the situation, and he was also unaware that the new assistant secretary of defense for manpower and personnel, John A. Hannah, had taken a gradualist approach to the carryover issue from the Truman administration since coming into office. Furthermore, the president was oblivious of the number of schools involved, let alone the number of children in attendance. As Morris J. MacGregor Jr. has observed, Eisenhower probably thought that the schools in question resided only on military bases. Some did, but others did not. Had Eisenhower's comments to Dunnigan stood, he would have had to integrate all schools that received federal funds. His gradualism prevented him from taking such a bold step.[31]

Ultimately, the president delegated the matter to Secretary of Defense Charles E. Wilson, who quickly corrected Ike's gaff by ignoring those schools receiving funds that were not on federal lands. Instead, Wilson focused on racially integrating schools that resided on federal property. Under his leadership, the Department of Defense integrated ten out of eleven schools on military installations. The lone outcast, a school at Fort Benning, Georgia, proved recalcitrant, but after the secretary of the Army applied further pressure, it integrated.[32]

For the most part, the eleven on-base schools integrated quickly because federal personnel staffed them. But schools of this type, staffed by federal personnel, represented only a small amount of those utilized to educate the schoolchildren of military personnel. In the armed forces there were sixty-three on-base schools. Of the sixty-three, twenty-one, the majority in the Jim Crow South, remained racially segregated. Those schools not staffed by federal employees relied upon the use of local citizens who had received state teaching licenses. It was highly unlikely that Southern states, prior to the mandate placed upon them by way of the *Brown* decision, would budge on the issue. Further complicating the matter was the way that racial segregation in Southern states was enforced. Since the era of Southern Redemption, Southern states used different methods to maintain the social and economic subjugation of African Americans. For example, the racial segregation practiced at the federal arsenal in Pine Bluff, Arkansas, relied on a state statute, while institutions on Army and Air Force bases in Texas justified segregation through provisions in the state's constitution.[33]

With no overarching solution available, the administration debated over what course to follow. This debate led to a firestorm of controversy involving one woman, the secretary of the Department of Health, Education, and Welfare (HEW), Oveta Culp Hobby. During World War II, Hobby commanded the Women's Army Corps (WACS). In that position, she commanded white and Black WACS, and though they did the same work, they remained strictly racially segregated. This led to a notable African American civil rights leader, Mary McLeod Bethune, to fight on the behalf of Black WACS to achieve better treatment. Her efforts achieved some change, as white and Black WACS attending Officer Candidate School in Iowa at Fort Des Moines did so in an racially integrated fashion. Some whites, however, objected to this development. The general manager of a Shreveport, Louisiana, radio station, John C. McCormack, reached out to the city's upper crust and complained:

Miss. Tucker's sister enlisted in the WAAC [WACS] about six weeks ago. After completing her basic training, she applied for administrative school and was transferred over last weekend to the Chamberlain Hotel in Des Moines. A couple of days after moving into this hotel, she wrote Miss Tucker a letter commenting very strongly on the situation between the negroes and whites in the WAAC. She said both negroes and whites were station in the Chamberlain Hotel, although they were on separate floors. They use the same dining room even though they have a section for the negroes and section for the whites. She said she had seen them working side by side serving food, and it was her understanding that they did KP [kitchen police] duty together. . . . I feel a little bit guilty in that we have . . . influenced so many girls to join this thing who no doubt find themselves in an unhappy situation after they arrive due to misrepresentation.

In her response to McCormack's concerns, Hobby draped herself in the cloak of Jim Crow segregation and sympathized with him: "The number of Negroes who receive officer candidate training is so small that they cannot be formed into company units, and are consequently placed in regular officer candidate companies. . . . I am satisfied that such occurrences as you mention are infrequent, and when they do happen are temporary and practically unavoidable." Instead of defending her Black personnel, Hobby lamented that she had no choice but to temporarily integrate them with whites while they trained.[34]

Several years later, as the first secretary of HEW (let alone the first woman to occupy the office), Hobby maintained her acceptance of racial segregation. During consultation with the Department of Defense over the remaining segregated on-base schools, Hobby suggested a gradualist approach. She wanted to wait and see what the Supreme Court, even though its deliberations over the *Brown* case were moving at a snail's pace, was going to decide on the issue. Hobby also advised caution on the matter, as "invoking full Federal operation of the schools might easily lead to serious adverse action on the part of the Congress as it considers the two pending bills for extending aid to schools in federally affected areas."[35]

Not willing to sit idly by as Hobby stonewalled racial progress, Adam Clayton Powell Jr. entered the political scrum by charging that Hobby "has virtually countermanded your order [Eisenhower's] abolishing segregated schools on Army posts." Meanwhile, Hobby found herself engulfed in a full-blown circus over another related matter. Civil rights groups pounced on the beleaguered HEW secretary's actions toward her assistant Jane Spaulding, the first Black woman to serve in HEW. During Hobby's feud with Powell, the HEW chief allegedly attempted to force Spaulding to sign a letter, which she did not pen, refuting any racial bias by the HEW chief. Spaulding, though, did not give in to Hobby's pressure.[36]

As time went on, Spaulding and Hobby clashed again. At the center of their final struggle was the issue of federal funding for a Houston hospital that practiced racial segregation. Hobby, a native Texan, supported the project, but Spaulding, who was becoming seen more and more as a "problem child" because of her continued championing of civil rights, did not and sided with civil rights groups that sought racial integration of the facility. Shortly thereafter, Hobby moved to remove Spaulding from HEW. Shortly after her termination, Spaulding managed to fire a parting shot at Hobby over the issue of racially integrating on-base schools, stating "there never has been any difference of opinion between the President, Secretary Wilson and myself" on the matter. Her omission of Hobby was deliberate.[37]

"BUT MAX, BABY . . ."

Spaulding's dismissal and her parting comments forced Charles Wilson to do a little political cleanup. He did so by claiming that there had been no conflict between the two departments on the matter. But the question remained: What was to be done about the schools? And while Eisenhower would have rather had his staff hammer out a solution, behind closed doors their struggles to do so were becoming public knowledge. Something had to be done. The president decided that the member of his staff best suited to handle the situation was Maxwell Rabb, his Jewish cabinet secretary and czar on minority affairs.[38]

To fringe elements in society, Rabb was no better than the allegedly pro-Jewish and communist leadership of the NAACP, whose roster of supposed communist members included men who played a role in the racial desegregation of the military, including Congressman Powell, W. E. B. Du Bois, Roy Wilkins, and Thurgood Marshall. Later, the Supreme Court appeared to be another tool of the "Invisible Government" after rendering the *Brown* and other pro–civil rights decisions. The *American Nationalist* declared that "not even David Niles, the Rasputin of the New Deal, enjoyed such an advantage" as Rabb did. But Rabb was not blind to the criticism being hurled at him from those on the radical right. On a Wednesday in June 1954, Rabb received a memo from his friend and fellow Eisenhower administration official James Lambie. Attached to it was the latest copy of *Human Events*, an anti-Semitic conspiratorial paper that lashed out against those elements—whether Jewish, communist, or liberal—that it perceived manipulated the American government and people. Although this was not the first time he had appeared in a publication of this kind, Lambie teased Rabb for his inclusion, but he also warned him: "But Max, baby, this sheet actually sells. People read it. Presumably people even believe it. They pay 10.00 a year for it."[39]

How many read *Human Events* or the various works of other conspiratorial tracts like it remains largely unknown, but some did, and as Lambie cautiously reminded Rabb, they believed it. In a sense, the racial diatribes of these authors provided a scapegoat for a segment of the white population that feared and loathed the social changes unfolding in America from 1948 to 1968. It meshed well with the American obsession of charting the growth of global communism during the Cold War—Russia gets the atomic bomb, China goes red, the Berlin Crisis, Sputnik, and eventually the conflicts in Korea and Vietnam—while also providing ample insecurity during the domestic Red Scare highlighted best by the witch hunts of the House Un-American Activities Committee and the terror unleashed repeatedly by the unsupported accusations of Republican senator Joseph McCarthy of Wisconsin.

Despite the undercurrent of right-wing resistance to his reform efforts in the military, Eisenhower dispatched the much-maligned Rabb to handle the situation involving on-base schools. Rabb's efforts netted results, as Secretary of Defense Wilson announced in January 1954 that the twenty-one segregated schools and any new schools under construction on military bases must be integrated by September 1955. Rabb's prodding notwithstanding, Wilson knew that racially integrating the rest of the schools would likely be rough going and that, if necessary, he might have to provide educational alternatives for military dependents in case some schools refused to change. Once the deadline arrived, though, nineteen of the twenty-one schools had racially integrated. The remaining two, one in Florida and one in Texas, lost their funding and closed because of their failure to comply. In the meantime, Southern segregationists in Congress assailed the administration's action. "We'll not take it lying down; we'll fight it," Democratic congressmen Arthur Winstead of Mississippi, a member of the powerful House Armed Services Committee, declared. The

Mississippian remained true to his word, as he later tried to introduce a public law to halt the funding of schools that operated in a racially integrated basis; the bill, however, never garnered enough support to come to fruition. While Winstead politically flailed away, others, such as Georgia representative E. L. Forrester, offered milder words of resistance, calling the racial integration of on-base schools a "mistake."[40]

SETTING THE EXAMPLE BEFORE BROWN

In 1955, journalist Lee Nichols wrote a series of articles for the United Press that covered the racial integration of on-base military schools in the South. From these articles a few themes emerged that carried on throughout the history of the racial integration of the armed forces. The first was the continued belief that the military could serve as a successful sociological laboratory where the experiment of racial integration could be conducted. He observed that "some southern educators and observers are watching the military experiment closely as a pilot operation that may help point the way to eventual compliance with the US Supreme Court's anti-segregation edict." Furthermore, Nichols believed that racial integration was working. To illustrate this point, he introduced his readers to a young African American boy in one of the on-base racially integrated schools. According to his account, the boy had been struggling to make a mask for Halloween. His crafting woes did not go unnoticed, and his teacher asked for volunteers to help the boy with his project. Soon, a constellation of mask-makers, including white children, eagerly volunteered their services. Nichols also noted the outcome of a racial incident between a Black student and white student. The white student called his Black classmate a "nigger." According to the parents of the Black child, once the white student's classmates heard about what he had said, they "shunned" and ostracized him for his behavior.[41]

Even though racial acceptance began to take place on base, racial exclusion off base remained the social norm. Out of a desire to maintain the anonymity of a town that resided near a military installation that had integrated its on-base schools, Nichols dubbed it "Blanktown." While in Blanktown, the reporter attended a local White Citizens' Council meeting. Originating in Indianola, Mississippi, as a direct result of the *Brown* verdict, White Citizen's Councils sprung up all over the South and were often led by respected local officials who chaired meetings that focused on how to preserve the Southern racial status quo through the prevention of racial integration of the region, including its all-white school system. The historian Neil R. McMillen believed that the White Citizens' Council, though powerful and intimidating, was not another version of the Klan:

Disdaining exotic rituals, secret oaths, and paraphernalia of disguise, just as it eschewed the rope, fagot, and whip, it forswore lawlessness and pledged itself to strictly legal means of defiance. Whatever may have been the theoretical relationship between the explosive atmosphere it often created and the actual outbreak of violence, there is no tangible evidence which suggests that it engaged in, or even overtly encouraged, criminal acts. From time to time individual Council members were implicated in acts of vigilantism, including homicide and bombing, but the organization itself was never directly linked with these things.

Still, that might have made it even more dangerous than terroristic organizations such as the Ku Klux Klan. The Klan operated in secrecy, while the White Citizens' Council acted more openly and legitimately as they espoused resistance to the *Brown* ruling and racial integration in general.[42]

To be sure, council members believed that the amalgamation of the races was a threat to their very way of life. During the meeting at Blanktown, one of the speakers declared: "Integration of the races in our schools will lead to inter-marriage and mongrelization of the white race." To prevent this heinous future from taking place, a Council member, alluding to the liberal agenda of some Northerners, suggested an educational remedy: "We must educate our children not to be taken in by the propaganda of the Northern politicians and the Northern Press." Additionally, the group cautioned that it would be wise if the town limited the African American vote.[43]

While the Council's stance was clear, at no point did it broach the topic of the racial integration of the base's schools. Afterward, the chairman of the Council, who also happened to be the town's judge, admitted to Nichols that the relationship between the base and the town "means a lot to us economically." Curious about the omission of what typically would be a nonstarter item for the White Citizens' Council in the public realm, Nichols later questioned the principal of the on-base school and why he felt that the Council could turn a blind eye to the matter. The principal replied succinctly: "Money talks." A lesson can be gleaned from Nichols's reporting on Blanktown—one that would be learned by the government and by those seeking to address America's civil rights discrepancies and as such would be repeated in the future: the potential of using the economic power of the federal government and military to coerce locals into changing social behaviors or at the very least forcing them to accept a racially integrated military within the confines of their region.[44]

INTEGRATING ON-BASE COLLEGE CLASSES

The integration of military schools was not limited to just K-12 children; it also applied to college students. In the spring of 1956, New York Democratic senator Herbert H. Lehman received a letter from an African American airman stationed at Donaldson Air Force Base in South Carolina. Airmen from his post, he informed the New Yorker, could enroll in on-base college courses offered by the University of South Carolina. The problem was that these courses remained restricted to white personnel only under university policy. The African American soldier, perhaps knowledgeable about the on-base school fight, wondered if these courses relied on federal funding. If it turned out that the government was supporting these classes, it meant that they were financially funding racial segregation within a racially integrated military reserve. With his interest peeked, Lehman wrote to the secretary of defense and questioned him about it.[45]

Shortly after the senator became involved in the issue, the Army suddenly became interested and decide to launch their own probe into the matter. The timing of the Army's investigation is quite peculiar and lends credence to the theory that it did so only because of the senator. Whether it was Lehman or not, the Army and Pentagon proved reluctant to give the senator any information about what they had found. During the Army's initial inquiry, the branch identified two bases that indeed practiced racial segregation in college classes: Fort Benning, Georgia, and Fort Jackson, South Carolina—later a third installation, Fort Gordon, also in Georgia, was identified. According to the Adjutant General (AG) J. P. Sullivan of the Army, it was customary for military installations to host higher-education classes for soldiers during off-duty hours, as it afforded them the opportunity to better themselves. Still, if these classes were to continue, the AG felt they "would . . . have to be open to all military personnel." Although the solution was clear, the AG recognized that the Army could not tell a public university in the American South what to do. Nonetheless, he advised base commanders to bring the courses in line with the Army's racial integration policy. After base commanders informed the universities involved of the Army's stance, the universities ended their contracts with the Army. And by July 1956, the head of the Troop Information and Education Division, Colonel Harold C. Lyon, reported that the problem had been eliminated.[46]

Throughout the entire episode, Lehman remained out of the loop. In another letter to the secretary of defense, the senator reminded Wilson that he still had not received a definitive answer on the matter. According to his sources, the senator discovered that the Department of Defense had paid for

75 percent of the cost of educating soldiers in college classes. The New Yorker believed that the DOD was therefore funding racial segregation. "I cannot conceive of a more shocking affront to the law and conscience of our land than for the Department of Defense to continue a policy under which Federal funds are used to enable educational institutions to enforce local," he declared, "indeed unconstitutional, discriminations against United States personnel in military installations."[47] Along the same lines, Lehman was puzzled as to why the military, which prided itself on its ability to repel communism, would deny African Americans the right to better themselves educationally while serving. To make his point, he cited an Air Force policy letter, which had provided a Cold War rationale for the continued education and training of its airmen:

This letter notes that "Advanced military techniques and modern equipment require formal knowledge never before considered essential." It emphasizes that today's American military personnel, "surrounded by conflicting ideologies and propaganda, *must have sufficient education* to provide them with insight, vision and self-confidence to defend the principles of American democracy in times of stress."

The nature of warfare had changed, the senator contended. In the world of the 1950s, soldiers needed not only great physical strength but also the necessary wits to ward off communist rhetoric and subversion. It made no sense whatsoever, he believed, to deny Black soldiers this right. To do so was tantamount to sabotaging the national defense.[48]

With little hope that the department was going to act on its own, Lehman released his letter to the press. With its feet now to the fire, the Department of Defense quickly responded to Lehman's requests for information. Assistant Secretary of Defense for Manpower and Personnel Carter L. Burgess informed the senator that the department had already discussed and rectified the problem as far as the Army was concerned. He also provided Lehman with a report that had catalogued the Army's progress on the issue. Burgess believed that "this report shows that, in addition to the installation concerning which you made inquiry, agreement has been reached to permit no segregated classes, University extension or otherwise, on any military post or installation."[49] When it came to the issue of the Department of Defense funding racially segregated classes, Burgess passed the blame from the department onto Congress, which provided the funding for soldiers to attend on-base classes.[50]

On October 30, 1956, the matter ended for Lehman, as he released a statement that praised the Department of Defense and the Army for its decision to end its relationship with Southern universities that practiced racial segregation. The senator expressed hope that the Department of the Air Force would also adopt this same policy, as Burgess's letter made no mention of the Air Force's on-base classes. It was possible that Burgess expected all the branches of the armed forces to comply with the stance taken by the Army.[51]

Unfortunately, that does not seem to have been the case; three years later, the problem of segregated college classes returned. Roy Wilkins, who was then the executive secretary of the NAACP, received a letter from a resident in Mississippi that alleged that the University of Mississippi and Mississippi Southern College taught segregated courses to personnel at Kessler Air Force Base in Biloxi, Mississippi. Unlike the earlier incidents, the universities conducted the college courses off base and did so likely out of a deliberate effort to prevent African American personnel from attending, and potentially complaining about, the situation. The Mississippian also informed Wilkins that any Black airmen who protested the situation would reportedly be "shipped out." The controversy would continue into the 1960s, when Congressman Charles Diggs continued the fight to racially integrate the educational programs tied to Kessler.[52]

KEEPING THE NAVY ON COURSE

During the Eisenhower administration's first few months, it confronted a handful of racial issues in the Navy. The first was a self-inflicted wound that needed healing. In 1952, under the auspices of a naval directive, OIR Notice CP75, the handiwork of Chief of the Office of Industrial Relations Rear Admiral W. McL. Hague, the Navy, always cautious on environmental or social issues, bowed to the preexisting racism of communities surrounding its installations by deciding to racially segregate civilian employees who worked on base. The scope of the order was immense, as it affected several Southern naval installations, including several larger ones, such as those at Norfolk, Virginia, and Charleston, South Carolina, to operate in a racially segregated manner. After learning of the order, James C. Evans, spokesman for the Department of Defense, drafted a memo to Anna Rosenberg that the Navy's actions were tantamount to a return to racial segregation. Nearing the end of the Truman administration, however, the issue had not been redressed.[53]

After Eisenhower's arrival in the White House, the situation resurfaced, as the civil rights community objected to what they perceived to be an outright rejection of Executive Order 9981 and Eisenhower's promise to finish the racial integration of the military. Clarence Mitchell of the NAACP had reached out to Secretary of the Navy Robert Anderson seeking clarification on the issue. In response, Anderson informed the NAACP representative that the Navy would

continue to follow the order, as it would not risk upsetting the local population by driving the issue of integration any further than society would allow.
Dutifully, Mitchell reported Anderson's gradualist response to the head of the
NAACP, Walter White. After learning of Anderson's comments, White went
on the offensive. Taking a page out of Adam Clayton Powell Jr.'s playbook on
how to handle Eisenhower, the head of the NAACP charged that Secretary
Anderson was blocking the president's desire to complete the racial integration
of the military, which the venerated civil rights organization believed included
civilian personnel who worked on military installations. Interjecting himself
into the proceedings, Congressmen Powell further goaded the president into
action by calling into question the blatant "insubordination" of his lieutenants.
The congressman seemed to reason that, if his assault on the lack of discipline
with the administration did not jolt the old general into action, perhaps the
Cold War would. Powell reminded the president that "the free world is looking
to you as its last hope."[54]

A perturbed Eisenhower responded to his critics by asserting that he was
looking into the matter and that his administration had "not taken and we shall
not take a single backward step," as the president believed that "there must be
no second-class citizens in this country." To forestall any further embarrassment, Eisenhower once again dispatched Maxwell Rabb to intercede on a civil
rights issue that his staff had either failed to rectify or, as in this case, had made
worse. Rabb quickly applied pressure on Anderson—as did Dennis D. Nelson,
who worked in the Pentagon and warned Anderson of the embarrassment his
acceptance of the order would have on the president—with the result being
that the secretary quickly performed an about-face on the issue and rescinded
the order.[55]

Another leftover of civil rights dilemma in the Navy from the Truman years
was the continuing racial disparity of the Steward Branch. In 1952, Black stewards still made up the majority (65 percent) of that branch. The man placed
in charge of dealing with this problem was Anderson, the civilian head of the
Navy. The besieged naval chief squared off against a man familiar with the
racist history of the Navy, Lester Granger, the longtime head of the National
Urban League. In 1945, James Forrestal, then secretary of the Navy, had commissioned Granger to research race relations within the branch. Since that initial investigation, the Navy had made improvements, but the National Urban
League chief remained concerned about the blatant racism still present in the
Navy. Other civil rights groups were also concerned. The American Civil Liberties Union felt that little had changed and that "pockets of discrimination
and segregation" still existed in the Navy.[56]

After hearing Granger's concerns and his remedy for the problem—the rapid procurement of white recruits to serve in the Steward Branch, which he believed could balance the racial composition—Anderson ordered the chief of personnel, Vice Admiral James L. Holloway, to remedy the situation. Holloway consulted with a panel of naval experts to come up with a solution. Many ideas arose, including merging the Steward Branch with the traditionally all-white Commissary Branch. The Navy decided instead to end the practice of recruiting separately for the Steward Branch. By doing so, it was widely believed that the overall population of African Americans in the Navy would go up, while the amount in the Steward Branch would go down. And, in fact, this change, along with the ability of stewards to transfer out of the branch, led to significant results. By 1958, the percentage of Blacks in the Steward Branch dropped from 65 percent to 23.4 percent. A similar plan surfaced to address the racial lopsidedness of the Marine Corps Steward Branch. It too netted impressive results, as by 1961 Black stewards made up only 20 percent of the Marine Corps Steward Branch. In the civil rights community, the integration of the Steward Branch in both the Navy and Marine Corps was a cause for both celebration and regret. While the number of Black stewards decreased, the number of Filipinos and Asians in the branch increased, leading to the consternation of civil rights advocates who observed that all the Navy had done was trade one race for another.[57]

RACISM AND AMERICAN MEDICINE

During the early twentieth century, social scientists with little connection to Charles Darwin loosely applied his theories to the realm of social sciences; the result of their controversial endeavor was the creation of social Darwinism, which reinforced the preexisting racist white belief of the racial supremacy of the Anglo-Saxon race over all others, including the African and African American races. Embracing this questionable theory, social Darwinists such as Frederick L. Hoffman contended that the lower-ranked African American race was destined for extinction. Indeed, according to others who followed this line of thought, the only reason that Blacks even continued to exist was because of the beneficial and paternalistic nature of slavery. According to social Darwinists of the time, slavery had provided African Americans with an "unfair advantage," as their food, clothing, and shelter were provided to them by white slave owners. With the sanctuary of slavery removed and with African Americans relocating to cities that were highly unsanitary, it was only a matter of time until the race would fall into ruin, social Darwinists believed. These quasi-theories did not remain isolated to the realm of the social Darwinists; some American medical professionals subscribed to them as well and even suggested that it was in the best interest of white America to expedite the end of the African American race.[58]

Not all members of the American medical community, however, subscribed to this racist ideology. Henry Butler, an African American physician and a founding member of the National Medical Association, along with a few others, argued that the issue was not one of racial inferiority but was the natural outcome of an unequal society that denied Blacks the opportunity to develop mentally and socially. Butler and his colleagues, though, had a hard time convincing their profession otherwise. Working against his effort to set the record straight was the continuing spread of racist medical studies that argued the contrary. One of the most important American medical journals of any era, the *Journal of the American Medical Association*, had published articles that displayed questionable science, if not blatant racism. According to one article from 1910, Black men were walking, talking, tragic figures who were easily corrupted by political intoxicants, or real ones such as alcohol, who lusted for sex, and who carried in their bodies the diseases of their sexual handiwork and spread them among those they fornicated with; in a word, they were deemed to be wretched and lost:

Whatever the motive that guided the pen which decreed absolute suffering, it stands as one of the world's greatest tragedies, for now the Negro was free, not to live but to die, and he took advantage of his freedom. He was free indeed—free as the birds of the air—free to get drunk with cheap political whiskey and to shiver in the cold because his scanty savings went to purchase flashy and flimsy garments, free never to bathe, and sleep in hovels where God's sunlight and air could not penetrate—absolutely free to gratify his every sexual impulse; to be infected with every loathsome disease and to infect his ready and willing companions, and he did it—he did it all. The result is the Negro of 1909, the Negro of today.

The works of social Darwinists and the racist articles that appeared in the nation's preeminent medical journals worked in tandem to encourage white doctors to shy away from treating Black patients and toward embracing the pseudo-scientific racism of the era.[59]

White doctors' refusal to treat African Americans had disastrous results for the race. Around 1900, it was estimated that the average white lived to be about fifty years in age, while the average African American made it only to their early thirties. In part this activity helped encourage an already growing Black medical community, which worked to establish its own hospital system. While Black doctors struggled to build their own medical profession, some whites decided to change course and treat African American patients. They did not do so out of fear of competition but out of a fear of germ-based disease—thus, out of a desire to protect the white community from the supposed pitfalls of the Black one. Equally important, some white doctors felt compelled to treat African Americans because of their own elite status in society; throughout American history, the wealthier classes, in a paternalistic fashion, believed it was their responsibility to care for the poorer classes. Though whites started to treat Blacks, they did so only in a segregated manner; African American patients still did not receive the same quality of health care as whites.[60]

There were notable exceptions to the rule, however. Consider the story of Dr. Charles R. Drew, a brilliant African American physician and researcher and the man most responsible the creation of the blood bank, which transformed in perpetuity the way blood was harvested and stored for medical use and was especially critical during World War II. Brilliant though he was, greedy he was not. Drew did not appear to crave the monetary rewards of his exceptional talents and instead preferred the life of the physician dedicated to the Hippocratic oath to care for patients while also making sure to train successors. For Drew, it meant training the next generation of Black doctors.[61]

Much like his life, his untimely death sent reverberations. On a trip to Tuskegee, Drew fell asleep at the wheel of the car he was driving and wrecked. Those who were with him, including several doctors, quickly assessed his situation as grim. They received aid from some of the white motorists who passed by and got word to an ambulance; soon the badly injured Drew and his party were on their way to Alamance General Hospital. Charles R. Drew, whose efforts saved the lives of countless others, died succumbing to the totality of his fatal wounds. But Drew—really his death—lived on in an unfounded form of conspiratorial mythmaking that emerged over how he was supposedly *really* treated. The historian Spencie Love discredited the falsehoods of the mythmaking surrounding Drew's treatment and subsequent death. She demonstrated that the African American physician had, in fact, been treated fairly by white physicians—some of whom recognized who he was—as they labored to save his life. The reason the myth persisted was because, for African Americans, it fit with the realities that they had faced as a people. While Charles Drew did not face this reality in his dying moments, others, likely many of their race, had. And so the untruths and lies surrounding Drew's death fit and provided an answer that the African American community, one that had suffered countless racial indignities and had grown in many ways untrusting of white society because of them, could accept.[62]

THE CRUSADE FOR RACIAL EQUALITY IN VETERANS MEDICAL CARE

There was little mythmaking about the terrible treatment of Black veterans after their military service had ended. For that matter, the health care of all-American veterans was putrid at worst, ad hoc and inconsistent at best. In the years following World War I, however, that changed when President Woodrow Wilson sought to rectify the situation. His efforts led to the establishment of the Veterans Bureau. Under the leadership of Secretary of the Treasury Andrew Mellon, a governmental committee was formed—the White Committee, named after its chair, Dr. William Charles White—to grapple with the difficult problems that came with designing a hospital system charged with the task of meeting the needs of the nation's veterans. This uniquely veteran-focused medical care system by the 1930s became the Veterans Administration (VA).[63]

While a Progressive Era initiative, the VA operated for a time as a racist one as well. Gauging the social, cultural, and racial sentiment of the era, Mellon and his panel opted against the racial integration of the VA and instead created a solitary African American hospital dedicated to the treatment of the nation's Black veteran community. Located in Tuskegee, Alabama—the home of the Tuskegee Institute and future home of the Tuskegee Airmen and, more regretfully, the Tuskegee Syphilis Study—African American veterans now had a place where they could receive treatment. By placing the hospital in Alabama, the VA disregarded the concerns of the NAACP and those of African American veterans at the time who did not want the medical facility located in the racially segregated South. The concern was that Black veterans were likely not to receive as good of treatment in the segregated South, where Jim Crow ruled, whether it was a federal facility or not.[64]

It turned out, however, that the Tuskegee hospital was not the lone VA hospital to care for Black veterans. Most of the VA hospital system, which comprised 127 hospitals, practiced racial integration. Only a handful, twenty-four, with nineteen in the South, did not and racially segregated its patients. It seemed that the economic impracticality of running a racially segregated hospital, along with mounting pressure from civil rights groups and members of the African American medical community, contributed to the decision of the majority of the hospitals to operate in an integrated fashion. As for the twenty-four racially segregated hospitals, the "local customs" of the towns where the facilities resided prevented racial reforms from taking hold. But what that meant differed from town to town. In some cases, the social norms of a locality meant that African Americans seeking treatment would be racially segregated, while in more extreme situations it meant the prohibition of Black veterans receiving any aide at a facility.[65]

This inconsistent form of Jim Crow segregation in the VA continued unabated under the stewardship of General Carl J. Gray Jr., who led the institution during the Eisenhower years. That was until Congressmen Adam Clayton Powell Jr.—Powell had learned of the depths of racial despair within the VA from his wife, the talented pianist, singer, actress, and activist Hazel Scott—found out about it. To get to the bottom of what was going on in the VA, he initiated a dialogue with the VA's chief medical director, Admiral J. T. Boone. In his response to the congressmen from New York, Boone parroted the VA's long-standing acceptance of racial segregation based on the desires of the local community and "for the protection and safeguarding of patients." Boone's answer only aggravated Powell more, however. In a spirited letter to the Eisenhower administration, Powell dramatically informed the chief executive that "negro citizens are free to fight all over the world on an integrated basis for the cause of democracy," but when they returned home they were not rewarded for their efforts and instead faced segregation in the treatment of the wounds they had earned by serving their country. Worse yet, Powell observed, this situation jeopardized Eisenhower's racial reform agenda in the government and military.[66]

The VA was not, and has never been, a part of the Department of Defense or its armed forces and as such did not fall under the guidelines of Executive Order 9981. When Eisenhower acted on the VA issue, it appears that he did so with Executive Order 9980 in mind. The sibling order of Truman's racial integration edict, Executive Order 9980 was designed to eliminate racism in the staffing practices of the federal government. The Veterans Administration was part of the federal government and as such fit within the order's guidelines. With pressure mounting from civil rights advocates such as Powell, the Eisenhower administration conducted a survey in August 1953 that sought to understand the scope of racial segregation at the VA. According to the study's findings, the number of racially segregated VA hospitals had increased to forty-seven out of 166 hospitals. Unsurprisingly, the 1953 investigation noted that most of these hospitals resided in the South. After consuming the report,

Eisenhower once again called upon Maxwell Rabb to work his magic. Rabb then instructed Gray's replacement, Harvey Higley, to racially integrate the rest of the VA.[67]

In an abrupt about-face, Higley found that he could now suddenly count on the support of the once-reticent Boone. Whether Powell's political threats intimidated him, or feared alienating himself with the president, Boone informed Higley that "my responsibilities encompass the physical and mental care of the veterans of the Nation, irrespective of race, creed, or color." Hardly an impassioned response, but it was one in the affirmative. So Higley ran with it. On October 26, 1954, Higley informed the president that he had completed the racial integration of the VA hospital system. Eisenhower was grateful: "In making the success of your program possible," he told Higley, "our people have once again demonstrated their social maturity and their determination to have in America fair play and equal opportunity. In your accomplishment, Americans everywhere can take a great and justifiable pride."[68]

THE HOWLS OF RACIALLY INHOSPITABLE SOUTHERNERS

While a monumental victory for civil rights advocates and liberal reformers, the integration of the VA faced a stiff challenge from Southern segregationists in Congress. In an accusatory letter to Higley that was cosigned by fifty Southern congressmen, they howled that the racial integration of VA hospitals in the South was a "violation of state and local statutes." On the ground, grassroots political operators employed rhetoric that borrowed from the prevailing regional narrative that a liberal/communist conspiracy against the South that was tantamount to the renewal of Reconstruction was underway and the racial integration of the VA proved it. "Not since the end of the War Between the States has the South faced such a dark future. Integration was only the first phase of the Communists to take over our government," ominously warned C. A. Barnett, a Third Judicial District state judge and guest speaker at a Veterans of Foreign Wars (VFW) meeting in Jonesboro, Louisiana. Building on Barnett's comments, Louisiana VFW state commander Milton Frazier claimed that the racial reform in the VA was a part of a budding "communist-inspired political system of forced integration." So heinous was the federal government's actions that the VFW's 13th District and the 4th District of the American Legion denounced the effort underway in the VA hospital in Shreveport and throughout the rest of the state.[69]

One white veteran's story became proof in the minds of some Southerners of the evils of racial integration in the VA. C. D. Broughton of Homer, Louisiana, a World War II veteran and a patient at the Shreveport VA, took umbrage with the facility's embrace of Eisenhower's mandate to racially integrate. In seemed that Broughton found it deplorable and despicable that he had to share a room with a recently injured African American veteran. He then complained about this situation to the nurse on duty; the nurse then apprised him that he had to accept the facility's policy to receive treatment. After he refused to accept the policies of the VA, the Shreveport facility (which had not considered him to be in any medical danger) discharged the disgruntled white veteran. In response to this social atrocity against the white veteran, the Homer post of the American Legion went on the offensive. In a resolution against the facility, the membership of the Homer post declared "racial integration is un-Christian, undemocratic, and established in its origin as a Communistic plot designed to breakdown our morals and resistance, bring about a classless, raceless society, and result in the overthrow of the government of our country." Indeed, it went against the grand experiment of the South—racial segregation—which they believed had netted positive results for all: "Several hundred years of progressive race relations have definitely established that separate facilities for each race is the only social order that is in keeping with the laws and the cherished traditions of the South and in the best interest of both races."[70]

Louisianans were hardly alone in their disdain and dismay over the issue of racial integration of the VA. Neighboring Mississippi, no stranger to social unrest, also piped up with objections. A year after the rage in the VA over racial integration, Mississippi's racism once again was on display, this time garnering national attention. On August 28, 1955, in the small town of Money, Mississippi, Emmett Till, a fourteen-year-old African American boy, was savagely beaten and murdered for allegedly insulting the Southern societal honor of a white woman. Over fifty years later, the woman at the center of the controversy, Carolyn Bryant—who at the time claimed that Till had touched her hand, at one point cornered her in her family's store, and put his hands around her waist, all while having the temerity to aggressively flirt with her and even ask for a date—admitted to the historian Timothy B. Tyson that she had lied while under oath about the matter. Though a tragedy, Till's lynching galvanized a generation of civil rights reformers in the 1950s and 1960s.[71]

About two hours south of Money is the capital city, Jackson. Jackson was the home, as it still is today, to a Veterans Administration hospital. Almost a year after the Till lynching, the ugliness and racial bigotry of the era rose its head once again. A white female veteran of World War II who served as a member of the Women Accepted for Volunteer Emergency Service, R. G. Beckwith alleged that she was admitted into a ward with Black men. Especially galling for Beckwith was the idea that an African American veteran had a room right across the hall from her own. Angered, her husband, who was also a veteran, wrote to a couple of the state's defenders of white superiority, Democratic senator James O. Eastland and Democratic representative John Bell Williams, to investigate the matter.[72]

But other groups that supported the notion of white over Black also answered the call to arms over the alleged racial transgression. Ellis Wright, president of Jackson's White Citizens' Council, expressed publicly his revulsion to the situation, declaring that it was a "gross insult" to Beckwith and that fellow Council members should "make it their first order of business to demand that action be taken by our national, state and city officials" to address the continuing insult to Southern society that racial integration of the VA imposed. Privately, Wright reached out to another titan of racial segregation from Mississippi, Democratic senator John Stennis. While he sympathized with Wright's feeling on the matter, Stennis, who had complained to the VA's leadership about the Beckwith case, admitted that the only person with the power to change the situation was Eisenhower. It was, in Stennis's estimation, unlikely that anything would be done. There are political hills worth dying on, but for Stennis it appears this was not the political hill he wanted to die on. He informed Wright: "I do not think it advisable for me to issue a statement to the press on the matter at this time."[73]

While Stennis backpaddled from the controversy, Sidney Russell, state commander for the VFW organization in Mississippi, charged straight into the fracas by launching an investigation, which he led personally, into the situation at the Jackson VA. At the end of his inquiry, he surmised that "it looks like they're trying to do more for integration here than for treatment of the sick." Russell's comments proved so inflammatory that it forced the state quartermaster for the VFW in Mississippi, Alison M. James, to walk back Russell's erroneous statement. After recognizing the problems that Russell's comments could cause the VFW, James claimed to the press that Russell's remarks allegedly came from a white patient who had relayed the information to him and that the head of the state VFW shared it without fact-checking it.[74]

While racial conservatives, including Mississippi state senator Earl Evans Jr., who called for the state to care for those veterans who sought to be treated in a segregated fashion, railed against the VA, the head of the Jackson VA, A. W. Woolford, went on the defensive. On several occasions, including a talk before a Kiwanis Club meeting, the beleaguered manager apologetically outlined the situation at the VA hospital in Jackson, explaining that "the hospital is forced to carry out the policy of the federal government," and flatly rejected Beckwith's accusation by pointing out that "sex [i.e., gender] segregation" was practiced in the hospital and that her room was in fact not across the hall from that of a Black veteran but instead that of an "elderly white patient."[75]

Military bases, VA hospitals, and other federal facilities are often coveted by local, state, and national officials because of the revenue and employment opportunities they can provide to the communities where they reside. In early 1957, it was announced that a new VA hospital, which would replace the existing one in Jackson, had been approved by the House Appropriations Committee. By May that year, the State Sovereignty Commission of Mississippi, a body dedicated solely to maintaining and preserving racial segregation, approved the granting of state land to the VA to build the new hospital. Presiding over this commission, and the State Building Commission, which had already approved of the transfer of land, was the governor of Mississippi, J. P. Coleman, a Southern segregationist Democrat. But even racists must bow from time to time to economics. Recognizing there was a real-world cost in money and veterans care for Mississippians and other veterans who traveled in from neighboring Southern states, Coleman admitted that the hospital, though it rankled the white population, had to be racially integrated or the federal government would not foot the bill for it. As he put it succinctly: "We grabbed a tiger we can't handle."[76]

The angst felt by Mississippi politicians was best articulated by the only person to vote against donating the land, state senator Earl Evans Jr. "It would be ridiculous," the senator from Canton suggested, "to try and maintain segregation and then contribute land for an integrated hospital." But they were in a bind, because if they did not vote for it they would likely lose out on providing health care for the state's veteran population, not to mention the fallout they would face for the lost jobs that would result. Still, Evans voted the measure down; Coleman, who could not vote on the matter, wanted it known that he would have voted for it.[77]

Not all Mississippians, however, agreed with the logic of Coleman's leadership on the matter. The *Jackson Daily News* editor Jimmy Ward lambasted the commission for "swallowing the lure of Federal funds like a hungry bass at dawn," stating that it might as well rechristen itself the "State Surrender Commission." Coleman, perturbed and upset over the editorial because "some inkslinger called me an integrationist," decided it was high time that he responded in kind in his own editorial. Titled "An Answer to the Editorial Entitled 'Munich Day in Mississippi,'" Coleman went after his critic. "This editorial is so absurd in its concocted statement of facts and so fantastic in its contorted conclusions that possibly I should reply, purely for the benefit of the record," he began. He blamed his rival Evans for getting the commission involved in the first place, when the senator knew full well that the state could do little about the racial composition of the VA hospital. Coleman then proceeded to pose a series of questions to the offending editor and his paper. Does he desire to rob Mississippian veterans of their right to health care and treatment within the state as opposed to burdening them to travel? Does he want to shut down all federal offices, which were also racially integrated, such as the post office or the various military bases within the state? Would he and his paper have politically roasted the two committees for not approving the land and purloining Mississippian veterans of their right to treatment?[78]

At the conclusion of his rant, Coleman claimed that the *Jackson Daily News* and its ink-wielding editor jealous of the fact "that this administration has scored a 100 percent success in the maintenance of segregation in all areas where the state possessed any authority." He also alleged that he had it on good authority that the editor was in fact on vacation in Europe at the time of the publication of the piece, which led to the governor offering a bounty, which amounted to a charitable donation by the governor to all of the veterans organization in Mississippi, for "the name of the ghost writer who gave birth to this libel."[79]

White Citizens' Councils fanned the flames of controversy surrounding the building of a new racially integrated veterans' medical facility in the capital city. The Veterans Administration, in their opinion, wielded "naked power" in its desire to force integration on the good people of Mississippi, while also causing tremendous "humiliation" to the "physically helpless [white] war veterans which could greatly injure their health and [well] being in a way likely never to be undone." Thus, they called for Congress to act and respect the local "customs, traditions and laws of the states" where VA Hospitals resided. While they waited for Congress to act, they also wrote a letter to Eisenhower. In it, the executive secretary of the White Citizens' Council, Robert B. Patterson, blamed the death of two white veterans on the racial integration practiced by the VA:

One Mississippi veteran of World War I was placed between two negroes. In his sickness, he would awaken and look at the negro beside him and then break into tears. Another Mississippi veteran of World War I, who served as a Captain in France, had an aggravated heart condition. He was place in an integrated ward, also, between two negroes. He was bathed in the tub immediately following the bathing of a negro, and he told me that the humiliation made his heart skip several beats.

Both of these gentlemen, residents of Indianola, Mississippi, have now passed to their reward, and I believe that integration hastened their passing.

But there was a way out of this dilemma that Patterson alleged was leading to the untimely demise of white veterans. He suggested that Eisenhower issue an executive order that allowed veterans the right to choose whether they stayed in a racially integrated or segregated ward. To support his suggestion, Patterson—though he provided no evidence in support—claimed that Black veterans felt the same way that racist white veterans did about the situation: they wanted to be segregated when receiving treatment. Eisenhower never responded to the letter or the suggestion.[80]

While the White Citizens' Council led the revolt, others that opposed the VA's actions sought a pound of flesh as well. It was nothing more than "federal 'blackmail'" according to the VFW, which declared that it would rather have no hospital at all as opposed to having racial integration forced upon it. The state's white contingent of the American Legion engaged in a civil war of sorts over the issue. The commander for the state Legion, Jack Pace, had threatened Black posts and Black Legion members with being expunged from the ranks if they continued to support those within who were considered to be "racial agitators"—namely, those championing the VA's actions as well as the larger racial problems present in Mississippian society. Responding to his commander's statement was Albert Powell, an African American post commander, who countered: "So long as there is an American Legion we shall work to make our country a living democratic reality. It is the responsibility of Negro and white servicemen alike to help save America from Hitler-like movements from within." He openly asked Pace: "Is freedom of speech and freedom of assembly for white Americans only?" And he concluded on the importance of America winning the Cold War: "Shall we allow deep-seeded prejudices to make it impossible for our ambassadors to sell democracy abroad?"[81]

In the end, white racist angst over the issue was all for naught. It did not prevent the VA from placing a racially integrated hospital in Jackson to replace the outgoing racially integrated hospital that was already there.

CONCLUSION

Serving in the executive branch of the Eisenhower administration, E. Frederic Morrow was a racial anomaly, as he was the lone Black man. Morrow had come over from the Department of Commerce after the *Brown* decision to serve as Eisenhower's administrative officer for special projects, a position he would hold until 1961. Operating in that capacity, Morrow was privy to the civil rights actions the administration took publicly and behind the scenes. He understood better than most Eisenhower's rationales, limitations, and abilities on civil rights issues. His assessment of the president, which appears in *Black Man in the White House*, remains important, as it strips away the varnish of Eisenhower's accomplishments, which in Morrow's eyes were very little, to get at the heart of the man as a civil rights leader:

President Eisenhower's lukewarm stand on civil rights made me heartsick. I could trust this man never to do anything that would jeopardize the civil rights or the personal dignity of the American Negro, but it was obvious that he would never take any positive giant step to prove that he unequivocally stood for the right of every American to walk this land in dignity and peace, clothed with every privilege—as well as every responsibility—accorded a citizen of our Constitution.

His failure to clearly and forthrightly respond to the Negro's plea for a strong position on civil rights was the greatest cross I had to bear in my eight years in Washington.

Morrow's sorrow over Ike's inability to get out of his own way on the issue was not without rationale. He understood then something that many of the president's biographers would come to understand later: Eisenhower was "a man of his time." "Whatever his defects, they were not those of indifference or lack of dedication. They were the faults that may have come out of past or present environment, out of the generation in which he was born, or out of the tastes supported by his own lifetime of experience." Eisenhower, according to Morrow, was a failure in the realm of civil rights because he could not understand what it *meant* to be Black in America. He could not understand that the tremendous achievements earned—the racial desegregation of schools in the civilian and military realms, the racial desegregation of Washington, DC, and the end of Jim Crow in the Veterans Administration health care system—meant very little when African American citizens and veterans alike were still being treated in a substandard and racist fashion.[82]

But when reading over the papers of the Eisenhower years, especially on the issue of civil rights, it becomes apparent that the administration did not share Morrow's feelings about the president. The administration missed entirely Morrow's point about dignity. Instead, the Eisenhower administration recognized politically the importance of the president's accomplishments and sought to harvest them in a fashion that enabled them to sell this information to the African American community and progressive reformers alike.

In 1956, the administration did this deliberately to win the Black vote. Referring back to the 1952 campaign, and a document released at the time titled "The Republican Party and the Negro," the administration, and the Republican National Committee, highlighted Eisenhower's accomplishments, which included the completion of the racial integration of the armed forces. Byproducts included the victories for the children of service personnel seeking a racially integrated education on base, as well as the triumph for minority veterans seeking the racial integration of the VA, including hospitals situated in the segregated South. To be sure, these were important victories for Eisenhower, and African Americans of the era rewarded him with sizeable support.[83]

Such victories were also important, as far as the president was concerned, to the greater clash against communism. He noted in 1956 that "the stature of our leadership in the free world has increased through the past three years because we have made more progress than ever before in a similar period to assure our citizens equality in justice, in opportunity and in civil rights." And in 1961, during his final State of the Union address, Eisenhower thought that more must be done in America's continuing struggle against communism: "This pioneering work in civil rights must go on. Not only because discrimination is morally wrong, but also because its impact is more than national—it is world-wide."[84]

In a sense, Eisenhower—much like Truman before him—had a right to be proud of what he had achieved. For over a decade, the American armed forces, more than professional sports or the Supreme Court, had led the way in civil rights reform. By the end of the 1950s, Truman's and Eisenhower's approaches to reform—which revolved around the notion of equality of opportunity, Cold War necessity, and presidential action—had achieved great change in the military and the Veterans Administration. But the failure to eradicate, let alone try to contend with, continuing racism within the military and how that affected the dignity of African Americans were not something that Eisenhower or Truman ever truly dealt with. Their accomplishments were iconic, but at the same time superficial, as they failed to deal with the root of the problem: American racism. Instead, as with so many problems, it was left for another president to rectify.

CHAPTER 5

From Image to Action: Kennedy, Johnson, and Reform

"I'm just saying that it's [the presidency] the center of power. . . . I'm not talking about personal [power]—I'm just saying it's the center of action," mused Senator John F. Kennedy during an interview with writer James M. Cannon in early 1960. Kennedy firmly believed "the presidency is the place to be in a sense if you want to get anything done." Undeniably, the thing that the soon-to-be president from Massachusetts wanted most to get done was the Cold War. America's racial woes, though, proved to be a continuing hinderance to that goal, an unwelcome annoyance that, although connected to the bigger dilemma at hand—unchecked Soviet communist expansion—got in the way of the action.[1]

The administration and its president realized that America's civil rights record was a problem. They also understood that if they failed to act on civil rights, it would gift the Russians with a ready-made propaganda message crafted from American racial hypocrisy, a message that would resonate profoundly with its targeted audience in the predominantly nonwhite Third World. But it was not a moral issue for Kennedy, at least early on; instead, it was a matter of political and international optics. The *image* of a flailing America under his guidance was unacceptable to Kennedy. And thought he had several civil rights stalwarts on his staff, when Kennedy acted on civil rights issues, he did so to preserve his administration and the nation's image above all else.

THE COAST GUARD KERFUFFLE

During the inaugural parade of his administration, image was certainly on the mind of the young president when he noticed that the contingent from the United States Coast Guard Academy was made up of entirely white cadets. Kennedy recoiled at what he saw, but not because he was personally offended by the all-white display before him; it was because of what it *looked like* to the nonwhite world. He pounced. "Call the commandant [of the Coast

Guard Academy]," the president bellowed to Richard Goodwin, an aide to the president, "and tell him I don't ever want to see that happen again." If it was immediate satisfaction that the president hoped for—after all, he believed that the presidency was the apex of all American political power—Kennedy was about to learn a tremendous lesson in the great limitations of his office when dealing with the bureaucracy of the lethargic and often plodding machinations of government.[2]

Responding to the initial inquiry was not the secretary of Treasury—Treasury controlled the Coast Guard at the time, a legacy of its founder, Alexander Hamilton, the first secretary of the Treasury—Douglas Dillon but instead the special assistant to the secretary of Treasury, Theodore L. Eliot Jr. Though the lack of African Americans in the academy caused a good measure of consternation and stress within the administration, Eliot believed that racism had nothing to do with it. In his opinion, it was simply the reality of the situation. According to Eliot, the Coast Guard had one African American officer, nine African American warrant officers, and a little over seven hundred African American enlisted personnel. This meant that the Coast Guard had approximately 742 African American personnel among its ranks. The total compliment of the Coast Guard was 30,900. While Eliot claimed "there is no distinction made in the Coast Guard on the basis of race, creed or color," the evidence suggested otherwise.[3]

While reformers in the Kennedy administration recognized that something was going on at the academy, Secretary Dillon continued the narrative that his junior, Eliot, had begun. That did not mean nothing was wrong or that it was smooth sailing for the Coast Guard. Dillon recognized that since 1955 only two African Americans had qualified for entrance into the academy. Out of the two, Javis Leon Wright Jr., was admitted, but ultimately the Black cadet and track athlete left the institution for health reasons. Dillon offered a series of reasons for why this was likely the case. First, he observed that applicants to the academy were not required to racially identify themselves on their application forms. Additionally, Dillon conceded to the president that a lack of institutional effort or desire existed within the leadership of the Coast Guard on the matter. He also suggested that perhaps the smaller size of the branch prevented the interest of the African American community in joining it or trying to attend the academy. What he did not do, though, was declare that systemic racism was the culprit behind the continued lily-white nature of the Coast Guard and its academy.[4]

Though the head of Treasury tried to defend his departmental turf and explain away the situation, civil rights reformers within the administration were not buying what he was selling. Frank Reeves, one of Kennedy's African American appointees, had learned that the Coast Guard did not require a "Congressional sponsor . . . [and that] admission is on basis of written examination given in February and subsequent screening on basis of numerical standing by an [Academy] Board." He also learned that two potential Black candidates to the academy existed, were interested in attending, and needed only to take the entrance exams. While they prepped for the test, Frederick Dutton and Harris Wofford, advisers to the president on civil rights matters, requested that Dillon provide more information about the admission process. Dutton was intrigued by the interview process of potential cadets, which was conducted by white men and, he believed, was likely systemically prohibiting the acceptance of minority candidates. He encouraged Dillon to reform the process and suggested that more minority candidates be allowed to take the entrance exams. In response to Dutton, Dillon claimed that the interview process took place after the completion of the entrance examination and that a preselected board, not the interviewers, decided which candidates were accepted.[5]

Regardless of whether he believed racism was present in the Coast Guard Academy, Dillon, under increasing political pressure from the White House throughout the spring of 1961, initiated a desperate search for any minority candidate, especially a Black one. The reason that the search had expanded from just finding an African American candidate to any minority candidate was Dutton, who had requested from Carlos McCormack, a member of the Democratic National Committee, a list of potential Latin American recruits for the academy and had informed Dillon that "we should move beyond the question of whether there exists racial discrimination by the Academy and consider how to get competent Negroes, Spanish-American, Japanese-American, Puerto Ricans, and others considered for admission there." To his credit, Dillon seemed receptive to this request.[6]

In the meantime, another Dillon deputy, Assistant Secretary of the Treasury A. Gilmore Flues, reported to Dutton some needed good news. A measure of progress had been achieved, as two Asian Americans were already enrolled in the academy. More important, Flues reported to Dutton that the Coast Guard Academy may have finally found the elusive potential Black Coast Guard cadet. There was one potential hang-up: he might not, in fact, be Black. Flues noted:

He has listed himself as a Latin American but the interviewer states *he is very dark and gives evidence of colored blood*. This *boy* was 28th on the list of alternates, which would ensure his going into the Academy if he desires to do so. I have had him covered personally at his home on Long Island by a Coast Guard officer who reports the *boy* is apparently anxious to go and seems like a very fine type. I have been notified this morning he has now passed his physical and unless the security checkup shows a defect everything is in line for him to report to the Academy on June 15. His scholastic record and his standing on the examination indicate this *boy* can well carry the academic program. [Emphasis added]

A couple things stand out about Flues's comments that are troubling. First, the absolute desperation of the Coast Guard was apparent and appalling. They were so desperate that the leadership of the Treasury Department thought it knew the racial makeup of a potential candidate to the academy *better than the person applying*. Additionally, and it seemed to have been done in an innocent fashion, Flues referred to the Latin American candidate, who he believed was really Black, and other potential Black candidates as "boy" or "boys." Though they seem innocuous, the use of these terms in regard to a minority candidate was racially insulting and emasculating and reflected part of the Coast Guard's problem: it lacked the understanding or the desire to understand the racial sensitives of American minorities in the 1960s.[7]

Equally disturbing, Flues's memo was sent to Frederick Dutton, a Black man, who had likely heard the derogatory use of the term "boy" before. Even if it was unintentional, it still reflected misunderstanding and a lack of sympathy. If this was what the leadership of the Treasury Department was sending to an adviser of the president, what was going on in the department and in the Coast Guard? Also, Flues was wrong. It turned out that the young man he was talking about really was Latin American, just as he had claimed, because he was never identified as a Black candidate to the academy. In the best-case scenario, it was an innocent mistake that reflected a part of a bigger problem. At worst, it demonstrates that the secretary of the Treasury was relying on racist identification techniques to ascertain if the Coast Guard had finally found a Black candidate.

As the search continued for the elusive Black cadet, the academy integrated in another fashion by appointing W. D. Waller, an African American graduate of Howard University, to the position of assistant professor of chemistry, which made him the first African American professor in the academy's history. Not until 1962, almost a year after the president made his request and after a vigorous advertising and recruiting campaign by the Coast Guard, did an African American cadet begin his studies at the academy. Cadet Merle J. Smith would graduate four years later, becoming the first of his race to do so. Smith, who passed away in 2021, never considered himself to be anything more than an officer in the Coast Guard. His wife recalled: "He considered all of his accomplishments as part of doing his job, as opposed to being a trailblazer or a pioneer." Nonetheless, Commander Smith earned the bronze star, commanded a ship in close-quarters combat, the first of his race to do so, and served in Vietnam.[8]

Kennedy's interest in the racial composition of the Coast Guard Academy prompted similar investigations of the nation's other service academies. According to data collected by the White House, African American representation in the service academies remained anemic, as the institutions hovered around "one percent." During the 1960/1961 academic year, for example, only twenty-two Black cadets attended West Point and the United States Naval Academy, while only four enrolled in the relatively young United States Air Force Academy. For that matter, the United States Military Academy at West Point would not have its first African American faculty member, James Stith, until the mid-1970s. Out of an effort to improve the low number of minority cadets, the Kennedy administration suggested the academies send recruiting information and members of the armed forces to high schools, colleges, the African American media, and the NAACP.[9]

While the White House struggled with rectifying the racial makeup of its service academies, the president also expressed frustration over the racial composition of the nation's military honor guards. Beginning as a senator and continuing into his presidency, Kennedy was intimately familiar with the struggles underway in Africa and actively sought an international and domestic policy to change America's image with African leaders. For example, his political staff often attempted to prevent African dignitaries from encountering the racism and indignities of Jim Crow segregation in American society. But this action was less about preserving their international rights as human beings or ostensibly as men; it was instead a calculated aspect of his larger Cold War first policy as president. Africa was a hot spot. Better to keep its leaders closer to the United States than the Soviet Union. One way of doing that was to not alienate African foreign leaders when entertaining them.[10]

While hosting the president of Ghana, Kwame Nkrumah, however, Kennedy noticed that very few Black soldiers appeared in the American honor guard. This oversight disturbed the president greatly, and he insisted to his cabinet that the situation be resolved. Kennedy was right to be concerned. The number of minorities in the honor guards was miniscule; only 15 percent were African American. The most egregious example came from the Navy, which already had a poor reputation among Blacks because of the Steward Branch; it had no African Americans in its honor guard at all. In response to the president's concerns, Robert S. McNamara, Kennedy's secretary of defense,

President Kennedy at Camelot—image was everything: President John F. Kennedy's obsession with how his administration and the nation looked in its battle with Soviet Union included ensuring that the nation's military honor guards were racially integrated. Here Kennedy reviews the Marine Honor Guard at Quonset Naval Air Station, Rhode Island, September 25, 1961. Source: KN-C18933, Robert Knudsen. White House Photographs. John F. Kennedy Presidential Library and Museum, Boston.

instructed Assistant Secretary of Defense of Manpower and Personnel Carlisle P. Runge to rectify the situation at once.[11]

Outside of these direct actions by the president, Kennedy preferred that the dedicated reformers within his administration handle the civil rights issues within the military. With the president's blessing, Frederick Dutton organized them into the Sub-Cabinet Group on Civil Rights. Operating under the leadership of Harris Wofford, the special assistant to the president for civil rights, it led the racial reform efforts of the administration. Wofford remarked about the group years later:

Above all, the group tried to see the administration's civil rights policy as a whole, and to recommend what we thought that policy ought to be. Since the president had given little specific direction, we did not sit around trying to guess what he would desire. Where there was a clear mandate, such as in federal employment, we moved as fast and far as we could. In areas where there was no specific mandate, but no reason to believe Kennedy would oppose action, we went ahead, reporting to the President or going to him for the authority when it seemed necessary. His attitude was that we had a mandate to do anything we could get away with without causing him undue political trouble. When we knew that the president was opposed or hesitant, as he was about early issuance of the order on housing or about legislation, we kept appraising the problem and from time to time would give him our best advice, even though he didn't enjoy hearing it.

An ally that the Sub-Cabinet Group relied on to achieve racial reform was the Department of Defense. In a sense, the new group was merely continuing the belief of its reforming predecessors who saw tremendous opportunities for the African American community by way of racially integrating and reforming the military. But logically speaking, it also made good sense to target changing the DOD, which controlled the American military. Gargantuan in size and, as Wofford quipped, "a world within itself," the DOD and the 8 million soldiers and citizens it employed, along with the various business that worked to support it, penetrated all aspects of American life.[12]

    A willing accomplice to the Sub-Cabinet Group and leading the charge for racial reform at DOD was McNamara's special assistant, Adam Yarmolinsky. Prior to his time in the department, the Harvard- and Yale-trained lawyer made a name for himself as a vigilant defender of civil rights, a fact that his boss, McNamara, admitted years later: "Adam was more sensitive to the subject [civil rights] in those days than I was. I was concerned. I recognized what Harry Truman had done, his leadership in the field, and I wanted to continue his work. But I didn't know enough." Yarmolinsky believed that McNamara, though his interest and input were evolving slowly, had the capability to do more. In 1971, Yarmolinsky recalled to Daniel Ellsberg that, after his first meeting with McNamara, "I got the impression of extraordinary intelligence and vigor, and I knew that he was a man of real intellectual substance who was concerned about public issues to an extent that was quite unusual in an automobile executive."[13]

    Mutual admiration aside, McNamara, when it came civil rights reform within the ranks, was not quite there yet. In the interim, he relied heavily on the expertise of his special assistant during those early months and years of his tenure. So trusting was McNamara in Yarmolinsky that, when the latter presented his boss with an item for reform, the secretary rarely rejected it. An example of this trust in action was when Yarmolinsky objected to the use of the integrated military police to remove African American soldiers from segregated civilian establishments off base, which reinforced the notion among whites and Blacks that the military was complicit with the tenets of Jim Crow. Instead, the military needed to be a more active protector and educator of its Black personnel; Yarmolinsky believed it should supply lawyers for African American soldiers in these situations so that they could be fully educated on their rights. In the meantime, the armed forces could provide on-base alternatives to off-base racially segregated civilian businesses, the special assistant advocated, that catered to all personnel. After Yarmolinsky presented this idea to McNamara, it was quickly and quietly made the policy of the Department of Defense.[14]

A CASE OF INCONSISTENT LEADERSHIP

Instrumental though Yarmolinsky would prove to be for McNamara, he could not do everything. When it came to larger issues, such as the implementation of presidential executive orders on civil rights, the defense chief usually took the lead and often muddled his way through. Whether it was because McNamara was too focused on reforming the Pentagon, his self-admitted lack of clarity on the issue of civil rights, or because he did not wish to take any steps that were out of line with the president, a leadership style emerged that was absentee in nature and lacked the confidence needed to drive meaningful and consistent change. This created a befuddling atmosphere for commanders who operated below the secretary and had to contend with implementing vague policies.

The first of the two presidential executive orders on civil rights, Executive Order 10925, was released in March 1961. This order merged the committees of governmental employment with that of governmental contracts into a solitary group, the President's Committee on Equal Employment Opportunity (PCEEO). Vice President Lyndon B. Johnson, who in the coming years would play a larger role in the racial reform of the military, chaired the committee, composed of government employees—including the secretary of defense and the heads of the armed forces—and private citizens. During the committee's first meeting, Kennedy observed: "All of us agree that Federal money should not be spent in any way which encourages discrimination, but rather should be spent in such a way that it encourages the national goal of equal opportunity."[15] The federal government doled out millions of dollars in business contracts annually. The president, by way of his executive order, decided to use the economic power of those contracts to accelerate civil rights reform in the nation, which as a byproduct would foster a positive image abroad. If the PCEEO uncovered a business relationship between a branch of the federal government and a racially discriminative company, the administration reserved the right to terminate the contract if the offending party did not resolve the issue.[16]

Upon the order's release, McNamara failed to offer any guidelines to his subordinates on how to carry it out; instead, he simply issued a statement declaring that the department would comply with the president's wishes. One month later, in April, in a rare moment of further involvement and clarification, Kennedy insisted that action take place straight away: "I want immediate and specific action taken to assure that no use is made of the name, sponsorship, facilities, or activity of any Executive Department or Agency by or for any employee recreational organization practicing discrimination based on race, creed, color, or national origin." Once again, McNamara dutifully informed Department of Defense personnel that they were to comply with this additional aspect of the order; but at no point did he offer any guidance or limits to its implementation. Subsequently, it was up to his assistants, Adam Yarmolinsky and Carlisle Runge, and to the respective base commanders of the armed forces to handle the situation.[17]

This approach was problematic, as it dumped responsibility for carrying out change onto two assistants with differing philosophies on governance. A noted liberal reformer, Yarmolinsky envisioned the armed forces in the same manner as the reform-minded advocates who had proceeded him. It could offer, he believed, a "second chance" at life. In his work *The Military Establishment*, Yarmolinsky explored the socioeconomic transformation that came with military service. As a result of his investigation, he was convinced that those who served benefited from military service; however, those from poorer economic backgrounds, notably African Americans and poor whites, benefited even more, as it allowed them an opportunity to gain technical and life skills that they would have not gained in a career outside the military. In a deeper and more historical sense, Yarmolinsky believed that Kennedy's executive order offered the socially lethargic armed forces an opportunity to push into a new era of reform. Here, he sought to seize upon the moment for change. Because of Yarmolinsky's aggressiveness on the issue, powerful conservatives throughout the nation would brand the Ivy Leaguer as a communist meddler.[18]

Assistant Secretary of Defense for Manpower and Personnel Carlisle P.

Runge, a Wisconsin Democrat, had a political worldview that tended to follow the more conservative side of the party on social issues and viewed the executive order in a more traditional and conservative fashion. He worried that, if the Department of Defense acted on Kennedy's executive order too aggressively, it would become responsible for reforming large segments of the civilian community off base, something he did not feel the department was geared to do. Runge expressed these concerns at length in a letter to the Sub-Cabinet Group in July 1961. The elephant in the room for Runge was the matter of controlling the flow of federal funding from the Department of Defense into businesses that discriminated. When Runge spoke about federal funding tied to the DOD, he meant *everything*, from the flow of capital that came *indirectly* from American military personnel utilizing off-base services in local communities surrounding bases to *direct* aid from the federal government to defense contractors, schools, and more. Both understood the potential of the president's order, but where Yarmolinsky saw an opportunity, Runge viewed it as an overreach that was bound to bring trouble. To avoid that potential pitfall, Runge opted for an approach that removed a great deal of the responsibility from the department and sought to instead place it on other agencies inside the government.[19]

With no clear or consistent leadership emerging from the civilian handlers of the military, base commanders' interpretation of the president's order depended on their own personal beliefs as opposed to a set policy dictated from above that they could follow. Some commanders simply refused to act, while others interpreted the president's order liberally.

The later appeared to be the case for the base commander of Maxwell Air Force Base, located in Montgomery, Alabama. The base allowed racially segregated youth baseball teams to use its facilities. Following the issuance of the president's order, however, the base commander halted the practice and even canceled a racially segregated American Legion Baseball luncheon. It was then that Southern segregationist senator, Lister Hill of Alabama, intervened and sent a complaint to the Department of Defense. Hoping to avoid a confrontation with forces on the political right in Congress, Runge informed the senator that the commander had acted too broadly in his interpretation of the order.[20]

While he worked to defuse the political bomb to his right, Runge also had to neutralize challenges from his political left as he faced pressure from the bipartisan United States Civil Rights Commission (USCCR), within the government, which had maintained throughout the era a dogged interest in the civil rights activities of the military. After learning about the situation in Alabama, the USCCR queried the department on how it would deal with the use of military bases for racially segregated civilian activities elsewhere. After conferring with Yarmolinsky, Runge responded that the Department of Defense did not investigate the racial composition of every recreational activity on their bases; neither did it prohibit on-base groups, such as softball teams, from playing against a racially segregated civilian group. The answer satisfied Hill but proved wanting for the USCCR. But it was the best that Runge and Yarmolinsky could do without the support of the secretary of defense behind them. Therefore, instead of forging a cohesive statement against racism, the department hesitated and punted, which was more along the lines of Runge's approach to the issue.[21]

In Mobile, Alabama, at Brookley Air Force Base, the post commander prohibited the purchase of baseball tickets to the town's local minor league baseball team. The team's management operated its stadium in a racially segregated manner, and since it was the civilian employees of the base selling tickets to the airmen, the base commander interpreted this activity as a clear violation of the president's executive order. Fortunately for the Department of Defense and the officer, Senator Hill did not interject into the situation, which partly explains, along with McNamara's lack of leadership, why it was handled differently. The lone objection to the base commander's actions instead came from within the DOD; conservative lawyers in the Pentagon questioned the validity of the base commander's action, as it was the baseball team, not the airmen buying the tickets, that had committed the act of racial discrimination. Downplaying the concerns of the legal department, Yarmolinsky moved swiftly to rectify the situation. He neatly upheld the commanding officer's decision by suggesting that the White House should use its influence on the ownership of the team to encourage it to racially integrate a portion of the stadium. Economics, not executive pressure, ultimately carried the day. The team relied on the attendance of base personnel to make profit. To in any way jeopardize that support was fiscally irresponsible. With little alterative available, the organization followed the suggestions outlined by Yarmolinsky and racially integrated a portion of the stadium to maintain a steady attendance of military personnel.[22]

RACIAL DESEGREGATION IN THE DEFENSE INDUSTRY

While inconsistency marred progress on military bases, clear direction and leadership emerged to lead to reform off the bases—namely, within the private defense industry. Much of this activity occurred under the Plans for Progress program, which was headed by the PCEEO and backed financially by one its members, Robert Troutman. But it also occurred in coordination with the NAACP and the Department of Defense, whose efforts led to the racial integration of some of the nation's largest defense contractors including Lockheed and General Electric plus a handful of smaller firms. The leader of the PCEEO, Lyndon Johnson, had informed the nation's defense contractors that reform need not come by force but that racial change was necessary when considering Cold War calculations and moralistic concerns, suggesting that it was "the right thing to do."[23]

There can be no doubt that this program netted tremendous results. Using the Air Force as an example, it is easy to see how the DOD implemented Executive Order 10925 in a broad and effective manner. From the start, the Air Force was clear that it would not tolerate racial segregation among civilian contractors and would terminate any contract with an offending company. To meet the Pentagon's guidelines, a civilian contractor could "not discriminate against any employee or applicant for employment because of race, creed, color, or national origin." Complying with the order proved insufficient. Every contractor also had to advertise, through flyers and posters, that it was an equal opportunity employer. Making the order even more potent was the requirement that contractors had to ensure that their subcontractors also operated in an integrated fashion. The latter, when queried over the issue, had to submit their "books, records, and accounts" to the PCEEO to ensure compliance.[24]

Historically, Plans for Progress has been seen in a negative light. The historian James Giglio noted that NAACP representative Herbert Hill had felt that the program was "one of the great phonies of the Kennedy administration's civil rights program." Further, he observed that the alleged failure of Plans for Progress only deepened the emerging feud between Robert Kennedy and Johnson, the former blaming entirely the situation on the latter. There are some merits to this line of thinking, as Carl Brauer noted that the PCEEO rarely used the power it had to end contracts. The reasons for not doing so were many. The president had created the committee without congressional approval, which meant that, if it acted out of place too much, it would likely irk Southern segregationists in Congress who likely were already frustrated with its existence. Furthermore, if the PCEEO would have acted, it likely would have led to a dispute in the courts. There was something else to consider: the image-driven leadership of John Kennedy, who sought to achieve change with as little negative consequences as possible. While criticism existed within the administration, including Kennedy's own frustrations with Johnson and the PCEEO, it was likely that the vice president, in the mind of Giglio, was simply "reflecting the administration's cautious style and approach."[25]

Other scholars such as Randall Woods have pointed to the problematic role that the great benefactor of the program, Robert Troutman of Georgia, played. One member of the PCEEO, the African American businessmen John Hervey Wheeler, warned that Troutman's association with Sibley Law Firm of Atlanta bore trouble for himself and the PCEEO. Wheeler observed that the law firm was "famous for infiltrating Negro causes and rendering them impotent by working from within." What followed was a political and leadership clash between Johnson, who wanted to expunge Troutman from the PCEEO, and Robert Kennedy, who backed Troutman. Johnson would win, and Troutman eventually resigned from the committee.[26]

Troutman's resignation letter was telling, as he informed Kennedy that he had "accepted [originally his place on the committee] because you asked." And though he would find some merit in his work, Troutman largely considered his time on the committee to be something akin to a punishment; he referred to it as "an unenthusiastic assignment" that he was unagreeably a part of for "fifteen long, arduous months." Though he did not air his issues, he certainly had them with Johnson; but he was also frustrated with the Black community, who he felt was not grateful enough with what Troutman believed was his success:

You did not request nor did I expect to be consumed by this assignment. It came largely by accident—when my study showed me (a) the real nature and gravity of the nation's Negro problem and (b) how little the past approaches of well -meaning people had bettered the situation. I fashioned a venture and approach which made sense to men. And its results (in terms of goal, efforts and expense) are amazing, if not miraculous. While the venture became immediately impressive to those (the nation's key employers) who could achieve great nationwide success, it became equally unimpressive to those who speak for the people whom Plans for Progress sought to aid (the nation's large Negro population). Incredible but true!

Not only did Troutman feel under appreciated by all involved; he was also done with being the benefactor for Plans for Progress, as he sought to be reimbursed for the $50,000 he had put up to support the program. While Kennedy thanked Troutman for his service, he said nothing to the Georgian about repaying the money.[27]

Although controversy surrounded the Troutman affair, and the feud with Bobby Kennedy was starting to heat up, the PCEEO was not a total failure under Lyndon Johnson's leadership. It increased the number of Blacks in high-level government positions by 35 percent, netted a 20 percent increase in middle-tier governmental jobs, and resolved 72 percent of 1,610 racial complaints in favor of the complainants. The PCEEO also aided in integrating segments of the American Federation of Labor and the Congress of Industrial Organizations (the famed AFL-CIO labor union), which allowed Blacks into coveted skilled-labor apprenticeship programs. These victories meant significant gains for the civilian and military realms. And while not a perfect resolution to the situation, many civilian defense occupations became open to African American workers because of the effort.[28]

OFF-BASE EDUCATION

In a letter to James Evans, an African American graduate of the Massachusetts Institute of Technology then serving as the civilian assistant in the Office of the Assistant Secretary of Defense for Manpower and Personnel, Waddie L. Hall lamented the second-class treatment that her son, the child of a military personnel member, experienced in his pursuit of an education because he happened to be Black:

As a military wife, whose husband has nearly fourteen years service, I am very displeased with the segregated school system on Shaw Air Force Base (South Carolina). My husband and I often talk about the people who were our enemies during World War II, and how they as aliens are able to come to this country and be treated as first class citizens. Here we are born citizens and also our son, yet our son can't attend the school which is most convenient for him. He has to travel 7.3 miles one way to school when the school here at Shaw is [approximately] one mile [away]. By the time he walks to the bus stop which is off the base, and on a busy highway, he could ride his bicycle to the school here at Shaw. . . . There is only one solution to this problem, and that is to push for admission of my child and other children similarly located to Shaw View Elementary School, which is the school they should attend. This school was built with and supported by heavy federal contributions. This present system is causing my husband and I to spend more money, and needless emotional stress. Why is the government moving so slow to do away with segregation, especially when its been against the law for over eight years[?].

Waddie Hall's consternation underscored a remaining issue for African American armed forces families that was unresolved during the Eisenhower administration, which was the question of federal authority over federally funded off-base racially segregated schools that catered to military dependents.[29]

At the time, the Eisenhower administration believed it had little course of action available to redress the situation. Its conservative approach to the issue was especially frustrating for African American families living in a post-*Brown* world, where implementation in the South was proceeding at a gradual pace. Kennedy's Executive Order 10925, though, empowered the HEW to take on the issue. The secretary of HEW, Abraham Ribicoff, a Connecticut Democrat, interpreted Public Laws 815 and 874—both were products of World War II and provided aid for construction and staffing of schools located in "federally impacted" towns and regions—in a more progressive manner than his Eisenhower-era predecessor. Ribicoff reasoned that those funds could not support racially segregated schools, as that did not fit within the guidelines of the president's executive decree. Informed that they had to racially integrate, the schools received a stern warning from HEW. If they failed to voluntarily comply, HEW would halt funding to those institutions and remove military children from the schools. In January 1963, HEW took the matter one step further, declaring that the federal government would not only cease funding schools that were noncompliant but also build new schools for the affected children.[30]

It became increasingly apparent that HEW, though it sought to meet the letter of the law, was operating counter to the political prudency of the president. In March 1963, United States Attorney General Robert Kennedy, a top adviser and sibling of the president, called his brother to discuss the matter. The cost of erecting eight new schools was going to cost about "three million bucks," the younger Kennedy reported to his older brother. In the attorney general's opinion, it was going to be a waste of money because the Justice Department was already hard at work on a suit that the attorney general had filed in 1962 involving military schools in Prince George County, Virginia, that dealt with this very issue. Eventually, the attorney general would expand the suit to include military children who lived on and off base and expanded its scope to include schools in Alabama, Louisiana, and Mississippi: "It makes no sense that we should ask military personnel to make sacrifices and serve away from home and at the same time see their children treated as inferiors by local requirements that they attend segregated schools." If the federal government followed HEW's lead, he explained to the president, it would spend $3 million for about fifty to sixty Black students for only a year or two.[31]

After hearing out his brother, Jack was confused as to why HEW made this move in the first place: "What we should have done is just left it with the legal case. I don't know how we got beyond that." From the president's perspective, the matter should have been simply and quietly addressed. While he struggled to understand how this could happen, the answer was clear: the problem was a lack of cohesive leadership from his office on the issue of racial reform in the military. The situation involving dependent children of minority personnel is illustrative of this point. With the president deliberately, for political reasons, out of the picture, HEW acted on its own accord on the issue and with little consultation, it would seem, with the Justice Department. Thus, as this occurred the Justice Department—namely, Robert Kennedy—sought its own resolution in the courts that would have allowed the law to work in the favor of minority families and spare his brother blame for the reform it would unleash. But with little leadership, communication, and coordination, the issue became muddled; both efforts collided into one another.[32]

Meanwhile, implementation of the HEW policy fell to the Department of Defense and base commanders to carry out. To bring a measure of leadership to the rudderless reform endeavor, the DOD provided instructions to its base commanders to be knowledgeable enough to "counsel parents on the procedures available for the transfer of their children to integrated schools, on how to appeal assignment to segregated schools, and on legal action as an alternative to accepting local school board decisions to bar their children." Despite the flawed nature of the lack of communication and colliding visions of reform that emerged, the HEW effort netted some results in Texas, Georgia, Tennessee, Florida, and Virginia, where base commanders successfully achieved the racial integration of schools in areas around their bases. In total, fifteen schools racially integrated, and in areas where schools failed to do so new schools were built. This represented a quasi-victory, but not the total victory desired by the Department of Justice, HEW, or the DOD on the matter; Morris J. MacGregor Jr. observed that "in the long run any attempt to integrate schools through a program of voluntary compliance appeared futile." As such, the issue of off-base school education for military dependents remained inconsistent from region to region and base to base on whether or not the children of military personnel received a racially integrated education. Not until the passage of the Civil Rights Act of 1964 would the efforts to bring an end to off-base racial segregation of dependent schools be achieved.[33]

OFF-BASE HOUSING

Military installations could not always accommodate the housing needs of all its soldiers, and whenever this happened personnel had to search off-base for housing. The unrelenting racism of American society made the process exceedingly difficult on African American servicemen. Denied the right to equal housing, African American soldiers often ended up in the most impoverished sections of town. In 1956, Ira W. Jayne, a judge from Michigan, complained to Roy Wilkins about the housing accommodations available to African

American soldiers stationed at Fort Polk, Louisiana. Having monitored the situation for some time, Jayne reported that "they are housed in the segregated district [off-base] and restrained by some kind of a curfew from leaving the district after 9 o'clock at night."[34]

According to Bill Current, a member of the US Navy and the nephew of the NAACP's director of branches, Gloster B. Current, racism was also prevalent in the Norfolk, Virginia, housing community of Ben Moreel. Living in a racially segregated community, Current and his compatriots faced continuous white police harassment. But the concern emerging within the white community in the greater Norfolk area was not directed toward the indignities African Americans, military and civilian, faced in acquiring a home; it instead focused on the damage that racial integration was supposedly doing to the value of their homes. A white citizen in Norfolk wrote to Mississippi Democratic senator James Eastland about the unfairness thrust upon white citizens because of attempts at racial integration of housing:

It certainly does not seem fair to the white home owner for a Negro to come into an all-white section and buy a house, thereby causing the value of the white persons home to be cut about 50% overnight. Seems as though the true blooded Americans have given up and are ready to give the Negro's anything they ask for. I am not prejudiced against the Negro nor do I hold any malice in my heart against them, but in all fairness I don't advocate the mixing of these two races. Frankly I don't think it will work, now or EVER.

While white citizens howled that their property values were declining, African Americans military personnel, with little opportunity to live elsewhere, were more often than not being stuffed into segregated neighborhoods.[35]

If they were not there, Black soldiers, sailors, airmen, and Marines found themselves living a considerable distance from base. As members of the military, however, they were required to be at the base by a certain time each morning. If they arrived late for duty, they faced reprimands and potential punishments. In the early 1960s, the US Civil Rights Commission contended that the presence of racism in off-base housing prohibited the military from existing in a state of maximum readiness because it forced Black military personnel to live too far from their duty stations. And little help was on its way; the recently signed Housing Act of 1961, which focused more on urban renewal efforts, failed to address the issue, and the much-ballyhooed bill creating a Department of Urban Affairs proved to be dead on arrival.[36]

Ever reluctant to risk too much political capital on the issue, Kennedy nonetheless had promised to do something about racial segregation in housing while on the campaign trail in 1960, even going so far as providing a statement full of gusto and political arrogance when he promised the African American community that the housing dilemma could be dealt with by a simple "stroke of the presidential pen." The problem seemed to be that Kennedy had misplaced his pen. It took pressure from the Black community, which had instituted an "ink for Jack" campaign, to get him to move on the issue two years later. The release of Executive Order 11063 in November 1962 elicited great praise from the Black community. But their cheers quickly turned into jeers. The greatly anticipated order proved limited in its scope, as it failed to rectify racism in federally funded public housing. Instead, it addressed only future federally funded housing projects. "We've gotten the best snow job in history. We've lost two years because we admired him," a civil rights advocate voiced in frustration over the president's inability to put forward strong civil rights legislation. Dr. Martin Luther King Jr. warned the Kennedy administration that its failure to field significant reform was leading to the growth and rise of a cynical view, though he did not share it, within the civil rights movement. "The most cynical view holds that it [the Kennedy Administration] wants the votes of both [civil rights reformers and racial segregationists] and is paralyzed by the conflicting needs of each."[37]

And the problem was not going away anytime soon. On the same day that Kennedy signed the executive order, the NAACP sent him a memo that detailed the racial discrimination facing Blacks, both civilian and military, in their desire to own a home outside Cape Canaveral near Patrick Air Force Base. The NAACP informed the president that the African American community in the area, a region dominated by military personnel and their families, "are beginning to equate the whole broad pattern of this suppression and denial [in acquiring federally funded housing] with the policy of the federal government." This situation was not limited to Florida or the South; it affected African Americans servicemen all over the country. Ira Harrison, a writer for Syracuse's *People's Weekly*, penned a letter to the president about the plight of Captain James Anderson. Anderson, an African American doctor in the Army, struggled to find a suitable apartment in New York for his family. Flagrant racism seemed to be the culprit as Harrison claimed that a "gentlemen's agreement" existed that barred Blacks from federally funded housing in the area.[38]

From across the country, Dr. Paul Muller, president of the Sacramento Committee for Fair Housing, who was in support of an order that ended racial discrimination in public housing, dispatched a letter to Kennedy that informed him of not only the housing woes facing Black soldiers but also the economic impact on those builders trying to help these servicemen build a home. One contractor observed that "if builders get out of line by selling to the wrong party

[African Americans], the lending institutions will call in the notes on all other unsold property. If a builder has many unsold homes where the property has been subordinated to construction loans, the builders does not have sufficient capital to meet the notes." As contractors dealt with economic punishments if they tried to aid Black personnel or citizens, the situation fared little better for real estate professionals. One female Realtor who had attempted to aide an African American officer in the Air Force in purchasing a home recalled that the company she worked for informed her that "if I were to submit the Negro's name for this home I could possibly lose all further listings with the owning company." Through at great financial risk to herself, she ended up aiding the Black officer and submitting his information anyway, without mentioning his race, to a lending institution. Ultimately, his VA loan application was denied.[39]

Given the nature of the president's lackluster solution to the overall housing situation, it was only natural that the DOD's interpretation of the order also proved insufficient. Under Secretary McNamara's guidance and using what little cover came from Kennedy's largely ineffective order, the Pentagon inserted a nondiscrimination clause in all contracts between the armed forces and off-base rental properties. Additionally, the civilian leadership of the military required base-level leadership to collect data on all available nonsegregated housing within their respective areas. African American personnel could use this information when searching for suitable housing within the local community. Though a necessary first start, McNamara's policy had minimal impact, as it failed to address the issue of private housing, which represented the majority of available dwellings. With no alternative available to them, Black military personnel continued to live in many of the most dilapidated parts of a community or farther and farther away from their post.[40]

Any action, no matter how weak, of this sort elicited a reaction from the South, where political orators assailed the president's order as economically irresponsible, potentially unconstitutional, and autocratic. The chairman of the Senate Banking Committee, Democratic senator Absalom Willis Robertson of Virginia, who wondered about the constitutionality of the order, chided the president over an action that he believed "hurt real estate values all over the nation—not just in the South." The junior senator from Georgia, Democrat Herman E. Tallmadge, went further than his colleague by calling the order "a grave disservice to the economic welfare to impose upon an industry expending 6 per cent of the gross national product and employing 2.2 million workers the political burden of implementing a partisan viewpoint on human relations." It was an "audacious usurpation of power," John Stennis, the stalwart segregationist Democratic senator from Mississippi, believed, one that mirrored the oversight found in a totalitarian communist nation by challenging "the right of every American to choose his own associates."[41]

THE VETERANS ADMINISTRATION AND RACIAL REFORM

Though its hospitals had racially integrated, the Veterans Administration remained riddled by the resistant nature of the civilian communities that supported its institutions by way of contract labor. For example, some medical schools and state homes that worked with the VA continued to operate in a segregated fashion. Forcing them and others to integrate to match the federal standard of the VA might lead to the termination of contracts with the government, which could jeopardize the quality of health care that patients received. The VA opted to avoid confrontation and instead embraced a familiar strategy: it embraced the cultural norms of the local population and did not challenge racial segregation. Furthermore, it doubled down on the notion that change could come only by way of congressional legislation. Operating under the auspices of Kennedy's Executive Order 10925, the VA did make some gains. It halted segregation in beneficiary travel and lodging, racial segregation in ambulance transportation, and racial discrimination in its burial practices. The institution also investigated and resolved complaints of racial discrimination in its hospital in St. Louis and at its insurance center, located in Philadelphia. Additionally, the VA distributed equal employment opportunity posters throughout its hospital system and promoted voter registration drives among African American veterans.[42]

While the VA's goal was to make changes where it could and as quietly as it could, the attempt to eliminate federal dollars going to institutions that operated in a racially segregated fashion did not always occur silently. When it came to the VA's treatment toward the burial of the dead, for instance, which began with the dispatchment of VA Circular 62-6, the effort created a brush fire when it was implemented in Georgia. And anything happening in the Peach State, especially if it effected the military, meant that Senator Richard Russell, the long-standing member of the Senate Armed Services Committee and general bane to all those who strove for racial justice in the armed forces, would soon get involved. And it did not take long for him to get involved, as Russell received a letter from Poteet Funeral Home located in Augusta that called his attention to the matter. The proprietors of the funeral home had catered to whites and felt that the effort to force them to racially integrate was criminal and reeked of authoritarianism:

We are not only being done a great injustice by the Veterans Administration, but the veterans will be done the greatest injustice of all. When it comes to the point that the government can tell us who we have to bury, we feel that it is time that the control of this country be given back to the people. If this is an indication of the type of administration we have and are going to have in the future, it is time we all made a move, even if it is to Russia.

Not to be outdone by one of its members, the Georgia Funeral Directors Association penned Russell as well. In the complaint, it alleged that, since whites would not bury Black soldiers and that Blacks would not bury white soldiers, the reform effort underway was bound to fail. The latter part of the statement, though, was dubious as only one example of a Black funeral home that refused to bury a white solider in an all-white cemetery was provided. As the letter ended, and in a clear moment of sympathy—not for the dead but instead for Russell and themselves in that they had to deal with this intrusion on Southern racial and societal norms—James H. Fletcher, the secretary of the association, remarked:

We realize that these are difficult times, and that the problem arising from the liberal viewpoints taken by some heads of government bring pressure to bear in the most unexpected places, however, we feel that this particular situation has created an impasse in Georgia which is not acceptable on any basis, and it is in this light that we are asking for your consideration of the matter so that some solution might be forth-coming in the future.

In time, and ostensibly because of pressure being applied by Russell and others, the order was adjusted in 1963. Now, instead of the VA taking the lead on setting up a burial, it was up to the veteran's family. This deft move allowed the survivors to choose "a funeral director of their choice" to oversee the burial. The policy still called for the use of directors who did not discriminate, "regardless of race, creed, color or national origin," in their business practices. But the arrangement was not considered to be a government contract, and payment was "a matter between the funeral director and the survivor." Reimbursement from the VA would happen afterward. While not blatantly saying it—as the VA claimed to work only with those that would abide by its nondiscriminatory credo—this adjustment allowed for the possibility of working with institutions that claimed to follow the VA's racial guidelines while in reality operating in a racially segregated fashion.[43]

In the politically and emotionally charged arena of housing, the VA maintained a conservative course. In August 1961, Roy Wilkins, chairman of the

Leadership Conference on Civil Rights and executive secretary of the NAACP, along with his colleague Arnold Aronson, secretary of the Leadership Conference on Civil Rights and director of program planning and evaluation for the National Community Relations Advisory Council, presented Kennedy with a report titled "Proposals for Executive Action To End Federally Supported Segregation and Other Forms of Racial Discrimination." The sixty-page Wilkins-Aronson report targeted everything from racial discrimination in general military affairs (in particular in the National Guard) to agricultural affairs.[44]

But housing, according to the report's authors, might have been the most important issue of them all: "In no area of civil rights is the need for Executive action more compelling than in the field of housing. For segregation in housing virtually assures segregation in schools, in recreation and in other community facilities." The problem was that the government was a complicit agent in the perpetuation of racial segregation in housing. As the situation applied to veterans specifically, the civil rights community argued that the VA "does not enforce an anti-discrimination policy in its housing loans." Indeed, they were correct. According to the work of the historian Ira Katznelson, racist lenders throughout America refused VA housing loans filed by Black veterans, which meant the prohibition of an important boon from the Servicemen's Readjustment Act of 1944, better known as the G.I. Bill, which was the right to file for a loan to purchase a home.[45]

In response to inquiries into the matter from the Kennedy administration, the VA attempted a good bit of misdirection. To counter the charge of complicity in the racial discrimination of Black veterans seeking a home loan, the VA argued that since February 15, 1950, a policy existed that prevented the use of a "direct loan" in a fashion that was racially discriminatory. It contended further that it maintained relationships with five states that individually prohibited the sale of homes on a segregated basis and that it was working to build relationships with two more states. In the states it had reached an understanding with, the VA retained the right to prosecute those that discriminated against veterans. Of course, this meant that in forty-three states the VA had no such arrangement in place to protect the rights granted under the G.I. Bill to its Black military personnel. Instead of forging a brave and bold new path, the VA demurred. In areas where state law prevented racial discrimination in the sale of homes, the VA refused to act: "In states where no such laws exist, however, the VA position has previously been that the Administrator has no legal or administrative authority to act against builders, sellers, or lenders who exercise racial discrimination in sales or loans involving veterans housing." Although the VA sought to review its standing on the issue, no reversal of policy emerged during the Kennedy years.[46]

An area where the VA excelled as a leader for civil rights reform within the military industrial community was in the employment of African Americans. And while it is difficult to ascertain how many of these individuals were prior-service military, that many of those employees were Black veterans cannot be doubted. During the early 1960s, most African American employees within the VA fell under the Wage Administration. Spanning the pay grades of GS-1 to GS-18, Wage Administration employees were primarily semiskilled labor positions. Some were janitors or maids; others were gardeners or maintenance employees; and some served as receptionists. Of the 37,337 employees within the Wage Administration, almost half—14,139—were Black.[47] Equally noteworthy was the appointment of African Americans into Title 38 positions. Title 38 classified employees consisted of doctors, nurses, dentists, and other medical professionals. There were 5,873 employees within this classification; 516 of them were African Americans, with the majority (472) serving as nurses, while the remainder were either physicians or dentists. To be sure, the number of African Americans serving in low-level positions brings up questions of the socioeconomic status of the African American community, but because the Veterans Administration was a part of the federal government it is also true that the vast majority worked in a racially integrated environment where they received the same pay and health benefits as their white counterparts, which likely surpassed what Blacks working in the private sector received.[48]

CHARLES DIGGS

An African American veteran of World War II, Charles C. Diggs Jr. encountered firsthand the racism of the military while stationed in Tuskegee, Alabama. The handful of African Americans officers, among them Diggs, found that their rank meant little in the eyes of white servicemen. Part of military tradition was saluting higher-ranking officers as a sign of respect and acknowledgment of one's superior. But in the 1940s, white servicemen went out of their way to avoid having to salute Black officers. For that matter, German prisoners of war housed in stateside facilities such as Tuskegee even received better treatment than Black officers. Years later, Diggs was the first Black man elected from Michigan to Congress and played a role in the attempt to bring to justice those who lynched Emmett Till. President Eisenhower dispatched Diggs, who carried his memories of the ill treatment of African American personnel during

World War II within him, on a fact-finding mission that scoured military bases on America's West Coast and in the Far East Command.[49]

For a veteran of American racism in the armed forces, what Diggs discovered on American military installations near and far was likely unsurprising to him. But it was clear after touring, meeting, and speaking with Black personnel that Diggs came away with the impression that though some reform had been achieved from his time in service that the African American warrior of the 1960s still faced racial discrimination. He believed this to be the case because the African American military personnel he visited with told him it was still there. Among their many accusations, they contended that the promotion rates of white personnel were higher than those of Black soldiers. While the accusation was a difficult one to prove, that they believed it was true and were willing to state it openly was all that mattered. Whether true or not, when personnel believe or feel they are being excluded or wronged in some manner, that carries weight with fellow soldiers, which leads to deleterious harm to morale. When it is a matter of race, it carries weight within their own racial community, which impacts the military's ability to recruit in that community. Put simply, if Black military personnel lacked trust in the military to do right by them, then so would future recruits from the Black community.[50]

At the heart of the issue of trust, the historians Sherie Mershon and Steven Schlossman contend, was a lack of consistent leadership. Though some measure of racial reform had been achieved over the years, the leadership of the armed forces had largely failed to achieve consistent success in the carrying out of its changes. Sometimes, it was as simple as lack of oversight over a reform on one base, whereas another received it. For that matter, civilian and military leaders' willingness to allow the reform to do the heavy lift of change without following up on it in a consistent manner was also a problem. This lack of oversight stemmed in part from the armed forces' engrained belief that military discipline could curtail individualism. Thus, a troubling assumption remained within the leadership of the military: if military personnel followed one set of guidelines, they would follow all of them without question.[51]

Coinciding with this was a feeling of professional ambivalence toward the issue of civil rights reform. Certainly, some officers, noncommissioned officers, and enlisted men, regardless of their race, embraced the civic, religious, humane, and frankly the blatant necessity of the Cold War that supported the cause of racial reform. But even those who were compelled to act were never judged by it *professionally*. Furthermore, officers in the armed forces stayed at military installations for short periods, rotating in and out quite frequently. This meant that any given officer had a brief amount of time to prove himself to superiors. So why waste that time dealing with civil rights issues off base when it would not help them receive a promotion? Conversely, if officers had wanted to act, their actions in theory could easily be undone after their departure, as there was no metric to keep the ball rolling for successors, let alone the creation of a peer pressure–based social environment that compelled them to act. It was not as if some officers in the military did not care about the issue. Undoubtedly many did, but the armed forces did little to compel them professionally or foster the creation of a social environment to marry their morality with their professional duties as leaders. The lack of a desire to measure leaders by their desire to support civil rights reforms within their command added to the inconsistency on the issue and brought the pacing of potential reforms to a crawl.[52]

With no regard for oversight or any professional reason for concern, some officers in the military allowed flagrant displays of racism to exist. One example involved the declaration of certain villages in Okinawa as a "Negro area," such as the Koza Four Corners Area, while the situation was different in "white areas" for Black men. A Black airman reported upon entering "white areas" that he found it difficult to find female companionship without possibly incurring a potential racial confrontation. He noted:

In my attempt to find the truth in this matter, I proceeded to patronize some of the so called "white areas," such as Goya, Kamahara, Koza, Nakanomachi, Yoshihara, and other such areas. I entered a number of bars in these areas and upon my entrance into these bars, I was served, but none of the "barmaids" would associate with me. I on some occasions asked some of the "barmaids" to dance and was on all occasions, refused, but I noticed that when ever [sic] a Caucasian entered, a "barmaid" went immediately to his table and sat, drank, and danced with him. I have not seen this happen when a Negro enters one of these bars. The only place that a Negro can go for Social activities and feel comfortable and at ease, is the "Koza Four Corner area." To go anywhere other than there might constitute a race riot.

It appeared that Jim Crow segregation was alive and well in East Asia, but that did not mean it would go unchallenged. In 1960, during the Fourth of July weekend celebration, a race riot between white personnel and Black personnel occurred in Japan. Differing accounts emerged from the military, which viewed it as a minor affair, and from locals, who deemed it a riot. The *Morning Star Okinawa* reported that the riot involved a small force of forty African American military personnel, who in their pursuit of ending racial segregation in Japanese social establishments locked horns with whites and the military police.[53]

Another glaring example, and one that persisted throughout the 1960s and beyond, was the defiant flying of the Confederate flag by white American soldiers. The Stars and Bars served as a rebellious symbol for whites who were openly against racial integration. With no clear-cut order or coordinated movement among commanders to tackle the problem, the flying of the flag of a defunct and defeated state lived on in the racially integrated armed forces. After African Americans in the Far East Command complained about the display of the flag, racist whites, embracing the terroristic trademark of the Ku Klux Klan, burned crosses in the yards of their fellow Black military personnel. At times, the situation became so venomous and full of vitriol that it caused some African American performers to halt their shows. During a performance at the Golden Dragon Yokohama Officers Club, Chubby Checker ended his act early because of "the sight of guests sitting ringside in blackface, the residue of the [tasteless] amateur minstrel show which preceded him, along with an array of hanging Confederate flags." According to Diggs, the military was aware of these incidents and more of racial discrimination within its ranks but refused to do anything about it.[54]

THE GESELL COMMITTEE

In 1962, Diggs reported his findings to Kennedy. But the matter and the pressure on the president to do more did not stop there. While Diggs needled and chided the president in the foreground, a grassroots movement originating within the civilian arm of the DOD's leadership was underway in the background to do more on the issue. Leading this endeavor was Adam Yarmolinsky. The ubiquitous special assistant to McNamara worked on convincing his boss of the need for a new fact-finding committee, one similar to the Fahy Committee of years past, to investigate racism in the military. McNamara agreed and proposed the idea to the president.[55]

On June 24, 1962, Kennedy established the President's Committee on Equality of Opportunity in the Armed Forces. Heading up the seven-member committee was Gerhard Gesell, a well-traveled Yale-trained lawyer who had spent much of the New Deal and Cold War era working for the Securities and Exchange Commission and as a member of Congress's Joint Committee on the Investigation of the Pearl Harbor Attack. The other members of what became known as the Gesell Committee represented an eclectic collection of civil rights proponents of varying degrees of notoriety. Perhaps the most well known of the group were Whitney Young, the head of the National Urban League, John

The Gesell Committee: Pressed by his civil rights advisers to do more about racism remaining in the ranks of the armed forces, Kennedy established the Committee on Equal Opportunity in the Armed Forces on January 23, 1963, the Gesell Committee. The seven-person panel included several key members of the civil rights community. *Left to right*: attorney Laurence I. Hewes; NAACP attorney Nathaniel S. Colley; journalist Benjamin Muse, head of the Southern Regional Council's Southern Leadership Project; attorney and committee chairman Gerhard Gesell; President Kennedy; executive director of the National Urban League Whitney M. Young; publisher of the *Chicago Defender* John H. Sengstacke; and attorney Abe Fortas. Source: ST-49-2-63, Digital Identifier: JFKWHP-1963-01-23-A, White House Photographs. John F. Kennedy Presidential Library and Museum, Boston.

H. Sengstacke, the longtime publisher of the Black newspaper the *Chicago Defender*, and Abe Fortas, who, besides a reputation as a brilliant legal mind in the fields of civil rights and the First Amendment, had the tremendous good fortune of befriending a young Texas Hill Country Democrat named Lyndon B. Johnson, who would eventually nominate the Memphis-born lawyer to the Supreme Court. Rounding out the group were Benjamin Muse, the "fighting moderate," a political journalist, head of the Southern Regional Council's

Southern Leadership Project, and the author of *Virginia's Massive Resistance*, a work designed to combat the blatant opposition in the South to racial integration; and another Yale-trained lawyer, Nathaniel Colley, who at this time was serving as an attorney for the NAACP; Laurence I. Hewes III—not to be confused with his father, Laurence I. Hewes Jr., who had worked throughout his career in various aspects of governmental regulation over agriculture—served as staff director and counsel to the group.[56]

The purpose of the Gesell Committee was to serve as an advisory body to the Pentagon. It could make suggestions, but it lacked the political clout of its predecessor, the Fahy Committee, which had a direct line to the president for action. Any action was going to come from the DOD, not the chief executive. Though not wielding the same power, the group's charge was no less daunting, as it investigated many areas of racial concern within the military: the promotion rates of African Americans, the remaining problems in the Navy's Steward Branch, and the lack of Black officers in the armed forces.[57]

In June 1963, the group submitted its initial report to the president, which supported Diggs's earlier findings and belief that racial discrimination was alive and well in the armed forces. The problem, according to the committee, was clear: there was a clear lack of leadership and governance on the issue. With no clear guidelines from the Department of Defense, commanding officers of military installations addressed racial discrimination off base in an ad hoc and uncoordinated manner. It further meant that the gradualism of the 1940s and 1950s would persist into the 1960s, especially regarding problems in the local community, where military commanders lacked the authority to deal with incidents off base.[58]

Through direct oversight, the establishment of legal guidelines, and the use of educational programs, the Gesell Committee felt that the racial problems of the military could be resolved. Oversight would come through the adjustment of promotion requirements. If an officer, regardless of race or rank, desired advancement, then that officer had to become a more active force against racial discrimination. It also suggested that each base should have an officer detailed to deal with racial incidents. It would be the duty of this officer to investigate racism on base and off base and report them to the base commander for remediation. On the very important front of off-base discrimination, the committee advocated the creation of an integrated base-community council to replace the old lily-white councils that had dominated this role in the past. These councils were charged with the task of encouraging the local community to voluntarily cooperate with the military on the matter.[59]

Volunteerism, however, would go only so far. In most cases, local communities needed a compelling reason to alter their past behavior. The committee suggested using off-base sanctions as an economic prod to force the more reluctant communities into action. If a local business discriminated against African American soldiers, the base commander had the power to prohibit soldiers from frequenting the establishment. This would create an economic motivation for local businessmen to racially integrate their establishments while also sending a clear message to the community: the military would no longer tolerate racial discrimination toward African American personnel. If none of these methods worked, the Department of Defense had the right to shut down the installation.[60]

After mulling over the committee's suggestions, McNamara established a new directive that implemented most of its proposals; the major omission was the threat of closing bases to achieve racial integration, which, given the power of Southern segregationists in Congress, made a great deal of political sense but demonstrated the lackluster leadership from the president and his defense chief on the issue. Policy Directive 5120.36 made civil rights abuses of African American soldiers, on base and off base, the responsibility of a new civil rights hierarchy within the Department of Defense. To establish a semblance of oversight, Alfred B. Fitt became the first assistant secretary of defense for civil rights. McNamara subordinated this new office to the assistant secretary for manpower. Operating under these guidelines, the armed forces created equal-opportunity divisions within their respective branches that coordinated efforts with the assistant secretary of defense for civil rights.[61]

Not all, though, were willing to cooperate. Much of the military's officer corps, regardless of branch, rejected the idea outright. Some questioned whether the armed forces had the authority or the social right to get involved in the affairs of a local community. And some believed it was unfair to place these additional duties on base commanders. This included some civilian leaders of the military who were champions of civil rights reform. The most noteworthy was Secretary of the Air Force Eugene Zuckert, who had served as a willing foot soldier in Secretary of the Air Force Stuart Symington's quest to racially integrate the branch during the Truman administration. It was not the issue of civil rights reform that he objected to; it was the methodology of tasking Air Force commanders, who largely objected to this new role, with implementing changes off base. Better, he reasoned, to wait until legislation was passed, such as the civil rights bill pending in Congress. In the face of such steep resistance, the department retreated and declared that sanctions to be applied only when all other methods had failed and that they required the approval of the secretary of defense before going into place.[62]

THE TOTALITARIAN NATURE OF IT ALL

Shortly after the release of Gesell Committee's report, Southern Democrats and conservative Republicans denounced vigorously its recommendations. The ranking majority member of the House Armed Services Committee, Lucius Mendel Rivers, a Democrat from South Carolina, the first state to secede from the Union, was aghast. The report was "inflammatory, vicious, and extremely prejudiced . . . [and] . . . will seriously affect if not destroy the combat efficiency of your Armed Forces." Channeling the firebrands of his home state's radical past, the South Carolinian forewarned that the ideas of the Gesell Report would "destroy the morale of our Armed Forces and will do more to divide the singleness of purpose of our Armed Forces than the fall of Fort Sumter in 1861, and I know something about that, if you catch the point." Exasperated by the role this would play in segregated communities surrounding military bases, Rivers's Democratic colleague from Louisiana, Felix Edward Hébert, chimed in that "this is a scythe held over the head of every community, the everlasting sword of Damocles over its economic future and its survival." Moving quickly from recounting tales of Greco-Roman tragedy to those of the growing communist menace within the country, he believed that this was "the beginning of the police state and the commissar program in America, the United States of America." "Mr Speaker, God forbid that we have an OGPU [the predecessor to the KGB] or an SS [the Nazi Schutzstaffel] in our military," Durward Gorham Hall, a Republican representative from Missouri, observed. Many agreed with the statements made by Democratic representative John James Flynt Jr. of Georgia:

The recommendation contained in this report would seem to have come more from a totalitarian group such as existed in Germany between 1933 and 1945 under the Government headed by one Hitler, the head of the Nazi party, and contemporaneously the head of the German Government. It would appear more likely to have come from a Communist totalitarian government whereby the Armed Forces of the nation might be used to destroy rather than to protect individuals and citizens and the rights and liberties of its citizens.

Democratic representative Alton Lennon of North Carolina also agreed that it reminded him of the dastardly actions of the Third Reich. "They go into a community and put a swastika on the window and say you don't cross these doors, its off limits." The inflammatory language demonizing the actions as totalitarian continued when McNamara issued his directive to try and carry out the Gesell Committee's recommendations. The *Augusta Herald* called the

McNamara directive "Hitler-like" while also alleging "it is a barefaced exhibition of Stalinism, because it brings into our Armed Forces at last the Soviet function of the political commissar." Attempting to trump its crosstown rival in the demagoguery department, the *Augusta Chronicle* assailed the directive this way: "Worse still, if that be possible, is the almost complete lack of concern the Committee evidences for the irreparable harm that can befall the Nation as a result of its socialistic and unholy presentments."[63]

Words quickly turned into political action. Carl Vinson, Democratic representative from Georgia and chair of the House Armed Services Committee, was not going to stand for any meddling from the DOD into Southern affairs. In a statement to the press that upheld the totalitarian fears of his colleagues, Vinson warned that "if it is social reform today, it may be direct participation in national elections tomorrow; if it is race today, it could be religion tomorrow." He schemed to attack the problem at the source. In this case, the best way to get at McNamara politically and force him to reconsider was to punish commanders who carried out his marching orders. Vinson attempted to pass a bill that would court-martial any base commander trying to implement the directive, an endeavor that would have circumvented the entire military chain command, let alone the power of the president. Though his effort failed, Vinson's endeavor to halt the civil rights directive demonstrated the steely resolve of segregationists who believed the whole episode to be outrageous and an unlawful use of the military as a tool for social justice, which as a byproduct threated the very mission of the institution and transformed it, in their fearful estimation, into something akin to a political police force reminiscent of those found in totalitarian states.[64]

As Vinson and others in the House thrashed away at the DOD, Southern senators joined their Southern colleagues and Republican conservatives in the lower chamber in denouncing what they considered to be a blatant violation of the rights of man. "It has been apparent for some time that the more extreme exponents of revolutionary civil rights actions have wanted to use the military in a position of leadership to bring about desegregation outside the boundaries of the military bases, and have desired that the full economic weight of military bases be manipulated by the base commander to reverse local laws, customs, and policies," the long-tenured Democratic senator from Mississippi, John C. Stennis, believed.[65]

Echoing the era of Reconstruction, Georgia Democrat Herman Talmadge proclaimed that the McNamara directive was "strangely reminiscent of the orders in Reconstruction days when the South was occupied by troops and was divided into military districts under troop commanders who exercised authority in those areas." Furthermore, the Georgian declared: "We live in a nation of law, and not of man, and certainly not under a military dictatorship." The attempt to redress civil rights off base also caught the attention of the chairman of the Senate Foreign Relations Committee, Democrat J. William Fulbright of Arkansas. The Arkansan agreed with his Southern segregationist colleagues in the Senate that the actions of the Department of Defense were akin to the dark days of Reconstruction:

I am aware of the fact that the military departments have used the off-limits sanction to safeguard the health and welfare of personnel, and do not question the propriety of limited use of this power. The directive appears to go far beyond this normal and limited use, to make it the affirmative duty of military commanders to seek changes in local custom or even laws, in one of the most delicate and sensitive areas of our national life, putting the military back in the business of "educating" or even coercing the public. There are many defects in our society, I agree . . . but the cure for these social defects is not [the] use of the military, either by force or the threat of boycott.

Once Fulbright's appeals to reason gained no traction, he and his Southern colleagues attempted to block McNamara's directive, but their efforts failed.[66]

WHEN IN DOUBT, BLAME THE STAFF

Segregationists and conservatives in Congress sought other scapegoats to blame for the policy other than Gesell Committee or McNamara. Often they pinned blame for the directive on Alfred Fitt and Adam Yarmolinsky, who they held responsible for boondoggling the armed forces. Citing an article from the *Washington Star*, Senator Stennis cast Fitt, the assistant secretary of defense for civil rights, as a liberal meddler who was out to put his stamp on the affairs of the department. According to the article, Fitt had remarked: "I came over to this building [the Department of the Army] because I was excited at the prospect of doing something about eliminating discrimination in the Army. Now I will have a chance to do this throughout the whole Defense establishment." This was proof for Southern segregationists of Fitt's unholy role in this endeavor. Concurring with his senatorial colleague that something foul was going on in the Department of Defense was Republican senator Barry Goldwater of Arizona. The Southwesterner was an anti–New Deal and probusiness conservative who despised unions and sought to privatize Social Security; he was no stranger to the occasional mingling with those who believed in the conspiratorial, and on occasion he dabbled in it himself. Fitt was not alone in his actions, Goldwater warned. He had a powerful and dangerous accomplice: Adam Yarmolinsky. The Arizonan declared his "full support to a complete investigation into Mr. Fitt and Mr. Yarmolinsky and other persons in the Pentagon who are forcing Secretary McNamara—I am convinced against his will—to take this dangerous step," he told his colleagues. In September, Senator Strom Thurmond of South Carolina, citing the *Shreveport Journal*, confirmed and supported Goldwater's conspiratorial accusations. According to the paper: "The man who authored the Defense Department Directive . . . is none other than Adam Yarmolinsky."[67]

Throughout his tenure in the Kennedy and Johnson administrations, Yarmolinsky faced the same fate as Anna Rosenberg and Maxwell Rabb, and the intellectual and civil rights defender from the Northeast became a convenient target for powerful and vocal conservatives in American society. The right-wing conservative radioman and journalist Fulton Lewis Jr. attacked McNamara's failure to conduct a thorough background check of his special assistant, a man who "was a Vice-President of the notorious Fund for the Republic, in charge of its Washington operations, and unless Mr. McNamara is very stupid indeed, he must know that the Fund for the Republic is the most anti-anti-communist organization in the country." The Fund for the Republic, which Lewis and his right-wing audience feared religiously, had been established by the Ford Foundation in 1952. The purpose of the foundation was to examine the impact of the Cold War on American civil liberties. During the Second Red Scare and the assault on liberalism waged by Republican senator Joseph P. McCarthy of Wisconsin, the efforts of the group—which were diametrically opposite of the actions of the Wisconsin senator—came under the watchful eye of dyed-in-the-wool conservatives who sought to cast the foundation as sinister, corrupt, and possibly communistic. A decade later, Lewis, a longtime enemy of the Fund for the Republic, continued his offensive against the group, his sights set on slandering Yarmolinsky.[68]

So desperate were Yarmolinsky's political enemies to smear him that they often choose to attack the character of his parents. Conspiratorial peddlers such as Lewis uncovered what they alleged was the Yarmolinsky family's stained communist past. Yarmolinsky's father, Dr. Avrahm Yarmolinsky, was a Russian literature scholar who had received his doctorate from Columbia University. He had spent most of his career working for the New York Public Library as head of its Slavonic Department. His career represented that of an expert in Russia literature and culture, not that of an underhanded communist sympathizer and agitator. Neither was his mother a secret communist agent. Dr. Babette Deutsch was a renowned poet, a peace advocate, and politically active, all while educating the students at Columbia University on the finer aspects of poetry. According to Lewis, though, these were mere covers, as both "were affiliated with the subversive John Reed Club in 1930." John Reed Clubs were named after their namesake, John Reed, a member of one of the most preeminent families in a Portland, Oregon. But instead of following the ways of the elite American aristocracy of the Pacific Northwest, Reed pursued the ways of Karl Marx and Vladimir Ilych Lenin and the quest to raise the communist proletariat to great heights in its battle against the bourgeoise, the captains of capitalist industry. The clubs that eventually emerged from the 1920s through the 1930s bearing his name by way of its literary arm, *New Masses*, would serve to help bring the message of the communist revolution to America. By linking Yarmolinsky's parents to groups like the John Reed Clubs and more,[69] Lewis essentially argued that the apple does not fall too far from the tree to paint Adam Yarmolinsky as a red disciple.[70]

The slandering and scapegoating of a prominent and well-educated Jewish family such as the Yarmolinskys, resonated in anticommunist communities throughout the country, critically so in the South. As it decried the audacity of the Gesell Report, the Plaquemines Parish Commission Council in Pointe à la Hache, Louisiana, also went after Yarmolinsky and his parents:

"The Gesell Report" . . . implemented by a Department of Defense directive, written by one Adam Yarmolinsky, son of Avirhim [*sic*] Yarmolinsky and Babette Deutsch, both members of record of the John Reed Communist Club, would extend the "lateral" political control system of the United States military by putting "trained" individuals with bi-racial staffs skilled in dealing with racial discriminations with additional expert consultants in racial problems, with the right to negro personnel to make secret anonymous complaints against superior officers and post commanders, and encourage them to go over the heads of their superior officers and to make such anonymous complaints against their Military Officers to Civilian Agents of the Defense Department. . . . This Gesell-Yarmolinsky Report and military directive would surrender the Nation's military to systematic harassment and persecution by a Communist dominated NAACP . . . so that in the not too distant future, all semblance of discipline, morale and organization in our Country's Military would be destroyed, and our military potential and national defense so weakened as to endanger our National security, and make this Country an easy prey to world communism, all in accordance with the Stalin plan that finally, the last [bastion] of Capitalism, the United States of America, would fall into their hands without firing a shot . . . [i.e., Khrushchev's] threat that they would "bury us."

Perhaps the most disdainful opinion[71] from the conservative point of view on

Yarmolinsky's character and trustworthiness came from Democratic congressmen Felix Edward Hébert of Louisiana: "He has what I think is a satanic-like zeal to force these things (integration) upon an unwilling people."[72]

Whether the Southern red-baiting accusations against the Kennedy administration's staffers had any real merit was not the point. It was part of a larger strategy that included Southern threats to restrict military funding, questioned the proper role of the defense department, and even threatened to court-martial those who acted in support of McNamara's directive. While their successes perhaps bought some time, Southerners along with some conservative republicans continued to rely on their strategy of demagoguery to fend off change on base and off base.[73]

"GOING INTO NUT COUNTRY"

On June 11, 1963, after the events surrounding the racial desegregation of the University of Alabama, which relied heavily on the president's involvement, Kennedy addressed the American people on the need for civil rights reform. For many, it constituted his best and perhaps most sincere plea for the nation to finally come to grips with the sinister shadow of its past. In it, Kennedy spoke of a topic he had focused the most on: the impact racism had on Americans of all races fighting abroad against communism. But this time, the Cold War was not the main reason for action. He returned in the speech to a subject he had touched upon during his presidential debates with Nixon back in 1960—namely, the statistical realities of African Americans living under the grim systemic racism of Jim Crow. In June 1963, the issue was not just about America triumphing over the threat of global communism but the threat racism posed to the nation's future. To avoid the prospect of that dismal tomorrow, the president believed that the future of America required all its children to have the equal opportunity to grow:

This is one county. It has become one country because all of us and all the people who came here had an equal chance to develop their talents. We cannot say to 10 percent of the population that you can't have that right; that your children can't have the chance to develop whatever talents they have; that the only way that they are going to get their rights is to go into the streets and demonstrate. I think we owe them and we owe ourselves a better country than that. . . . As I have said before, not every child has an equal talent or an equal ability or an equal motivation, but they should have the equal right to develop their talent and their ability and their motivation, to make something of themselves.

In the end, it seemed that Kennedy had finally abandoned his political, coldly calculated cautiousness to embrace the emotional morality of the moment: "We are confronted primarily with a moral issue. It is as old as the scriptures and is as clear as the American Constitution." It was a critical moment for the president on an issue that he had struggled with throughout his presidency. It proved to be short-lived.[74]

Months later, and with his civil rights package making its way through Congress, where racist Southern segregationists eagerly waited to decimate and weaken it, Kennedy found himself in Texas, once again on the campaign trail. During the early hours of November 22, 1963, the president observed wearily to his wife, Jackie Kennedy: "We're heading into nut country today." His rebuke of the Dallas–Fort Worth region was not without some measure of justification, as it had become a haven of right-wing Republican politics, an area that aided in the overall creation of the "Southern Strategy" that Richard Nixon would later capitalize on.[75]

It also did not shy away from embracing the conspiratorial. An avid consumer of the news, the president had just finished perusing that day's copy of the *Dallas Morning News*, which sported an ad from an ultra–right wing anticommunist organization, the John Birch Society. The group touted the economic successes of the region because of its conservative values while simultaneously admonishing Kennedy for his communist-like actions as president. The Birchers and their fanatical claims were no stranger to the president or his administration. A year prior, the Kennedy administration had clashed during the racial integration of the University of Mississippi with one of the Birchers' most ardent followers, the retired general Edwin Walker, whose fight to keep Ole Miss segregated, endeared him with Southern segregationists and conspiracy theorists alike.[76]

The story of Walker is a complicated and confounding one, but the former World War II veteran, who at one point had aided in the racial integration of Little Rock High School, had fallen from grace by the early 1960s, as he had been caught distributing anticommunist material, including material steeped in the conspiratorial tenets of the John Birch Society, to members of his military command in Europe. This type of activity was verboten in the armed forces and ultimately led to his trial and his decision to resign his commission. From that point on, he became a rising star of the radical right. Whether the

Birchers' article reminded Kennedy of the altercation with Walker is unclear; more likely, the president, according to Edward Miller, was thinking about Ted Dealey, publisher of the *Dallas Morning News*, at that moment. Nonetheless, Kennedy went into "nut country" to win over hearts and minds for his reelection. The result was far, far different; he was assassinated by Lee Harvey Oswald hours later.[77]

In the moments following the president's death, several machinations of government kicked into gear, including the somber and peaceful transfer of power to a Texan, who had grown up just south of Dallas in the scenic Hill Country, Lyndon B. Johnson. But it also meant the transportation and guarding of the president's body as it returned to the White House to lay in repose. There it met with an unmistakable irony. Though his time as a civil rights leader and reformer in the military was inconsistent and often noncommittal, Kennedy had, nonetheless, on the rare occasion, acted. On his first day on the job, the president had laid into the Coast Guard Academy for lacking a splash of racial color during the inaugural parade. Now, at the end of his presidency and life, the same man was guarded by a group of racially integrated American military personnel. With his death, Kennedy, imagery, and the racial integration of the armed forces had come full circle.

THE JOHNSON TREATMENT

"Congress," Lyndon Johnson wryly observed to biographer Doris Kearns Goodwin, "is like a dangerous animal that you're trying to make work for you. You push him a little bit and he may go just as you want but you push too much and he may balk and turn on you. You've got to sense just how much he'll take and what kind of mood he's in every day. For if you don't have a feel for him, he's liable to turn around and go wild. And it all depends on your sense of timing." Timing, though critical, was not always enough for Johnson to get the job done. The former Senate Majority Leader, vice president, and now president, through blatant manipulation, in acts of persuasion often referred to as the "Johnson treatment," emotionally and spiritually cudgeled Southern segregationists in Congress into submission on the issue of civil rights reform:

I knew that as President I couldn't make people want to integrate their schools or open their doors to blacks, but I could make them feel guilty for not doing it and I believed it was my moral responsibility to do precisely that—to use the moral suasion of my office to make people feel that segregation was a curse they'd carry with them to their graves.

John F. Kennedy in repose at the White House: The recently slain President John F. Kennedy returns to the East Room of the White House to lay in repose. In a moment of irony, the military honor guard that shepherded him into the room and stood post was racially integrated. November 23, 1963. Source: ST-C415-3-63, Digital Identifier: JFKWHP-1963-11-23-B. White House Photographs. John F. Kennedy Presidential Library and Museum, Boston.

To play on the emotional heartstrings of Southern segregationists, he not only shamed them into action; he blatantly used the image of the dead president to do so. Five days after the president's death, and one day before Thanksgiving, Johnson gave an address that was both eulogy and call to action, directed at the American people but also to his Southern friends and rivals in Congress:

We meet in grief, but let us also meet in renewed dedication and renewed vigor. Let us meet in action, in tolerance, and in mutual understanding. John Kennedy's death commands what his life conveyed—that America must move forward. The time has come for Americans of all races and creeds and political beliefs to understand and to respect one another. So let us put an end to the teaching and the preaching of hate and evil and violence. Let us turn away from the fanatics of the far left and the far right, from the apostles of bitterness and bigotry, from those defiant of law, and those who pour venom into our Nation's bloodstream.

I profoundly hope that the tragedy and the torment of these terrible days will bind us together in new fellowship, making us one people in our hour of sorrow. So let us here highly resolve that John Fitzgerald Kennedy did not live—or die—in vain.

The speech was quintessentially Johnson, rife with shame, hope, and patriotism—and he was at the center of it all.[78]

But Johnson knew that he had to move beyond just moral rationales or guilt to get things going. And that was why he used the Cold War to also make his case. His rationale for doing so was sound. The United States Information Agency was providing the incoming president with analysis that reminded him that the eyes and ears of the world remained fixated on the issue of civil rights in America. Instead of lamenting the problem, the avid legislative dealmaker seized upon the issue of American imagery during the Cold War to remind segregationists in Congress who sought to block his civil rights package that uplifting Blacks brought with it more than domestic prosperity and harmony; it also strengthened and enriched the nation's international image during the Cold War. In a sense, he was offering segregationists in Congress a justification for action: waging the Cold War and defeating godless communism. Johnson's methods, though questionable, were no less effective and netted the passage of the Civil Rights Act of 1964 and the Voting Rights Act of 1965. Though directly connected, his achievements in the civilian arena often mask what was also achieved in the military, which was equally impressive and often completed efforts that began and became mired during the Kennedy era.[79]

DESEGREGATING THE NATIONAL GUARD

"There are things here that are just not right," exclaimed the president of the University of Notre Dame and member of the US Civil Rights Commission, Father Theodore Hesburgh, to President John F. Kennedy. According to Hesburgh's sources, the Alabama National Guard, which resided in a Black Belt Southern state with a large African American population, did not have any Black soldiers among its ranks. Hesburgh's information was accurate; National Guard units not only in Alabama but also throughout the United States operated predominately in a racially segregated fashion, sometimes with no Blacks among the ranks at all. The issue was a holdover from the Truman administration that had never gained any serious traction toward reform likely because of the complexity of the state versus federal nature of the National Guard.[80]

A dozen years later, the racial segregation of the National Guard, which ran afoul of Executive Order 9981 and, for that matter, President Kennedy's efforts to rid the United States of negative racial imagery that could fuel Russian propagandists, remained a problem. But for Kennedy it was a problem for another day. The president believed that now was not the time to act: "Look, Father . . . I may have to send the Alabama National Guard to Berlin tomorrow and I don't want to have to do it in the middle of a revolution at home." Civil rights leaders such as Hesburgh were not surprised. It was a classic pragmatic, but no less cold, Kennedy response, almost on parallel with his brother Robert Kennedy's comments to Dr. Martin Luther King Jr. and others during the climatic conclusion of the Freedom Rides when the younger Kennedy was forced to dispatch United States Marshals to First Baptist Church in Montgomery, Alabama, to protect those protesting the violence the activists had faced. Both moments were about image and American foreign policy; morality and the equitable treatment of others need not apply.[81]

Though Kennedy was reluctant to do so, civil rights advocates kept after him on the issue of racially integrating the National Guard. In a letter to the president, Roy Wilkins said that racial exclusion in the branch was "humiliating" for Blacks and that "the disregard of the potential of trained Negro American manpower comes very close to being sabotage of the national interest."[82] In order to resolve the situation, Wilkins suggested that Kennedy withhold funding from Guard units unwilling to integrate. To its credit, the NAACP aided in the eventual integration of the Guard in Missouri and Texas, but it was not the sea change the organization had hoped for throughout the country.[83]

Pressure to act was also heaped on the president by the American Veterans Committee (AVC), which wrote to Robert McNamara in December 1962 about the issue. In 1962, the Guard was going through a restructuring; the planned change, the AVC believed, was a window of opportunity for the racial transformation of the branch: "The American Veterans Committee calls on you to use your authority to its fullest extent and your good offices in areas to which federal authority does not reach in order to make the reorganization a vehicle for integration wherever possible." Sometimes the pressure to act came directly from frustrated African American personnel, such as the artillery commander Captain James Johnson Jr., who wrote to the president complaining about the lack of opportunity he found leaving the active military for the Reserves. As he relayed to the president, it took some time before he had found a unit in Jacksonville, Florida, that would accept him. After that struggle, Johnson got tougher in his war for equality in the Guard. He faced a Guard that offered little opportunity for Black personnel; the "social club" nature of the organization ostracized him because of his skin color, and Johnson was punished for speaking out against the blatant segregation that existed within it by being transferred to a paratrooper outfit. Though he pleaded for Kennedy to act, Johnson planned to take it in stride, just as so many of his race had done before him, to prove his dedication to the country he loved: "Mr. President, I have no desire to jump from an airplane and even less because someone else desires it. Nevertheless, I will, because I am very pleased to be allowed to serve with this unit even though the assignment has another injustice [in mind]."[84]

While outside groups and individuals sought to pressure the president into action, the Department of Defense, which would ultimately be responsible for carrying out any reforms, opted for a less confrontational approach. Instead of forcing the issue, it attempted to persuade the Guard to voluntarily integrate. The department had a reason to rely on voluntary integration: jurisdiction. The Guard was both a federal and a state body. Many leaders within the federal government—including those at the Pentagon, most notably Assistant Secretary of Defense of Manpower and Personnel Carlisle Runge—along with racial segregationists within the states that hosted Jim Crow Guard units, argued that the government could not do anything to change the racial makeup of the branch unless it was called up to federal duty, which led to an important question: What would happen when that call-up concluded and the federal government restored power over the Guard back to the states?[85]

With little leadership or progress emerging during the Kennedy years, the National Guard remained a bastion of racial exclusion when LBJ came to office. But reform was on the horizon. In November 1964, the Gesell Committee presented Johnson with its final report, an account that included the investigation of racism at overseas military installations and examined the racist practices of the National Guard; of the two issues, the examination of the Guard took precedence. While the committee wanted to avoid generalizing—as the actions of one Guard unit in one part of a state did not reflect those in another—it was clear that the organization overall was continuing to racially discriminate. The ability to serve in the National Guard was an opportunity that all Americans should have, the committee asserted. To deny African Americans this chance was unfair and unjust. Furthermore, the committee noted, once a Guard unit was federalized it was amalgamated with an active-duty component, which meant that all-white units would be mixed with integrated active-duty units. If whites in the Guard did not learn how to work alongside Black soldiers, the cohesiveness of the force would be impaired when it was called to action. As with its first report, the committee believed that voluntary means should be utilized to encourage the Guard to racially integrate; however, if that failed to net the desired result, the president—now possessing the power granted under the Civil Rights Act of 1964—should use sanctions on nonintegrated Guard units. To figure out who was racially integrated and who was not, the committee suggested that the Department of Defense collect statistical data from all states to ascertain how many African American soldiers were serving in their respective state's Guard.[86]

Overall, the committee felt that the president needed to make the issue national in focus and to avoid partisanship if possible; the issue had to be sold to the American people as necessary for the well-being of the nation. However, while Johnson supported the idea of racially integrating the National Guard, he never made a sweeping declaration on the matter. Instead, Johnson decided to allow the Pentagon to continue to handle the matter. And perhaps it was not necessary for him to get involved directly after all. Since the inception of the Gesell Committee and its investigation into discrimination in the Guard, ten Black Belt states had racially integrated their units; for these, the body's presence was catalyst enough. As the Gesell Committee had predicted, the passage of new civil rights legislation became a powerful tool against racial segregation within the Guard. Under the auspices of Title VI of the Civil Rights Act of 1964, which prohibited the use of federal funds in any manner that discriminated, the Department of Defense now had the legal ability to force change in the organization. In early 1965, the department compelled the parent organizations of the Guard—the Army and the Air Force—to draw up new regulations that halted racial discrimination within the Guard. Slowly, the National Guard began to racially integrate its forces by the end of 1965.[87]

CLOSING THE DEAL: OFF-BASE HOUSING REFORM

In 1963, the DOD had requested that the respective branches of the armed forces submit reports on incidents of off-base racial discrimination. A year later, Alfred Fitt shared the report's conclusions with Lee White, the White House counsel. Overall, the report provided a justification for further off-base activity in areas such as housing that still haunted African American personnel. As Fitt observed to White: "Wherever [base] commanders have acted affirmatively on behalf of their men, positive, beneficial results have been obtained . . . no matter how rigidly segregated or tension-ridden the local civilian community."[88] In some cases, if a base commander simply inquired into the manner, that was often enough to compel businesses and schools to begin racially integrating immediately. What were the motives of those commanders who acted? They acted for the same reasons that they did during the Kennedy administration: it was the right thing to do for their command and men. Why did civilians, including Southern segregationists, listen? They recognized that base commanders wielded incredible economic power, a weapon that could cut and slash away at the economic prosperity of those communities surrounding bases. The report also demonstrated that the fear among some leaders within the armed forces and politicians that using the military for reform off base would likely end up in unleashing hostility was unfounded. The "affirmative anti-discrimination efforts by commanders have nowhere generated hostility or controversy in military-civilian relationships," the report declared. There was great potential here, Fitt insisted to White; the administration just needed to harness it. However, political needs temporarily trumped further reform off base. Fitt was informed by the White House to put a lid on further civil rights activities until after the passage of the Civil Rights Act of 1964. After its passage, the department was again told to halt its civil rights activities until after the 1964 presidential election.[89]

While the Johnson administration waited for the political stars to align before pursuing further reform, other civil rights groups continued to demonstrate why change was needed. One such entity was the American Friends Service Committee (AFSC), which operated in Washington, DC. In its report "Negro Military Servicemen and Racial Discrimination in Housing," the AFSC detailed the fluid nature of military life, in which a soldier and his family remained continuously on the go, moving from one area of the country to another; in some cases they were forced to find housing off base. The AFSC observed that many civilians had capitalized on the need for off-base housing by renting homes or apartments to soldiers. In what should have been a bounty of available housing, African Americans were excluded. Since the department had failed to act, African American military personnel had been forced to live in the poorest sections of towns in substandard, dilapidated housing. Some even had to drive incredible distances just to get to their base: "One Negro airman at Andrews AFB still, after three months, is being forced to drive 104 miles *daily* between his mobile home and the base because he cannot find a court in a closer location that will rent a space to him." The situation had to be resolved. And the only way to resolve the issue was to empower base commanders. The belief was that base commanders should give priority to African Americans and their families when it came time to find available on-base housing. In addition to this change, the AFSC suggested that more nondiscriminatory off-base housing should be leased by the military. Finally, base commanders should utilize the economic power of their position by prohibiting any member under their command from renting or buying a house from any business or individual practicing racial discrimination.[90]

Since the Eisenhower administration, African American military personnel had been waiting for reform in off-base housing. And to be sure, Johnson, who had been Senate Majority Leader during the Eisenhower years, was aware of it. In a 1966 speech, Johnson noted the importance of providing equal housing for Black personnel: "Negro Americans comprise 22% of the enlisted men in our Army combat units in Vietnam—and 22% of those who have lost their lives in battle there. We fall victim to a profound hypocrisy when we say that they cannot buy or rent dwellings among citizens they fight to save."[91] One year later, the wait for reform ended. In 1967, the Department of Defense sent out a survey to thirteen communities—including one in Washington, DC—designed to gauge the troubles facing African American military personnel in their search for suitable housing off base. Not surprisingly, the survey showed that the Department of Defense's past reliance on civilian volunteerism had been ineffective.[92]

While McNamara digested the report's conclusion, a group known as the Action Coordinating Committee to End Segregation in the Suburbs (ACCESS) staged a sit-down demonstration in his office. For years, McNamara had been consumed by his quest to transform the lethargic and inefficient Department of Defense. Throughout, he had often been inconsistent on racial integration of the armed forces, often letting Yarmolinsky take the reins. McNamara, though, would not pass the buck on this issue and took full responsibility for his failure to act. In 1967, the Secretary of Defense observed "there are thousands of our Negro troops, returning from Vietnam, who are being discriminated against in off-base housing. . . . The Negro serviceman has been loyal and responsible to his country. But the People of his country have failed in their loyalty and responsibility to him." It seemed that the failure of his early housing programs, the ACCESS protest, and the thought of Black soldiers, who he had a direct responsibility to, all had come to weigh heavily on his conscience.[93]

Now prepared to act, McNamara ordered Deputy Secretary of Defense Cyrus Vance to order the military conduct a fact-finding mission on the availability of off-base housing surrounding military installations that contained a minimum of 500 servicemen. Next, McNamara dispatched Assistant Secretary of Defense for Manpower Thomas D. Morris to tackle the issue as it applied to the available off-base housing surrounding the nation's capital. With incoming reports showing that the situations off base were bleak, McNamara prohibited all servicemen from staying in any rental or lease-based housing that practiced racial discrimination. It was not, however, a national embargo on housing, as McNamara anticipated that some communities, fearing the economic fallout of being blacklisted by the Department of Defense, would comply and thereby end racial discrimination in off-base housing. He also expected some to refuse to reform. To show he was serious, McNamara relied on the threat of sanctions. Once word got out that he was willing to use sanctions, the Secretary of Defense believed that the rest of the communities would snap in line behind the department's wishes. He justified his actions by claiming that racial discrimination against Black personnel had an adverse effect on them and thus affected the efficiency of the military during the Cold War. After leveling sanctions on the civilian community surrounding Andrews Air Force Base, which was located in Maryland, he argued that the inability of Black Vietnam veterans to find off-base housing was sapping the morale and impairing the "effectiveness of the base."[94]

By early September, McNamara threatened to expand his program of sanctions to include all bases within US borders. Along with sanctions, housing referral offices sprung up on military installations throughout the country. This simple yet effective program ordered all servicemen who were married to consult with and receive permission from referral offices before they sought off-base housing. In this fashion, these offices could prevent soldiers of both races from even looking into an apartment complexes or real estate firms that practiced racial discrimination.[95]

In late December, Fitt, who had replaced Morris as chief of manpower, informed McNamara that his new approach to civil rights reform in housing was paying off. According to the data, the amount of housing for African American soldiers nationwide had gone from 59 percent to 73 percent. In fact, Maryland and Virginia, where McNamara first launched his campaign to address racism in off-base housing, had demonstrated significant change: "Maryland has risen from 5,600 open units (4%) to 39,400 (27%)," and "Northern Virginia has risen from 9,100 open units (10%) to 33,400 (36%)."[96] An area of special concern for the secretary of defense was California, which over the years had proven to be a hot spot of racism in housing, but it was also demonstrating some growth: "California's open [housing] units have grown from 206,100 (71%) to 253,800 (83%). [Housing] Listings have increased from 37,300 (13%) to 147,500 (51%)." While the department had made great strides, it would ultimately have to continue the integration of off-base housing without its chief. In the spring of 1966, McNamara had begun to express reservations about American involvement in Vietnam, which he was considerably responsible for. The war no longer seemed worth the blood and treasure that the nation was expending on it, and

McNamara now felt that America's efforts in Vietnam were only hurting its ability to halt communist expansion.[97]

With McNamara out, Johnson turned to the ever-capable Clark Clifford to run the Defense Department. After taking office, Clifford, who had advised Harry Truman in his famous upset victory over Thomas Dewey in 1948 and had been instrumental in the creation of Executive Order 9981, made his intentions as the new secretary of defense clear. On the twentieth anniversary of Truman's racial integration of the armed forces, the defense chief declared that extraordinary progress had occurred in the military. Yet racial discrimination in off-base housing was having "a corrosive and damaging impact on Black Americans wearing this country's uniform," Clifford lamented. In order to address this situation, he was "determined to push forward with our campaign to achieve 100 per cent housing justice for all servicemen."[98]

Clifford had an advantage in the fight for equality in off-base housing that his predecessor, McNamara, did not: the passage of the Civil Rights Act of 1968. For several years, the Johnson administration had labored to push through Congress an act that would provide African Americans with a chance at fair and equal housing. In addition, the Supreme Court's decision in *Jones v. Mayer* (1968) upheld the government's ability to prohibit businesses from practicing racial discrimination while trying to sell or rent a home. With legislative and judicial momentum providing a terrific tailwind at his back, Clifford ordered Fitt to come up with a plan that expanded upon McNamara's earlier reforms. First, the DOD under Clifford continued to use sanctions against offenders that racially discriminated against military personnel. But now the DOD would also provide advice and legal council to service personnel facing racism in housing. The Department of Defense additionally worked closely with the Justice Department and Department of Housing and Urban Development to seek out nondiscriminatory housing for Black military personnel. By the close of 1968, a new set of statistics emerged from the Department of Defense. According to the data, there were now 1.17 million homes and apartments available to rent for all members of the armed forces. Though the problem of racism in housing would continue for years to come, the dramatic gains of 1968 for military personnel demonstrated a marked shift in how the DOD handled the issue.[99]

CONTINUED REFORM IN THE VA

Since the 1950s, the VA hospital system had operated in a racially integrated manner and included a sizeable African American contingent among its employees. During the Johnson administration, the organization built upon these accomplishments. VA recruiters traveled across America, including stops at Historically Black Colleges and Universities, to recruit the best and the brightest that the Black community had to offer. This was an important development for civil rights advocates, as it showed the VA's determination to hire African Americans for upper-level positions as opposed to just hiring them for menial work. By the mid-1960s, *Ebony* magazine was willing to declare the VA the "Government's Most Integrated Agency." Indeed, "by the end of FY [fiscal year] 1968, Negroes made up 25.99 per cent of the total VA employment." Considering that the VA was "the Federal Government's third largest employer," the achievements of the organization during the 1960s were impressive.[100]

An important subject for all veterans was benefits. Not all veterans had access to existing benefits. For example, various requirements, such as time in service, type of service, and so on, determined whether or not one received aid from the VA. This was a problem for all veterans from the era of the Korean War onward. In 1966 and 1967, President Johnson signed two acts that worked in tandem to address this issue. The Veterans' Readjustment Benefits Act of 1966—it became known as the Cold War GI Bill—focused on Korean War era veterans; and a year later, the Veterans' Pension and Readjustment Assistance Act of 1967 expanded the coverage of the Cold War GI Bill to include those serving during the Vietnam War. Prior to signing the 1966 act into law, Johnson vacillated over whether he would sign the bill. His hesitation was not because he objected to helping veterans but because the president, a master of political calculus, believed that he could have likely achieved the same results without having to ask Congress—which was already funding the war in Vietnam and the Great Society—for more money. As he explained: "I had felt that we could start the new GI program, and that we should, by providing special funds for soldiers who served in combat areas . . . [fund] others . . . through the Higher Education Act. . . . In that way . . . we would not ask for more than we could get, or bite off more than we could chew in educational costs." In the end, Johnson signed both, which opened benefits to millions of veterans.[101]

This was critical moment for the nation's veterans, but it also did something else. When considering the history of the G.I. Bill, it becomes clear that the Cold War iteration was arguably the first true G.I. Bill for the African American soldier. The racism of the 1940s and 1950s had largely prevented Blacks from consistently claiming the benefits provided by the first G.I. Bill, especially in the prickly area of housing.[102] During the Johnson era, African American personnel came to enjoy access to benefits that had been prohibited from them for decades. And as Johnson observed, it was a chance to give back to those who served and were serving the country, regardless of race or gender. "We are saying to the brave Americans who serve us in uniform, in camps and bases, in villages and jungles, that your country is behind you; that we support you; that you serve us in time of danger."[103]

The administration also expanded benefit programs that aided veterans' children. The War Orphans Education Assistance Program, which was originally designed to provide funding to the children of deceased World War II and Korean War veterans, was expanded by the administration to include soldiers fighting in Vietnam. Moreover, the administration modified the program to also include children whose parents had been "totally and permanently disabled" during warfare or through a training accident. Intended for young adults aged eighteen to twenty-six, the program covered four years of education. By late 1968, the program was now considered to be a "scholarship," which meant that it became tax-free. Although not specifically designed to cater to African American soldiers, this program ensured that Black children whose parents were either killed or permanently injured still had an opportunity for social advancement.[104]

CONCLUSION

The nature of the dilemmas that the Kennedy and Johnson administrations faced, whether it was the Cold War, the conflict in Vietnam, persistent poverty, or the growing power of a vocal but splintering civil rights movement, has ensured that they are historically examined in conjunction. But all pretenses of similarities between the two presidents disappear when examining how they handled these situations. For the issue of racial integration and continued racial reform of the armed forces, this matters greatly. While both were aware of the damage that racial segregation and continued racism caused the Republic in its battle with global communism, Kennedy remained fixated on repairing any such disparity in the armed forces quickly and superficially. And when one considers the Freedom Riders episode, he wanted to do this in civilian realm as well. Thus, if there were no Black cadets in Coast Guard Academy, or if there were no Blacks in the honor guards of the armed forces, both need to get some because of the damage it did to the image of Kennedy's administration and to that of the nation.

The deeper issues of systemic racism that allowed for continued racial problems on base and off base were not truly addressed by Kennedy; instead, to duck any political fallout, he allowed his staffers, who were gifted and capable people sensitive to the issue, to press for change. Despite their goodwill and marginal successes, they lacked the clout of the presidency to drive change and reform. For Kennedy to become more involved, it required the dogged efforts of a Black military veteran and congressman, Charles Diggs, and entailed the diligent efforts of the civil rights staffers of his office and the DOD, notably Adam Yarmolinsky, to convince Kennedy to convene a special committee to investigate lingering issues of racism in the military. And though he would peruse the first report of the Gesell Committee and some minor changes were instituted, Kennedy largely avoided dealing with racial segregation in the National Guard and the continuing issue of racial desegregation of off-base housing.

The man who would assume the presidency, Lyndon B. Johnson, inherited those issues, along with many others, and successfully obtained progress where his predecessor could not. Why could Johnson do that which Kennedy could not? First, Johnson did not seem hesitant to take action. After assuming the presidency, he went straight to work on fulfilling the former president's wish for civil rights reform. Coinciding with a lack of hesitancy was his belief that he had a martyr's mandate that perhaps only he could use to its maximum. As the former and arguably most influential and powerful Senate Majority Leader in the body's history, Johnson was a far more successful political horse trader than just about anyone in Washington. The political virtuoso from the Hill Country of Texas knew who to see and who to bludgeon with reason, morality, and shame; sometimes this included sparring with old friends and mentors like Richard Russell. Johnson knew who to coax and who needed something in exchange for their vote. This talent or knack afforded Johnson civil rights victories that were, outside of the Reconstruction Amendments, unprecedented in their scope and depth.[105]

Those victories also opened the door for additional triumphs in the military. But it should be noted that for all of Johnson's talents he did not do this alone. The president inherited and chose to keep much of the Kennedy cabinet. This included gifted staffers in various government entities. While certainly questions remain over this decision when it comes to the Vietnam War, for the continued racial reform of the military it was a critical important decision and likely the right one. Johnson inherited not only McNamara, whose own views on the importance of civil rights reform were changing, but also many of his dedicated assistants, most notably the civil rights champion Yarmolinsky and the new assistant secretary of defense for civil rights, Alfred Fitt. Yarmolinsky early on, and Fitt as the Kennedy administration entered its twilight, had worked to lay the groundwork for further change.

Once Johnson's civil rights package fell into place, these advisers, under the leadership of McNamara and then Clark Clifford, acted in a more active and consistent fashion than they had during the Kennedy years regarding reform of the military. To put it another way, Johnson's arrival to the presidency provided a missing component to existing DOD efforts to reform the military: an active and openly involved president who had the wherewithal and ability to achieve necessary changes in the law, which provided enough political muscle for the civilian leadership of the DOD to address some of the remaining civil rights issues in the armed forces, such as segregation in the National Guard and racism in off-base housing. Without Johnson's leadership, it would have been more of the same for the DOD, which would have meant that racial reforms would have remained stalled by the inconsistent and uninterested leadership of the Kennedy presidency.

CHAPTER 6

The Decrescendo of Cold War Racial Reform: Vietnam, Johnson, and Nixon

Richard Barnett had been in the thick of it in Vietnam, and if there were any doubters he had two Purple Hearts to prove it. The Jackson, Mississippi, native was proud of his service, proud of his nation for fighting the war against communist aggression, and proud to have served with "a few good buddies." But when the Vietnam veteran heard General William Westmoreland, the head of all combat operations in Vietnam, praise the Black soldier, his blood boiled. In a statement designed to highlight the growing camaraderie between the two races, the general had observed that "you can't tell the difference between the negro and white soldiers." A year later, Westy told Ethel L. Payne, "the First Lady of Black journalism," that African American personnel "are performing in magnificent fashion and are a credit to our country as all our troops are." "It is a truly dramatic story," Westmoreland continued, as he recalled his first experience commanding Black troops in Korea. As compared to Korea, he believed that the "morale [between the two races] is high and there are relatively few complaints." That, however, was not how Private First Class (PFC) Barnett had seen it; in his view "solidarity—the old fighting spirit has broken down." What had caused this to happen? Barnett believed that the racial integration of the armed forces was at the heart of problem. "Every unit flooded by the recent waves of Negroes knew this terrible and drastic change," the veteran grumbled.[1]

"The waves of Negroes" that Barnett referred to so disparagingly were a result of the disproportionate number of African American soldiers serving in combat units in Vietnam. A noted scholar of the African American military experience during the war, James Westheider observed that several reasons emerged to help explain this situation. First, it was the unintended result of the military's desire by way of the Selective Service Act of 1948 to curb the amount of personnel accepted into service, while also trying to improve the overall quality of those who were inducted. After the conclusion of the Korean War, the DOD incorporated a deferment system that emphasized drafting men from the ages of eighteen to twenty-five. Coinciding with this change, the military's leadership also raised the physical and mental entrance requirements of the armed forces. Dubbed by the DOD as "manpower channeling," this deferment system additionally "exempted students, professionals, and skilled workers." Though these changes were meant to benefit all American society, such deferments ended up largely protecting middle- and upper-class whites from seeing duty in Vietnam.[2]

Meanwhile, those same deferments did little for African American men who largely did not qualify for the exemptions because they lacked the opportunity, whether it was because they were poor or undereducated, to pursue an education or a skill. This issue was especially crucial considering that a "Euro-cultural bias in the AFQ [Armed Forces Qualification] tests" existed that prevented Blacks for qualifying for other positions outside the combat arms within the military. Compounding the situation was the lily-white racial composition of local draft boards. Roughly 1.3 percent of all draft board members were Black, while the vast majority were white. Additionally, Black men found that they lacked ready access to the same sanctuary that some whites had used to avoid service in Vietnam: the National Guard and Reserves. Though the Department of Defense worked to force the Guard to racially integrate and had enjoyed some success, the pace of racial integration proceeded slowly and gradually, especially in the American South.[3]

While systemic racism and lack of leadership from the white command structure of the armed forces tells a good bit of the story, it ignores the reality that African American men were not solely the victims of a categorically conniving and wholly unfair system designed to send them off to war to die. Part of the situation that they faced in the military was the inadvertent result of a decision their community had made decades earlier. Historically, the civil rights community and its leadership—such as W. E. B. Du Bois (though he would later question his logic), Walter White, Whitney Young, and A. Philip Randolph along with scores of others—had deliberately schemed to have Black men serve during times of war, especially in combat units, to prove unequivocally to whites their worth as racial and societal equals. This strategy helped net results, but it also aided in the number of Blacks serving disproportionately in combat in Vietnam.

Another reason for the disproportionate number of Black soldiers serving in combat units was themselves. For many, their service in the military represented not only their patriotism—they were Americans, after all, who loved their county—but also the need to adhere to a greater legacy. The Black community understood well its history of military service to the republic, one that went all the way back to Crispus Attucks during the Revolutionary War. Though that service was intertwined with the larger civil rights goals of achieving freedom and equality for the Black community, it also aided in defining who they were as a race, as a gender (specifically aiding in shaping African American masculinity), and as citizens to the republic. It had to be preserved. This led the Black community to embrace the self-preservation and promotion, as Christine Knauer observed, of their own military history. While they worked to preserve their military heritage, others within it likely felt that they needed to continue it by serving. That certainly would explain why so many Black men sought service in elite combat units, with many becoming Marines, Airborne troopers, and Army Rangers.[4]

There is also the economics of the matter to consider. Though questions and concerns had arisen within the African American community over the years about military service, Blacks generally still viewed a life in the military as a viable option and did so even during the Vietnam War. In a 1966 *Newsweek* poll, 47 percent of African Americans believed that the military provided a better way of life for their children than one in the predominately segregated civilian world. As Ethyl Payne surmised:

In the society of today, with all its revolutionary changes, the U.S. is lagging behind the military services in the pace of integration. Hence, there is a disproportionate higher ration of Negroes in uniform than whites. Denied the rights and opportunities to advance at home, they flock to the Armed Forces in search of a "better shake" than they can get in civilian life.

Years later, Christian Appy agreed with Payne's premise that Black service during the war provided greater opportunities for African Americans than they were likely to receive in the civilian world: "There were people who would say—older [African American] uncles and fathers who would say—'Listen, in our society, yeah, the military might be authoritarian and hierarchical, but it's more of a meritocracy, there's more opportunity for people like us than practically any other area of American society. . . . If you do your job, you're going to get a steady paycheck, you might get promoted. You might learn some skills.'" Those African Americans who sought to earn even more volunteered for combat service willingly. This was not about greed; certainly for most Black soldiers it was not about that. It was about doing what it takes to earn a better way of life for themselves and their families. If that meant a tour or two in a combat or special operations unit, so be it.[5]

Regardless of the reason for their service, willing or otherwise, controversy soon enveloped the disproportionate number of Black men serving in combat units, as they were also dying disproportionately. In 1966, the *New York Times* declared that Black deaths in the Army "from 1961–1965 was 18.3 percent," while the amount in the Marine Corps was 11.3 percent.[6] By 1968, the problem had grown so large that the DOD instituted "a cutback in front-line participation by Negroes." Still, that did not end the senseless and controversial loss of life of Black men. For example, a year after the cutback was instituted, a young Black Marine, PFC Dan Bullock, was killed. Bullock had joined the Corps, after falsifying his birth date, at the tender age of fourteen. The Brooklyn native traded his chance to go to high school and maybe even the prom for the opportunity to serve his country in Vietnam. He was killed in 1969 in Quang Nam Province, the victim of a North Vietnamese sapper's deadly satchel charge. Bullock was fifteen years old at the time of his death and is believed to be the youngest American killed during the war.[7]

By the time of the Vietnam War, the military had racially integrated. Racial change came with a cost, however. Though it had implemented racial integration, the military had done so in a way that was reflective of its unique and distinctive nature. It *ordered* and *demanded* compliance with racial reform just as it would any other directive. Sometimes this approach worked, as some whites readily embraced their Black colleagues after spending time with them on and off the battlefield. But compliance, though necessary to function, does not mean unilateral understanding of the plight of the Black community, let alone its soldiers, or the racial *acceptance* of them.

As time passed, and with the racial integration of the National Guard and Reserves, there were fewer and fewer places for racist and segregationist-minded white soldiers to hide. This meant that, instead of the military ferreting out racist white soldiers within the racially integrated ranks of the American military, they remained—and their attitudes and beliefs remained with them. Thus, soldiers such as PFC Barnett remained and penned letters to Southern newspapers or politicians and decried the growing Black presence in the military. Worse, soldiers of his ilk scapegoated African American colleagues and blamed any racial strife in the military on them: "It's the constant fights and tensions [between the races]—the impossibility of integration ever working— that is tearing our Army apart," Barnett frustratingly recalled to the *Daily News* of Jackson, Mississippi.[8]

It also meant the perpetuation of racial stereotypes, some as old as the republic, about the abilities of Black men as people and soldiers. According to Barnett, African American personnel were "cowardly," unwilling to sacrifice themselves for the greater good, made lousy officers (meaning they lacked intelligence in his eyes), and were acting in a confrontational manner—one time a "bunch of Negroes in camp tore down the flag which Governor [George] Wallace sent us and burned it up." After the incident, they even had the temerity to chant, "We will overcome you." In a sense, Barnett's quip reflected an old racist stereotype that whites during slavery held about slaves they considered to be rebellious, such as the infamous Nat, who was seen as problematic because he challenged his place in a racist society. But it also was emblematic of a generational shift in attitude occurring between the older and newer African American soldiers and Marines serving in Vietnam.[9]

OLD BREED VS. NEW BREED

When studying this era, it is easy to get into the mindset that once racial reforms in the military were complete Black soldiers became just like white soldiers and all that really mattered to them at the point was their pay, the quality of food they received, that their time off or leave was not infringed upon, and that their benefits remained acceptable to themselves and their families. For some this might have been the case. But that approach ignores the generational shift that was afoot in the military's Black community. In fact, a split was occurring between the older and the younger Black soldiers.

The first traces of the "new breed" of African American soldiers can be found in 1961. In a series of articles by Leonard W. Malone for the all-Black *Pittsburgh Courier*, the veteran African American journalist investigated the racial integration of the armed forces in Europe. He discovered that not all Black soldiers were alike in their feelings and beliefs about the current racial state of the military and were in fact made up of two different groups. There was the old breed of African American soldier—those who had served prior to, during, and after the golden age of racial integration and reform that had occurred from 1945 to 1960. Their racial experiences in the military ran the gamut. They had gone through the hell of racial segregation that was still in play at the end of World War II, relished in the prospect and promise of Harry S. Truman's Executive Order 9981, fought in a more increasingly integrated fashion in Korea, made real gains during the Eisenhower administration in the education of their dependents and themselves, and even received integrated health care from the once racially segregated VA hospital system. This older group appreciated, because they knew what it had been like before, the improvements in the military. Was their situation perfect? No, they admitted; they understood more reform was likely needed to continue the progress that had already been made. But a sense of acceptance, perhaps even compliancy, did seem to exist. As Malone noted, they even recognized that racial violence between the two races, white and Black, would still break out from time to time. But instead of making this a dealbreaker, or a bridge too far, the old breed accepted it as par for the course of life in a racially integrating military. As one member of the old breed reasoned: "Sure the fellows [white and Black soldiers] fight once in a while, but it's nothing. They usually say, 'Why are we fighting . . . let's have a beer' . . . and it's finished."[10]

The second group, made up of younger African American military personnel, was not as forgiving. As Malone observed, the young Black men of this group had been raised and educated in a more racially inclusive environment and thus expected to encounter a more accepting and advanced racial environment in the racially integrated military. It is important to remember that the American military, whether it wanted to be or not, was at the vanguard of race relations for many in the Black community. So expectations of it were high for some Blacks. That said, token acceptance would no longer cut it for these men, as the average member, Malone reported, "wants acceptance as a human being, first, and as a Negro, incidentally; not merely only on a working level, but at all levels."[11]

Six years later, in 1967, Ethel Payne also observed the change in the attitudes of Black soldiers serving in Vietnam. While covering the Vietnam War for the *Chicago Defender*, Payne encountered what she would call the "new breed" of African American soldier. "He [the old breed] has been replaced by the new breed—younger (average age 18–22), more aggressive, more militant, more confidence in himself, surer of what he is fighting for and surer of what he expects if he makes it back 'to the world.'" Expectations had changed from the older to the younger, not only about the change in the military but also how future reform could be achieved. In her investigation, she discovered that a split existed within the new breed on the issue of civil rights. Those who fell between the ages of eighteen to twenty were "skeptical of the effectiveness of the non-violent philosophy of Martin Luther King . . . they are not black power advocates, but they feel that Stokely Carmichael has succeeded admirably in shaking up 'the man.'" Those over the age of twenty-one supported the nonviolent strategies of Reverend King and deplored the racial violence exploding in cities across the nation, most notably in Detroit. Violence, in their view, was a self-created obstacle to racial equality that did more harm than good.[12]

BLACK SOLIDARITY

Some Black soldiers became so jaded over the racism still present in the American military that they turned inward to their Black friends and away from their white colleagues to find solidarity and brotherhood. As a result, Black solidarity grew and aided in fostering the belief in Vietnam that there were really two American armies serving there—one Black, one white. When it was time for war, those armies interacted and did the job. When it was time for downtime, rest, and play, those armies retreated to their own separate encampments. Some white military personnel, though, were able to penetrate the racial boundaries and become close friends with Black soldiers. One African American soldier bluntly observed: "I got some white friends who are 'For Real' studs, and hell, they could call me anything they want, because I know they are for real. I know some Chucks [racist white soldiers] I'd most likely punch in the mouth if they said good morning to me because I know they are some wrong studs." Even so, some Blacks had grown so cynical about race relations within the military that they distrusted the motives of even those whites seeking to be their friends. Of course, part of the reason they felt this way was the continued separation of Black and whites during off-duty hours. White soldiers had been known to get into altercations with African American soldiers who tried to go to whites-only bars, especially when the possibility of interaction with Vietnamese women or white American military women was likely to occur.[13]

Continued separation from white comrades only hardened African American feelings toward whites and the war. In a show of solidarity, Blacks began to wear slave bracelets made of boot strings, while at other times they saluted African American officers with the Black Power salute. And finally, Black soldiers engaged in "dapping." Dapping, in the simplest terms, was a type of handshake that showed solidarity and love between Black soldiers. For African Americans, it was another aspect of their own unique culture that they maintained while serving. While some whites were amused by the practice, others found it to be annoying, as it often took place during the most inconvenient times, such as during meals. As the war carried on, white company commanders tried to eliminate forms of Black self-expression such as dapping because they believed it interfered with the cohesiveness of the unit.[14]

THE STARS AND BARS OF CONTROVERSY

Considering this change in the makeup of the Black combat soldier in Vietnam, the controversy that existed within Barnett's unit over flying what was likely the Stars and Bars, the battle flag of the Confederacy, comes into a clearer focus. For Black military personnel in general, but especially the new breed of Black soldier, the flag was a symbol of oppression and enslavement and left them feeling, as one African American solider noted, "like an outsider." Conversely for Alabama governor George Wallace, who had supplied the flag, and other Southerners, it was a deliberate display of disrespect to the Black community, a symbol of white resistance against those who sought to end the white-over-Black nature of the South, and overall it gave them a unique sense of Southern regional pride in their defiant stand to preserve Dixie.[15]

Before a raucous crowd in 1965, Wallace, a man who had once opposed the racial integration of his state's flagship University of Alabama, defended his and other white Southerners' embrace of the flag of the fallen Confederacy: "They tell you we're traitors. They tell you we're wrong to fly this flag." "Whenever you see the Confederate flag flying, you will see people who will fight for their country with more zeal than anywhere else." Secretary of Defense McNamara deemed flying the Confederate flag to be a problem. And though he moved to sanction against its use, his efforts were undercut by two intertwined forces: Southern states that contained the flag in their state flags, and reticent Southern soldiers, officers, and enlisted men who refused to comply with or carryout DOD directives against the display of the flag.[16]

It was not unlikely to see the Confederate flag flown over hooches in Vietnam or even make its way to the Air Force Academy at Colorado Springs, Colorado. Even in the instances where the Confederate flag would be policed and removed, the state flags of the South that had the battle flag encased within it, such as the state flag of the Magnolia State, Mississippi, continued to fly high. Whenever there was an attempt by the military to police the flagrant display of state flags with the offending symbol within it, it was quickly challenged by Southern segregationists in Congress. For example, four years after Barnett's plea to reverse the racial integration of the military, PFC Leonard D. Smith, an enlisted Marine from Shelby, Mississippi, was forced to take down from his post his state's flag. It was, Smith felt, a "Slap to my face" as well as a "Slap to the face [of] two million Mississippians."[17]

Indignant to the slight of a citizen of his home state and to the state itself, Democratic senator James O. Eastland took up the cause of Smith and his home state by asking the Commandant of the Marine Corps, General Leonard F. Chapman, about the matter. "I can truly say that two million Mississippians take a deep sense of pride in their state flag," Eastland opined. Officially, the Marine Corps declared that lowering the flag was not about policing the state flag of Mississippi but preventing the use of the flag as a marker for enemy assaults against American military units. The military assured Eastland that the same action was taken when it came to other state flags that were flying. This response satisfied Eastland and John Stennis, who had joined the cause with his fellow senator from Mississippi, and they ended their inquiry. But controversy still swirled around the issue; PFC Smith, who had originally complained about the slight to his state, died by way of what appeared to be an accidental self-inflected "gunshot wound to the head." The Marines hurriedly assured the senators from Mississippi that his death was indeed an accident and in no way a suicide or tied to the flag issue.[18]

MLK AND LBJ

Black soldiers were not the only ones changing. The leaders of the civil rights movement—which had contained in its past many advocates not only for America's wars but also the use of such contests to prove the racial and societal worthiness of their race to whites—were changing by the mid-1960s on the notion of Black military service. The principal figure to break with the African American community's embrace of war to achieve social equality was Dr. Martin Luther King Jr.

A onetime supporter of the American cause in Southeast Asia, King's stance began to shift in 1965, as he believed that the war was becoming an increasing distraction. The focus of the nation should be on racial equality and justice for all, not on war in a foreign land against a colored population. While he understood the importance of defeating global communism, King believed "we won't defeat communism by guns or bombs or gases. We will do it by making democracy work." "Making democracy work" meant tackling the remaining injustices of American racism; failure to do so would continue to damage America's "moral standing in the world," he reasoned. Defeating racism at home would, King felt, aide in thwarting communist propaganda that was plaguing the hearts and minds of the Third World. Ideological concerns aside, King recognized that wars cost money. Vietnam was no different, and every dime spent on it robbed the nation of the ability to continue to wage President Lyndon Johnson's War on Poverty. Furthermore, the American approach to waging the Vietnam War went against the nation's heritage. King declared that American activities in Vietnam were "anti-revolutionary" and reeked instead of "white colonialism." How could a nation that had achieved its own freedom through revolution dare to halt the efforts of another trying to do the same? Finally, he wondered why African American soldiers should fight to free the South Vietnamese when Blacks themselves did not enjoy the fruits of racial equality in the United States?[19]

LBJ and MLK—a fraught partnership: From the onset of their relationship and despite their differences in approach, the two leaders managed to deliver in a spectacular fashion during the so-called Second Reconstruction. The partnership ended abruptly in 1967, however, when King publicly broke with Johnson over the Vietnam War. Source: A2134-2A, 03/18/1966, LBJ Library. Photo by Yoichi Okamoto.

His evolution on Vietnam reached its nadir in 1967, when King delivered his "Beyond Vietnam" speech. Giving the speech came with a cost; it meant breaking with President Lyndon Johnson, who he had partnered with during the early years of the decade to achieve spectacular racial reform. Though it was always a respectful relationship, it was not always the most fluid of political partnerships, as they differed greatly in their approaches to reform. Johnson preferred working the tools of the machination of politics, where he was a master and could control all aspects of the process; King relied on moral, ethical, Christian and grassroots persuasion, directly challenging immoral racist laws in the South, often going to jail for it, and conducting mass demonstrations designed to force the nation to face its sinful and racist past.[20]

But the two men were at loggerheads over Vietnam. Johnson could project the image of a confidant lion, always on the prowl, always on the hunt. But inside he often harbored the doubts and concerns of a gazelle being hunted by one. Johnson often spoke with bravado, but every now and then he would drop his guard and tell the truth. It can also be said that Johnson told *a version of the truth*. When he spoke to Doris Kearns Goodwin about Vietnam, he told her the political truth: he knew that, whether or not he got involved, he was screwed either away. For Johnson, a cold warrior in his own right, "that bitch of a war," Vietnam, cost him dearly, and like something out of a Greco-Roman tragedy, he trudged befuddling onward into his political demise. He did so because, for Johnson, a foreign policy disciple of the era of World War II American fears over appeasement and all the trouble that came with it, Vietnam was a line that had to be drawn—even if went against his best judgment and reservations, even if it threatened the Great Society that he cherished, even though he would harbor doubts about his decisions throughout. He felt he had to do it.[21]

For King, it was equally as much a war that he had to fight against. He offered seven reasons in his "Beyond Vietnam" speech—a nod to the seven deadly sins of the Christian bible—for his decision to make a stand against the war. Overall, a connection existed between the war and the racial crisis in the United States, King informed his audience. It seemed to him that the former was robbing the latter from resolution: "And I knew that America would never invest the necessary funds or energies in rehabilitation of its poor so long as adventures like Vietnam continued to draw men and skills and money like some demonic, destructive suction tube." The cost was too cynically high in its irony for King, as the war hungered for more and more. Its ravenous appetite for destruction consumed economically, spiritually, morally, ethically, and physically from both races, white and Black. And throughout it all, the war in Vietnam continued to divide the very American soldiers, white and Black, who paid the highest price while carrying out its deadly mission: "We watch them," King stated, "in brutal solidarity [white and Black] burning the huts of a poor village, but we realize that they would hardly live on the same block in Chicago."[22]

A champion of nonviolent protest, one who had schooled those within the movement against the use of violence and intimidation, though he himself faced it constantly, King felt compelled to go after "the greatest purveyor of violence in the world today: my own government." It was time, King told those before him in attendance at the Riverside Church in New York City, to save the soul of America: "Now it should be incandescently clear that no one who has any concern for the integrity and life of America today can ignore the present war. If America's soul becomes totally poisoned, part of the autopsy must read 'Vietnam.'" As a man of faith and a practitioner of the teachings of Jesus Christ, he felt compelled to do it. King could not turn his back on any man, enemy or not: "We are called to speak for the weak, for the voiceless, for the victims of our nation, for those it calls 'enemy,' for no document from human hands can make these humans any less our brothers." In the end, he called for the madness of Vietnam to end because it was, as he would call it, "a symptom of a far deeper malady within the American spirit, and if we ignore this sobering reality . . . we will find ourselves organizing 'clergy and laymen concerned' communities for the next generation."[23]

Joining King in his cry against the war was the controversial leader of the Student Nonviolent Coordinating Committee, Stokely Carmichael. For Carmichael, the war in Vietnam was just more of the same for the Black man: "Black people have always been cannon fodder for the wars of imperialism." A vehement opponent of the war, Carmichael had even traveled illegally to Hanoi; while there he pledged the support of his race to the North Vietnamese. During a subsequent visit to Paris, Carmichael built on his actions in Hanoi by calling for American defeat in Vietnam: "We do not want peace . . . we want the Vietnamese to defeat the United States." His call for American defeat was a new twist on an old favorite. Just as American civil rights internationalists had done before him, Carmichael intertwined the domestic racial problems of the nation with aspects of its foreign policy.[24]

In the past, Carmichael's civil rights predecessors had condemned the fact that Black troops were involved in wars for freedom, while not being free themselves, just as King had recently done with Vietnam; however, these same advocates because of their embrace of the potential of the nation still supported its wars. Indeed, their pursuit of racial reform for the African American community within the American system prevented them from doing anything but support the nation's military activities. Carmichael, though, felt no obligation to follow this well-trodden pathway to reform that emphasized working within the system. A generation of younger African American soldiers hungry for greater equality agreed with him.[25]

GUNS AND BUTTER

As the flames of racial animosity in the armed forces continued to burn, the Johnson Administration threw gas on the fire when it launched Project 100,000, a controversial racial reform effort in the military that received equal damnation from the leadership of the armed forces and the civil rights movement. Designed to meet America's commitment to wage the Cold War—namely, by shoring up the nation's military manpower shortage during the 1960s—this guns-and-butter effort also doubled as a social welfare program, as it aided President Johnson's effort to wage a War on Poverty by accepting into the military the socially downtrodden, many of whom were African Americans who had failed to pass the Armed Forces Qualification Test (AFQT) and gain entrance into the military and escape poverty.[26]

Oblivious to the concerns of the military or the civil rights community, a political triumvirate formed to make the controversial program a reality. The intellectual father behind Project 100,000 was Daniel P. Moynihan, a social reformer who coupled his social science background with his political acumen to unleash the power of the federal government to become an agent of reform. President Kennedy himself had tabbed Moynihan, the assistant secretary of labor for policy planning and research; he would be assisted by other members of an assembled task force to study the military's manpower woes during the early 1960s. The result of the task force's effort, one that was dutifully penned by Moynihan, was released in 1963 as *One Third of a Nation: A Report on Young Men Found Unqualified for Military Service*. In time, *One Third of a Nation* became Moynihan's foundation for Project 100,000, but that was yet to come. At the moment, the report discovered that an alarming number of young men were failing to pass the AFQT: "If the entire male population of draft age were examined, about one-third would be disqualified," the report declared. The reason for such a high failure rate? American poverty. Poverty affected Americans of all races, but *One Third of a Nation* focused specifically on the unfortunate fate of young African American males. It observed that, of the men interviewed for the study, 31 percent were out of work; of these, 29 percent were minorities. Those Black males who were employed fared little better, as the majority of them (75 percent) worked primarily as unskilled laborers and made less on average per year ($1,563) than the national average ($2,656). The report noted a multigeneration cycle of poverty had formed that often forced young Black men to abandon their chance to get an education so that they could join the labor force, often in low-paying jobs, to aide their families and survive. Once finished, the troubling findings of the report did not land on Kennedy's desk, who had been slain in Dallas, but instead on Lyndon Johnson's.[27]

"WHAT THE HELL IS THE PRESIDENCY FOR?"

As his advisers debated the costs of striving for civil rights reform, something his slain predecessor had begun to push for late in the last year of his life, Lyndon Johnson listened. The advice, while unambitious, was sage. No twentieth century president, even when considering Truman's efforts in the military, had tried to do what Johnson was trying to do. The only one who could rival Johnson was Abraham Lincoln during the Civil War and Reconstruction, when he freed the slaves and helped shape the political environment that would lead to the passage of the Reconstruction Amendments. Any effort Johnson made akin to Lincoln, his advisers warned him, was likely to be crushed by Southern segregationist Democrats, men who the president knew well, and conservative Republicans. Why should the president waste his political capital, which he had very little of, on it? Johnson did not hesitate or waiver in his response: "Well," he offered, "what the hell is the presidency for?" Ambition, vision, overcoming difficult challenges and setbacks, and the confidence, though he certainly had his insecurities, which likely fueled him on, were never a problem for Lyndon Johnson, who suffered from what the biographer Randall B. Woods diagnosed as a serious case of a "messiah complex." Johnson not only *believed* in the promise and potential of his Great Society, which included significant civil rights reform; he *believed*, through all his personal doubts, that he was the only one who could deliver it to the American people.[28]

For Moynihan, having his report land on the desk of Lyndon Johnson as opposed to that of John F. Kennedy was a godsend. Where Kennedy would have weighed the political calculus of embracing the notion of using the military as a tool against poverty and likely would have decided against doing so, Johnson relished the idea. The program offered the possibility of uplifting the poor, which paired well with his War on Poverty, helped rectify civil rights issues in the Black community, and solved the military manpower shortage plaguing the ranks during the Cold War. And it did all of this through a stint in the military, which meant it was going to be on the cheap. Of course, the socially conscious—he did, after all, genuinely care about the intertwined issue of American poverty and racism—and politically savvy—he was also quite good at political calculus—Johnson would embrace it.[29]

But to do this, Johnson needed help. And to get it, he turned to his secretary of defense, one of many Kennedy holdovers, Robert S. McNamara. Though the president had the utmost confidence in his secretary of defense, McNamara was an unlikely accomplice in the president's mission to make Moynihan's plan to save the poor a reality. During the early years of his reign over the DOD, McNamara had repeatedly relied on his special assistant, Adam Yarmolinsky, to spearhead the department's civil rights efforts. But with time the defense chief evolved. In his memoir *The Essence of Security*, published after his exodus from the Department of Defense, he counted among the "new missions" of the United States military the need to recognize that poverty was not only a national security issue for the United States during the Cold War but also a social malady that withered away the creative genius and ambition of human beings. Because of his evolution on the subject, McNamara became the face of Project 100,000.[30]

The exaggerating and impassioned Johnson never doubted that he had the right man for the job. "I've seen these kids all my life," he mused during a cabinet meeting. "I've been with these poor children everywhere" Johnson continued. Who could save them from the depths of despair? The president believed that Bob McNamara could. "I know that you can do better by them than the NYA [National Youth Administration] or the Job Corps can." The DOD, Johnson concluded, "can do the job best."[31]

Once the leadership of the armed forces got wind of what was coming—thanks to an article in the *Journal of the Armed Forces* that leaked the program—they did not like what they heard and immediately rejected the notion outright. They called it the birth of the "Moron Corps," a title that eventually was also used later to describe Project 100,000 personnel. Despite their criticism, McNamara announced that the armed forces, through the Special Training and Enlistment Program (STEP), would accept 60,000 recruits previously rejected from military service. How it would do so proved to be as controversial as the admission of these men into the ranks. The program proposed turning the military into a social instrument, whether it was as a school that provided STEP personnel with the remedial educational training necessary to gain admittance into the military or as a hospital that could correct any medical ailments that had prevented a disqualified applicant from being inducted.[32]

Johnson loved the idea that the social program promised to instill military discipline in inductees, which in essence meant that the armed forces would teach the downtrodden to pull themselves up by their own bootstraps. In a phone conversation with McNamara, the president told him a story about a White House staffer who had stolen a few items from his secretary's desk. He was not a bad young man or a lost cause, Johnson felt. With a little help and some discipline, the boy could be reclaimed and become a man. What Johnson then described to his defense chief amounted to an extreme character-building exercise for the poor, one brought on by way of the ridged discipline of the American armed forces:

I think you've got to take boys like that and give them some discipline. I just don't believe [in] that all the vocational training. . . . I never really seen a kid that came out of any of those vocational schools that is equipped to be a carpenter or mechanic or anything else, he learns a little basic stuff, but I don't think he is really prepared for it. . . . But I think, your people, you have the discipline built in there, you have the camps built in there, you have the cooks built in there, and if they don't do a damn thing but count trucks for you or something, you can keep them, you have the teachers.

Disciplining the downtrodden struck a chord with the task-focused McNamara, and he heartily agreed: "We can teach them work discipline. When you're supposed to be at a place at eight o'clock in the morning, by god they get there or they get disciplined." The idea that a lack of military discipline was what ailed the poor, especially regarding the African American poor, missed entirely the larger points about racism, lack of education, and how the burden of society prevented the poor of both races from escaping the cycle of poverty.[33]

Regardless of the potential to instill character and discipline into the downtrodden, some congressmen vigorously objected to the premise of STEP. Southern segregationist Democrats—who opposed the use of the federal government to uplift Blacks in any meaningful way—joined with fiscally minded and socially conservative Republicans—who opposed the price of the proposed program, which was estimated at $135 million—to block it from passing. Once again leading the resistance was the head of the Senate Armed Services Committee, Senator Richard Russell of Georgia. But Johnson, ever the dealmaker, was resolute to his cause. And the president believed that he could get Russell, his mentor, friend, confidant, and sometimes adversary, to come to the table and hammer out a deal.[34]

In March 1965, Johnson called the Georgian to discuss several matters with him. During the phone call, and likely by design, Johnson steered the conversation toward the issue of lowering the Navy's induction requirements, leading the president to muse with his longtime colleague over the idea of lowering the requirements across the board for all the armed forces. Johnson's effort, though, to get Russell into a conversation about STEP failed. So Johnson tried a different type of bait: he poked at Russell's racism. "It seems to me that you're paying a mighty big price on an Anglo-Saxon white man to make his boy go and fight Vietnam," the president opined, "but none of the others can because . . . they don't have the exact IQ." Johnson's verbal catfish noodling worked. "I held up the whole thing for years, when they tried to cut it back. . . . Smart boys, black and white—you're killing them, and the damn dumb bunnies [low-IQ inductees] escape!," Russell lamented to Johnson. With the Georgian nibbling on the line, Johnson made his move:

Well. . . . I think we can improve them [low-IQ inductees]. . . . The Navy has said that all this talk about the draft—[Barry] Goldwater is going to repeal it and all that kind of stuff—has ruined their program. They can't get people for it now. So, they're going to have to lower their physical and mental standards to get them. . . . If they do that then we'll have to lower them for the others [armed services]. . . . But just the borderline. In other words, if you say I can't come into your committee and testify unless I've got a B average, I would modify it to B-minus, that's all. I wouldn't drop it to D or F. I wouldn't take a second-grader, but I would just gradually do a little. And you don't have to move it much to pick up ten thousand.

As Russell pondered what Johnson suggested, Democratic senator Gaylord Nelson of Wisconsin submitted a new proposal backing STEP. Immediately, it met sharp opposition from two of Russell's most powerful segregationist allies, Strom Thurmond of South Carolina and John Stennis of Mississippi. They argued it was not the armed forces' responsibility to get citizens up to snuff for military service; neither should it serve as a sociological laboratory to uplift the impoverished.[35]

During his debate over the matter, Nelson seemed to understand that there was no point in highlighting to two well-known racial segregationists the gains that could be netted for the Black community through a program of this ilk. Instead, he decided to metaphorically grasp the flag and conjure up images of patriotism. Nelson reasoned that STEP provided a chance to serve for those who loved their country but had been disqualified from doing so. And besides, this made more sense, he argued, than relying on the allegiance of draftees who were forced to serve for two years and were likely to leave at the end of their commitment. Though Nelson's argument purposely downplayed the social reform aspect of the program, even he conceded: "There can be little question that STEP, like any program of education, will help to reduce poverty; but that is not its main purpose." Indeed, Nelson made it clear that "the main purpose of STEP is to reduce the Army's training costs, and to secure a higher caliber of manpower for the Army." The Southern segregationist trio of Thurmond, Stennis, and Russell—the Georgian had decided after all to remain firm in his stance—were not buying Nelson's argument; they all voted against STEP once again.[36]

"NINE PAGES OF DYNAMITE"

While the congressional battle over the STEP program waged on, Moynihan turned his attention to a more controversial project, "The Negro Family: The Case for National Action," an investigation into the African American community. Internally, members of the Johnson administration referred to the Moynihan Report, as it was commonly known, as "nine pages of dynamite" because it made the bold and controversial claim that young African American males suffered, as did their community and the nation, when they were denied the potential of a traditional family upbringing based on the principles of deference and discipline. As Moynihan put it: "The breakdown of the Negro family is the principal cause of all the problems of delinquency, crime, school dropouts, unemployment, and poverty which are bankrupting our cities, and could very easily lead to a kind of political anarchy unlike anything we have known."[37]

As with McNamara and Johnson, Moynihan drew inspiration from the very same belief in the benefits of military discipline. But Moynihan lionized a racially integrated, male-driven brand of discipline toward young Black men, which he believed could serve as a cure-all for poverty and the woes facing the Black community. He outlined his solution to the dilemma facing young Black men in seven steps, one of which included their increased induction into the armed forces. Service in the military would provide young African American males, Moynihan believed, with a social sanctuary from the distractions of the urban ghetto. They especially could break away from the influence of a female-driven household and Jim Crow segregation and instead be transferred to a place where a modicum of white and Black equality existed "run by strong men of unquestionable authority, where discipline, if harsh, is nonetheless orderly and predictable, and where rewards, if limited, are granted on the basis of performance."[38]

Moynihan's cure-all for what ailed the Black community met with a mixed response. There were those internally—for example, the Department of Labor—that believed his report was flawed. There were some in the civil rights community—like the NAACP's Robert Carter—who did not outright reject it and instead viewed it as a reminder of facts already known. Others, however, viewed it as "anti-negro" and claimed that Moynihan was nothing more than a "subtle racist," a charge that the longtime civil rights crusader Bayard Rustin found to be "silly." Though Rustin came to Moynihan's defense, he questioned the juxtaposition of the state of Black families to that of white ones, observing that what may seem unhealthy to one (whites) might not be considered as such by the other (Blacks). Meanwhile, James Farmer, the founder and leader of the Congress of Racial Equality, appreciated the sentiment and sincerity of the report, but he wondered if it had not opened the door for "a new racism."[39]

Despite the mixed response about the Moynihan Report and STEP's failure to pass, Moynihan continued to agitate behind the scenes for racial reform of the military. In a 1965 memo to Harry McPherson, special assistant and counsel to the president, he claimed that "the biggest opportunity to do something about Negro youth has been right under our noses all the time." That opportunity was to use the American armed forces as an instrument of social reform.

According to his data, Blacks made up 11.8 percent of the nation but only 8 percent of the armed forces.[40] The underrepresentation of African Americans in the military was an obstacle to their escaping poverty. Recognizing that the unemployment rate for African American men aged seventeen to thirty-four was 11.5 percent, Moynihan proposed what amounted to be a ledger swap: "If 100,000 nonwhite men were added to the Armed Forces, and resulted in a decrease of 100,000 in the unemployed, that unemployment rate would drop from 11.5 percent to 6.4 percent." Excited about this potential solution, Moynihan buoyantly declared:

If there was a proportionate racial balance in the Armed Forces, the unemployment rate from young Negro men would be lower than that for whites! That has not occurred for two generations. In truth, if you exclude agriculture, it has never happened in American history.

He also understood that his idea would stir up Southern segregationists in Congress. Instead of making the same mistake as they made with STEP—namely, that the administration had sought for additional funding to pay for it, which put the program on the radar of Southern segregationists—Moynihan suggested that the DOD, with as little fanfare as possible, should alter the AFQT to allow a greater number of low-scoring inductees into the military. And for good measure and a bit of political insurance, Moynihan suggested that the Johnson administration should "say nothing" to Congress or anyone else about what they were doing.[41]

Moynihan's proposal sounded good on paper; reality was a different matter. And McNamara knew it: as before with STEP and other racial reform initiatives, it was only a matter of time before Richard Russell got involved to muddy up the waters. And McNamara shared his concerns with the president. Referring to Russell, the Pentagon chief said matter-of-factly: "He's just reluctant to see anything done that takes more Negroes into military service." But the president was determined. Johnson wanted the program to succeed because the Vietnam War's growing economic cost was robbing potential funding from the Great Society. Project 100,000, though, could help him achieve both—reform and war—at the same time. To alleviate McNamara's concerns, the president offered a solution: "[Tell Russell] we'll take these Negro boys in from Johnson City, Texas [Johnson's hometown] and from Winder, Georgia [Russell's hometown]. We get rid of the tape worm and get the ticks off of him and teach him to get up at daylight and work to dark and to shave and to bathe. . . . When we turn him out we'll have him prepared to at least drive a truck."[42]

Though Johnson offered McNamara a folksy Southern narrative to spin

Senator Richard B. Russell of Georgia—gentleman segregationist: Since the conclusion of World War II, no Southern segregationist in Congress had done more to slow, stymie, and attempt to halt the racial integration of the armed forces than Russell. He met his match, however, when he crossed political swords over the issue with President Lyndon B. Johnson, his protégé and friend. Source: 9347-30, 04/03/1968, LBJ Library. Photo by Frank Wolfe.

for Russell, it would ultimately be the president himself—the dealmaker from Johnson City—who would go on another political angling adventure trying desperately to ensnare his wily opposition from Georgia. During a conversation with Russell regarding the manpower demands of the Vietnam War, which included the possible call-up of the Reserves to active duty, Johnson lured the senator into a discussion of Project 100,000:

Let me make a deal with you. I'll work on the reserve thing, follow your suggestions on that, if you follow mine on letting me call up everybody, letting me draft all of them, give me a little STEP program like you promised me one time; you made me a firm commitment and ran out on me. . . . But you just let me call up these damn folks, get them off the marijuana and out of the jungles, and out of the rats eating on them, and let me put them out in these damn camps.

"You can work the hell out of them if you want to," Russell retorted. "Work the hell out of them and feed them, I'm going to do it . . . but I don't want you cussing at me," the president responded. "I won't say a critical word, not one," the senator promised his old friend. But the Georgian did quip: "I think you're going to waste a lot of money on them, though." Such an exchange begs the question: Why would Russell now acquiesce to Johnson on the issue? Perhaps their friendship, mutual admiration for one another, the reality that the president was going to do it anyway, and maybe even party loyalty offer viable possibilities. The biographer Jeff Woods, though, suggests another reason: Russell's patriotism. As a hawkish cold warrior, Russell, as he had years before during the Korean War, likely acquiesced to Johnson's request, solely to put more boots—regardless of race—on the ground in Vietnam to battle against godless communism.[43]

PROJECT 100,000

McNamara announced to a crowded gathering before the Veterans of Foreign Wars that the US armed forces—the most powerful in the world—had a new, pugnacious, irascible, and intractable enemy to fight: poverty. So much for the sageness, if not the blatant suggestion, to cloak the program from critics in Congress, as counseled by Moynihan. Instead, McNamara confidently went for the throat and unveiled STEP's successor: Project 100,000. Divided into five classifications based on performance on the AFQT, recruits either scored above average (Categories One and Two), average (Category Three), or fell within the ranks of those who scored below average (Categories Four and Five). Much like its predecessor, Project 100,000 proposed that the military would now admit men whose scores placed them among Category Four recruits—not quite the bottom of the barrel, but still too close to the bottom rung for some critics.[44]

Any criticism was nothing more than white noise to the supremely confident McNamara. He believed that American society had failed these men, but he would not. Through their service in the military, they would reap benefits and take part in its vast educational network. McNamara believed that the armed forces would transform them, and with renewed confidence they would "return to civilian life with skills and aptitudes which for them and their families will reverse the downward spiral of human decay." Toward the conclusion of his remarks to the VFW, McNamara returned to the civilian realm of American society and admonished those who had given up on these men: "Too many instructors look at a reticent, or apathetic, or even hostile student and conclude: He is a low-aptitude learner." "In most cases," the defense chief argued, "it would be more realistic for the instructor to take a hard honest look in the mirror and conclude: 'He is a low-aptitude teacher.'"[45]

McNamara's scorched-earth razing of segments of America's educational system certainly did him no favors within that realm or with those who wrote about it. Fred M. Hechinger, a *New York Times* editor who specialized in discussing education, took note of McNamara's comments and Project 100,000. Though he came away impressed within the potential of the endeavor, Hechinger wondered if what was being posed was even possible. After all, he opined, the educational system within the military was being oversold a bit by McNamara:

The statistical review of the Armed Forces' educational effort is highly idealized—as apparently omnipotent on paper as the prospectus of any civilian school system. The overseas dependents' schools, for example, sound numerically impressive but they have a long history of academic deficiencies. Moreover, although under military auspices, they are essentially civilian schools, run by temporarily recruited public school teachers and administrators.

And the quality of the training that those recruits might receive was not as good as McNamara made it sound. Hechinger argued that the training and materials used were substandard:

As for the training materials used by the Armed Forces, they are often to paraphrase the description of military training manuals in "The Caine Mutiny," designed by geniuses but used by idiots. Academic quality control is hard to come by in civilian classrooms; it is even more difficult in a setting of military command where the basic mission is not educational.

And finally, he posed the obvious question: *Should* the military be doing this?

Such a mission would be quite different from the fine tradition of bringing education into the American military establishment; it would actually invite the military establishment to become a substitute school system. Those who, with General Eisenhower, see dangers in a military-industrial complex might be even more concerned by a military-educational complex or, since the educational technology is intimately involved, ultimately a military-industrial-educational complex.

Criticism aside, McNamara genuinely believed that the program could work and remained committed to the socially uplifting aspects of it. And though it doubled as a manpower program, he, along with program administrator Thomas Morris, had no intention to throw these men to the wolves. They privately had their reservations and concerns, however. Both were concerned that the poor educational standing of Project 100,000 recruits would lead to them being dumped into combat units. To protect "New Standards Men," the official designation for Project 100,000 personnel, from this ill-begotten, morally troublesome, and politically unsavory fate, McNamara required that the Navy and Air Force be required to take some of these men. While service in both branches came with its own risks, they were seen as more acceptable. After all, the Navy and the Air Force were more technically oriented outfits as opposed to the Army or Marine Corps. And therefore, because of the nature of service in the Navy and the Air Force, it would presumably provide a haven from the perils of ground warfare in Vietnam. Equally important to the tech-driven McNamara, New Standards Men were more likely to acquire a lifelong and life-changing technical skill because of their service in the Navy or the Air Force.[46]

"MORONS" AND "CRIMINALS"

From the jump, the armed forces largely rejected Project 100,000's use of sub-standard manpower. The rejection of these men meshed well with the long-running tradition of the military's leadership to object to any racial reform that it believed would threaten military efficiency. How they vocalized it, however, ranged from the polite to the dehumanizing. For example, the *Army Times* wondered: "Is this any time to require the services to take on a large scale 'poverty-war' training mission? We would think not." While the newspaper remained civil, the rank and file of the armed forces did not. New Standards Men became known as "McNamara's Morons," "McNamara's Moron Corps," "Stupid and Super-Stupid," and "McNamara's Million." The debasement of these men was not limited to the average soldier, as it made its way into the highest echelons of the military. General William Westmoreland bitterly excoriated Project 100,000 and its personnel. New Standards Men, in his opinion, were stupid. "Category four is a dummy. You can probably make a soldier out of ten percent of him," he opined, and they were nothing more than a crop of criminals who were responsible for the lion's share of discipline problems and the festering drug culture in Vietnam. In a good bit of scapegoating, the general believed that their inclusion undercut the American war effort in Southeast Asia.[47]

Echoing the thoughts and feelings of Westmoreland, the battalion commander Charles Cooper bemoaned: "Thanks to Project 100,000 they were just flooding us with morons and imbeciles. It doesn't mean they couldn't eat and talk and move around, but they couldn't learn well and they'd get frustrated and become aggressive." One veteran, Richard Bowen, agreed and recalled a story revolving around two individuals with nefarious backgrounds. One was a car thief, the other a lockpick. Though he did not offer proof, Bowen believed them both to be New Standards Men, and that they were in the military largely because they choose that fate over incarceration. While Bowen understood the logic behind the military's recruitment of such men, he remained convinced that most Project 100,000 personnel were criminals:

So I think in this group, there was a high percentage of people who had had some type of background with the law, and they were in our unit. For the most part, they had skills (laughs) that the rest of society wished they didn't have, and they were not afraid to use them. It turns out that we had other people who were arsonists, who had burned or tried to set people's houses on fire, so they got caught doing stuff like that. We had a lot of those kinds of people who were in the military during this time period.

Serving as a company commander of an engineer outfit in Vietnam, Lloyd Brown recalled that part of his command included a small naval component, which he believed to be a "dumping ground for people." Within its ranks were "27 Project 100 Thousand people . . . [which] included 2 people who had been convicted of voluntary manslaughter." He specifically remembered an incident where he almost lost his life at the hands of a substandard soldier. According to Brown, this soldier worked in supply and faced continuous slandering from his colleagues. One night, the solider finally lost his temper. He apprehended and threatened his belittling comrades with a loaded M-14. When Brown tried to reason with him, the soldier responded: "Don't you get near me, Sir, I will blow you away, along with all these other Sons of Bitches." Eventually, Brown diffused the situation and sent the man to the unit's psychiatrist for evaluation instead of the stockade. After the psychiatrist cleared him and returned him to duty, Brown, out of an effort to keep an eye on the soldier, made him his driver—a capacity, the commander recalled, that he excelled in.[48]

A CASE STUDY: PROJECT 100,000 AND THE MARINE CORPS

During the Vietnam War, the United States Marine Corps dispatched disproportionately more men to the fight than any other branch of the armed forces. According to its records, 30 percent of the Marine Corps was committed to Vietnam; indeed, from 1967 to 1970, 58.5 percent of all New Standards Men in the branch served in combat roles. Historical manpower needs that were always present within the Marines, along with the needs of the war in Vietnam, should have equaled a willing acceptance for these men. But that was not the case.[49]

Historically, the Marines Corps has been a proud and elite outfit that cultivated exclusiveness. But that also meant they had come to racial integration the hard way—they *had to do it* because of the necessity of war. Though they had reluctantly come to embrace the Black Marine, the Marines still clung to conservative tradition regarding the branch's use as a social instrument. This, along with the combat burden it bore in Vietnam, as David Dawson has observed, led its leadership to not only avoid using these potential New Standards Marines but also to resist them completely. Initially, the leadership of the Marine Corps largely grumbled that it should not have to accept New Standards Men while rejecting potential Marines that scored higher on the AFQT.[50]

When griping about it proved to be noneffective, the Assistant Chief of Staff (G-1) of the Marines internally suggested to leadership that they should manipulate Project 100,000 to their favor. Two pools of participants, mental and medical rejectees, made up Project 100,000. The stigma, of course, surrounded the former. As such, the Marines opted to cherry-pick from the latter. The majority of Project 100,000 medical rejectees were either overweight or underweight, which the Marine Corps believed was a correctable and more palatable condition to deal with. Surely a Marine Corps drill instructor, skilled in various forms of motivation, could get a young private to drop weight. The catch was that less than 1 percent of all New Standards Men came from the medical pool. Once it became obvious that there would not be enough recruits entering the Marines from this group to satisfy the DOD, the branch quickly abandoned the plan.[51]

If it could not cherry-pick who it reaped from the program, then maybe, the Marines believed, it could demonstrate how bad Project 100,000 really was and why they should not have to be a part of it. The Corps attempted to do this by scrutinizing an internal performance evaluation that pitted New Standards Men versus those from a control group. Simply, the Marines believed that New Standards Men were inferior to Marines who had achieved higher AFQT scores. As for overall performers, the examination determined that 35 percent of New Standards Men received lower-quality ratings from their commanders; in comparison, only 20 percent of Marines from the control group received similar ratings. A little over 20 percent of New Standards Men proved unable to complete their contracts, the report found; many washed out after eighteen months of service. Additionally, one-third of them recycled, which meant they had to redo a portion of their initial training. Most important, New Standards Men in the Marines perished at twice the rate of their counterparts, the report surmised.[52]

The Marines' handiwork, though damning, blatantly ignored the fact that most of these men met expectations; instead, the report was deliberately slanted to the negative, especially for the issue of death rates, which was used to allude to the fact that the Marine Corps believed that New Standards Men could not mentally hack it. Decades later, Dawson disagreed with the Marines assessment of New Standards Men. Certainly they struggled, he readily admitted, but not because they lacked heart or ability; they lacked the education necessary to net technically oriented positions in the Marines that could have allowed them to serve in noncombat roles. And even if they had the ability, the Spartan-like nature of the Marines, he observed, offered few opportunities for them to escape combat. Therefore, it was likely, he postulated, that they perished at such an alarmingly high rate because there was nowhere else in the branch for them to serve.[53]

The needs of the war were not on the side of Marine leaders eager to avoid using New Standards Men. As the war went on, the Johnson administration found itself waging an increasingly unpopular conflict, which meant that the social reform aspects of the program took a backseat to the *need* for warfighters to go to Vietnam. From the start, Marine recruiters believed they needed to steadily maintain their quota of New Standards Men entering the branch; if they did not, they worried, the Department of Defense might just end up drafting such men into their ranks anyway. If these men were the bottom of American society, as the Marines believed them to be, then what the branch was trying to do was skim the cream off the top of the bottom. That said, the necessity of Vietnam eventually led Marine recruiters to accept *more* New Standards Men into their ranks than the Department of Defense had called for. For Dawson, it highlighted a reality for the Marine Corps that it was unlikely to admit at the time but was no less true: "To fill its ranks, the Marine Corps would have been forced to lower enlistment standards and accept large numbers of recruits scoring in Mental group IV with or without Project 100,000." In a sense, Project 100,000, though bemoaned and detested by the Marines, prevented it from doing that which it would have had to do anyway.[54]

If New Standards Men had to be there, the leadership of the Marines reasoned, then it was going to limit the damage they could cause. Throughout the branch, commanding officers actively sought to remove or block New Standards Men from leadership positions. The problem was that the DOD utilized a code system that masked the participants in the program. Nonetheless, some motivated Marine commanders attempted and eventually claimed to have cracked the code. Historically speaking, no one can confirm whether they had accurately done so, let alone the number of times they falsely identified Marines as part of the program when they were not.[55]

A troubling development occurred during the guesswork of who was in Project 100,000 and who was not: racial justification as membership. Many white Marines erroneously believed that most Project 100,000 men within the branch were Black. The actual amount of Black New Standards Men in the Marines was 40.3 percent, while the majority, 58 percent, were white.[56] The reason for their flawed supposition was based almost entirely on the remaining racism within the branch. Though Vietnam was the first truly racially integrated war for the American military, the armed forces still struggled with issues of racial prejudice. In *Semper Fidelis*, Alan Millett observed that, while the policy of the Marines was one of nondiscrimination, the reality was the contrary. During off-duty hours, Marines of both races engaged in a good bit of rest and relaxation and often did so at bars, brothels, or any place that alcohol, drugs, and women, whether prostitutes or not, could be found. These social gatherings could turn violent. Regardless of who started a fight, African American Marines, whether Project 100,000 men or not, often shouldered the blame.[57]

Furthermore, the Marine Corps fell in line with the thinking throughout the military, highlighted by General William Westmoreland's comments years after the war that most New Standards Men were Black and they were all thugs and criminals. One white Marine veteran bitterly complained: "They were a crime wave in themselves." To an extent, as noted by William Allison, there were certainly some concerns, as "39 percent of Project 100,000 participants received nonjudicial punishments, compared to 19 percent for regular marines of similar rank and tenure." Allison wondered, however, how many of these charges were potentially racially motivated? The question is a viable one, as Dawson's research demonstrated that less than 10 percent of New Standards Men had a criminal conviction on their record before entering the military. And it begs a question: Why would they become a criminal by joining the military? That idea seemed counterproductive to the overall concept that the military can serve as a path to a better life. The belief that most Project 100,000 men were Black and criminally minded lived on, no matter how inaccurate the idea was.[58]

GUILT BY ASSOCIATION

Joining in the criticism of the program were African American civil rights leaders who condemned Project 100,000 to be nothing more than racial genocide. But was it? The majority of the program's participants were not Black but white. African American men made up only 36.7 percent of the project.[59] Neither, as critics of the program (then and now) believe, were they all victims of the draft. The slight majority of participants (54 percent) volunteered for the program and the chance to serve their country. With frustration mounting over the domestic inequalities still present in American life and with the terrible burden Black men were paying in Vietnam, though, members of the Black community and the civil rights movement soured on Project 100,000, which they believed was a result of the equally terrible and racist draft.[60]

The actions of the nation's outspoken and opinionated head of the Selective Service, General Lewis B. Hershey, aided in fostering this belief. A conservative Indiana Republican, Hershey was seen as a pariah in the civil rights community. To be sure, the man was no social reformer like Moynihan, but to the nation's longtime Selective Service chief racial reform in the armed forces mattered because he recognized the damage racism had done to the military. He believed, much like Johnson, McNamara, and Moynihan, that instilling military discipline in the downtrodden of America could aid in their uplifting. Hershey, in fact, had been a member of the task force that researched the nation's growing manpower problems in the early 1960s and that led to the writing of *One Third of a Nation*.[61]

Whatever ideas he may have harbored about social uplift, for Hershey the critical focus was always about fielding the strongest army he could. Those who got in his way, most notably antiwar protesters, faced his wrath. As opposed to jailing them as some conservatives championed, Hershey would rather draft them. His attitude and comments in this regard did not do himself or the Johnson administration, who was increasingly waging battle against the growing antiwar movement, any favors in the fall of 1967. During that autumn, Hershey unleashed a political firestorm. He announced that all branches of the Selective Service should reexamine all war protestors' draft status. Though the Supreme Court a year later reversed this action, the conspiratorial belief that the government was using the draft as a weapon against civil rights and antiwar protesters surfaced and remained cemented in the popular consciousness of many.[62]

Within every conspiracy are nuggets of truth used to support the belief of something nefarious happening. The issue of using the draft as a weapon against civil rights leaders does have some measure of credibility to it. Take, for example, the case of the celebrated civil rights icon John Lewis. Lewis, a strict advocate for nonviolent protest, for years had sought to achieve Conscientious Objector (CO) status; initially, he failed at the local level when an all-white draft board in Pike County, Alabama, rejected his request; subsequently, the larger board governing of the state did as well. This forced him to take the matter to the federal level. In 1965, he was granted CO (referred to as "I-O") status.[63]

As the civil rights movement evolved and the war in Vietnam unfolded, the former Freedom Rider, a man who had been beaten savagely on "Bloody Sunday" on the Edmund Pettus Bridge and the longtime leader of the Student Nonviolent Coordinating Committee, changed with the times. Lewis signed the controversial "Declaration of Conscience Against the War in Vietnam" and came out against the war. Then he openly empathized with those who sought to avoid military service by ducking the draft. "We are in sympathy with and support, the men in this country who are unwilling to respond to a military draft which would compel them to contribute their lives to United States aggression in Vietnam in the name of 'freedom' we find so false in this country," he argued. Shortly thereafter, and with little explanation available, Lewis's draft status changed; he was now considered to be "available for service" (1-A). Once again, he appealed his status with the federal government, most notably by way of a request to Senator Robert F. Kennedy and Burke Marshall, who headed the Civil Rights Division within the Department of Justice, which led to his new designation as "morally unfit" for duty (4-F).[64]

And certainly there were racist Southern congressmen, such as Louisiana representative Edward Hébert, who believed that the draft and Project 100,000 were a means to an end to fight against outspoken Blacks, whether it was over civil rights or antiwar issues. After hearing about the launch of McNamara's social reform program, Hébert quipped: "Maybe now they'll get Cassius Clay," referring to the legendary boxer who later changed his name to Muhammad Ali. While Hébert schemed to dethrone the heavyweight champion of the world, it was also possible that all-white draft boards in the South, and likely elsewhere in the republic, viewed the draft, and maybe even Project 100,000, as a weapon against the civil rights movement and Black social ascendancy. While the potential for this happening at the local level remains plausible, there is not enough evidence to definitively argue that Project 100,000 was co-opted in a grand scheme within the federal government to suppress African American civil rights advocates.[65]

To a community bereft over the loss of so many Black fathers, brothers, uncles, cousins, and sons who had perished in Vietnam, Project 100,000 was received, understandably, with great cynicism, skepticism, and ultimately disdain. While the NAACP and the leadership of the Southern Christian Leadership Conference offered no comment, older names in the struggle for civil rights reform in the military joined with new faces to the cause to denounce it. New York congressman Adam Clayton Powell Jr., a seasoned champion of racial reform, deemed it "genocide." "It's brutal," he reasoned. "It's nothing more than killing off human beings that are not members of the elite." While Powell condemned it, others met in New York to speak out against it. In a moment where the goals of the program were overshadowed by its image, the chairman of the New York City Human Rights Commission, William Booth, argued that Project 100,000 was "another attempt to get more Negroes into conflict." "They should," he added, "escalate the war on poverty instead of the draft." Stokely Carmichael, who in 1966 had supplanted Lewis as leader of the Student Nonviolent Coordinating Committee, disparaged the program as a deliberate and scandalous attempt by "the [white] man to get rid of black people in the ghettoes." It was nothing more than "a cynical method to punish black youths for the social ills imposed on them by the major society," added Black Power advocate and leader of the Congress of Racial Equality, Floyd McKissick.[66]

"NO SKILLS BEFORE. NO SKILLS AFTER."

Civil rights critics of the program received new grist for the mill when it was announced in the fall of 1966 that the remedial education portion of Project 100,000 would be voluntary. Indeed, over the life of the program, only 6 percent received any sort of technical training. For Black civil rights leaders this reeked of a bait-and-switch. But it turned out that it was not as simple as that, argued the authors Lawrence M. Baskir and William A. Strauss. Both had served on President Gerald Ford's clemency board after the war's conclusion. Using their unique knowledge of the draft and the manpower situation in Vietnam, they contend there was a different reason for the change in Project 100,000. The war, it would seem, was robbing the Great Society and the War on Poverty of the ability to carry out their missions. Project 100,000, which situated itself right in the middle as a manpower and social uplift program, was not immune. And as the war progressed, it just got worse. Baskir and Strauss noted that, as the needs of the war grew, the "rehabilitation programs [including Project 100,000] became a shadow of what McNamara originally had in mind."[67]

Meanwhile, while the civil rights community admonished the administration for the educational change to Project 100,000, a pocket of veterans emerged within who equally viewed the program as a moral outrage.[68] "I think

McNamara should be shot," exclaimed Herb DeBose, an African American lieutenant who had served in Vietnam and commanded Project 100,000 men. McNamara and the military, in his mind, had erred by sending men to fight who were not capable, and they were morally corrupt because they shirked on their promises of additional training once the fighting concluded:

Many weren't even on a fifth grade-level. And the Army was supposed to teach them a trade in something—only they didn't. Some were incorrigible, always fighting, and *did not belong there.* They brought their mentality with them. I had people who could only do things by rote. I found out they could not read. No skills before. No skills *after.* Disciplinary problems while in the military. Like any other guy in that war, they began to ask *why,* and when *they* asked *why,* it was often viewed as a discipline problem.

Gary Roberts, who served as infantry platoon leader in Vietnam, concurred: "They took 100,000 basically not very smart kids, eighteen [years old], put them through basic training, gave them a rifle and sent them to Vietnam." Once in country, they made their way out into the field, where their lackluster intellects did them little good. "That's just criminal," Roberts felt.[69]

PROJECT 100,000'S DEMISE

President Lyndon B. Johnson, a man known for his ability to finesse or force congressional leaders into seeing his way on legislation, had displayed throughout the War on Poverty tremendous frustration with those who criticized his efforts. Back in 1965, during a telephone conversation with Bill Moyers, he raged about those attacking him: "I'm ready to kill [the poverty program] quietly through George Mahon [chair of the House Appropriations Committee]," the president angrily informed Bill Moyers, "and get the damn thing out of the way if the niggers are just going to be that mean to me and [Sargent] Shriver's group is going to be disloyal." But Johnson did not end the program or Project 100,000. As for the latter, he let it continue because Johnson believed the program for the African American poor was working. And the president believed that it was working because his, assistant secretary of defense for manpower, Alfred Fitt told him it was working. In fact, Fitt lauded the program to the president: "By applying to these men the Defense Department's experience in educational innovation and on-the-job training, we are transforming them into competent military personnel, serving in such diverse occupational areas as electronic equipment repairmen, medical and dental specialists, as well as in combat arms."[70]

A 1968 study supported Fitt's praise of Project 100,000, as 96 percent of New Standard Men graduated from basic training. One year later, a follow-up report demonstrated that the program, now in its third year, was still graduating New Standards Men at a high rate (94.6 percent). These statistics even applied to the reluctant Marine Corps, which had waged a long battle against its own involvement in the program. Nonetheless, 88.9 percent of New Standards Men became Marines. In addition, 92 percent of these men, often considered to be too criminal, too stupid, and too Black to be in the Marine Corps, received ratings of either Good, Excellent, or Outstanding.[71]

For all the negativity surrounding the program in the military, there were those who expressed satisfaction with Project 100,000. "If the country is faced with formidable problems such as poverty and lack of education, and the armed forces can help, they should," an unnamed commander believed. Meanwhile, an Air Force officer observed:

I've heard no complaints about the Air Force's accepting rejects. In fact, many people think it's a hell of a good idea. . . . There are two categories of the guys who don't make it in the service: those who could but won't, and those who would but can't. We may be getting a group of people who can, but who never have had the chance to prove it.[72]

Some officers began to believe in the program after they saw New Standards Men in action. Colonel Walter Olson, an artillery commander in Vietnam, recalled his initial apprehension of New Standards Men; a concern, he admits, that was quickly alleviated after working with them:

My fears were unwarranted because they came around brilliantly, were probably the best soldiers that I've ever had to lead, although I went to Vietnam with some great fears that they were going to disintegrate and crumble and would not be able to do the job. I was absolutely astounded when I gave up my command in Vietnam how well they actually did. They were outstanding. They weren't the smartest people in the world, but they did their job and they did it very well.

It was going to be a little bit more work to get New Standards Men up to speed, admitted the infantry officer Ralph Hagler, but he felt it was worth the time and effort: "I must honestly say that for being a grunt in Vietnam during that time frame, 1966–1967, they were more than adequately equipped from the duty-honor-country standpoint to carry the mission out very well." It also seemed that some officers on the ground in Vietnam believed that a soldier with less education had less ego, and therefore less opinion, which theoretically meant they would not question orders: "These men make the best infantrymen, mortar men and mechanics. . . . Practically all will do their best to do a good job.

I'd prefer a company of riflemen with fifth-grade educations over a company of college men anytime."[73]

This theory, though terribly flawed, about undereducated soldiers making for better and arguably more complicit warriors was a theme that the investigative journalist Seymour Hersh, writing in 1970, picked up on. In a book on the My Lai Massacre, the famed reporter drew a straight line between the massacre of Vietnamese innocents to the undereducated soldiers of Project 100,000. The presence of thirteen New Standards Men along with their equally inept and undereducated lieutenant, William L. Calley, created, to Hersh's mind, a walking, talking death squad programmed to kill and thus "to take orders, not question them." The eventual Peers Commission investigation into the atrocity, and the much later work of Michal Belknap, aided in debunking this idea. But like so many fallacies surrounding Project 100,000, the myth lived on.[74]

Positive reports and observations aside, the triumvirate behind Project 100,000 was rapidly fracturing. The first to go was the grand architect of the program, Daniel Patrick Moynihan, whose Moynihan Report had caught fire in the West Wing. Many of its findings even made it into Johnson's speech before Howard University in 1965, but it also caught the attention of many members of the civil rights movement for all the wrong reasons. And in that same year, Moynihan was out of politics and back in the friendlier confines of academia. For a reformer and visionary tempered, criticized, and defeated by the realities of the government system and the limit of its power, Moynihan found in the academic world a safe space to dress his wounds, reexamine his philosophies, and reassess his past actions. As Greg Weiner's work on Moynihan observes, the man behind One Third of a Nation and the Moynihan Report changed as he melded the "hues associated with both liberalism (possibilities linked with governmental action) and conservatism (limitations born of respect for social complexity) to form a unique shade of political thought." Unlike his other compatriots in the cause to turn the military into a weapon for social justice and uplifting the poor, however, Moynihan would return to government service.[75]

While Moynihan contemplated his past actions, McNamara was out of office two years later. Disillusioned and frustrated with the war, the former Ford Motor Company executive was granted no reprieves. McNamara was struggling to work with a president he clashed with over how to wage the war. The defense chief was also facing a society questioning his actions and was offered no relief when coming home, as he faced a hostile reception there—his children, it was known around the Beltway, were antiwar and opposed their father's actions.

While observing McNamara, Johnson was reminded of the ill fate of James Forrestal, the embattled defense chief during the Truman administration who had committed suicide. Not desiring a repeat of history, Johnson saw to it that McNamara was installed at the World Bank. Though he had left Washington, McNamara would never escape the blame for the war or Project 100,000.[76]

The last one standing was Johnson. The political horse trader from Johnson City had spent the better part of his life in Washington. Despite all his achievements with the Great Society, most notably by way of civil rights reform, he believed that, even though time was not on his side, he still had work to do. In 1968, Johnson accomplished civil rights reform in housing, which not only aided the civilian realm but also directly impacted the efforts of the DOD when challenging the racism African American soldiers faced off base. For any other president, Johnson's achievement in housing would have been a triumph. But it was 1968, a telling time, a hard time, when Johnson's omissions and flat-out lies about the Vietnam War had come home to roost. He knew, likely before anyone else—even Walter Cronkite, with his famous broadcast about the Tet Offensive and the unsatisfactory nature of the war—that the likelihood of him getting reelected and potentially reunifying the nation had long since passed. On March 31, 1968, Johnson announced to the country that he would not run for reelection or accept the nomination to do so from his party.[77]

With its founding fathers gone, Project 100,000 also began to fade. Its death was the result of a combination of events. Certainly, losing those at the top—Moynihan, Johnson, and McNamara—who had championed it hastened its demise. But the reality was that Vietnam increasingly was becoming an unpopular war. The draft that aided in delivering the manpower necessary to wage it was also rejected more and more by civilians and the military. Real questions surfaced during the latter years of the war within military leadership about the quality of soldiers fighting in Vietnam. In time, this led to a desire to move toward an all-volunteer force and away from the draft. A program that relied partly on drafting substandard manpower—though, as the researcher Thomas Sticht has demonstrated, the number of Project 100,000 men was *less* than the number of similar substandard recruits used to fight in Korea—was low-hanging fruit for those who sought to abandon the draft and had despised Project 100,000 all along. The number of New Standards Men serving in the military gradually declined. Project 100,000 was a casualty of an unpopular war fought during a time of racial unrest that stalemated against poverty and communism. By the early 1970s, the great social engineering experiment under Moynihan, Johnson, and McNamara ended mired in controversy.[78]

RACISM WITHIN THE RANKS

Throughout the early years of the war (1965–1969), the leadership of the American armed forces continued to insist that race relations in the military were in excellent shape. But the reality emerging during that period tells a different tale. For example, consider the difficulties African American soldiers faced earning promotions. In an organization such as the armed forces where white officers dominated the leadership, it was more than possible that a racist white officer could greatly impair the ability of Black military personnel from advancing in their careers—everything from writing poor evaluations, even if they did not deserve it, to not providing important information about upcoming promotion boards. According to the research of James Westheider, by 1972 Black personnel in the Army made up 17 percent of all E-1s, the lowest noncommissioned rank, 3.5 percent of all E-8s, and just 7 percent of all E-9s, the highest noncommissioned rank.[79]

The numbers were equally problematic throughout the services. While many white officers, and even some Black soldiers, questioned whether or not the low numbers were really a matter of racist activity, the numbers in the Army are nonetheless important. Since African Americans disproportionately served, with most doing so in combat units, and died in Vietnam, the entrapment of much of their race in the lowest rank possible only reaffirmed the perception that some of them already had and that was being repeatedly broadcast by members of the Black Power subsection of the civil rights movement—that is, Black military personnel were nothing more than cannon fodder for a white war against another race.[80]

Their treatment by the military justice system did not alleviate this belief. The notion that Blacks had not been getting a fair shake in the courtrooms of the military had existed since Thurgood Marshall's investigation of the Army during the Korean War. When examining the punishment of Black soldiers, an alarming trend emerges. Black soldiers were not at all treated equitably by the military justice system, regardless of the level of infraction. During the Vietnam War, African American soldiers received more "nonjudicial punishment" under Article 15 than whites did.[81]

An Article 15 action can be anything from a written reprimand to time in the stockade to deductions in pay or a reduction in rank. It should be noted that Article 15s can be given out only by higher-ranking noncommissioned officers and by commanding officers. It can safely be assumed that an Article 15 action, in the wrong hands, could be a powerful means to limit the professional advancement of an individual or a race, when considering its use during the

Vietnam War toward Black troops. Take the case of the 193rd Infantry Brigade. Black personnel made up over one-quarter of all troops serving in it. Still, though they were not a clear majority of the outfit, they received 39 percent of its Article 15 punishments. Were the African American soldiers of this brigade just poor, degenerate, and thuggish? No. It was more likely that many of these men were victims of racial discrimination.[82]

As for more serious disciplinary situations, the evidence demonstrates that Black military personnel once again were treated in an unfair and unbalanced manner as compared to their white colleagues. In 1970, the Department of Defense conducted a special investigation into the military justice system. The department's task force discovered that 34.3 percent of Black personnel, out of a sampling of 1,441 individuals, had been court-martialed out of the military. Of those, 41 percent had been charged with either disobeying a direct order or assaulting a superior officer. For these soldiers, their return to "the world" was made even harsher, as their ability to find employment was reduced because of their discharge status. Reforms began to roll out in 1968 to deal with this issue, but as had always been the case, the drive and desire within white leadership to carry out the reforms were lacking.[83]

When considering the guidelines for dress and grooming, the military believed it had created a system of racial equality. But the perceived belief that a "soldier was a soldier" overlooked the reality of the situation. Because of its long-standing white majority, the American armed forces operated in a fashion that mirrored the larger cultural needs of that population, which meant that the way it established its guidelines catered to whites. By doing so, it compounded the growing lack of trust emerging among Black military personnel of the Vietnam era who felt culturally ostracized within the ranks. For instance, hairstyles, which might seem to be a nonissue for some, proved to be a cultural slight for many African American soldiers. Put simply, many Blacks did not maintain their hair in a fashion akin to whites. Perhaps worse, most white barbers, while adequate in the art of cutting the hair of white personnel, proved woefully inadequate in cutting the hair of Black soldiers. The inability of barbers to cut the hair of African American personnel became so bad that Black military personnel often turned to their Black compatriots to get a haircut so they would not be punished for failing to toe the line of military regulation.[84]

Further cultural slights revolved around music and entertainment. This included booking white entertainment acts as opposed to Black musicians of the era, or playing white music over the base's radio stations as opposed to giving fair and equal time to Black artists. Even the goods stocked in post exchanges (PXs) ignored the Black personnel's grooming and general lifestyle needs.[85]

A CAULDRON OF RESENTMENT

These slights, whether deliberate or not, combined to create a cauldron of racial resentment within the military. In the late summer of 1968, the cauldron bubbled violently as incarcerated American military personnel attempted to burn down the "LBJ" stockade, which, given the negativity surrounding the war and its leader, could easily and understandably be confused to mean the Lyndon Baines Johnson stockade. However, this referred to the Long Binh Jail, a military corrections facility in Long Binh, South Vietnam. At the heart of the riot was racism. "Black and white being in Vietnam was no different than black and white being in America," recalled Jimmie Childress, an African American veteran, prisoner, and member of Project 100,000 who had become disillusioned with the war. "We weren't separated by the military, we were separated by the *want* to be separated," Richard Perdomo, a white solider who was also incarcerated at LBJ, acknowledged. "There's always tension between races in a prison. You can control this with adequate staff. When you have control, the tension becomes dormant," admitted an African American officer, one of the supervisors over the compound. Part of the problem, he mused, was inadequate staffing. "We needed more people. None came."[86]

Fueling the deadly struggle that took place was the murder of Dr. Martin Luther King Jr., who was assassinated on April 4, 1968, months prior to the riot. Many people in America and Vietnam, white and Black, were saddened by his untimely passing, but some white soldiers were gleeful and donned the regalia of the Klan, while others waived the Stars and Bars of the fallen Confederacy in joyous and raucous triumph. All this tension resulted in unleashing racial carnage in America and Vietnam. At LBJ, the frustrations of the war, King's death, and the continued racism of the military led to a ninety-minute racial brawl that ended with the deployment of tear gas, the death of one prisoner, Private Edward O. Haskett, who "was beaten to death," the hospitalization of twenty-four others, and the injuring of five guards.[87]

Almost a year later, during the summer of 1969, the cauldron bubbled over again; this time it exploded into racial violence at Camp Lejeune, North Carolina. During a going-away party for members of the 1st Battalion, 6th Marine Regiment, a horrendous racial brawl took place between white and Black Marines. The "Rumble," as it was dubbed, resulted in several Marines being injured and one killed. A month later, right around the time of the Woodstock concert, a Marine report was published in the *New York Times*. It turned out that prior to The race riot the authors of the report, which was dated April 22, 1969, believed that "a racial problem of considerable magnitude" existed in the 2nd Marine Division.[88]

The reasons for it were many, they had found. White Marine officers and noncommissioned officers largely shirked their duties in upholding racial equality within the Marine Corps. They also cracked racist jokes that permeated official and unofficial memoranda and conversations. Facilities in the areas surrounding the 2nd Division remained racially segregated. For example, the existence of racist policing off base was equally bad on base, the investigators discovered. Further troubling, Black Marines felt they had no avenue, and in essence no voice or advocate, they could appeal to. They were isolated. Though the Marines began to address the situation, their corrective actions proved too slow to prevent racial unrest and equally inept in preventing a military prison riot a year later, at Camp Pendleton, where a racial incident led to scrum between white and Black Marine inmates. The problem of racial violence within the military continued to plague the Marines and the rest of the armed forces throughout the remainder of the Vietnam War.[89]

NIXON

During the presidential campaign of 1968, the issue of "law and order" weighed heavily on the brow of white America. But what did that mean? What needed the law and the order that so many seemed to clamor for? In a word for white America: everything. The political scientist James Sundquist observed about this era that "Ghetto riots, campus riots, street crime, anti-Vietnam marches, poor people's marches, drugs, pornography, welfarism, rising taxes, all had a common thread: the breakdown of family and social discipline, of order, of concepts of duty, of respect for law, of public and private morality." Much of white America had little time for a racial reformer. Instead, they wanted a hero to ride into town and clean up the nation. Richard Nixon aimed to be that man. For some Republicans, Nixon was also the saner and safer choice. Thus, for stalwart supporters of Nixon, the biographer John Farrell believed, it was left to Nixon to right the ship, stop the advancement of the oncoming third-party candidacy of George Wallace—whose blatantly racist and unbridled form of political leadership gained him a substantial following in the Deep South and, if elected, would only stoke further racial division—and bring order to the already troubled nation.[90]

NIXON AND RACE: POLITICAL NECESSITY

While Nixon lacked the bravado and smoothness of John Kennedy, the respect of Dwight D. Eisenhower, the willingness to change of Harry Truman, or the mastery of the legislative process of Lyndon B. Johnson, he had the political ability to move from one side of the civil rights issue to the other. Given the occasion, he could pull off the persona of someone who was sympathetic to the cause. During a national broadcast, Nixon openly courted poor Blacks by sympathizing with their situation. At another time, he admonished affluent whites in Philadelphia for their blessed livelihood: "You are fortunate people, but you know that in the great cities of America there is terrible poverty."[91]

While he showed some sympathy, Nixon always knew where his political bread was buttered. If he was going to be a law-and-order candidate, he could not be Bobby Kennedy, who had shown tremendous sympathy to the African American community and whose last name invoked, whether deserved or not, images of the Second Reconstruction. To the contrary: if Richard Nixon were to net the Republican nomination to run and *win*, he had to appeal to the South, which meant he needed a strategy to capture that region. His "Southern Strategy," as it came to be called, was to appeal to the social and racial sensitives of the region by lumping antiwar protests and the civil rights movement together as nothing more than an insidious desire to unleash anarchy on the country.[92]

To do this, he had to win over the hard-right conservative leadership of the south, which meant currying favor from men such as Strom Thurmond of South Carolina and Mills Godwin Jr. of Virginia, both of whom had ditched the Democratic Party—once dominated by Southerners like Jefferson and Jackson and that included an adopted Southerner, Franklin Roosevelt—for the Republican Party of Eisenhower, Goldwater, and Nixon, which was increasingly aligning itself with states' rights values and limited government intervention in societal affairs. Of course, he had to also win the white people of the South. He went a long way to achieving that by working behind the scenes during the Republican National Convention to let Southern whites know that he would not fail the region. In no uncertain terms, Nixon let them know that *he* was their man and that *he* would "lay off [the] pro-Negro crap"—in this era, "pro-Negro crap" meant issues like forced racial integration of schools—of the Democratic Party. He cemented that pledge to them and their region by picking Spiro Agnew of Maryland, a border-state governor and firebrand best known for his criticism of Vietnam antiwar protesters, as his vice presidential running mate.[93]

NIXON AND RACE: PERSONAL RACISM

President Nixon's historical actions in the civil rights arena tend to surprise the uninformed and has led to a debate about who he was and what his feelings really were on the matter. During the Nixon years, the president raised the budget to enforce civil rights activities by 800 percent, funding for Historically Black Colleges and Universities doubled, the number of African Americans serving in the upper echelon of the federal government increased by 37 percent, and racial segregation in Southern public schools was dealt a heavy blow as the proportion of Black children attending all-Black schools went from 68 percent to 8 percent, which meant that those who had left were now in racially integrated schools. And he even dabbled a little in racial military affairs. After John D. Weaver's book *The Brownsville Raid* caught the attention of the Congress in 1970, Nixon pardoned the men of the 25th Infantry Regiment for the Brownsville Affair.[94]

Small had observed that Nixon personally "believed in ending legal desegregation but opposed forced [racial] integration." But was Nixon's presidency, as Small had dubbed it, simply "schizophrenic" in its delivery of reform? While Nixon may have wanted to end racial segregation, he remained a racist throughout his presidency, especially in the African world, which he often described in remarks that reeked of Old World colonialism. Nixon once quipped that "there has never in history been an adequate black nation, and they are the only race of which this is true." At other times Nixon was more bigoted. He once informed his National Security Advisor and eventual secretary of state, Henry Kissinger: "Henry, let's leave the niggers to Bill," referring to Secretary of State Bill Rogers; "we'll take care of the rest of the world." And in 1971, he laughed at the racist rantings of his eventual successor of the neoconservative movement, California governor Ronald Reagan. During a telephone conversation with the actor-turned-politician, a chortling Nixon readily agreed with Reagan's assessment of the situation involving the betrayal, as the governor saw it, of several African nations in the UN that sought to admit China into the venerated body. "To see those," the Golden State's highest-ranking official cracked, "those monkeys from those African countries [to act in this fashion]—damn them, they're still uncomfortable wearing shoes!"[95]

The fall of 1971 was a challenging time for Nixon. There was his campaign for reelection, which of course led to the Watergate scandal, the defeat at the UN that Reagan had ranted about, welfare reform, and the issue of racially integrated school busing. The last two, Tim Naftali has written, "apparently

President Nixon, as Lincoln looms: As opposed to Lincoln, the standard-bearer
of their party, President Richard Nixon is not remembered as an important civil
rights reformer, but he did achieve some milestones, whether in the civilian
or military realm. Perhaps the most important civil rights reform that he was
directly involved in was the ending of the draft and the creation of the All-
Volunteer Force, a maneuver that reflected more his political acumen than any
desire to alleviate the disproportionate number of black men that served and
died during the Vietnam conflict, let alone to combat racism within the ranks.
Source: 37-whpo-9461-17-a, 6/23/1972, Richard Nixon Library.

inspired Nixon to examine more deeply his own thinking on whether African
Americans could make it in American society." From this emerged a dark racist belief for Nixon that the African American race was simply incapable of being good enough. In a conversation with Daniel Patrick Moynihan, the liberal
reformer who became a Harvard professor and Nixon confidant, the president
revealed that he believed the questionable research of the era—much of it coming from the psychologists Richard Herrnstein and Arthur R. Jensen—stating
that IQ and race were inseparable. This controversial research believed that
race defined the limits of one's intelligence. From that, it emerged in Nixon's
mind that a hierarchy in fact existed with whites firmly on top—an idea that
harkened back to the old social Darwinist beliefs about the inferiority of all
races minus that of the Anglo-Saxon.[96]

THE ALL-VOLUNTEER FORCE

Nixon's actions out of *political necessity* and his *personal racism* define him as a domestic, international, and military leader. The order of importance to him depended on the situation. For instance, ending the draft was not about the immoral racial ramifications of the manpower apparatus to the African American community. Instead, it provided Nixon a potential two-for-one political elixir for the tenuous situation that his administration faced—namely, the growing cries from antiwar and antidraft protesters, which included segments of the civil rights movement. While not a perfect solution, it had its benefits, and he found it too tempting to pass up. As Beth Bailey observed, the time was right for this type of calculated political maneuver. Some congressmen and Republican-dominated organizations, such as the Wednesday Group, had called for the end of the draft two years prior to Nixon's first year in office. So on the campaign trail in 1968, Nixon announced his intention to end the unpopular draft. When Nixon talked to the American people about ending the draft, he sold it as a necessary change. It was about the *necessity* of waging war on the Cold War atomic battlefield. No longer was it feasible, Nixon contended, to maintain massive glacially paced conscription armies in the shadow of Mutual Assured Destruction; what the country needed now was smaller, nimbler, and faster strike forces staffed by volunteer warriors who were deadly earnest in the art of counterinsurgency and nuanced in the sophisticated weapons of the era.[97]

The other justification for jettisoning the draft relied on the rights of the individual—namely, the idea of individual liberty and a person's ability to embrace that liberty and make a decent living in a competitive capitalist environment. The draft, however, circumvented that liberty, Nixon argued. The way to restore individual liberty was to create a "market-driven all-volunteer force." And in the months and years to come, America followed Nixon's advice and ended its draft and embraced a volunteer model for its armed forces. It was arguably Nixon's greatest racial reform in the military; after all, it ended the power of all-white draft boards over African American civilian personnel, the controversial Project 100,000, and the heinous number of Black men being drafted to serve and die on the battlefields of Vietnam. Those accomplishments were indirect bonuses, however, not the main goal. The main goal was to get out of Vietnam and silence the political left.[98]

With little meaningful leadership emerging from the top, the weight of further racial reform in the military fell on the shoulders of its leaders. But they struggled. Though it sought to field a more successful fighting force post-Vietnam, the creation of the All-Volunteer Force struggled against one of the great enemies of the republic: racism. In 1971, racial fighting had broken out between white and Black soldiers stationed in West Germany. *Ebony* magazine reported on it, and the DOD and the NAACP investigated the brawl. As a result, a year later the Army established the Race Relations School, designed to carry out the training now deemed necessary by the branch to educate its troops on racial differences and experiences in American society. Orders, it seemed, were no longer enough. It was now about understanding and respecting those whose skin color and beliefs differed from one's own.[99]

While the Army worked to train its way out of the situation, the Navy sought to extinguish the flames of racial confrontation that exploded onboard an aircraft carrier, the USS *Kitty Hawk*. No military outfit, once in the fray, is ever sparred the rigors of war. The *Kitty Hawk* was no different. Having its shore leave curtailed and rushed into action off the coast of Vietnam, it took part in some of the most strenuous air operations of the war, including aiding in conducting Operation Linebacker I, which sought to halt North Vietnamese operations below the 17th parallel and end long-stalled peace negotiations with North Vietnam.[100]

Offered little reprieve from their duties, the enlisted personnel of *Kitty Hawk* labored extensively throughout. Though the overall compliment of Black sailors onboard was small (7.2 percent), many of these men (46 percent) were new to the ship, which meant they were unfamiliar with how the vessel typically operated. When combining the two, a lack of trust emerged among the African American personnel. This distrust was compounded by the fact that most African American personnel onboard the *Kitty Hawk* were E-1 to E-3. Only a small number held higher noncommissioned officer ranks, let alone the handful who were officers. Racial integration of sleeping quarters and living spaces was not enforced. Though the captain and his officer cadre worked to enforce racial integration, a sort of benign racial neglect set in based on the feelings of the crew. As one officer put it: "If they're happy [living in segregated quarters], leave them alone." This allowed for development of what the scholar John Darrell Sherwood dubbed a "gang culture," where allegiance was not linked to the traditional chain of command but to those among the Black personnel deemed worthy of leadership.[101]

It must also be remembered that a segment of the Black community in the military was no longer willing, because of the rise of Black Power activism during this era, to turn a blind eye toward racism within it. Then there was the problem that caused havoc throughout the Navy: drugs. Drug use aboard ship was not only an African American issue; it plagued all races in the Navy.

All these factors combined provide the necessary ingredients for a racial explosion.[102]

Through the summer and into the fall of 1972, unrest onboard the vessel began to simmer, which only fostered further resentment, unrest, and lack of trust. After completing air operations that began at 1 p.m. on October 11 and concluded at 6 p.m. on October 12, a tired and weary crew sought a respite; instead, the distrust and resentment of the Black military personnel, fueled in part by the continued racial segregation that prevented contact and communication with white colleagues, led to total bedlam. Violence and fighting broke out. When it was over, at least sixty were injured. In a moment that harkened back to the existence of the "old breed" and "new breed" of African American servicemen, an older Black sailor afterward admitted that he was "shocked" by the incident, while a younger Black sailor simply quipped that the "blacks just got tired of being treated like dogs." When the *Kitty Hawk* returned to its home port of San Diego, California, several of its African American sailors were asked while disembarking from the vessel what started the problem. Their responses, though meant to explain their own experiences, would resonate for all Blacks who had served throughout this era of tremendous racial reform in the armed forces but who remained terribly frustrated about their experiences in a racially integrated military: "Racism," they replied.[103]

CONCLUSION

Throughout the racial reform of the military, the Cold War remained ubiquitous. Much like the Korean War before it, Vietnam played a role. Unlike Korea, which could be seen as positive because of the gains made in the Army and Marine Corps, Vietnam, which was waged in a more complex social and racial moment in American history, was often seen as a negative era for the racial reform of the military. Great gains had been made on behalf of African American military personnel and their families. Yesterday's gains, no matter how important, did not resolve the issue of acceptance and understanding of the Black community. The reason that was so was because the president and the military they led had never really tried to do so.

Johnson

Lyndon Johnson's status as a presidential reformer is largely unparalleled, with no disrespect to Abraham Lincoln; outside of Franklin Delano Roosevelt, nobody matched what he achieved legislatively as a president. Neither was the former Master of the Senate completely tone-deaf on civil rights, but he was operating in a time where the civil rights movement had shifted directions on Vietnam and African American military service. If it had been earlier in the century—say, the 1950s—Johnson's controversial approach for continued racial reform in the military (Project 100,000) might have been accepted, perhaps even welcomed, within the civil rights community. But this was the 1960s. The African American community and the civil rights movement, whether it was King's or Carmichael's version of it, had soured on the war in Vietnam. To be sure, some Blacks maintained an undying desire to serve in the military for reasons of patriotism and socioeconomic escape. But there was growing objection to Black military service as a means of social uplift.[104]

While he recognized the shift, Johnson's actions as president still missed the mark. Instead, he tried to do that which he understood best: making deals. He and his advisers thought they knew what was best for the Black community and sought to launch programs that carried forward their ideas. And that was why Johnson, to his detriment, supported Project 100,000. It would provide uplift, discipline, and aide in bolstering the Cold War American military. For Johnson, what was not to like? It was guns and butter. For African Americans, they disliked almost everything about it.

Though African Americans did not make up the majority of it, and no matter how noble the intentions of the Johnson administration, Project 100,000 smelled most foul to the Black community. Whether it was because of an inherent distrust of the government built up by years of frustrations and failures in the attempt to achieve more, or that reform was not proceeding at a pace fast enough to satisfy those who had desired desperately for more, members of the African American community and civil rights leadership viewed Vietnam with tremendous cynicism. It was not that they were sympathetic to communism; they sympathized with the Vietnamese people, who they saw in some ways to be like themselves. And they worried over the fate of their own people, who were waging a war that was eradicating their brothers, husbands, and sons at an alarming rate.

The way Vietnam was unfolding for their people, plus the increasing desperation, frustration, and the emergence of Black Power activism, all combined to shade their view of Project 100,000. How was dressing undereducated African Americans in the uniforms of the Army and Marine Corps, handing them a rifle, and dispatching them to win a war against godless communism in a foreign country dominated by a colored population going to change the fate of the Black man in America? It sounded more like genocide for the Black man at the expense of killing Vietnamese soldiers and citizens. It was killing two races with one racist stone. When it was announced that Project 100,000 jettisoned its educational component, not because of the pressing need to uplift men but instead to send them into war, it just made the program and the situation in Vietnam look worse to Black America.

In general, Johnson never corrected course in his understanding of what the African American community needed. Project 100,000 was only one example of this. He largely acted in a transactional fashion, one that tried to satiate the issue as he saw it, which was that racial segregation, no matter how morally irreprehensible, denied equality of opportunity for Blacks. If he could achieve that in protecting their rights as citizens, if he could restore the Southern Black vote, if he could weed out racism in housing, they would be grateful. And they largely were, but by Vietnam it was also about being accepted socially as a race on par with whites.

The desire for social and racial respect from whites was not new. During the 1960s, though, the issue took on even greater importance within Black America. In the military this is best reflected in the clash between the "old breed" and "new breed": one would tolerate slights, since so much had been done and achieved, but the other, which had grown up in a world far more inclusive, could no longer stomach the role of being a second-class citizen and human being. Serving in a racially integrated, but no less racist, military was a daily reminder of the lack of respect that their race received from their white brothers-in-arms.

Nixon

For Richard Nixon, none of this seemed to matter, civil rights and the war in Vietnam were means to a political end that would lead to victory at the polls. On civil rights, he catered to Blacks, but his promise to be a law-and-order leader overshadowed any sympathy he truly had for them, as it catered directly to the fears and consternation of conservative white America. With Vietnam, it was the same. In his 1969 "Silent Majority" speech, Nixon, in a good bit of dramatic flag-clutching, appealed directly to those he felt he needed the most—namely, the white conservative right—by blaming all the woes of America, and especially in Vietnam, on those he despised the most: the political left at the heart of the antiwar and civil rights movements.[105]

It was high political drama and manipulation at its finest, and it was all by design. As his biographer Melvin Small observed, Nixon knew the war was lost or not worth the effort, and he admitted to a staffer: "I've come to the conclusion that there's no way to win the war. But we can't say that of course. In fact, we have to say the opposite just to keep some degree of bargaining leverage." As he excoriated the left, a foil that the right could focus on, he moved toward that which the antiwar movement had wanted all along: withdrawal. But he did so not for the sake of Blacks, or for the sake of saving lives, but because the continued waging of an unwinnable war was politically stupid and costly for Nixon.[106]

If he did help Blacks and saved American lives, that was just an additional political gain, not the main goal. Nixon's main goal was to get out of Vietnam and silence the left. To be sure, the Vietnam War and the civil rights movement had coalesced to became a political problem for Nixon, and he understood that, by withdrawing from the former, it would ease the latter to a degree. Ending the unpopular draft would also help him, but it never led to a desire by Nixon to rid the military of the continuing issue of racism within the ranks. And Nixon's racism would not allow it to happen. A lifetime member of the NAACP who had befriended Jackie Robinson and once referred to the Little Rock Crisis as a "moral issue," Nixon disparaged Blacks behind their backs every chance he could get. From joking with Reagan to the time that Nixon confided to a colleague that African Americans were "just down out of the trees," he ridiculed and made fun of them.[107]

And much like Eisenhower, his onetime boss, Nixon never acted with the full power of his office to carry out racial change. For Ike, it was the *Brown* decision; for Nixon, it was the 1965 Voting Rights Act, which he never supported or encouraged the Justice Department to enforce. When he did act with the Justice Department, it was to go after a segment of the civil rights movement that had been deemed to be a societal problem—namely, Nixon's wholehearted support of the FBI in its investigation of the Black Panthers. And Nixon did not support racial change within the military as much as Eisenhower did. Instead, he seemed content during the era of the All-Volunteer Force to let the military reform itself. The main goal for Nixon was to escape the heat from the antiwar movement, not to appeal to Blacks about the benefits that could come their way if the military moved to a model that celebrated talent over skin color.[108]

Conclusion

The Cold War was a global version of the Hatfield–McCoy feud except with nuclear weapons. Both sides—Western democratic capitalism versus Eastern communism—declared the other the enemy and launched propaganda attacks against one another to rally those sympathetic to their side, while also seeking to secure the hearts and minds of Third World countries. They both used the notion that peace was out of reach to justify the incredibly reckless buildup of arsenals of annihilation dedicated to the eradication of one another. The leadership of this era, and the populations they represented, largely survived the Cold War because of the sobering effect stemming from the threat of Mutual Assured Destruction (aptly known as "MAD"). Therefore, instead of becoming a full-on shooting war, the Cold War would be one predominantly of an ideological nature with the occasional costly and dangerous flareup in places such as Korea, Vietnam, and Afghanistan.

American civil rights leaders certainly understood the power of fear that the Cold War invoked among the American people, and they sought to use it to force racial reform in the nation and military. Civil rights leaders from Du Bois to White, and African American congressmen from Powell to Diggs, took up the issue. The meaningful contributions of African American military personnel made it more and more difficult to ignore them, and the stalwart commitment of the Black community to carry out change played a critical role in the story of the racial integration of the armed forces. Despite the nobility of their efforts, civil rights leaders were not American presidents. They could encourage, plead, pressure, and even threaten presidents with nonviolent protests, but without presidential buy-in—which is exactly what civil rights leaders had sought for decades—the racial reform of America and its armed forces would never have gotten off the ground.

EQUALITY OF OPPORTUNITY IS NOT RACIAL ACCEPTANCE

American presidents supported racial reform in the military because of the necessity of the Cold War. The threat of antidemocratic propaganda from Russia forced presidents to engage in a counteroffensive that sought to demonstrate the superiority of the American way of life. But that also meant that presidents, whether or not they wanted to, had to recognize and address the greater predicament of American race relations throughout the nation and its military. Mirroring the struggle itself, presidential action in the military was not just about answering Moscow's verbal barbs; it was also about preparing the military for the day that the talking stopped and the fighting on the atomic battlefield began in earnest.

Of the six presidential administrations examined in this study, the administrations of Harry Truman, Dwight Eisenhower, and Lyndon Johnson accomplished the most. As Cold War presidents, they were driven and fueled to an extent by the larger struggle facing them. But how far each was willing to go to bring about reform was determined by their own beliefs. For Truman, it was a case of the political and the personal.

As a World War I veteran and a firm believer in the Bill of Rights, Truman could not allow African American veterans to be beaten and blinded simply because they were Black. Neither could he, as a president seeking election in his own right, ignore them or risk their allegiance to him if he did nothing. Truman was imperfect. He did not always deliver racial justice. The effort to prosecute Isaac Woodard's attackers had died at the hands of a racist white court, and even the sitting president could do nothing further about it. And he still held some level of racial animosity at times toward certain members of the Black community; the story of the feud between Truman and Adam Clayton Powell Jr. resonates in this regard. But despite all his faults, he delivered something few expected: Truman racially integrated the military.

The racial integration of the armed forces was a stunning achievement for the African American community and the president, but it was not without limitations. Truman did not believe that perfect racial equality could ever be achieved. But he did believe in equality of opportunity. Often, equality of opportunity meant a chance for African American men to serve in a racially integrated combat unit, attend a racially integrated training school, live on a racially integrated post, and become an officer in a racially integrated military. These were important and meaningful changes that civil rights reformers within and outside the armed forces had sought for decades.

For African Americans, "equality of opportunity" resonated with them as a people because they believed it provided a path to a better way of life for their race; seemingly, they also viewed it as the way to achieving racial acceptance from whites. The problem was that equality of opportunity by way of racial integration of the military never guaranteed that racial acceptance for Blacks as a people would follow suit; neither did it ever make it a priority to do so. It was *hoped*—largely by the African American community and white reformers who supported them—that it would occur. But those hopes were often dashed as American presidents from Truman onward, their staffs, and leaders in the military largely focused on achieving racial integration by way of equality of opportunity.

Eisenhower inherited a great many things when he took office from Truman: the Korean War, the larger Cold War, the budding civil rights movement of the 1950s, and the racial integration of the armed forces, which relied on the mantra "equality of opportunity." These issues were interlaced and help explain why Ike did more than most of those who would succeed him on the issue. The continued racial integration of the armed forces was a no-brainer for Ike. It was already underway and successful and was unfolding in a fashion that emphasized equality of opportunity, which was likely far more socially comfortable for Eisenhower, as that approach did not call for complete racial equality, which he, like Truman, did not seem to believe the president or the government could achieve acting alone.

Additionally, Eisenhower, again like Harry Truman, faced continuous pressure from the civil rights community to act. Where Truman had the ability to weather this provocation to action, Eisenhower seemed to be more reactive to it as opposed to proactive. For that matter, it could be argued that getting Adam Clayton Powell Jr. off his back was just as important a motivation for Ike as the desire to defeat global communism.

Befitting Ike's racial gradualism, it was a matter of whether or not he personally believed he had the political power to act. This ruling philosophy dovetailed with his social and cultural upbringing in the late nineteenth and the early-twentieth-century American Army, where he had little interaction, or desire to interact, with Black soldiers. After all, he had used them during the Battle of the Bulge only when he needed them. Still, and though he was often a great disappointment to those in the African American community who had voted for him, the reluctant Eisenhower, when he felt he could, achieved astounding victories for those who championed racial reform in the military during the Cold War. Of the three presidents who achieved the most reform, he may be the best example of the idea that a leader's actions need not meet the moral merit of the moment to be successful. The problem, of course, with his approach was that equality of opportunity continued to carry the day and that racism, because it was not dealt with, lived on; everything was kicked down the road for someone else to deal with. The problem, of course, was that the presidents of this era never really addressed it.

Of the three, Johnson had the least hesitation to act; neither did he have any reservations about using his power to reform. Dressed in a martyr's mandate and fueled internally by his own ego and insecurity, Johnson, a gifted political operator, acted in a more calculated political fashion—one that used morality as a weapon to achieve reform but still did not actually deal with the morality of the issue—than his predecessors. He believed without reservation that he would be able to shame the Congress and the American people into action. The problem with Johnson was that his ego and absolute certainty led him to rely on programs at times that were questionable in nature, which only added fuel to the internal fight that was splintering the civil rights movement between those who were working with Johnson—King and company—and those who saw him conducting racial genocide in Southeast Asia—Carmichael and others.

Within the military realm of Johnson reform, no effort looms larger than Project 100,000, which remains the most Quixotesque and controversial. Though not the abysmal failure critics allege, it did fail to do what the larger War on Poverty sought, which was to defeat poverty outright, to uplift Black men from the urban ghetto, while also supplying a stream of manpower to fight the battles of the Cold War. Project 100,000 had always been both a manpower and an antipoverty program. The costs of fighting the war in Vietnam, however, superseded the needs of the training aspect of the program. When that happened, Project 100,000 went from a revolutionary effort to harness the power of the military to go to war with poverty and instead became what was seen as a cynical endeavor designed to kill Black men—the very group the program had promised to save.

Under Johnson, McNamara, and Moynihan, the equality-of-opportunity approach of Truman lived on. Their mission—for Moynihan it might have even been obsession—centered on trying to level the racial playing field as opposed to eradicating the racism that underpinned it. Project 100,000 sought to uplift the poor, especially Blacks, though they did not make up the majority of the program, from the vicious and cyclical nature of poverty. Seeking racial uplift for Blacks, itself antiracist, is not entirely the same thing as targeting racism. And thus, it continued to argue, as had white and Black reformers throughout the twentieth century, that the strict deference and discipline of the military would be enough to overcome racism and achieve manhood for those Black men trapped in the impoverished pockets of the urban ghetto or rural America.

In some ways, they were led by Moynihan on this idea. He believed that what African American men needed was to get out from under a matriarchal environment to become men. The place that they could go to learn about deference, discipline, and manhood was the racially integrated American armed forces. Of course, there were problems with this approach. It relied on the belief that deference to the rules of the military, which in the 1960s was operating in a far more racially integrated fashion than before, ensured that racism would be defeated. The reality was that it was not. It also deeply offended some African Americans, as it blatantly argued that their community was broken and crime-ridden because of the lack of a patriarchal presence for Black men; though the motives behind this sentiment were pure, the description of Black America as broken was racist, as it tried to impress white ideas of what society should look like on African Americans. Still, while some Blacks might have accepted what Moynihan had to say, it completely ignored the reality that the matriarchal nature of Black society was not the problem but that instead it was the systemic racism that entrapped them in pockets of poverty.

Out of fairness to the trio of Truman, Eisenhower, and Johnson, all presidents of this era opted to treat the symptoms of racism in the military as opposed to completely removing the cause. But that did not mean that their approach did not net results. Furthermore, if the trio of reforming presidents had followed the pace established by the politically handcuffed Franklin Roosevelt, or the image-conscious John Kennedy, or the politically focused but morally devoid Nixon, the military would not have progressed nearly as far as it did.[1]

IT TAKES A VILLAGE

American presidents did not achieve racial reform of the military on their own; they always needed help. Franklin Roosevelt and Truman needed a General Eisenhower. Though not a major driver of racial reform during World War II, Eisenhower was responsible for giving the order to racially integrate fighting forces during the Battle of the Bulge. Truman, Eisenhower, Kennedy, and Johnson need a "Lighting Joe" Collins, an "Old Iron Tits" Matthew Ridgway, and a William "Westy" Westmoreland (though he howled that Project 100,000 was a destructive force that aided and abetted in robbing American victory in Vietnam) to support the idea of racial integration and reform in the military. They also needed the army of officers, noncommissioned officers, and military personnel who found a way to overcome the generational existence of racial segregation and limitations on the ground that prevented the military from acting in an efficient fashion. Sometimes these unnamed warriors of yesterday's past even achieved some measure of racial acceptance.

If the adage "the suit makes the man" were applied to presidents, it would go something like "the advisers make the president." Operating within the realm of the executive branch, civilian staffers of the president and in the War Department and later the Department of Defense made all the difference. At every turn of this story, staffers' activities behind the scenes explode off the page. During the early throes of World War II, Franklin Roosevelt had Eleanor Roosevelt and Anna Rosenberg. As the Cold War raged and the propaganda attacks from Russia showered down, Truman had Clark Clifford, who in turn had Phileo Nash, who helped craft Executive Order 9981.

While Eisenhower attempted to the dodge the issue until he could no longer, he turned to Maxwell Rabb to achieve the continued racial integration of the military, the Veterans Administration, and its hospitals and to cool the flames of his critics. Adam Yarmolinsky, Carlisle Runge, Alfred Fitt, and Moynihan, along with a handful of others, achieved limited success under Kennedy, but under Johnson they thrived and sought to end racial segregation in the National Guard and went to war with American poverty while also protecting the rights of African American military personnel as they sought housing for their families. Nixon's greatest adviser was himself. He understood the reality of waging an unpopular war that his country was losing, while also dealing with continued angst over civil rights. Though it was not created for this purpose, the All-Volunteer Force offered a cure-all, and Nixon used it as such. For him, it was another weapon against the hippies, the Black civil rights activists, and the antiwar crowd of the counterculture in American society that grated him so much. But if it looked like it was helping the Black community, he would not fight that image.[2]

THE PECULIAR AND STRANGE MIND OF THE SOUTH

During the Cold War, the South's fears over racially integrating the military— an institution they felt an incredible bond with—were multifaceted and enmeshed with one another. While not all white Southerners were racists, many feared racially tinkering with the military, as they believed erroneously that the racial integration of the armed forces would lead to total mayhem within the ranks—a fear that much of the military, from the lowest to the highest in rank, shared with them. The reason that many in the South felt this way was owed to the region's remaining racism from the sins of its past, one that oscillated from a warped form of racist paternalism over Blacks to that of a more callous and bigoted rejection of them. Consider the story of Ned Almond, a white graduate of VMI, who because he was a Southern white man—which in the eyes of the

Army meant that he supposedly knew how to *handle* them best—was tabbed to lead Black men into the calamity of World War II.

Living during the era of the so-called White Man's Burden, Almond seemed to behave in a somewhat paternalistic fashion toward his men as he sought to train them, despite their supposed racial shortcomings, to the best of his ability. Once his command fell apart during combat in Italy, though, Almond embraced the most hardened of racist beliefs from this region and blamed and condemned his men for lacking the basic intelligence or courage to fight. He went so far to declare, despite the examples within his own command or historically, that Black men did not have what it took to be warriors for America. Ned Almond never stopped blaming them, but he was hardly alone. For those Southerners who followed this societal mantra of racism, segregation, and hate, they just could not accept the former slaves of the region or their ancestors as societal equals, let alone as combatants for the region or the country.

The concerns over military efficiency and the racism that supported it hint at why some white Southerners could not accept racial integration. The reality was that some white Southerners could not accept racial integration because it challenged what they thought the South was—at the vanguard—and what they thought American society—more like the South—should be. The region's bravado over its religious devotion, wholesomeness, family focus, military prowess, and more has always served as a cultural shield that protected the region from facing its historical problems, such as substandard education and lack of opportunity for many of its poorest citizens, whether white or Black; the monopolization of the region's wealth in the hands of the few; and the role racism and slavery had played in shaping the region's identity. These insecurities, along with the region's defeat during the Civil War, led to the necessity of a narrative that reinforced the region's importance to itself and the rest of the country: the Lost Cause.

From the smoldering ruins of defeat, the Lost Cause allowed the South, and those Southerners who embraced it, to see themselves as a noble and vanquished people who fought for individual (minus minorities) and states' rights against the greedy and meddling desires of a tyrannical government. Put simply, even if it had lost, it did the right thing by standing up and fighting. The South's inherent distrust of outsiders—whether they were Northern Yanks, carpetbaggers, liberals, communists, or today's cultural Marxists—and their motives is a surface-level example of this phenomenon in practice throughout Southern and American history. All of this protected the South's conscience against the sins of its past, but it also granted the region an inflated view of itself.

This was why the South trembled at the thought of the racial integration of the armed forces, because not only would it spill over into local communities and potentially encourage Southern African Americans to join with the civil rights movement and shed themselves of Jim Crow and seek racial equality; it would remove an important social and cultural barrier between white racist Southerners and the uncomfortable truth about their past and present. It would challenge not only the South's way of life; it would upend what they believed to be the region's role as a social, religious, and cultural North Star for the rest of the nation. Though it was flawed and terribly bigoted, it is easy to see how frightening and terrifying racial integration of the armed forces, and America as a whole, was for racist white Southerners of the era who held these beliefs and why, with their world once again upside down, they came roaring back against any change to their way of life and perceived importance to the country.

While the South reckoned with its social and cultural future, some presidents trembled at the notion of upsetting the region socially, culturally, and politically. They feared it so much that they would not act aggressively on civil rights reform in the military or, for that matter, outside of it. And as such, they *incarcerated themselves* in the Southern cage because they feared the result to themselves politically (JFK and Nixon), their programs (FDR), and the country (Eisenhower) that could result if they acted. But while some feared upsetting the region, others defied the South anyway. Harry Truman was one of them. But it did not come without a cost for him. In the fall of 1948, after he had begun the process to racially integrate the military, he had to square off against a sizable Southern defection from his party. Johnson, a Southerner, further agitated the white people of his region by his victories in the civilian realm, while also racially integrating the National Guard and improving housing conditions off base for Black service personnel. Of the three presidents who achieved the most reform in the military, Eisenhower is the odd duck of the group. In a sense, he incarcerated himself in the Southern cage as a civilian leader out of concern of another civil war. But much like Kennedy, Ike was forced to act on matters he just could not ignore, such as the Little Rock Crisis. Yet Eisenhower acted to racially reform the education apparatus of the military and integrate the VA. For this, Ike faced his fair share of slander and vitriol from conspiracy theorists and Southerners alike. Perhaps it is best to surmise that Eisenhower was under some sort of house arrest, where at times he could act more freely but did so with a cautious eye toward not offending the South too much.

Meanwhile, the participants in the 1960 presidential contest, John Kennedy and Richard Nixon, proceeded in a more guarded fashion, one that was akin to Franklin D. Roosevelt's approach. They both appreciated and respected the power of the region. Being a man so focused on his and the nation's imagery, Kennedy, much to his consternation, repeatedly found himself in civil rights situations that forced him to act in direct conflict with the South; prominent examples in the civilian realm include the Freedom Rides and the racial integration of Ole Miss and the University of Alabama.

When he did act in the military arena, Kennedy's actions were consistently calculated. Racially integrating honor guards and the Coast Guard Academy, both low-hanging political fruit, were great for international relations and the image of the nation, but they were not quite as politically dangerous as racially integrating the National Guard or fighting against racial prejudice in off-base housing, which was why neither occurred during his presidency. Similar to Eisenhower, Kennedy it seems wished that the civil rights movement would just disappear, but since that was not going to happen, he proved agreeable to the idea of letting his staffers take the lead on the issue, which allowed him the opportunity to deflect blame and keep his eye on the Cold War. Even when the findings of the Gesell Report pressed for further change, Kennedy never used the full weight of his office to get behind the reforms or direct McNamara to carry them out. As a result, instead of acting aggressively, McNamara, who was also facing blowback from within the military, hesitated and limited the scope of the reform that occurred. When Kennedy finally came around on the morality of the matter and seemed ready to get behind civil rights reform, it was too late; he was assassinated five months later.

Recognizing the power of the Southern voting bloc, Nixon went to the South directly and willingly kowtowed to their wish to preserve their way of life and self-perceived importance to curry their political favor. Though he ended the draft and ushered in the era of the All-Volunteer Force, these reforms have often been viewed historically as weapons that the president used against the left as opposed to anything meaningful. Put simply, the South had very little to worry about from a man who sought their favor, who promised to bring law and order back to the land, which meant keeping the hippies and civil rights activists in check, and who generally believed that African Americans were inferior.

FOR THE NECESSITY OF THE MILITARY AND THE SOCIETY IT PROTECTS

The world has a problem with racism; the United States is not immune. It has been with the republic and its military since the very beginning when slaves were brought over to Jamestown and, years later, when George Washington struggled to use Black troops, whether free or enslaved, against the superior British forces the young country faced. But Washington, then Lincoln decades later, and then Franklin Roosevelt almost a century after that, all came to a solution about the use of African American military personnel. It is one that Truman and his successors followed during the period under examination in this study: *necessity*. They needed Blacks to fight for the country to win the contest it was engaged in at the time. Regardless of whether it led to temporary, limited, or expansive reform within the armed forces, presidents continuously relied on the necessity of the moment brought about by the nation's enemies to justify not only the use of Black soldiers but also the racial reforms that were deemed equally necessary to secure victory.

While necessity drove the issue for presidents, reformers within their administrations and civil rights operatives in the civilian community believed that racial integration of the armed forces was an important step toward ending Jim Crow segregation throughout the country. The reason they felt so confident about having the military do this was because of its strict adherence to discipline, doctrine, and command structure. Those who sought a better way of life for African Americans within and outside the military gambled that racism could be ordered out of the military completely. In a sense, when one considers the scope of the gains made for the average African American members of the military and their families, that gambit paid off. The payout of their wager was racial integration of all aspects of the American armed forces, integrated education on base for the children of military personnel, integrated health care after their career was over, and even efforts to improve access off base to nondiscriminatory education and housing. But it was not a total victory over the forces of hate and racial discrimination, and it was never designed to be.

During World War II and the Cold War, the military certainly acknowledged the issue of racism, as both the Nazis and the communists used it against the Americans, but it did so in a fashion that was dependent on the necessity of defeating a foreign enemy or idea, not one that worked continuously to protect the racial inclusivity gained by change. Instead, presidents and others within their realm continued to reform the military out of a desperate desire to thwart their enemies but did not do enough to maintain the acceptance they hoped would come from those reforms or from their power to order change among the personnel of the armed services.

The result of this approach that sought to rectify this image, and served to bolster the ranks further during times of war, led to a racially integrated military but not a racially accepting one. Decades of tremendous reform had been achieved, but not all whites or Blacks trusted one another. By the time this story reaches the era of the Vietnam War, this lack of trust manifested itself in often dangerous and deadly ways.

Why did universal racial acceptance not occur? The great failure of the racial integration and reform of the military was that there was never a concerted and consistent desire to hunt out and eliminate racism from within the armed forces. The failure to do so not only robbed the armed forces of fielding an even more efficient and talented fighting force during the Cold War; it also may have prevented those moments where racial magic could occur, where whites and Blacks could congeal, remain uniquely different, but emerge out of the crucible of war and race as something much stronger together.

This was frustrating to be sure for reformers of the era, who were witnessing this very racial magic before their eyes. A white veteran of the Korean War from Mississippi reflecting on his time in battle, an experience he shared with a fellow Black soldier, felt that "I don't hold with this stuff about 'niggers.' I had a colored buddy in Korea, and I want to tell you he was all right." Waged during the height of the civil rights movement, through the deaths of Martin Luther King Jr., Malcolm X, and Robert Kennedy, the Vietnam War was no stranger to racial tensions. But at times the forging power of war—or, as Jeremy Maxwell called it, the "establishment of a brotherhood"—created a bond among many of each race. Specialist Charles Strong was a Black man fighting what many of his race believed to be a white man's war in Southeast Asia. Yet after his time in the military was over, he reflected a great deal on a white friend he had from Georgia who died in the bush:

It hurt me bad when they got Joe. Joe was an all right guy from Georgia. . . . If you were to see him the first time, you would just say that's a redneck ridge runnin' cracker. But he was the nicest guy in the world. . . . Some of the brothers would automatically take offense at him saying hi there brother man, but I always told them Joe was all right. There was no room for racism in the field.

Such emotional moments that brought the races together were perhaps the best possible outcome that could be achieved by the racial integration of the military because it superseded economic and political equality and cut straight to the quick and achieved some measure of racial acceptance. But the rub was that the racial integration of the military by way of equality of opportunity never intended to do this directly.[3]

It has often been anecdotally stated that the American military prepares for the next war by examining the prior one. While that is an overly simplistic statement about war planning, there is some truth to it. And to an extent, modern presidents, their staffs, the Department of Defense, and the military itself could all gain by examining the changes it made for its African American personnel during the Cold War. But to win today's battle over racism, gender discrimination, sexual discrimination, white nationalism, and conspiracy that presently infest aspects of the American armed forces, replicating that same strategy will not carry the day for them or the republic. The bitter truth about reform in American society, as with any society, is that it is irregular in nature; it lacks perfect harmony or symmetry or a semblance of continuous progress. True reform—lasting change—requires as much failure as it does success and does not happen overnight. Sadly, and frustratingly so for those who seek it, true reform takes generations to achieve.

Racial integration of the armed forces for the better part of the twentieth century was a noble goal, and it still is, but societal inclusivity and acceptance must be the goal now. To achieve a victory of some sort for the American military against all the problems that dog it—the threat from foreign powers, as they have done in the past, to use the nation's racial problems as a way to drive a wedge within the ranks, but also the intertwined issues of domestic white nationalism, racism, and conspiracy—presidents and the leadership of the armed forces must continuously attack the dilemma in a multifaceted way. It begins with leaders at the executive level clearly identifying the enemy as if at war. White nationalism, conspiracy, and racism, let alone the other dilemmas it faces, within the United States and its military should be approached just as presidents treated fascism and communism—as a grave threat to American democracy.

While a good opening salvo, presidential proclamations emerging from the White House calling for reform are rarely as effective as pressure from the president directly on the military to comply with change. During the Cold War, when the commander in chief was at the helm and applying pressure, whether it was direct or by way of a subordinate individual or group, change was achieved in the military. Likewise, if a president or the Department of Defense called for a change in policy to offer guidance and leadership, the policy was carried out uniformly. But when leadership failed to materialize, when the reform and its guidelines were not clear and direct, the change achieved was inconsistent in nature, ad hoc at times, and often unsatisfactory in its results. The former, not the latter, must be the way.

The leadership of the military must fight for acceptance of all within. Complacency or just following the regulations without an earnest desire to promote change will just lead to the problem remaining and to its spread throughout.

Likely it will lead to a backlash that will appear both discreetly and indiscreetly in the backdrop by those who do not wish to change. To be fair to the leaders of the armed forces, it is debatable whether they can achieve this without the help of the society that they protect. After all, the most gifted, creative, and talented leaders of the military—people who respect as best as they can the differing races, sex, or genders under their commands—cannot control the upbringing and unique social dynamics of their personnel. Education and training can help, but that alone cannot sway the most ridged of racists and conspiracy theorists. Nonetheless, it equally means that the leadership of the armed forces should not tolerate the existence of ideas or personnel, regardless of their talents, that seek to divide by way of race or other erroneous justifications.

The mantra of the American armed forces must revolve around a *professional* dedication to the eradication of bigotry from within. The military prides itself on its professionalism, often highlighted by its ability to give and follow orders and regulations. But in this matter it is equally important that the leaders of the military, officers and noncommissioned officers alike, make the issue of bigotry a matter that tarnishes their own professional and personal pride. This means that the leaders and soldiers of the American military cannot merely rely on presidents to act and force them to change; they must be held accountable for the elimination of this issue, which directly affects readiness, just as they would any other matter that would affect the ability to lead.

For the leaders of the armed forces, it will mean making hard choices and taking difficult stands against prejudice, and for many this will be uncomfortable, but it is no less critical to them and the military's mission. Individuals have a right to their own thoughts and feelings; this is a right that can never be taken from them. That is not what it is being suggested. What is being proposed is discharging personnel who may have great gifts but whose attitudes and inability to congeal with others, for whatever reason, risks the sanctity, camaraderie, and efficiency of the military they serve.

And finally, it is also a matter of self-preservation for the American armed forces. The twenty-first century American military is a volunteer organization dependent on its ability to recruit inclusively the best and brightest that the United States has to offer. The military of the United States today looks a bit different than it used to, but its mission for the nation remains unchanged. It is no longer feasible for the leaders of the armed forces to look away from prejudice—whether out of ignorance, bigotry, or apathy—within the ranks, as the military must juggle the needs of all the races, genders, and sexual orientations among its personnel. If it fails to respect and protect the equality and also the *acceptance* of its personnel, their families, and their loved ones, its ability to field the absolute best and most talented force possible will be threatened. Just as the racial segregation of the armed forces was considered inefficient and undemocratic, so, too, is allowing those within who continue to spread racism and sexism and engage in general prejudice toward their fellow soldiers, sailors, airmen, and Marines. It is time for the military to overcome and adapt to the greatest adversary it has ever faced: bigotry and discrimination. To borrow a line from a World War I combat veteran who became a Cold War president, Harry Truman: the military knows the way, it only needs the will.

Epilogue

Throughout the decades of racial reform in the military, advocates for maintaining racial segregation came and went, but Richard Russell, head of the Senate Armed Services Committee, remained a stalwart of racist opposition who never deviated or wavered. For a moment, in 1957, he stopped thinking about his battle against racial integration of America and its military. Instead, he turned his attention to another issue: the war over historical memory. Russell wondered about future historians who had yet to begin their work and what stories they would tell about the racial integration of American society, the military, and the role the South played in it all. "The honest historian of the future," Russell began, "in attempting to write a history of this period is certain to meet confusion and frustration. His bewilderment will be greater than that of Alice in her adventure in Wonderland." He continued:

When he commences his study of governmental affairs he is bound to draw the inference from all of the public records that this was an age of oppression and persecution. He will read pronouncement after pronouncement from the self-designated White Knights of politics [liberal reformers], spurred and booted for the political arena, that they were embarked upon a campaign to slay a dragon which lurked in the Southern section of this land who was oppressing and persecuting a minority group called Negroes by subjecting them to all kinds of unfair and brutal treatment,—Indeed denying them their most elemental rights as human beings.

He will be shocked by the picture that is painted by the [lamentations] of those who temporarily occupied positions of great responsibility and leadership, accompanied by the boasts of each champion that he and he alone was chosen and anointed for the role of dragon slayer and rescuer of the oppressed.

But there was hope. Russell believed that the historians of tomorrow might see things clearly, as the South saw them—but only if they were noble, Russell surmised. "If our historian is worthy he will recognize a sour note to some of the claims which was described in the parlance of this then ancient age as phony and self-serving." What Russell was trying to do was what all racist advocates of his time—whether they were conspiracy theorists, white nationalists, or supporters of the Lost Cause narrative—tried to do: control the narrative and make the South look like a noble victim of Northern liberal oppression, while ensuring that Jim Crow lived on throughout. And therefore Russell himself, a champion of segregation, was writing in a "phony and self-serving" fashion.[1]

A year earlier, another Southerner and former president, Harry Truman, was also thinking about the future. In his case, Truman was thinking about how the history of racial integration of the armed forces would play a role in shaping the future of America. In an address before the Platform and Resolutions Committee of the Democratic National Convention in 1956, Truman took his audience back to the 1860s to justify the findings of *To Secure These Rights*, the report that had been penned by his special committee when he was president almost a decade earlier and that led in many ways to Executive Order 9981. As he recalled the story of racial progress over the years, Truman knew it was likely that members of his own party, including Southerners who had defected from the liberal cause by joining the Dixiecrat revolt, had still not read, or intended to read, its findings. The ever-blunt Truman told them that they should. In a statement that was both a slight and a joke, the former president informed his audience: "That document is a Government document, printed by the United States Government Printing Office at Washington in 1947, and I think for a quarter you can get a copy of it." Then his comments turned more serious and pointed:

It would do you good to get it and read it. You would find out then that all these proceedings which have taken place, including the decision of the Supreme Court [referring to *Brown v. Board of Education*], about which there is so much controversy, was only an enforcement of the law which has been a part of the fundamental and basic law of this United States since the late 1860's.

It was sage advice for those within the party who recognized it was changing on the issue of civil rights reform; but it was also plain-old common sense for a nation that sought to battle global communism. He was essentially arguing that the white and Black races operating together, not segregated, in the military and society was the way forward. But for those Southerners in the room steeped in their own conspiratorial web and reared in the Lost Cause school, did what they had always done: they turned a deaf ear to Truman's advice and continued to rail against the societal changes that threatened their racial zeitgeist.[2]

Those who seek to understand the remaining racial issues plaguing the military and American society, and the dangerous tide of rising white nationalism in the country today, could learn a great deal from the long-standing battle that Russell, Truman, and others waged during the Cold War over the racial integration and reform of the military. That battle is ongoing.

RENAMING MILITARY BASES

Recently, aspects of that struggle can be found in the fight over renaming military bases named after former Confederate officers. Considering the social unrest spurred by Black Lives Matter (BLM) protests against the continued discrimination that African Americans face in society, and because the leadership of the American armed forces sought to reckon with its own racist past, it embarked on a mission to change the names of those bases. This shift might seem natural, even commonsensical, in our own era, but something had changed. During the Cold War–era racial integration of the armed forces, it was typically the president or his administration assuming ownership of the issue. But this time around, it was the military leading the way. For example, the Department of the Navy had investigated the issue of its relationship with Confederate images and the battle flag of the failed Confederacy *before* the controversy over the Army's base-renaming issue had emerged. The Navy had decided that its continued association with these symbols of the Confederacy "undermines the Navy's message of inclusiveness." Always cognizant of its racial image—a hangover from its earlier struggles during the Cold War to attract and retain Black recruits—the Navy worked to change and did so by prohibiting display of the Stars and Bars.[3]

Joining on the side of the armed forces were past military leaders including David Petraeus, the retired general and former head of the Central Intelligence Agency, and others who were also calling for change. By doing so they brought a certain level of military cachet with them. Several Southern bases were named, the former head of the CIA observed, after rather unexceptional Confederate leaders. To be sure, these bases—there were ten named after Confederate officers, all located in the South—were not named for these men for their military genius or astute prowess, Petraeus claimed. Instead, "Army leaders, to say nothing of political figures at the time, undoubtedly wanted to ingratiate themselves with the southern states in which the forts were located. They bowed to—and in many cases shared—the Lost cause nostalgia that sponsored so much civilian statuary, street naming, and memorial building from the end of Reconstruction through the 1930s, when the trend tapered off but did not end completely."[4]

Once at the tail end of the reform movement, the United States Marine Corps sought to do more than the Army, Navy, and Air Force combined on the issue. Under the leadership of the Marine Corps Commandant, General David H. Berger, the Marines went to war with Confederate imagery and white nationalism seeking to use it to rally against the republic. The Marine Corps "banned public displays of the Confederate battle flag at all Marine Corps installations, to include paraphernalia such as mugs, posters and bumper stickers." US forces stationed in Korea and Japan followed suit. In an interview on the ABC news program *This Week*, Berger put his actions in plain terms and turned the old idea of "military efficiency," often used to fight racial integration and reform of the military in the past, on its head: "This is not an attempt to erase history. But the bigger symbol is the things that draw the team together so that we can operate with that kind of implicit trust. We have a flag, it's the American flag, we have the Marine Corps colors, we have things that unify us; anything that gets in the way of that is a problem." In essence, Berger was arguing for inclusion and that the racial integration and continued reform of the Marine Corps are necessary for it to do its job at a high level. But for Berger, that alone was not enough; more had to be done. And it began, as it always does, with self-examination and an unrelenting desire to improve as a person and an organization. "If we are actually honest with ourselves," Berger admitted, the first step is acknowledging that "we all have unconscious biases, admitted or not; we do." The Marine Corps Commandant believed that the way to deal with racism, as well as gender-based discrimination, within the billets was to stay alert and vigilant and to protect the talented assets in the service: "We have to pay a lot more attention, in other words, earlier on, deliberately, intentionally, managing the talent that we have and not let it sort itself out in the wash."[5]

For Berger, this meant assigning more female Marines to areas previously restricted from them, increasing the number of Black officers (at the time of the interview, the Marines had the lowest amount of African American officers, around 5.7 percent), and working on issues such as parental leave for all Marines, including those who identified as gay or lesbian. But in a branch with a tradition of exclusiveness and "whiteness," would this be enough? Cameron McCoy, a military historian and African American lieutenant colonel serving in the Marine Corps Reserves, while hopeful about the direction the Commandant was articulating, remained unsure about what that would mean for young Black men entering the Marine Corps: "The commandant has made an extremely noble and professional gesture," McCoy informed NPR, "But what does that really mean if I'm a young [African American] lance corporal and I've never seen anybody who's not white in charge of me?"[6]

DRAINING A RACIST SWAMP? OR PLAYING IN IT?

For a time, the Pentagon under President Donald J. Trump seemed receptive to changing the name of the Army bases; Secretary of Defense Mark P. Esper and Secretary of the Army Ryan D. McCarthy admitted they were open "to a bipartisan discussion on the topic." That position, however, did not square well politically with the president's. Conservative politicians of both parties—from Wallace to Thurmond to Nixon to Trump—have continuously stoked the issues of race and white nationalism to maintain favor within the largely conservative base of the American South. To change the name of the bases threatened Trump's sway over the region, and the controversial president knew it. His tweeted response was unique to him and reflected his confrontational and off-the cuff style; but it also mirrored past political pandering to the region: "My Administration will not even consider the renaming of these Magnificent and Fabled Military Installations."[7]

It was not enough to say no; the president felt compelled to play up the importance of the bases by referring to them, with capital letters, as "Magnificent and Fabled." To be sure, the bases had been a fixture of the Southern landscape for decades, but this was not about economics or social uplift or the historical role they played in the nation's wars. When the president made it a point to highlight their greatness, it carried a martial tinge, one designed to stoke the conservative wings of the Republican Party that venerated military service. But the political ground had been well-trod by conservative forebears. He deliberately relied on the trope of the Lost Cause narrative—honoring with eternal veneration the fallen Confederacy. In this case, Trump sought to preserve and honor Confederates leaders who were in fact traitors to the country yet memorialized in the bases' names.[8]

Politically, it made good sense for Trump. Moralistically and ethically speaking, his actions were abhorrent. Behind the scenes, staffers tried to reason with the president, but he remained rigid and unsympathetic to the effect the names had on the morale of minority personnel, let alone the bigger message it was sending to the growing Black Lives Matters protest movement during the summer of 2020. The controversy took a turn toward the personal for the president when a favorite political sparring partner entered the fray. Senator Elizabeth Warren of Massachusetts, a law professor before turning to politics, worked to attach an amendment to the defense spending bill making its way through Congress that required renaming the Southern bases in question, which the Senate Armed Services Committee approved in a bipartisan vote. When the president heard about the plan, he lashed out on Twitter: "I will Veto the Defense Authorization Bill if the Elizabeth 'Pocahontas' Warren (of all people!) Amendment, which will lead to the renaming (plus other bad things!) of Fort Bragg, Fort Robert E. Lee, and many other Military Bases from which we won Two World Wars, is in the Bill!" Trump did indeed veto the bill, but Congress overrode it. Shortly after the end of the Trump presidency, Congress created a board to carry out renaming the installations. The nation's first African American secretary of defense, Lloyd Austin, was responsible for assembling the board. Renaming bases may be the tip of the iceberg for the group; its ambitions seem larger. It also sought "to remove other names and symbols from Defense Department properties and assets honoring those who served the Confederate States of America."[9]

BLACK LIVES MATTER PROTESTS AND THE LAFAYETTE SQUARE INCIDENT

The American military has been used throughout history to quell domestic disorders. For many who study civil rights and race relations in America, the 1967 Detroit race riots come to mind. At that moment, the National Guard was used. The killing of several antiwar student protestors in 1970 by National Guardsmen at Kent State University is another infamous episode. Over fifty years later, the National Guard, once a bastion of racial segregation, was again used in a controversial fashion to clear out civil rights protestors, this time in Washington just blocks from the White House and Congress. In June 2020, Black Lives Matter supporters were in the nation's capital to protest the continued racial inequality present in American society, highlighted by the recent murder of George Floyd at the hands of Minneapolis police officers. During street-clearing near Lafayette Square, park police, the National Guard, and noxious gas were deployed; that evening, Blackhawk and Lakota military helicopters buzzed and hovered over protestors, creating, the *Washington Post* reported, "wind speeds equivalent to a tropical storm." At the time of the incident, it was speculated that President Trump ordered the crackdown himself. A report released by the Department of Interior's Office of Inspector General (among other IGs), however, attempted to absolve Trump of any wrongdoing, declaring: "We found that the Park Police made the decision to clear the park of protesters in order to install an anti-scale fencing to protect the park and US Park Police officers during those protests." To state the obvious, questions remain about his involvement and about the timing of the president's decision to take a picture before St. John's Church shortly after the park was cleared out. Chairman of the Joint Chiefs of Staff Mark Milley and Secretary of Defense Esper, among many other officials, participated.[10]

While aspects of the incident remain mired in controversy, another equally troublesome matter remains: Guardsmen called into service included Black soldiers. It is estimated that African American personnel made up 60 percent of the DC Guard personnel involved in the crackdown against the BLM protestors. As Black and white protestors suffered under the weight of anti-demonstration tactics, so, too, did those who had to carry out the process. "It's a very tough conversation to have when a soldier turns to me and they're saying, 'Hey sir, you know my cousin was up there yelling at me, that was my neighbor, my best friend from high school,'" remarked an African American lieutenant. Some admitted they would have been out there with members of their race and community had they not been activated for duty. "I was happy to see him [her brother] out there . . . to walk for me when I couldn't," remarked an African American female Guardsman. Major General William J. Walker, commanding general of the DC National Guard, an African American solider himself, recognized the dilemma Black soldiers faced carrying out orders that they wrestled with. "'I have some Guardsmen whose family members came out and criticized them. 'What are you doing out here, aren't you black?'" Walker said. "Of course, we're all hurting. The nation is hurting."[11]

WHITE NATIONALISM AND THE AMERICAN ARMED FORCES

Another troubling racial front for the republic's armed forces revolves around the growing white nationalism from within. In February 2020, the *Military Times*, which has tracked the rise of white nationalism in the armed forces over the years, declared: "More than one-third of all active-duty troops and more than half of minority service members say they have personally witnessed examples of white nationalism or ideological-driven racism within the ranks in recent months." Others were paying attention to the issue as well. In December that same year, Colorado Democratic representative Jason Crow, himself a former Army Ranger and Iraq and Afghanistan war veteran, and Representative Lori Trahan joined the fight against bigotry in the ranks by introducing a bill to revamp diversity training. At the time, Crow argued:

One of the strengths of our military is its diversity. In Iraq and Afghanistan, I served with men and women from every corner of the country and the team was stronger for our diversity. . . . I believe an important function of the military is to be a standard bearer for the values of our country and to lead by example. But I also know we have a problem in our military with sexual violence, racism, and homophobia. This bill is a powerful step forward to ensure our military is a place of equality, inclusivity, and integration.

Their efforts to police the rising hate and bigotry in the military was too late. On January 6, 2021, the Capitol Building was assaulted by an angry, predominately white mob that sought to overturn the lawful election of Joseph R. Biden, a Delaware Democrat and former senator and vice president. Among the rabble of white supremacist groups, QAnon conspiracy propagandists, and violent others were active-duty and retired members of the US military. Crow, a member of the House Armed Services Committee, felt that the issue of racism and white nationalism in the military was at tipping point and that it had been enflamed by the words and actions of its leader, specifically naming President Trump. Whether or not it was Trump's fault, *Politico* observed that "the overall problem of right-wing extremism has dogged the military for decades and tends to be more severe when there is a rise in wider society."[12]

And the problem was getting worse. Mark Pitcavage, a member of the Anti-Defamation League, testified to the House Armed Services Committee that "the number of extremists in the military has increased due to a higher percentage of white supremacists attempting to join the military and the development of white supremacist leanings among some currently-serving personnel. . . . To an even greater degree than in previous surges of extremism." What was aiding in its growth? "The Internet has played a role in the present one, with extremist content found on websites, discussion forums, chat rooms, social media, messaging apps, gaming and streaming sites, and other platforms." Meanwhile, the Pentagon dismissed accusations that it had failed. "We don't tolerate extremists in our ranks," Jonathan Hoffman, the chief Pentagon spokesperson, claimed. Pitcavage had his doubts: "That almost all of the extremists in these examples were initially exposed by journalists or anti-racist activists is another troubling sign that the military branches may not be engaged in sufficient self-scrutiny."[13]

THE BATTLE OVER INCLUSIVITY RAGES ON

Half a century after the *Kitty Hawk* race riot and in the wake of the turmoil at Lafayette Square and the Capitol, and given rising white nationalism in the United States, the racial integration and reform of the armed forces continues. In the middle are African American personnel, who still today serve their country disproportionately in its wars and its domestic disturbances at home. As it has always been, their story has been one of triumphs and setbacks. And in recent years, the stars of that story have largely been African American women.

In 2009, Command Sergeant Major Teresa King, an African American who escaped her family's sharecropping background in rural North Carolina, became the first woman to run the US Army Drill Sergeant Academy at Fort Jackson, South Carolina. Trouble soon emerged; after two years she was accused of running a "toxic command," and it was alleged by some that King was nothing more than a meddling "micromanager." Whether or not these accusations were fair, they led to her suspension as commandant of the school. Over time and with the evidence lacking, the accusations were dismissed and she was reinstated. Not too long after her reinstatement, King retired from the Army. According to her she did not do so willingly. Instead, King believed that the Army that she had capably served for thirty-two years had forced her out. The rationale? Because she, as John Lewis would say, "got into some good trouble." King set a standard that some did not believe they had to meet: "A lot of the combat arms guys (apparently) thought they didn't have to meet the standards to be drill sergeants—that I was going to give 'em a hat," she observed. Furthermore, they did not respect her as a leader: "And a lot of the male, combat arms officer[s], Ranger-types—they didn't think I should be in that position. So they defamed me. They wouldn't even talk to me." Ultimately, King reasoned, her ouster from the Army came down to three things: "It was because I was female, [had] no combat experience, and third because I was black. They wouldn't talk to me; they would talk to my deputy and send me a note. They refused to work with me." She would later sue the Army for damages. Since her ouster, King has been inducted into the Army's Drill Sergeant Hall of Fame and the Women in Military Service for America Memorial located at Arlington National Cemetery, Virginia.[14]

To be sure, King's exodus was a setback, but doors continued to open for African American women and men in the military. Sergeant First Class Janina Simmons blazed a new trail for her gender and race as the first female African American soldier to become an Army Ranger. Not too far behind was Lieutenant General Vincent Stewart of the Marine Corps, who became the first African American to head the Defense Intelligence Agency. Six years later, President Joseph R. Biden nominated a former US Central Command leader, General Lloyd J. Austin III, to become the first African American to serve as secretary of defense.[15]

PREJUDICE AND THE WAR TO REFORM

As with the earlier years of racial reform of the military, change spilled from the bases into other areas associated with the armed forces. Cedric T. Wins, a retired Army general and African American soldier, had already gone farther than many of his race in the military. But now, he had a new job that was taking him home: he was set to become the first African American superintendent of the Virginia Military Institute. There, he had to navigate difficult racial terrain, as VMI's history of racial inclusion was problematic at best and remained that way some thirty-five years after Wins's graduation. In June 2021, a state-funded independent investigation into the academy "found that institutional racism and sexism are present, tolerated, and left unaddressed at VMI. The racist and misogynistic acts and outcomes uncovered during this investigation are disturbing." Which was worse for those interviewed at VMI—racism or sexism—was debatable, but many believed the treatment of female cadets by male cadets was likely worse. Among those questioned, 14 percent of female cadets reported being sexually assaulted at the school. Further, the women at VMI felt that the cultural ambivalence of the institution would lead those in charge to do little about their plight. They also feared reprisal for even reporting that an assault took place.[16]

With pressure mounting at that time, and with the situation at VMI becoming more of a circus, Democratic governor Ralph Northam, a VMI alum, entered the fray. No stranger to controversy, Northam had weathered his own racial turbulence after a picture emerged allegedly depicting him in blackface, something he later denied. A subsequent inquiry failed to prove conclusively that it was him or how the racist image appeared alongside an image of Northam in his medical school yearbook. Despite his woes, the beleaguered governor had gained the respect of the African American community in Virginia by heeding the recommendations of many of the state's Black political officers. And he did so again, when he demanded that his alma mater, VMI, a state-funded institution, change.[17]

Superintendent Wins, already trying to reform the school's culture, took the criticism in stride and went back to work. Using the troubling findings of the report as a call to arms, Wins believed this moment offered VMI an opportunity to learn and grow from past mistakes: "VMI has a long history of improvement. Now is no different." When charges arose that critical race theory (CRT), which studies the persistence of systemic racism in American society—an academic theory, by the way, that has become a rallying cry and foil for the political right—was being taught at VMI, Wins went to war with one of his own: Carmen D. Villani Jr., a white VMI alum from the class of 1976. Villani had leveled the charge against the institution, questioned its call for extra funding, and openly wondered if the money was going to support teaching CRT. Wins then went on VMI's Facebook page and declared before the small but powerful VMI community; "Mr. Villani . . . you have no understanding of

[Diversity, Equity, and Inclusion] or what it means, or how much of the funding for DEI is represented in our request." Some sided with Villani, calling the actions of VMI and its Black superintendent "racist" toward whites; others drew from the familiar well of resistance often used by the South, proclaiming it was all communistic. As one commentor believed, this was the beginning of "the ascendency of cultural Marxism" at VMI. Another ranted about how this would lead to the loss of memory of the Confederacy, which VMI students during the Civil War had fought and died for. The "virtue signalers," this person alleged, using a common slur for liberals, "[were] beating down every last vestige of the [memory of the] Confederacy."[18]

Despite such wails of anguish, including from VMI cadets on the chat app Jodel, the institution has begun the process of reforming. It took down the statue of the Confederate war hero General Thomas "Stonewall" Jackson, a slave owner and VMI professor. Importantly, VMI has moved to alter aspects of a long-running but troubled tradition—the student-run "honor court." The notion of being judged by one's peers should reflect the height of professionalism and objectivity, but the honor court at VMI had operated in a terribly unfair fashion toward Black cadets, who were expelled from the academy disproportionately based on their numbers.[19]

While systemic prejudice has existed at the institution, it should be noted that not everyone at VMI is bigoted or stone-cold racist. Just like other institutions saddled with racial or gender or sexual scandals, VMI contains within its halls dedicated leaders, faculty, and staff who do not reflect or accept such behavior. Frankly, they are likely embarrassed or appalled by it. Neither are all its cadets willing accomplices to prejudice; many, in fact, came forward to speak out against behavior that tarnished the academy they loved. With these important groups in mind, VMI has an opportunity to embrace those within who dare to stand up and oppose prejudice by emulating the standard established by Superintendent Wins, an African American soldier who understands what it means to be a VMI graduate, who has likely experienced his fair share of racial discrimination, and who was a successful leader in the United States Army.

In effect, VMI has a wonderful opportunity to reverse its controversial past not only by emerging as a leader on the issue but also by also heeding a lesson that the American military has had to learn repeatedly since the first steps toward integration during World War II. "Equality of opportunity," while useful and a noble start, is not enough—and never has been. Simply allowing Blacks, other minorities, and women to attend VMI, without understanding the prejudices and obstacles they face daily, is not a solution. In the absence of the necessary spirit of togetherness, it is a half-step that allows prejudice, bigotry, and distrust to fester. Furthermore, it fails to challenge and eliminate the bigoted notion that inclusivity and acceptance of others hinder the national defense. Instead, VMI should highlight that which history has taught: there is strength in unity.

Notes

Abbreviations Used in Notes

DDE Library	Dwight David Eisenhower Library and Museum
EJI	Equal Justice Initiative
ETO	European Theater of Operations
HST Library	Harry S. Truman Library and Museum
	PCCR	President's Committee on Civil Rights
	To Secure These Rights	The Report of the President's Committee on Civil Rights (1947)
JFK Library	John Fitzgerald Kennedy Library and Museum
	CRPRF	Civil Rights Progress Reports File
	SCGCR	Subcabinet Group on Civil Rights
	WHCSF-E	White House Central Files Subject Files-Executive
	WHCSF-G	White House Central Files Subject Files-General
	WHSF	White House Staff Files
JWFP, UARK	J. William Fulbright Papers, University of Arkansas Libraries
LBJ Library	Lyndon Baines Johnson Library and Museum
	PCEOAF	President's Committee on Equal Opportunity in the Armed Forces
NAACP, LOC	National Association for the Advancement of Colored Peoples Papers, Library of Congress
NARA II	National Archives and Record Administration at College Park
OWC	Orson Wells Commentaries
RRL, UGA	Richard Russell Library, University of Georgia Libraries

Preface

1. Meyer Kestnbaum, "Citizenship and Compulsory Military Service: The Revolutionary Origins of Conscription in the United States," *Armed Forces & Society* 27, no. 1 (Fall 2000): 7–9. As compelling as the discussion over when Americans embraced the notion of citizen service, perhaps the more relevant conversation is the one that is unfolding today within military history circles. A discussion that the concept of the American "citizen-soldier" dutifully ready to serve his or her country is "dead." For more, see Elliot Abrams and Andrew J. Bacevich, "A Symposium on Citizenship and Military Service," *Parameters* 31, no. 2 (Summer 2001): 18–22. Indeed, Professor Adrian Lewis, in his landmark work *The American Culture of War*, added to this grim prognosis his belief that America today—devoid of a government able to compel or force the citizenry to action, with emphasis placed on the end of the draft—a "military cluster" has emerged to support the armed forces. Much like a well in a barren land, the American armed forces repeatedly draw personnel from this "military cluster" of

families. This is problematic because it is less inclusive in its scope and breadth, let alone its racial and gender composition. And with little regard or desire emerging from much of society, it further means that supplemental forces, such as those coming from private military companies or private military firms, have become more and more the norm. For more, see Adrian Lewis, *The American Culture of War*, 3rd ed. (New York: Routledge, 2018), 1–2.

2. Mary L. Dudziak, *Cold War Civil Rights: Race and the Image of American Democracy* (Princeton, NJ: Princeton University Press, 2000).

3. As Taylor notes, Truman, in a meeting with the Fahy Committee, understood his power in the military to be without question and that the unique nature of the military, with a vertical organization, ensured things would be achieved if he ordered them. Fascinatingly, Truman also sought to seize upon the momentum of the racial integration of the armed forces and carry it throughout the government. For more, see William A. Taylor, *Military Service and American Democracy: From World War II to the Iraq and Afghanistan Wars* (Lawrence: University Press of Kansas, 2016), 66.

4. Harry S. Truman, "Address Before the National Association for the Advancement of Colored People, June 29, 1947," online by Gerhard Peters and John T. Woolley, The American Presidency Project, www.presidency.ucsb.edu/node/231974.

5. Jon Meacham, *The Soul of America: The Battle for Our Better Angels* (New York: Random House, 2018), 12–13.

6. John Hope Franklin, *The Militant South, 1800–1861* (Urbana: University of Illinois Press, 2002).

7. Sir William Howard Russell, *Pictures of Southern Life, Social, Political, and Military* (New York: James A. Gregory, 1861), 8.

8. W. J. Cash, *The Mind of the South* (New York: Vintage Books, 1991), 136.

9. Richard Hofstadter, *The Paranoid Style in American Politics and Other Essays*, with a New Foreword by Sean Wilentz (New York: Vintage Books, 2008), 29, 39; Meacham, *The Soul of America*, 17.

10. Michel Paradis, "The Lost Cause's Long Legacy," *The Atlantic*, June 26, 2020, www.theatlantic.com/ideas/archive/2020/06/the-lost-causes-long-legacy/613288.

11. Paradis; Allyson Hobbs, Amy Davidson Sorkin, and Evan Osnos, "A Hundred Years Later, 'The Birth of a Nation' Hasn't Gone Away," *The New Yorker*, www.new yorker.com/culture/culture-desk/hundred-years-later-birth-nation-hasnt-gone -away. Wilson would also address the former Confederates. For more, see Woodrow Wilson, *The Messages and Papers of Woodrow Wilson*, vol. 1, edited by Albert Shaw (New York: The Review of Reviews Corporation, 1924), 408–411.

12. Sheila Miyoshi Jager, *Brothers at War: The Unending Conflict in Korea* (New York: Norton, 2013), 107.

13. Randall B. Woods, *Prisoners of Hope: Lyndon B. Johnson, the Great Society, and the Limits of Liberalism* (New York: Basic Books, 2016), 207.

14. James E. Westheider, *The African American Experience in Vietnam: Brothers in Arms* (Lanham, MD: Rowman & Littlefield, 2008), 22–23, 27, 34–36; James E. Westheider, *Fighting on Two Fronts: African Americans and the Vietnam War* (New York: New York University Press, 1997), 74–77, 85–93.

Chapter 1: A Faustian Bargain

1. The standard work on the African American experience during World War II remains Ulysses Lee, *The Employment of Negro Troops* (Honolulu: University Press of the Pacific, 2004 [Washington, DC: Government Printing Office, 1966]); Citations utilized, however, come from the University Press of the Pacific's paperback edition (2004) of Lee's classic. Page numbers provided reflect that edition and not the original. Lee, *The Employment of Negro Troops*, 141–143.

2. Benjamin Quarles, *The Negro in the American Revolution* (New York: Norton, 1961), 7; Judith L. Van Buskirk, *Standing in Their Own Light: African American Patriots in the American Revolution* (Norman: University of Oklahoma Press, 2017), 45–48.

3. Quarles, *The Negro in the American Revolution*, 9–17; Van Buskirk, *Standing in Their Own Light*, 53–59.

4. Quarles, *The Negro in the American Revolution*, 9–17; Van Buskirk, *Standing in Their Own Light*, 53–59.

5. Quarles, *The Negro in the American Revolution*, 9–17; Van Buskirk, *Standing in Their Own Light*, 53–59.

6. Eric Foner, *The Fiery Trial: Abraham Lincoln and American Slavery* (New York: Norton, 2010), 169–171, 176–180, 206–208, 240–249, 268–270; James M. McPherson, *Tried by War: Abraham Lincoln as Commander in Chief* (New York: Penguin Press, 2008), 7–8, 157–159, 201–205.

7. "Should the Negro Enlist in the Union Army?," Address at a Meeting for the Promotion of Colored Enlistments, July 6, 1863, *Douglass' Monthly*, August 1863; See also Frederick Douglass, "MEN OF COLOR, TO ARMS!," *Broadside*, Rochester, March 21, 1863.

8. E. Foner, *The Fiery Trial*, 169–171, 176–180, 206–208, 240–249, 268–270; McPherson, *Tried by War*, 7–8, 157–159, 201–205; Kestnbaum, "Citizenship and Compulsory Military Service," 7–9.

9. Theodore Roosevelt, *The Rough Riders* (New York: Charles Scribner's Sons, 1899), 143–145; Mark Lee Gardner, *Rough Riders: Theodore Roosevelt, His Cowboy Regiment, and the Immortal Charge Up San Juan Hill* (New York: William Morrow, 2016), 173–174, 244; Stacy A. Rozek, "'The First Daughter of the Land': Alice Roosevelt as Presidential Celebrity, 1902–1906," *Presidential Studies Quarterly* 19, no. 1 (Winter 1989), Part I: American Foreign Policy for the 1990s, and Part II: T. R., Wilson, and the Progressive Era, 1901–1919, 56.

10. Willard B. Gatewood Jr., *"SMOKED YANKEES" and the Struggle for Empire: Letters from Negro Soldiers, 1898–1902* (Fayetteville: University of Arkansas Press, 1987), 92–97.

11. Gatewood Jr., *"SMOKED YANKEES,"* 92–97; Willard B. Gatewood Jr., *Black Americans and the White Man's Burden: 1898–1903* (Urbana: University of Illinois Press, 1975), 240–244.

12. Deborah Davis, *Guest of Honor: Booker T. Washington, Theodore Roosevelt, and the White House Dinner That Shocked a Nation* (New York: Atria Books, 2012), 161–170, 187, 200–202; Edmund Morris, *Theodore Rex*, rev. ed. (New York: Random House, 2002), 39.

13. Davis, *Guest of Honor*, 207–213; Morris, *Theodore Rex*, 52–54; Thomas G. Dyer, *Theodore Roosevelt and the Idea of Race* (Baton Rouge: Louisiana State University Press, 1980), 105; Troy Kickler, "Albion Tourgee (1838–1905)," *NorthCarolinahistory.org: An Online Encyclopedia*, North Carolina History Project, https://northcarolinahistory.org /encyclopedia/albion-tourgee-1838-1905.

14. Davis, *Guest of Honor*, 207–213; Morris, *Theodore Rex*, 52–54; Thomas G. Dyer, *Theodore Roosevelt and the Idea of Race*, 105; Kickler, "Albion Tourgee (1838–1905)."

15. Davis, *Guest of Honor*, 207–208, 212; Doris Kearns Goodwin, *The Bully Pulpit: Theodore Roosevelt, William Howard Taft, and the Golden Age of Journalism* (New York: Simon & Schuster, 2013), 321; Morris, *Theodore Rex*, 54–56.

16. Davis, *Guest of Honor*, 212; Morris, *Theodore Rex*, 54–56.

17. Morris, 54, 172.

18. Morris, 56; Davis, *Guest of Honor*, 222–223.

19. Morris, *Theodore Rex*, 56; Davis, *Guest of Honor*, 222–223; See also Mark Twain, *Mark Twain in Eruption: Hitherto Unpublished Pages about Mean and Events*, ed. Bernard Devoto (New York: Harper & Brothers Publishers, 1940), 30–31.

20. Jeffrey T. Sammons and John H. Morrow Jr., *Harlem's Rattlers and the Great War: The Undaunted 369th Regiment and the African American Quest for Equality* (Lawrence: University Press of Kansas, 2015), 34–35, 157–158; John D. Weaver, *The Brownsville Raid* (College Station: Texas A&M University Press, 1992), 19–23, 25–28, 34–42; Bernard C. Nalty, *Strength for the Fight* (New York: Free Press, 1986), 91–97; Goodwin, *The Bully Pulpit*, 511.

21. Weaver, *The Brownsville Raid*, 25–28.

22. Sammons and Morrow Jr., *Harlem's Rattlers*, 34–35, 157–158; Weaver, *The Brownsville Raid*, 19–23, 25–28, 34–42; Nalty, *Strength for the Fight*, 91–97; Goodwin, *The Bully Pulpit*, 511.

23. Goodwin, 511–512.

24. Weaver, *The Brownsville Raid*, 17; Goodwin, *The Bully Pulpit*, 512–514.

25. Goodwin, 514–515.

26. Goodwin, 513–515.

27. Goodwin, 513–515; "Roosevelt's Hostility to the Colored People of the United States: The Record of the Discharge of the Colored Soldiers at Brownsville," Washington, DC, 1906, Library of Congress, www.loc.gov/item/rbpe.24001000.

28. Goodwin, *The Bully Pulpit*, 513–515; "Roosevelt's Hostility to the Colored People of the United States."

29. Sammons and Morrow Jr., *Harlem's Rattlers*, 157–158; Nalty, *Strength for the Fight*, 102–103; Jaime Salazar, *Mutiny of Rage: The 1917 Camp Logan Riots and Buffalo Soldiers in Houston* (Lanham, MD: Prometheus Books, 2021), 59–60.

30. Sammons and Morrow Jr., *Harlem's Rattlers*, 157–158; Nalty, *Strength for the Fight*, 102–103; Salazar, 59–60.

31. Nalty, *Strength for the Fight*, 102–103.

32. Nalty, 103–106; Sammons and Morrow Jr., *Harlem's Rattlers*, 158.

33. Nalty, *Strength for the Fight*, 103–106; Sammons and Morrow Jr., *Harlem's Rattlers*, 158.

34. Nalty, *Strength for the Fight*, 103–106; Sammons and Morrow Jr., *Harlem's Rattlers*, 158.

35. Allyson Hobbs, Amy Davidson Sorkin, and Evan Osnos, "A Hundred Years Later, 'The Birth of a Nation' Hasn't Gone Away"; Sammons and Morrow Jr., *Harlem's Rattlers*, 265–295, 356, 403–404, 460, 447–475.

36. Sammons and Morrow Jr., *Harlem's Rattlers*, 265–295, 356, 403–404, 460, 447–475; Equal Justice Initiative, "Lynching in America: Targeting Black Veterans" (2017), 25, https://eji.org/reports/targeting-black-veterans; "Medal of Honor: Sergeant Henry Johnson," Army.MIL Features, www.army.mil/medalofhonor/johnson. For more on the Harlem Rattlers and the role the war played in the expanding and evolving civil rights struggle, see Chad Williams, *Torchbearers of Democracy: African American Soldiers in the World War I Era* (Chapel Hill: University of North Carolina Press, 2013).

37. Robert H. Ferrell, *Unjustly Dishonored: An African American Division in World War I* (Columbia: University of Missouri Press, 2011), vii, 9–11, 13–41.

38. Ferrell, vii, 9–11, 13–41.

39. Equal Justice Initiative, "Lynching in America," 19; Adriane Lentz-Smith, *Freedom Struggles: African Americans and World War I* (Cambridge, MA: Harvard University Press, 2009), 169–205.

40. Equal Justice Initiative, "Lynching in America," 19; Lentz-Smith, *Freedom Struggles*, 169–205.

41. Equal Justice Initiative, "Lynching in America," 19; Lentz-Smith, *Freedom Struggles*, 169–205.

42. Equal Justice Initiative, "Lynching in America," 22–31.

43. Lee, *The Employment of Negro Troops*, 141–143.

44. Lee, 141–143; Morris J. MacGregor Jr., *Integration of the Armed Forces, 1940–1965* (Washington, DC: Center of Military History, United States Army, 1981), 23.

45. Sherie Mershon and Steven Schlossman, *Foxholes & Color Lines: Desegregating the U.S. Armed Forces* (Baltimore: Johns Hopkins University Press, 1998), 20.

46. Mershon and Schlossman, 35; Jonathan Rosenberg, *How Far the Promised Land? World Affairs and the American Civil Rights Movement from the First World War to Vietnam* (Princeton, NJ: Princeton University Press, 2005), 5, 39–43, 132.

47. Rosenberg, 5, 39–43, 132; Roy Wilkins, "Defending Democracy," *The Crisis*, October 1939, 305.

48. James G. Thompson, "Should I Sacrifice to Live 'Half-American?,'" *Pittsburgh Courier*, January 31, 1942, 3; Neil A Wynn, *The African American Experience During World War II* (New York: Roman & Littlefield, 2011), 40–41.

49. Roy Wilkins, "Now Is the Time Not to Be Silent," *The Crisis*, January 1942, 7.

50. Doris Kearns Goodwin, *No Ordinary Time: Franklin and Eleanor Roosevelt: The Home Front in World War II* (New York: Simon & Schuster, 1994), 168–169.

51. Goodwin, 168–169.

52. Ira Katznelson, *Fear Itself* (New York: Norton, 2013), 16, 128.

53. William E. Leuchtenburg, *The White House Looks South: Franklin D. Roosevelt, Harry S. Truman, Lyndon B. Johnson* (Baton Rouge: Louisiana State University Press, 2005), 28, 58–60, 62–63.

54. Leuchtenburg, 28, 58–60, 62–63.

55. Roosevelt on Lynching, quoted in Leuchtenburg, 64–65.

56. Goodwin, *No Ordinary Time*, 169.

57. Goodwin, 170.

58. Rosenberg, 138–140; Daniel Kryder, *Divided Arsenal: Race and the American State During World War II* (New York: Cambridge University Press, 2000), 15; Goodwin, *No Ordinary Time*, 247–251.

59. Benjamin Quarles, "Will a Long War Aid the Negro?," *The Crisis*, September 1943, 268.

60. Kryder, *Divided Arsenal*, 35–36; Henry L. Stimson and McGeorge Bundy, *On Active Services in Peace and War* (New York: Harper and Brothers, 1947), 461, 463–464.

61. Kryder, *Divided Arsenal*, 36, n.40; Stimson and Bundy, *On Active Services*, 461, 463–464.

62. Stimson and Bundy, *On Active Services*, 461, 463–464; Thomas A. Guglielmo, *Divisions: A New History of Racism and Resistance in America's World War II Military* (New York: Oxford University Press, 2021), 40.

63. Stimson and Bundy, *On Active Services*, 461, 463–464.

64. Throughout the war, Stimpson was an advocate of the use of Japanese American personnel. Often in racial terms, he described the military potential of the "yellow man." And it seems, according to the historian Thomas Guglielmo, that Stimpson had more faith in the immediate prospects of Nisei Japanese Americans than he did Black males. For more, see Guglielmo, *Divisions*, 65, 67, 71–72, 75, 86.

65. Kryder, *Divided Arsenal*, 35–36; Stimson and Bundy, *On Active Services*, 461, 463–464; Goodwin, *No Ordinary Time*, 169.

66. Kryder, *Divided Arsenal*, 35–36; Stimson and Bundy, *On Active Services*, 461, 463–464; Goodwin, *No Ordinary Time*, 169.

67. Goodwin, 164.

68. Goodwin, 164.

69. Goodwin, 27–30; J. Todd Moye, *Freedom Flyers: The Tuskegee Airmen of World War II* (New York: Oxford University Press, 2010), 51–53; Barbara A. Perry, "How John F. Kennedy and Eleanor Roosevelt Went from Rivals to Allies," *Dallas Morning News*, August 30, 2020, www.dallasnews.com/opinion/commentary/2020/08/30/how-john -kennedy-and-eleanor-roosevelt-went-from-rivals-to-allies.

70. Goodwin, *No Ordinary Time*, 27–30.

71. Kryder, *Divided Arsenal*, 66; Mershon and Schlossman, *Foxholes & Color Lines*, 42–43.

72. West Virginian comment quoted in Goodwin, *No Ordinary Time*, 172; Mershon and Schlossman, *Foxholes & Color Lines*, 42–43.

73. Mershon and Schlossman, 47–51.

74. Thomas W. Cutrer and T. Michael Parrish, *Doris Miller, Pearl Harbor, and the Birth of the Civil Rights Movement* (College Station: Texas A&M University Press, 2018), xii–xiii, 18–25; Chris Dixon, *African Americans and the Pacific War, 1941–1945* (New York: Cambridge University Press, 2018), 52–53.

75. Cutrer and Parrish, *Doris Miller*, xii–xiii, 18–25; Dixon, 52–53.

76. Ian W. Toll, *Pacific Crucible: War at Sea in the Pacific, 1941–1942* (New York: Norton & Company, 2011), 126; Cutrer and Parrish, *Doris Miller*, 26–29.

77. Toll, *Pacific Crucible*, 126; Cutrer and Parrish, *Doris Miller*, 26–29.

78. John C. Walter, "Congressman Carl Vinson and Franklin D. Roosevelt: Naval Preparedness and the Coming of World War II, 1932–1940," *Georgia Historical Quarterly* 64, no. 3 (Fall 1980): 294; Marjorie Hunter, "Carl Vinson, 97, Ex-Congressman Who was in House 50 Years, Dies," *New York Times*, June 2, 1981, 26; James Cook, *Carl Vinson: Patriarch of the Armed* Forces (Macon, GA: Mercer University Press, 2004), 23–24, 264–265.

79. Cutrer and Parrish, *Doris Miller*, 26–43.

80. Cutrer and Parrish, 26–43.

81. Cutrer and Parrish, 62–67; L. D. Reddick, "The Negro in the United States Navy During World War II," *Journal of Negro History* 32, no. 2 (April 1947): 208–211; Mershon and Schlossman, *Foxholes & Color Lines*, 47–51.

82. Cutrer and Parrish, *Doris Miller*, 62–67; Reddick, "The Negro in the United States Navy During World War II," 208–211; Mershon and Schlossman, *Foxholes & Color Lines*, 47–51.

83. Robert J. Schneller Jr., *Blue & Gold and Black: Racial Integration of the U.S. Naval Academy* (College Station: Texas A&M University Press, 2008), 4.

84. Jack D. Foner, *Blacks and the Military in American History* (New York: Prager, 1974), 21, 129; MacGregor, *Integration of the Armed Forces*, 100–112; Mershon and Schlossman, *Foxholes & Color Lines*, 47.

85. J. Foner, *Blacks and the Military in American History*, 21, 129; MacGregor, *Integration of the Armed Forces*, 100–112; Mershon and Schlossman, *Foxholes & Color Lines*, 47; Melton A. McLaurin, *The Marines of Montford Point: America's First Black Marines* (Chapel Hill: University of North Carolina Press, 2007), 1, 97–98.

86. J. Foner, *Blacks and the Military in American History*, 21, 129; MacGregor, *Integration of the Armed Forces*, 100–112; Mershon and Schlossman, *Foxholes & Color Lines*, 47; McLaurin, *The Marines of Montford Point*, 1, 97–98.

87. MacGregor, *Integration of the Armed Forces*, 18; Lee, *The Employment of Negro Troops*, 16–17.

88. On the debate, planning, and eventual actions that led to the development of a Black manpower policy for the armed forces prior to World War II, see Lee, *The Employment of Negro Troops*, 15–50, 51–87; and Robert F. Jefferson, *Fighting for Hope: African American Troops of the 93rd Infantry Division in World War II and Postwar America* (Baltimore: John Hopkins University Press, 2008), 47–61.

89. As Robert Jefferson observed, "Black 93rd Division members who managed to travel to the larger cities and towns of Tucson, Flagstaff, and Bisbee learned quickly to travel in groups, as they frequently found themselves embroiled in skirmishes against civilian police and white soldiers." For more, see Robert Jefferson, *Fighting for Hope*, 76–81.

90. Robert F. Jefferson, *93rd Infantry Division (1942–1946)*, BlackPast.org, www.blackpast.org/african-american-history/u-s-ninety-third-infantry-division-1942-1946; Ephrem Yared, *92nd Infantry Division (1917–1919, 1942–1945)*, BlackPast.org, www.black

past.org/african-american-history/92nd-infantry-division-1917-1919-1942-1945-0; Michael E. Lynch, *Edward M. Almond and the US Army: From the 92nd Infantry Division to the X Corps* (Lexington: University Press of Kentucky, 2019), 88–89; Nalty, *Strength for the Fight*, 164.

91. Jefferson, *Fighting for Hope*, 158–177; Jefferson, *93rd Infantry Division (1942–1946)*.

92. Jefferson, *Fighting for Hope*, 158–177; Jefferson, *93rd Infantry Division (1942–1946)*.

93. Jefferson, *Fighting for Hope*, 158–177; Jefferson, *93rd Infantry Division (1942–1946)*.

94. Jefferson, *Fighting for Hope*, 158–177; Jefferson, *93rd Infantry Division (1942–1946)*.

95. The Editors of *Encyclopedia Britannica*, "Bougainville Island," *Encyclopedia Britannica*, www.britannica.com/place/Bougainville-Island; Jefferson, *Fighting for Hope*, 157–158, 177–180. I say the artillery strike was risky because, considering the likely proximity of the Japanese from the Black men of Company K, it could be considered a "danger close" situation. A "danger close" situation is military parlance for when artillery rounds (or other types of munitions) were within a distance determined to be a possible risk to friendly personnel in the area.

96. Jefferson, *Fighting for Hope*, 178–189; Nalty, *Strength for the Fight*, 170; Lee, *The Employment of Negro Troops*, 512, n.35; Jefferson, *93rd Infantry Division (1942–1946)*.

97. Jefferson, *Fighting for Hope*, 178–189; Nalty, *Strength for the Fight*, 170; Lee, *The Employment of Negro Troops*, 512, n.35; Jefferson, *93rd Infantry Division (1942–1946)*.

98. Jefferson, *Fighting for Hope*, 185–186.

99. Jefferson, 186–187. For more on MacArthur and his racism and leadership on the issue of race, see chapter three of this book.

100. Jefferson, *Fighting for Hope*, 186–187.

101. Jefferson, 186–187.

102. Jefferson, 186–187; Jefferson, *93rd Infantry Division (1942–1946)*.

103. It should be noted that, although he had acted with the best intentions of his community at heart, White's actions in the South Pacific were heavily criticized by some of the soldiers of the 93rd Division. For more, see Jefferson, *Fighting for Hope*, 187–188.

104. Jefferson, *Fighting for Hope*, 186–187; Jefferson, *93rd Infantry Division (1942–1946)*.

105. Jefferson, *Fighting for Hope*, 186–187; Jefferson, *93rd Infantry Division (1942–1946)*.

106. Lynch, *Edward M. Almond and the US Army*, xii, 1–4, 14.

107. Lynch, 37–38; Rudyard Kipling, "The White Man's Burden," Modern History Sourcebook, Fordham University, https://sourcebooks.fordham.edu/mod/kipling.asp.

108. African Americans also played a role in this, but they were not always consistent about it. Some objected to the imperialism of the United States at the time, while others felt some measure of pride in the growing power of their country. Sometimes, Black soldiers looked down on the racial populations they were suppressing. Many African American military personnel, though, could not help but feel a measure of sympathy and empathized with those racial groups that they had helped white America conquer. See Gatewood, *Black Americans and the White Man's Burden*, 180–221, and Gatewood, *"SMOKED YANKEES,"* 184–235, 245–316.

109. Lynch, *Edward M. Almond and the US Army*, 37–38; William Shakespeare,

Henry IV, Part 2, edited by Barbara A. Mowat and Paul Werstine (New York: Simon & Schuster, 2020), 111.

110. Lynch, *Edward M. Almond and the US Army*, 62–64.

111. Lynch, 67–71.

112. Lynch, 67–71.

113. Lynch, 72–76.

114. Lynch, 1, 75–76; for more on the assessment of Almond as a fair-minded leader see 76–102.

115. Lynch, 103–109.

116. Lynch, 109–111.

117. Lynch, 109–111.

118. Lynch, 111–112.

119. Lynch, 113.

120. Lynch, 113; Robert Child, *Immortal Valor: The Black Medal of Honor Winners of World War II* (New York: Osprey, 2022), 240–244.

121. Lynch, *Edward M. Almond and the US Army*, 113–114.

122. Lynch, 114–125, 149.

123. Lynch, 126–129.

124. Lynch, 122, 126–129.

125. Lynch, 122, 126–129.

126. Lynch, 129–133.

127. Lynch, 129–133; Daniel K. Gibran, *The 92nd Infantry Division and the Italian Campaign in World War* II (Jefferson, NC: McFarland, 2001), 103.

128. Lee, *The Employment of Negro Troops*, 624, 688–689, 690–691; MacGregor, *Integration of the Armed Forces*, 51–53.

129. Lee, *The Employment of Negro Troops*, 624, 688–689, 690–691; MacGregor, *Integration of the Armed Forces*, 51–53.

130. South Carolina and Alabama soldiers' comments quoted in The President's Committee on Civil Rights, *To Secure These Rights: The Report of the President's Committee on Civil Rights* (Washington, DC: U.S. Government Printing Office, 1947), 83–84 (hereinafter *To Secure These Rights*); see also 85–87; European Theater of Operation questions and answers quoted in Morris J. MacGregor Jr. and Bernard C. Nalty, eds., *Blacks in the United States Armed Forces: Basic Documents*, vol. 5 (Wilmington, DE: Scholarly Resources, 1977), 518; Mershon and Schlossman, *Foxholes & Color Lines*, 163–165.

131. Mershon and Schlossman, 142–143.

132. Steven L. Ossad, *Omar Nelson Bradley: America's GI General: 1893–1981* (Columbia: University of Missouri Press, 2017), 21, 310; Mershon and Schlossman, *Foxholes & Color Lines*, 142–143.

133. Ossad, *Omar Nelson Bradley*, 21, 310; Mershon and Schlossman, *Foxholes & Color Lines*, 142–143.

134. Mershon and Schlossman, 142–149; MacGregor, *Integration of the Armed Forces*, 156.

135. MacGregor, 176–179; Mershon and Schlossman, *Foxholes & Color Lines*, 149–150; "Remarks of Howard C. Petersen, The Assistant Secretary of War, at Luncheon for Negro Newspaper Publishers Association, March 1, 1946," HST Library, Philleo Nash Papers, Box 55, Minorities, Negro General, Negroes in the Armed Forces.

136. MacGregor, *Integration of the Armed Forces*, 176–179; Mershon and Schlossman, *Foxholes & Color Lines*, 149–150.

137. Federal Records of World War II.: Military Agencies, United States, National Achieves and Records Service, January 1, 1951, U.S. Government Printing Office, 274; *Army Talk* #70, 5 May 1945, HST Library, RG 220, Box 7, Records of the President's Committee on Equality of Treatment and Opportunity in the Armed Services, General Correspondence, 1.

138. *Army Talk* #70.

139. Karl Gunnar Myrdal, *An American Dilemma: The Negro Problem and Modern Democracy*, vol. 1 (New Brunswick, NJ: Transaction Publishers, 1996), 422.

140. Mershon and Schlossman, *Foxholes & Color Lines*, 155–157.

141. *Army Talk* #70.

Chapter 2: "It Was Good Trouble, It Was Necessary Trouble"

1. Aspects of this chapter first appeared in my doctoral dissertation: Geoffrey W. Jensen, "It Cut Both Ways: The Cold War and Civil Rights Reform Within the Military, 1945–1968" (PhD diss., University of Arkansas, 2009), and again, several years later, in Geoffrey W. Jensen, "The Political, the Personal, and the Cold War: Harry Truman and Executive Order 9981," in *The Routledge Handbook of the History of Race and the American Military*, ed., Geoffrey W. Jensen (New York: Routledge, 2016); Isaac Woodard Affidavit, April 23, 1946 (NAACP Papers, Reel 28, Frames 1012–1013); here after referred to as Isaac Woodard Affidavit; Richard Gergel, *Unexampled Courage: The Blinding of Isaac Woodard and the Awakening of President Harry S. Truman and Judge J. Waties Waring* (New York: Sarah Crichton Books, 2019), 14–15.

2. Isaac Woodard Affidavit, April 23, 1946; Gergel, *Unexampled Courage*, 14–15.

3. Woodard incorrectly identified the town as Aiken in his affidavit, see Isaac Woodard Affidavit, April 23, 1946.

4. Conflicting accounts about Woodard, whether he was drinking or not and his behavior on the bus, emerged from his fellow passengers, including a while soldier and Black soldier, after the incident. See Gergel, *Unexampled Courage*, 15.

5. Isaac Woodard Affidavit, April 23, 1946; Walter White, *A Man Called White: The Autobiography of Walter White* (Athens: University of Georgia Press, 1995), 330–331.

6. Isaac Woodard Affidavit, April 23, 1946; White, *A Man Called White*, 330–331.

7. Orson Welles, *Orson Welles Commentaries*, July 28, 1946, Welles mss, LMC 2009, Lilly Library, Indiana University, Bloomington, Indiana, https://orsonwelles.indiana .edu/items/show/2169 (hereinafter "OWC"); OWC, August 4, 1946, https://orson welles.indiana.edu/items/show/2171; OWC, August 11, 1946, https://orsonwelles.india na.edu/items/show/2172; OWC, August 18, 1946, https://orsonwelles.indiana.edu/it ems/show/2174; OWC, August 25, 1946, https://orsonwelles.indiana.edu/items/show /2176; "Orson Welles," *NAACP Bulletin*, vol. 5 (August–September 1946): 1; Brian Do- linar, *The Black Cultural Front: Black Writers and Artists of the Depression Generation* (Jackson: University Press of Mississippi, 2012), 203–208.

8. OWC, July 28, 1946; OWC, August 4, 1946; OWC, August 11, 1946; OWC, August 18, 1946; OWC, August 25, 1946; "Orson Welles"; Dolinar, *The Black Cultural Front*, 203–208.

9. White, *A Man Called White*, 325–328, 331; Michael Gardner, *Harry Truman and Civil Rights: Moral Courage and Political Risks* (Carbondale: Southern Illinois University Press, 2002), 21–23.

10. Alan Rice, "Black Troops Were Welcome in Britain, but Jim Crow Wasn't: The Race Riot of One Night in June 1943," *The Conservation*, June 21, 2018, https://get pocket.com/explore/item/black-troops-were-welcome-in-britain-but-jim-crow-wasn -t-the-race-riot-of-one-night-in-june-1943?utm_source=pocket-; Linda Hervieux, *Forgotten: The Untold Story of D-Day's Black Heroes, at Home and at War* (New York: HarperCollins, 2016), 184; Nalty, *Strength for the Fight*, 154–155.

11. Rice, "Black Troops"; Hervieux, *Forgotten*, 184; Nalty, *Strength for the Fight*, 154–155.

12. Rice, "Black Troops"; Hervieux, *Forgotten*, 184; Nalty, *Strength for the Fight*, 154–155.

13. Rice, "Black Troops"; Hervieux, *Forgotten*, 184; Nalty, *Strength for the Fight*, 154–155.

14. Rice, "Black Troops"; Hervieux, *Forgotten*, 184; Nalty, *Strength for the Fight*, 154–155.

15. White, *A Man Called White*, 330–331; Equal Justice Initiative, "Lynching in America," 27, 44; Gail Buckley, *American Patriots: The Story of Blacks in the Military from the Revolution to Desert Storm* (New York: Random House, 2001), 337; Erica Sterling, The Georgia Civil Rights Cold Cases Project at Emory University, "Maceo Snipes," https://coldcases.emory.edu/maceo-snipes/#f2.

16. Scott Buchanan, "Three Governors Controversy," New Georgia Encyclopedia, October 5, 2021 update, www.georgiaencyclopedia.org/articles/government-politics /three-governors-controversy.

17. White, *A Man Called White*, 330–331; Equal Justice Initiative, "Lynching in America," 27, 44; Buckley, *American Patriots*, 337; Sterling, "Maceo Snipes"; for more on the Ford lynching, see Laura Wexler, *Fire in a Canebrake: The Last Mass Lynching in America* (New York: Scribner, 2003), and Anthony Pitch, *The Last Lynching: How a Gruesome Mass Murder Rocked a Small Georgia Town* (New York: Skyhorse, 2016).

18. White, *A Man Called White*, 325–328, 331; Gardner, *Harry Truman and Civil Rights*, 21–23; Truman letter to Tom Clark, September 20, 1946, HST Library, Papers of HST, General File, Box 113, Negro file; DOJ Press Release on Isaac Woodard, September 26, 1946, HST Library, Papers of Philleo Nash, Box 45, Isaac Woodard File.

19. White, *A Man Called White*, 325–328, 331; Gardner, *Harry Truman and Civil Rights*, 21–23; Truman letter to Tom Clark, September 20, 1946, HST Library, Papers of HST, General File, Box 113, Negro file; DOJ Press Release on Isaac Woodard, September 26, 1946, HST Library, Papers of Philleo Nash, Box 45, Isaac Woodard File; "Federal vs. State Issue at S.C. Trial," *Afro-American*, November 9, 1946; "Police Chief Freed in Negro Beating," *New York Times*, November 6, 1946.

20. John Lewis, "A President Who Got in Trouble—Good Trouble. Necessary Trouble," in *The Civil Rights Legacy of Harry S. Truman*, ed. Raymond H. Geselbracht (Kirksville, MO: Truman State University Press, 2007), 9.

21. David McCullough, *Truman* (New York: Simon and Schuster, 1992), 588.

22. Harry S. Truman, *The Memoirs of Harry S. Truman*, vol. 2, *Years of Trial and*

Hope, 1946–1953 (London: Hodder & Stoughton, 1956), 181, 269–273; Leuchtenburg, *The White House Looks South*, 151–152.

23. Leuchtenburg, 147–156; Jonathan Daniels, *The Man of Independence* (Columbia: University of Missouri Press, 1998), 339.

24. Leuchtenburg, *The White House Looks South*, 147–156; Daniels, *The Man of Independence,* 339.

25. Gergel, *Unexampled Courage*, 27.

26. Truman, *Memoirs*, 181, 269–273; Nancy MacLean, *Behind the Mask of Chivalry: The Making of the Second Ku Klux Klan* (New York: Oxford University Press, 1994), xi–xvii.

27. McCullough, *Truman*, 164–165; Gardner, *Harry Truman and Civil Rights*, 6–8, 20–21.

28. Gardner, 6–8, 20–21.

29. Gardner, 6–8, 20–21; Truman, *Memoirs*, 181, 269–273; *To Secure These Rights*, 7.

30. Alonzo Hamby, *Man of the People: A Life of Harry S. Truman* (New York: Oxford University Press, 1998), 433.

31. Hamby, 433.

32. *To Secure These Rights*, 7; Harry S. Truman, Address Before the National Association for the Advancement of Colored People, online by Gerhard Peters and John T. Woolley, The American Presidency Project, www.presidency.ucsb.edu/node/231974 (hereinafter "Truman's NAACP Address").

33. Truman's NAACP Address.

34. Daniels, *The Man of Independence*, 336; *To Secure These Rights*, 146–147; Dudziak, *Cold War Civil Rights*, 26–27, 80–81; also see Gardner, *Harry Truman and Civil Rights*, 34–36.

35. *To Secure These Rights*, 6–9, 21–46, 83–85; Gardner, *Harry Truman and Civil Rights*, 50–58.

36. Walter White Statement to PCCR, HST Library, Philleo Nash Papers, Box 194, PCCR Meeting Minutes [2], 200, 205.

37. *To Secure These Rights*, 47; Mershon and Schlossman, *Foxholes & Color Lines*, 165; MacGregor and Nalty, eds., *Blacks in the United States Armed Forces: Basic Documents*, vol. 5, 518–520; *To Secure These Rights*, 40–46.

38. *To Secure These Rights*, 147, see also 139–148; Jonathan Rosenberg, *How Far the Promised Land?*, 182–183; Mershon and Schlossman, *Foxholes & Color Lines*, 165.

39. Harry S. Truman, Special Message to the Congress on Civil Rights Online by Gerhard Peters and John T. Woolley, The American Presidency Project, www.presidency.ucsb.edu/node/232898.

40. Truman, Special Message to the Congress on Civil Rights.

41. Truman, Special Message to the Congress on Civil Rights.

42. Truman, Special Message to the Congress on Civil Rights; *To Secure These Rights*, 79, 150, 162; Mershon and Schlossman, *Foxholes & Color Lines*, 167; Gardner, *Harry Truman and Civil Rights*, 76–77.

43. Randall B. Woods, *The Quest for Identity* (New York: Cambridge University Press, 2005), 20–22, 64.

44. Cash, *The Mind of the South*, 136.

45. Cash, 136; Alan T. Nolan, "The Anatomy of the Myth," in *The Myth of the Lost*

Cause and Civil War History, eds., Gary W. Gallagher and Alan T. Nolan (Bloomington: Indiana University Press, 2000), 11–34.

46. Jeff Woods, *Black Struggle, Red Scare* (Baton Rouge: Louisiana State University Press), 35–38.

47. "Southern Newspapers Hit Civil Rights Report," *Washington Post*, October 30, 1947, 11; Comments about Rankin quoted in Stan Frank, "The Rancorous Mr. Rankin," *Liberty*, October 6, 1945, 19; Rankin comments quoted in "Civil Rights and the Election," *The Christian Century*, 65, no. 7 (February 18, 1948): 195–196; R. Woods, *The Quest for Identity*, 21.

48. Gardner, *Harry Truman and Civil Rights*, 72; Benn Steil, *The Marshall Plan: Dawn of the Cold War* (New York: Oxford University Press, 2018), 260.

49. J. Woods, *Black Struggle, Red Scare*, 36.

50. Kari Fredrickson, *The Dixiecrat Revolt and the End of the Solid South, 1932–1968* (Chapel Hill: University of North Carolina Press, 2001), 140; Mershon and Schlossman, *Foxholes & Color Lines*, 179–180.

51. R. Woods, *The Quest for Identity*, 48–52.

52. Hamby, *Man of the People*, 368–369.

53. Paula P. Pfeffer, *A. Phillip Randolph, Pioneer of the Civil Rights Movement* (Baton Rouge: Louisiana State University Press, 1990), 133, 137–144.

54. William A. Taylor, *Every Citizen a Soldier: The Campaign for Universal Military Training After World War II* (College Station: Texas A&M University Press, 2014), 58, 60–62.

55. Hamby, *Man of the People*, 368–369; Pfeffer, *A. Phillip Randolph*, 133, 137–144.

56. Pfeffer, 138.

57. Clark Clifford, *Counsel to the President: A Memoir* (New York: Random House, 1991), 209–210.

58. Gardner, *Harry Truman and Civil Rights*, 107, 109–111.

59. Harry S. Truman, Executive Order 9981—Establishing the President's Committee on Equality of Treatment and Opportunity in the Armed Services Online by Gerhard Peters and John T. Woolley, The American Presidency Project, www.presidency.ucsb.edu/node/231614; Mershon and Schlossman, *Foxholes & Color Lines*, 167, 183; "The Order Mr. Truman Did Not Issue," *Pittsburgh Courier*, August 7, 1948.

60. Clifford, *Counsel to the President*, 210–211.

61. Harry S. Truman, The President's News Conference of July 29, 1948, Online by Gerhard Peters and John T. Woolley, The American Presidency Project, www.presidency.ucsb.edu/node/232710; Mershon and Schlossman, *Foxholes & Color Lines*, 183–184, 187, 189.

62. Representative A. Leonard Allen (LA), "Anti-segregation Executive Order," *Congressional Record* 94:12 (July 27, 1948), A4653; Representative Overton Brooks (LA), "Segregation in the Armed Forces," *Congressional Record* 94:12 (July 27, 1948), A4650; (Rankin comments) PCCR General Correspondence, HST Library, RG220, Box 7, File "R"; Representative Ed Gossett (TX), "President's Executive Orders of July 26, 1948," *Congressional Record* 94:12 (July 27, 1948), A4645.

63. James Forrestal (edited by Walter Millis and E. S. Duffield), *The Forrestal Diaries* (New York: Viking Press, 1951), 439–440.

64. Speech of Senator Richard B. Russell, Untitled Speech, July 26, 1948, RRL, UGA, Series III, Box 30; Senator Richard B. Russell (GA), "Freedom of Selection Amendment to Selective Service Act—Personal Statement," *Congressional Record* 94:5 (May 12, 1948), 5665–5667.

65. Senator Russell, Untitled Speech, July 26, 1948; Senator Russell (GA), "Freedom of Selection Amendment to Selective Service Act—Personal Statement," 5665–5667; Senators Richard B. Russell (GA) and Burnet R. Maybank (SC), "Promotion of National Defense—Increase in Personnel of Armed Forces," *Congressional Record* 94:6 (June 8, 1948), 7355–7367; Senator Russell (GA), "Freedom of Selection Amendment to Selective Service Act—Personal Statement," 5665; for Russell and Maybank's renewed pursuit for "freedom of choice" in the armed forces in 1950, see Senators Richard B. Russell (GA) and Burnet R. Maybank (SC), "Extension of the 1948 Selective Service Act," *Congressional Record* 96:7 (June 21, 1950), 8988–8995; "Glancing Back at Certain Remarks," *The Nation* 171, no. 1 (July 1950), 1–2; Richard M. Dalfiume, *Desegregation of the U.S. Armed Forces: Fighting on Two Fronts: 1939–1953* (Columbia: University of Missouri Press, 1975), 166.

66. Mary Ethel Haldane Kindle to J. William Fulbright, February 22, 1948. Special Collections, JWFP, UARK, BCN 48, Box A256, Folder 1; Phil D. Poston to J. William Fulbright, February 22, 1948. Special Collections, JWFP, UARK, BCN 48, Box A256, Folder 1.

67. Phil D. Poston to Harry S. Truman, March 9, 1948. Special Collections, JWFP, UARK, BCN 48, Box A256, Folder 1; Letter, Mrs. B. E. Thomas to Harry S. Truman, OF 93, HST Library, Box 542, 2; Letter, Y. F. Stewart to Harry S. Truman, OF 93, HST Library, Box 542.

68. Correspondence Between Harry S. Truman and Ernie Roberts, HST Library, August 18, 1948, President's Secretary's Files, Truman Papers; Gardner, *Harry Truman and Civil Rights*, 131; also see Robert Ferrell, *Off the Record: The Private Papers of Harry S. Truman* (Columbia: University of Missouri Press, 1997), 146–147.

69. Correspondence Between Harry S. Truman and Ernie Roberts; Gardner, *Harry Truman and Civil Rights*, 131; also see Ferrell, *Off the Record*, 146–147.

70. Mershon and Schlossman, *Foxholes & Color Lines*, 20–22.

71. MacGregor, *Integration of the Armed Forces*, 227–229.

72. MacGregor, 227–229.

73. MacGregor, 229; Stephen Ambrose, *Eisenhower: Soldier and President* (New York: Simon & Schuster, 1990), 542.

74. Omar Bradley and Clay Blair, *A General's Life* (New York: Simon and Schuster, 1983), 485; Mershon and Schlossman, *Foxholes & Color Lines*, 143; MacGregor, *Integration of the Armed Forces*, 55.

75. Bradley and Blair, *A General's Life*, 485; Mershon and Schlossman, *Foxholes & Color Lines*, 143; MacGregor, *Integration of the Armed Forces*, 55.

76. Bradley and Blair, *A General's Life*, 485; Lee Nichols, *Breakthrough on the Color Front* (New York: Random House, 1954), 206; MacGregor, *Integration of the Armed Forces*, 317.

77. Bradley and Blair, *A General's Life*, 485.

78. Harry S. Truman, Address in Harlem, New York, Upon Receiving the Franklin

Roosevelt Award, online by Gerhard Peters and John T. Woolley, The American Presidency Project, www.presidency.ucsb.edu/node/233997; MacGregor, *Integration of the Armed Forces*, 317–318; "Negro Leaders Question Bradley on Segregation," *Philadelphia Bulletin*, July 29, 1948.

79. Senator Russell (GA), "Freedom of Selection Amendment to Selective Service Act—Personal Statement," 5666, and Senators Russell (GA) and Maybank (SC), "Promotion of National Defense—Increase in Personnel of Armed Forces," 7358, 7366, and Senators Russell (GA) and Maybank (SC), "Extension of the 1948 Selective Service Act," 8991–8995; Dalfiume, *Desegregation of the U.S. Armed Forces*, 173; "General Bradley's Stand," *Fort Worth Star Telegram*, July 29, 1948; "And Now-Military Rights Program," *Montgomery Advertiser*, July 29, 1948; "Army's Chief of Staff Defends Military Segregation," *Jackson Clarion-Ledger*, July 30, 1948. Bradley later claimed to regret the praise he received from Southerners over the incident; for more, see Bradley and Blair, 486.

80. Mershon and Schlossman, *Foxholes & Color Lines*, 188–191.

81. Mershon and Schlossman, 188–191.

82. Mershon and Schlossman, 191–192.

83. Hamby, *Man of the People*, 11–512.

84. Mershon and Schlossman, *Foxholes & Color Lines*, 192; MacGregor, *Integration of the Armed Forces*, 345–346.

85. Transcript, Stuart R. Symington Oral History Interview, May 29, 1981, by James R. Fuchs, 1–2, Truman Library, www.trumanlibrary.org/oralhist/symton.htm#subjects; James C. Olson, *Stuart Symington: A Life* (Columbia: University of Missouri Press, 2003), 134–135.

86. Transcript, Stuart R. Symington Oral History Interview, May 29, 1981, by James R. Fuchs, 1–2, Truman Library, www.trumanlibrary.org/oralhist/symton.htm#subjects; James C. Olson, 134–135; MacGregor, *Integration of the Armed Forces*, 338.

87. Mershon and Schlossman, *Foxholes & Color Lines*, 155–156, 193; MacGregor, *Integration of the Armed Forces*, 338–339

88. "Air Force Won't Give in to Dixie," *Pittsburgh Courier*, June 25, 1949; "Pilots Testing Alabama Jim-Crow Bus Seating," *Pittsburgh Courier*, July 2, 1949

89. Mershon and Schlossman, *Foxholes & Color Lines*, 194–195; Nalty, *Strength for the Fight*, 153.

90. Mershon and Schlossman, *Foxholes & Color Lines*, 195–197.

91. Charlene E. McGee Smith, *Tuskegee Airman: The Biography of Charles E. McGee: Air Force Fighter Combat Record Holder* (Boston: Branden Publishing Company, 2000), 81–83.

92. C. Smith, 79–80.

93. J. Foner, *Blacks and the Military in American History*, 5; Ian W. Toll, *Six Frigates: The Epic History of the Founding of the U.S. Navy* (New York: W. W. Norton and Company, 2006), 17; Nalty, *Strength for the Fight*, 19–21.

94. J. Foner, *Blacks and the Military in American History*, 5; Toll, *Six Frigates*, 17; Nalty, *Strength for the Fight*, 19–21.

95. Mershon and Schlossman, *Foxholes & Color Lines*, 127–130.

96. Mershon and Schlossman, 127–130; Milton Stewart memo to Robert K. Carr, HST Library, RG 220, Box 6, PCCR, April 1, 1947.

97. Mershon and Schlossman, *Foxholes & Color Lines*, 130–133, 199.

98. Mershon and Schlossman, 199.

99. Dixon, *African Americans and the Pacific War*, 52–53; MacGregor, *Integration of the Armed Forces*, 235–240.

100. MacGregor, 237–241.

101. Mershon and Schlossman, *Foxholes & Color Lines*, 200–202.

102. Mershon and Schlossman, 200–202.

103. Mershon and Schlossman, 200–202.

104. Mershon and Schlossman, 202–203.

105. Mershon and Schlossman, 202–203; Walter White Telegram to Harry S. Truman, Robert L. Dennison Files, Box 4, Segregation: Charleston and Norfolk Naval Yards, June 27, 1952; W. McL. Hague to Clarence Mitchell, HST Library, Robert L. Dennison Files, Box 4, Segregation: Charleston and Norfolk Naval Yards, February 4, 1952; W. McL. Hague to all Naval and Marine Corp Commanding Personnel, OIR Notice CP 75, HST Library, Robert L. Dennison Files, Box 4, Segregation: Charleston and Norfolk Naval Yards.

106. Mershon and Schlossman, *Foxholes & Color Lines*, 204–208.

107. Mershon and Schlossman, 204–208; Ken Royall statement to Fahy Committee, HST Library, RG 220, Box 2, Fahy Comm Mtgs, March 28, 1949, 1; Omar Bradley statement to Fahy Committee, HST Library, RG 220, Box 2, Fahy Comm Mtgs, March 28, 1949, 3.

108. Mershon and Schlossman, *Foxholes & Color Lines*, 208–209.

109. Mershon and Schlossman, 209–210.

110. Mershon and Schlossman, 210–214.

111. Mershon and Schlossman, 210–214; "Army Lags Behind Air Force and Navy In Ending Jim Crow," *Minneapolis Spokesman*, August 26, 1949.

112. MacGregor, *Integration of the Armed Forces*, 100–112; Mershon and Schlossman, *Foxholes & Color Lines*, 203–204; Ray Albert Robinson Statement to Fahy Committee, HST Library, RG 220, Box 12, Fahy Comm Mtgs, January 13, 1949, 1–8.

113. MacGregor, *Integration of the Armed Forces*, 100–112; Mershon and Schlossman, *Foxholes & Color Lines*, 203–204; Ray Albert Robinson Statement to Fahy Committee, 1–8; Memo, Al Smith to John Sengstacke, "Resignation of Lt. (Second) John Earl Rudder from U.S. Marine Corps," RG 220, Box 12, Fahy Comm Mtgs, February 10, 1949, 3–4; Lem Graves Jr., "Lone Negro Marine Officer Tenders Resignation," *Pittsburgh Courier*, February 19, 1949.

114. MacGregor, *Integration of the Armed Forces*, 100–112; Mershon and Schlossman, *Foxholes & Color Lines*, 203–204; Ray Albert Robinson statement to Fahy Committee, 1–8; Memo, Al Smith to John Sengstacke, "Resignation of Lt. (Second) John Earl Rudder from U.S. Marine Corps," 3–4; Graves Jr., "Lone Negro Marine Officer Tenders Resignation."

115. MacGregor, *Integration of the Armed Forces*, 100–112; Mershon and Schlossman, *Foxholes & Color Lines*, 203–204; Ray Albert Robinson Statement to Fahy Committee, 1–2, 9.

116. Carol Anderson, *Eyes Off the Prize: The United Nations and the African American Struggle for Human Rights, 1944–1955* (New York: Cambridge University Press,

2011), 3; Christine Knauer, *Let Us Fight as Free Men: Black Soldiers and Civil Rights* (Philadelphia: University of Pennsylvania Press, 2014), 53.

117. Anderson, *Eyes Off the Prize*, 96–98.

118. Jon E. Taylor, *Freedom to Serve: Truman, Civil Rights, and Executive Order 9981* (New York: Routledge, 2013), 129–130.

Chapter 3: Born out of the Necessity of War

1. HST Library, RG 220, Box 12, Rep. Jacob Javits Resolution, 1.

2. HST Library, RG 220, Box 12, Rep. Jacob Javits Resolution, 1.

3. Representative Adam Clayton Powell Jr., *Congressional Record* 96.6 (May 24, 1950), 7679.

4. Representative Jacob Javits, *Congressional Record* 96:6 (May 24, 1950), 7680.

5. Representative John Rankin, *Congressional Record* 96:4 (April 19, 1950), 5391; Representative John Rankin, *Congressional Record* 96:6 (May 24, 1950), 7680.

6. Representative Charles E. Bennett, *Congressional Record* 96:6 (May 24, 1950), 7680; Representative John Rankin, *Congressional Record* 96:6 (May 24, 1950), 7681; the debate over the Powell, Javits, and Bennett amendments can be found in *Congressional Record* 96:6 (May 24, 1950),7678–7682.

7. Dean Acheson's National Press Club remarks, HST Library, Papers of George M. Elsey, Box 101, Personnel Correspondence, Dean Acheson; Woods, *Quest for Identity*, 54–61.

8. On the subject of manpower issues in the post–World War II American military, see Lewis, *The American Culture of War*, 161–165.

9. Jager, *Brothers at War*, 71–73; Lewis, *The American Culture of War*, 115–116.

10. Dalfiume, *Desegregation of the U.S. Armed Forces*, 202–203; Andrew H. Myers, *Black, White & Olive Drab* (Charlottesville: University of Virginia Press, 2006), 77–82; Mershon and Schlossman, *Foxholes & Color Lines*, 229–230.

11. Myers, *Black, White & Olive Drab*, 80, 86–91; Strom Thurmond, Statement "[Segregation in the Armed Forces]" (Campaign Meeting), McCormick, S.C., May 24, 1950, 2, Mss100, Strom Thurmond Collection, Speeches, Box 7; Mershon and Schlossman, *Foxholes & Color Lines*, 229–230.

12. Myers, *Black, White & Olive Drab*, 80, 86–91; Mershon and Schlossman, *Foxholes & Color Lines*, 229–230.

13. Jager, *Brothers at War*, 103–108.

14. Mershon and Schlossman, *Foxholes & Color Lines*, 225, see also 223–225; Dalfiume, *Desegregation of the U.S. Armed Forces*, 204–205.

15. Dalfiume, 205; Senator Herbert H. Lehman, "Record of American Negro Combat Troops in Korea—Statement by Senator Lehman and Editorial Comment," *Congressional Record* 96:10 (August 23, 1950), 13184; Gail Buckley, *American Patriots*, 357–358; Mershon and Schlossman, *Foxholes & Color Lines*, 220–222; William T. Bowers, William M. Hammond, and George L. MacGarrigle, *Black Soldier, White Army: The 24th Infantry Regiment in Korea* (Washington, DC: Center of Military History, United States Army, 1996), xi–xii, 27–28.

16. Bowers, Hammond, and MacGarrigle, *Black Soldier, White Army*, 57–58.

17. Bowers, Hammond, and MacGarrigle, *Black Soldier, White Army*, 57–58; Curtis

James Morrow, *What's a Commie Ever Done to Black People: A Korean War Memoir of Fighting in the U.S. Army's Last All Negro Unit* (Jefferson, NC: McFarland, 1997), 34; Buckley, *American Patriots*, 357.

18. Mershon and Schlossman, *Foxholes & Color Lines*, 220, see also 223.

19. Morris J. MacGregor Jr. and Bernard C. Nalty, eds., *Blacks in the United States Armed Forces: Basic Documents*, vol. 12 (Wilmington, DE: Scholarly Resources, 1977), 172; Juan Williams, *Thurgood Marshall: American Revolutionary* (New York: Three Rivers Press, 1998), 169–171.

20. MacGregor and Nalty, *Blacks in the United States Armed Forces: Basic Documents*, vol. 12, 172; Williams, *Thurgood Marshall*, 169–171.

21. The convictions of the thirty-two African American soldiers breaks down as follows: one sentenced to execution, fifteen to life in jail, one to fifty years in jail, two to twenty-five years, three for twenty years, one for fifteen years, seven for ten years, and two for five years. The two white soldiers convicted of similar wrongdoing faced much lighter sentences: one white was sentenced to five years, a sentence that later was reduced; the other was sentenced to three years. For more, see MacGregor and Nalty, eds., *Blacks in the United States Armed Forces: Basic Documents*, vol. 12, 178.

22. Mershon and Schlossman, *Foxholes & Color Lines*, 222–223; MacGregor and Nalty, eds., *Blacks in the United States Armed Forces: Basic Documents*, vol. 12, 171–184.

23. Williams, *Thurgood Marshall*, 171–173.

24. Williams, 171–173.

25. Williams, 172; Geoffrey Perret, *Old Soldiers Never Die: The Life of Douglas MacArthur* (Holbrook, MA: Adams Media Corporation, 1996), 178; William Manchester, *American Caesar: Douglas MacArthur: 1880–1964* (New York: Back Bay Books, 2008), 132–133.

26. "Negro General for M'Arthur," *Chicago Defender*, July 15, 1950.

27. Ethel Payne, "The Last Time I Saw MacArthur," *Chicago Defender*, April 28, 1951.

28. Zhou Enlai comments quoted in Chen Jian, *China's Road to the Korean War* (New York: Columbia University Press, 1994), 180; Jager, *Brothers at War*, 113–114, 117–124; Woods, *Quest for Identity*, 57–58.

29. Hamby, *Man of the People*, 556; Woods, *Quest for Identity*, 58–61; for a more detailed examination of the decision-making behind MacArthur's removal, see Lewis, *The American Culture of War*, 158–161, and Jager, *Brothers at War*, 172–177.

30. For Adrian Lewis, it was not only a matter of MacArthur's ego or inability to take orders from Truman; it was also that the orders and instructions went against what he and many in the military understood to be a part of the American way of war. Lewis observed that "the Truman administration was not conducting the war [hence, it was doing so in a limited fashion] in accordance with the traditional American practice of war, and MacArthur knew only one way to fight war." MacArthur was angling for a total war solution. The problem was that he trying to do so during the early years of the atomic battlefield. For more, see Lewis, *The American Culture of War*, 159.

31. Manchester, *American Caesar*, 661 and 667; see also 666–672.

32. Manchester, 684–686; "M'Arthur Assails 'Jim Crow' in Army," *New York Times*, May 28, 1951.

33. "'Great Efforts' Have Been Made to Cause Race War, MacArthur Tells Negro Paper," *New York Times*, June 4, 1951.

34. Richard Dunlop, "A Story of the Airborne and Ridgway," *Chicago Tribune*, August 18, 1985, www.chicagotribune.com/news/ct-xpm-1985-08-18-8502230826-story.html; Mitchell Yockelson, *The Paratrooper Generals: Matthew Ridgway, Maxwell Taylor, and the American Airborne from D-Day through Normandy* (Lanham, MD: Stackpole Books, 2020), 145; Matthew Ridgway, *The Korean War* (New York: Doubleday & Company, 1967), 79–80, 192–193; Harold H. Martin and Matthew B. Ridgway, *Soldier: The Memoirs of Matthew B. Ridgway* (New York: Harper & Brothers, 1956), 205.

35. Dunlop, "A Story of the Airborne and Ridgway"; Yockelson, *The Paratrooper Generals*, 145; Ridgway, *The Korean War*, 79–80, 192–193; Harold H. Martin and Matthew B. Ridgway, 205.

36. Ridgway, *The Korean War*, 19.

37. Ridgway, 19.

38. Jeremy P. Maxwell, *Brotherhood in Combat: How African Americans Found Equality in Korea and Vietnam* (Norman: University of Oklahoma Press, 2018), 69, 81–82; Lynch, *Edward M. Almond and the US Army*, 113–114, 129–133.

39. Mershon and Schlossman, *Foxholes & Color Lines*, 228–229; MacGregor, *Integration of the Armed Forces*, 445–447.

40. Mershon and Schlossman, *Foxholes & Color Lines*, 231.

41. Mershon and Schlossman, 231.

42. *The Utilization of Negro Manpower in the Army: A 1951 Study* (McLean, VA: Research Analysis Corporation, 1967), S-4–5; Mershon and Schlossman, *Foxholes & Color Lines*, 230–232.

43. *The Utilization of Negro Manpower in the Army: A 1951 Study*, S-4–5; Mershon and Schlossman, *Foxholes & Color Lines*, 230–234.

44. *The Utilization of Negro Manpower in the Army: A 1951 Study*, S-4–5; Mershon and Schlossman, *Foxholes & Color Lines*, 230–234.

45. Nichols, *Breakthrough on the Color Front*, 122–123.

46. Mershon and Schlossman, *Foxholes & Color Lines*, 239.

47. Mershon and Schlossman, 241–243; Leo Bogart, ed., *Project Clear: Social Research and the Desegregation of the United States Army* (New Brunswick, NJ: Transaction Books, 1991), 151–156, 170–171.

48. Mershon and Schlossman, *Foxholes & Color Lines*, 241–243; Bogart, ed., *Project Clear*, 151–156, 170–171.

49. "Ltr from Mrs. Nellie Baker to Richard Russell, Dec 29, 1952" 1, Richard B. Russell Jr. Papers, X. Civil Rights: Segregation in the Armed Services, Correspondence 1952–1955, Box 184, RRL, UGA.

50. A brief examination of the following works can provide a good bit of illumination on the South's development of a martial identity: Franklin, *The Militant South*; Edward Ayers, *What Caused the Civil War? Reflections on the South and Southern History* (New York: Norton Books, 2005); Cash, *The Mind of the South*. A steady shift has occurred since the early 1970s that has amplified Southern enlistment rates in the military. For more, see Dave Philipps and Tim Arango, "Who Signs Up to Fight? Makeup

of U.S. Recruits Shows Glaring Disparity," *New York Times*, January 10, 2020, www.ny times.com/2020/01/10/us/military-enlistment.html.

51. For more on Pershing and the Army's concerns about fraternization between African Americans and French men and women, see "A French Directive," *The Crisis* 18, no. 1 (May 1919), 16–18.

52. "Ltr from Mr. George T. Laney to Richard Russell, May 30, 1951," Richard B. Russell Jr. Papers, X, Civil Rights: Segregation in the Armed Services, Correspondence 1952–1955, Box 185, RRL, UGA.

53. "Mr. J. T. Beverly to Richard Russell, March 13, 1951," Richard B. Russell Jr. Papers, X. Civil Rights: Segregation in the Armed Services, Correspondence 1952–1955, Box 185, RRL, UGA.

54. "Ltr from Reverend George Beasley to Richard Russell, March 1, 1951," Richard B. Russell Jr. Papers, X. Civil Rights: Segregation in the Armed Services, Correspondence 1952–1955, Box 185, RRL, UGA; "Typed Ltr forwarded to Richard Russell from Mr. Walter McClenny, October 10, 1951," Richard B. Russell Jr. Papers, X. Civil Rights: Segregation in the Armed Services, Correspondence 1952–1955, Box 185, RRL, UGA.

55. Mershon and Schlossman, *Foxholes & Color Lines*, 243–244.

56. Rose H. Hepp to Harry S. Truman, with attached memo, November 12, 1950. HST Library, Official File, Truman papers.

57. Bogart, ed., *Project Clear*, 243.

58. Mershon and Schlossman, *Foxholes & Color Lines*, 245; Bogart, ed., *Project Clear*, 242–246.

59. Mershon and Schlossman, *Foxholes & Color Lines*, 245; Bogart, ed., *Project Clear*, 242–246.

60. Bogart, ed., 241–242.

61. Bogart, ed., 241–242.

62. Bogart, ed., 241–242.

63. General J. Lawton Collins, *Lightning Joe: An Autobiography* (Novato, CA: Presidio Press, 1994), 110–111.

64. Mershon and Schlossman, *Foxholes & Color Lines*, 245–247; Nalty, *Strength for the Fight*, 260–261; MacGregor and Nalty, eds., *Blacks in the United States Armed Forces: Basic Documents*, vol. 12, 245, 252; Nichols, *Breakthrough on the Color Front*, 128–129; Collins, 357.

65. Maxwell, *Brotherhood in Combat*, 82–84; David Halberstam, *The Coldest Winter: America and the Korean* War (New York: Hyperion Books, 2007), 307; Mershon and Schlossman, *Foxholes & Color Lines*, 248–249; Melton McLaurin, *The Marines of Montford Point*, 160, 168, see also 161, 166–168; MacGregor, *Integration of the Armed Forces*, 472.

66. Maxwell, *Brotherhood in Combat*, 82–84; Halberstam, 307; Mershon and Schlossman, *Foxholes & Color Lines*, 248–249; McLaurin, *The Marines of Montford Point*, 160–161, 166–168; MacGregor, *Integration of the Armed Forces*, 472.

67. Mershon and Schlossman, *Foxholes & Color Lines*, 249–250.

68. MacGregor, *Integration of the Armed Forces*, 457, see also 456–457; for more on Russell, see Jeff Woods, *Richard B. Russell: Southern Nationalism and American Foreign Policy* (New York: Rowman & Littlefield, 2007), 32–33; Mershon and Schlossman, *Foxholes & Color Lines*, 248.

69. Samuel W. Rushay Jr., "Harry Truman's History Lessons," *Prologue Magazine* 41, no. 1 (Spring 2009), www.archives.gov/publications/prologue/2009/spring/truman -history.html.

70. McCullough, *Truman*, 584; Jeffrey M. Jones, "The Short Answer: Who Had the Lowest Gallup Presidential Job Approval Rating," Gallup, https://news.gallup.com /poll/272765/lowest-gallup-presidential-job-approval-rating.aspx..

71. McCullough, *Truman*, 584.

72. McCullough, 770–771.

73. McCullough, 860.

74. "'Integration' Is Destroying U.S. Army," *The American Nationalist* (n.d.), DDE Library, Maxwell Rabb Papers, Box 45, Fringe Groups and Publications Anti-Semitism (1).

75. "'Integration' Is Destroying U.S. Army."

76. Anna Kasten Nelson, "Anna Rosenberg, an 'Honorary Man,'" *Journal of Military History* 68 (January 2004): 133–138.

77. Nelson, 146, 155.

78. Nelson, 146, 155; Elizabeth A. Collins, "Red-Baiting Public Women: Gender, Loyalty, and Red Scare Politics" (PhD diss., University of Illinois at Chicago, 2008) (Ann Arbor, MI: ProQuest LLC, 2011), 77–84.

79. Nelson, "Anna Rosenberg, an 'Honorary Man,'" 146, 155.

80. Nelson, 156–157.

81. MacGregor, *Integration of the Armed Forces*, 487–488.

82. Hubert H. Humphrey, *The Education of a Public Man: My Life and Politics* (Minneapolis: University of Minnesota Press, 1991), 39–42.

83. MacGregor, *Integration of the Armed Forces*, 487–488.

84. Letter, Senator Hubert H. Humphrey to Anna M. Rosenberg, Assistant Secretary of Defense Manpower and Personnel, October 16, 1952, RG 319, Records of the Army Staff, The Integration of the Armed Forces, 1940–1965, Box 8, NARA II; Memo, Anna Rosenberg to Earl McGrath, January 10, 1953, HST Library, White House File, Nash Papers.

85. Letter, Earl McGrath to Anna Rosenberg, January 15, 1953, HST Library, White House File, Nash Papers; MacGregor, *Integration of the Armed Forces*, 488–490.

86. George C. Reinhardt, "No Segregation in Foxholes," *The Crisis* 60, no. 8 (October 1953): 457; Nichols, *Breakthrough on the Color Front*, 223.

Chapter 4: The Frustration of the Middle Way

1. Gina M. DiNicolo, *The Black Panthers: A Story of Race, War, and Courage—the 761st Tank Battalion in World War II* (Yardley, PA: Westholme Publishing, 2014), 123–125.

2. DiNicolo, 123–125.

3. Henry Louis Gates Jr., "Was Jackie Robinson Court-Martialed?," *The African Americans: Many Rivers to Cross with Henry Louis Gates, Jr.*, PBS, www.pbs.org /wnet/african-americans-many-rivers-to-cross/history/was-jackie-robinson-court -martialed.

4. Jackie Robinson, *First Class Citizenship: The Civil Rights Letters of Jackie Robinson* edited by Michael G. Long (New York: Holt and Company, 2007), 40.

5. Years after his death, Stephen Ambrose remains an important figure whose work has captivated audiences and encouraged a generation of military and political historians. His career, though, was not without self-inflicted missteps that have been used to chip away at his legacy. Perhaps, the most noteworthy of these misdeeds for my work is the relationship that Ambrose claimed to have with Eisenhower and whether the famed historian embellished upon it. Ambrose's son, Hugh Ambrose, has written on this issue and offered an essay in defense of his father on the *History News Network*: Hugh Ambrose, "Eisenhower and My Father, Stephen Ambrose," History News Network, George Washington University, https://historynewsnetwork.org/article/126907.

6. Ambrose, *Eisenhower*, 542–543.

7. Jean Edward Smith, *Eisenhower in War and Peace* (New York: Random House, 2012), 708.

8. J. Smith, 708.

9. Mershon and Schlossman, *Foxholes & Color Lines*, 266.

10. Mershon and Schlossman, 266.

11. Ambrose, *Eisenhower*, 367.

12. Ambrose, 367.

Stephen Ambrose, *Duty, Honor, Country: A History of West Point* (Baltimore: John Hopkins University Press, 1966), 231–233; Ambrose, *Eisenhower*, 23–24, 335, 367–368, 409–410; Mershon and Schlossman, *Foxholes & Color Lines*, 266–267.

13. Ambrose, *Eisenhower*, 409.

14. Ambrose, 446–448; Dudziak, *Cold War Civil Rights*, 121–123.

15. Ambrose, *Eisenhower*, 446–448; Dudziak, *Cold War Civil Rights*, 121–123.

16. Fred I. Greenstein, *The Hidden-Hand Presidency: Eisenhower as Leader* (New York: Basic Books, 1982), 62–64.

17. Herbert Brownell and John P. Burke, *Advising Ike: The Memoirs of Attorney General Herbert Brownell* (Lawrence: University Press of Kansas, 1993), 301; David A. Nichols, *A Matter of Justice: Eisenhower and the Beginning of the Civil Rights Revolution* (New York: Simon & Schuster, 2007), 13–15; Greenstein, *The Hidden-Hand Presidency*, 62–64.

18. J. Smith, *Eisenhower in War and Peace*, 709–710.

19. Dwight D. Eisenhower, *The Papers of Dwight David Eisenhower*, vol. 14, *The Presidency: The Middle Way* (Baltimore: Johns Hopkins University Press, 1970), 471; Michael Korda, *Ike: An American Hero* (New York: HarperCollins, 2008), 674; Mershon and Schlossman, *Foxholes & Color Lines*, 268.

20. Charles V. Hamilton, *Adam Clayton Powell Jr.: The Political Biography of an American Dilemma* (New York: Cooper Square Press, 2002), 199–205, 211–219; Timothy J. Hoffman, "The Civil Rights Realignment: How Race Dominates Presidential Elections," *Political Analysis*, vol. 17 (2015), Article 1, 5.

21. Hamilton, 199–205, 211–219; Hoffman, 5.

22. William Inbolden, *Religion and American Foreign Policy, 1945–1960: The Soul of Containment* (Cambridge: Cambridge University Press, 2008), 258.

23. Inbolden, 257–259.

24. Inbolden, 257–259; Dwight D. Eisenhower, "The President's News Conference,

October 30, 1957," online by Gerhard Peters and John T. Woolley, The American Presidency Project, www.presidency.ucsb.edu/node/233887.

25. Dwight D. Eisenhower, "Annual Message to the Congress on the State of the Union, February 2, 1953," online by Gerhard Peters and John T. Woolley, The American Presidency Project, www.presidency.ucsb.edu/node/231684; Dwight D. Eisenhower," Radio and Television Address to the American People on the Situation in Little Rock, September 24, 1957," online by Gerhard Peters and John T. Woolley, The American Presidency Project, www.presidency.ucsb.edu/node/233623.

26. Ambrose, *Eisenhower*, 15.

27. Chester Pach and Elmo Richardson, *The Presidency of Dwight D. Eisenhower*, 8th ed. (Lawrence: University Press of Kansas, 1991), 30–32.

28. Dwight D. Eisenhower, Annual Message to the Congress on the State of the Union (February 2, 1953); Nichols, *A Matter of Justice*, 1–2; Pach and Richardson, *The Presidency of Dwight D. Eisenhower*, 30–32.

29. For more on Mullins, see Graeme Wood, "Into the Psyche of Eustace Mullins," *The Atlantic*, September 23, 2010, www.theatlantic.com/entertainment/archive/2010/09/into-the-psyche-of-eustace-mullins/63457; "Eustace Mullins, Anti-Semitic Conspiracy Theorist, Dies at Age 86," *ADL*, February 4, 2010, www.adl.org/news/article/eustace-mullins-anti-semitic-conspiracy-theorist-dies-at-age-86.

30. Letter, A Factician to All the Members of the Manchester MFGS and Bankers Associations, and The Manchester County Councils of Foreign Wars, and The American Legion, Manchester, New Hampshire, Gentlemen and Fellow Buddies, March 4, 1952, DDE Library, Max Rabb Papers, 1938–1958, Box 5, Eisenhower Campaign, 1952 Correspondence (12); Flyer, "Impeach Eisenhower!," DDE Library, Max Rabb Papers, Box 40, Anti-Semitism Materials (3); Eisenhower on his power within the federal government quoted in Dwight D. Eisenhower, *The Papers of Dwight David Eisenhower*, vol. 14, *The Presidency: The Middle Way*, 471; Brownell on the Hidden-Handed nature of Eisenhower quoted in Herbert Brownell and John P. Burke, *Advising Ike*, 301; Greenstein, *The Hidden-Hand Presidency*, 62–64; Nichols, *A Matter of Justice*, 13–15; Ambrose, *Eisenhower*, 62–63; Mershon and Schlossman, *Foxholes & Color Lines*, 268.

31. MacGregor, *Integration of the Armed Forces*, 489–490; Dwight D. Eisenhower, The President's News Conference (March 19, 1953), online by Gerhard Peters and John T. Woolley, The American Presidency Project, www.presidency.ucsb.edu/node/231547.

32. MacGregor, *Integration of the Armed Forces*, 489–490; Humphrey, *The Education of a Public Man*, 39–42.

33. MacGregor, *Integration of the Armed Forces*, 490–491.

34. Brenda L. Moore, *To Serve My Country, To Serve My Race* (New York: New York University Press, 1996), 71.

35. Moore, 35–37, 73; Letter, Oveta Culp Hobby to Dwight D. Eisenhower, April 13, 1953, DDE Library, Ann Whitman File, Administration Series, Box 19, Hobby, Oveta Culp (6), 3.

36. Representative Adam C. Powell Jr. (NY), "Segregation," *Congressional Record* 99:11 (June 11, 1953), A3368; MacGregor, *Integration of the Armed Forces*, 492; "Oveta's

Negro Aide Fired—Fought Bias," *New York Post*, February 2, 1954; "Jane Spaulding Gets Third Top-Level Job," *Chicago Defender*, January 8, 1955; "Mrs. Spaulding Is Shifted to 3D Administration Job," *New York Herald Tribune*, December 30, 1954.

37. Representative Powell Jr. (NY), "Segregation," A3368; MacGregor, *Integration of the Armed Forces*, 492; "Oveta's Negro Aide Fired—Fought Bias"; "Jane Spaulding Gets Third Top-Level Job"; "Mrs. Spaulding Is Shifted to 3D Administration Job."

38. MacGregor, *Integration of the Armed Forces*, 492.

39. "NAACP Leaders with Their Communist-Front Citations!," *Common Sense*, August 1, 1957, 1–4; "The Supreme Court—Communism's Trojan Horse in the U.S.," *Common Sense*, July 15, 1957, 1; "Key Cabinet Post for Max Rabb," *American Nationalist*, March 25, 1954; Memo, James Lambie to Max Rabb, June 2, 1954, DDE Library, Max Rabb Papers, Box 41, Anti-Semitism Materials (6).

40. MacGregor, *Integration of the Armed Forces*, 492–493; "President Moves to End Army School Segregation," *St. Petersburg Times*, March 26, 1953; Representative Arthur Winstead (MISS) "H.R. 7984," *Congressional Record* 110:2 (February 18, 1954); Dwight D. Eisenhower, *The White House Years: Mandate for Change, 1953–1956* (New York: Double Day, 1963), 235–236.

41. Lee Nichols's articles from the United Press (UP) spanning the dates of November 13, 16, and 17, 1955, pp. 1–2, NAACP, LOC, Group III, Box A 327, NAACP Administration files 1956–65, General Office File, U.S. Army General (file), 1956–1957.

42. Neil R. McMillen, *The Citizens' Council: Organized Resistance to the Second Reconstruction, 1954–1964* (Champaign–Urbana: University of Illinois Press, 1994), 360–361; Stephanie R. Rolph, *Resisting Equality: The Citizens' Council, 1954–1968* (Baton Rouge: Louisiana State University Press, 2018), 2.

43. Lee Nichols's articles from the United Press (UP) spanning the dates of November 13, 16, and 17, 1955, NAACP, LOC, Group III, Box A 327, NAACP Administration files 1956–65, General Office File, U.S. Army General (file), 1956–1957.

44. Lee Nichols's articles from the United Press (UP) spanning the dates of November 13, 16, and 17, 1955, NAACP, LOC, Group III, Box A 327, NAACP Administration files 1956–65, General Office File, U.S. Army General (file), 1956–1957.

45. Letter, Senator Herbert H. Lehman to Charles E. Wilson, SOD, February 8, 1956, NAACP, LOC, Group III, Box A327, NAACP Administration files, General Office File, U.S. Army General (file), 1956–1957; Letter, Senator Herbert H. Lehman to Charles E. Wilson, SOD, May 15, 1956, NAACP, LOC, Group III, Box A327, NAACP Administration files, General Office File, U.S. Army General (file), 1956–1957.

46. Memo, AG, L. P. Sullivan to Commanding General Continental Army Command, "On-Post Civilian School Classes," May 14, 1956, NAACP, LOC, Group III, Box A327, NAACP Administration files, General Office File, U.S. Army General (file), 1956–1957; Memo, Chief of Troop Information and Education Division, Colonel Harold C. Lyon to Director, Office of Armed Forces Information and Education, Department of Defense, Washington, D.C., "Segregated Classes on Post," July 10, 1956, NAACP, LOC, Group III, Box A327, NAACP Administration files, General Office File, U.S. Army General (file), 1956–1957.

47. Letter, Senator Herbert H. Lehman to Charles E. Wilson, SOD, October 10, 1956, NAACP, LOC, Group III, Box A327, NAACP Administration files, General Office File, U.S. Army General (file), 1956–1957.

48. Letter, Senator Herbert H. Lehman to Charles E. Wilson, SOD, October 10, 1956; Letter, Carter L. Burgess, Assistant Secretary of Defense Manpower, Personnel and Reserve to Senator Herbert H. Lehman, October 15, 1956, NAACP, LOC, Group III, Box A327, NAACP Administration files, General Office File, U.S. Army General (file), 1956–1957.

49. Letter, Senator Herbert H. Lehman to Charles E. Wilson, SOD, October 10, 1956; Letter, Carter L. Burgess, Assistant Secretary of Defense Manpower, Personnel and Reserve to Senator Herbert H. Lehman, October 15, 1956, NAACP, LOC, Group III, Box A327, NAACP Administration files, General Office File, U.S. Army General (file), 1956–1957.

50. Letter, Senator Herbert H. Lehman to Charles E. Wilson, SOD, October 10, 1956; Office of Senator Herbert H. Lehman, "Senator Herbert H. Lehman Charges Discrimination Against Negro Service Personnel in Use of Defense Department Funds for Off-Duty Education Programs," October 11, 1956, NAACP, LOC, Group III, Box A327, NAACP Administration files, General Office File, U.S. Army General (file), 1956–1957; Letter, Carter L. Burgess, Assistant Secretary of Defense Manpower, Personnel and Reserve to Senator Herbert H. Lehman, October 15, 1956, NAACP, LOC, Group III, Box A327, NAACP Administration files, General Office File, U.S. Army General (file), 1956–1957.

51. Office of Senator Herbert H. Lehman, "Announcement by Senator Herbert H. Lehman on discontinuation of segregation in Army's off-duty education program at Southern Universities," October 30, 1956, NAACP, LOC, Group III, Box A327, NAACP Administration files, General Office File, U.S. Army General (file), 1956–1957.

52. Letter, Felix Dunn, M.D. to Roy Wilkins, May 19, 1959, NAACP, LOC, Group III, Box A326, NAACP Administration files, General Office File, U.S. Air Force General (file) 1956–1960; Letter, Charles Diggs to Eugene Zuckert, June 25, 1962, NAACP, LOC, Group III, Box A326, NAACP Administration files, General Office File, U.S. Air Force General (file) 1961–1962.

53. MacGregor, *Integration of the Armed Forces*, 483–487.

54. MacGregor, 483–487; Representative Powell Jr. (NY), "Segregation," A3368; Hamilton, 199–205, 211–219.

55. Mershon and Schlossman, *Foxholes & Color Lines*, 269–270; MacGregor, *Integration of the Armed Forces*, 483–487.

56. MacGregor, *Integration of the Armed Forces*, 420–425; "Navy Is Criticized on Bias 'Pockets,'" *New York Times*, June 17, 1955; "Bias Charged in the Navy," *New York Herald Tribune*, June 17, 1955.

57. Mershon and Schlossman, *Foxholes & Color Lines*, 256.

58. W. Michael Byrd and Linda A. Clayton, *An American Health Dilemma*, vol. 2, *Race, Medicine, and Health Care in the United States, 1900–2000* (New York and London: Routledge, 2000), 77–78.

59. Byrd and Clayton, 78–85; Vanessa Northington Gamble, *Making a Place for Ourselves: The Black Hospital Movement 1920–1945* (New York: Oxford University Press, 1995), 4–7.

60. Byrd and Clayton, *An American Health Dilemma*, 78–85; Gamble, *Making a Place for Ourselves*, 4–7.

61. Spencie Love, *One Blood: The Death and Resurrection of Charles R. Drew* (Chapel Hill: University of North Carolina Press, 1996), 13–30, 262.

62. Love, 13–30, 262.

63. Gamble, *Making a Place for Ourselves*, 71–79, 182–186.

64. Gamble, 71–79, 182–186.

65. Robert E. Adkins, *Medical Care of Veterans* (Washington, DC: U.S. Government Printing Office, 1967), printed for the use of the Committee on Veterans Affairs, 90th Cong., 1st sess., House Committee Print No. 4, 248–249; Byrd and Clayton, *An American Health Dilemma*, 257–258.

66. Byrd and Clayton, 257–258; Adam Clayton Powell Jr., *Adam by Adam: The Autobiography of Adam Clayton Powell Jr.* (New York: Kensington Books, 2002), 96–97; Letter, J. T. Boone to Adam Clayton Powell, May 18, 1953, DDE Library, Max Rabb Papers, Box 48, VA (3); Letter, Adam Clayton Powell, May 21, 1953, DDE Library, Max Rabb Papers, Box 48, VA (3); Nichols, *A Matter of Justice*, 45–46.

67. Adkins, *Medical Care of Veterans*, 249–250.

68. Adkins, 249–250.

69. Letter, W. Colmeer et al. to H. Higley, February 27, 1957, DDE Library, Max Rabb Papers, Box 57, VA (1); "Barnett Is VFW District Meet Speaker," *Shreveport Journal*, February 11, 1957; "Legion Action Hits Integration," *Shreveport Journal*, February 11, 1957.

70. "Veteran Protesting Integration at VA Hospital Denied Care," *Shreveport Journal*, November 17, 1956; Joan De Sardon, "VA Hospital Head Explains Desegregation Policy in Use," *Shreveport Journal*, November 21, 1956; "Resolution Scores VA Hospital Integration," *Shreveport Journal*, November 24, 1956.

71. Timothy B. Tyson, *The Blood of Emmett Till* (New York: Simon & Schuster, 2017), 2–6.

72. "Hospital Official Denies Accusation," *Commercial Appeal*, July 21, 1956.

73. "Integrated Hospital Criticized in Jackson," *Commercial Appeal*, July 24, 1956; Letter, John Stennis to Ellis W. Wright, August 10, 1956, John C. Stennis Collection, Series 26, Veterans Administration, Box 2, General Hospitals, 1955–1977, Jackson VA Hospital, Segregation Problem.

74. "Hospital Official Denies Accusation"; "VA Hospital Chief Says Only Whites in Beckwith Ward," *Clarion-Ledger*, July 21, 1956; "State VFW Leader Attacks VA Hospital," *Clarion-Ledger*, July 26, 1956; "VFW Not in Race Hassle," *Jackson State Times*, July 27, 1956; "State Hospital Aid Urged for Veterans," *Commercial Appeal*, July 27, 1956.

75. "Hospital Official Denies Accusation"; "VA Hospital Chief Says Only Whites in Beckwith Ward"; "State VFW Leader Attacks VA Hospital"; "VFW Not in Race Hassle"; "State Hospital Aid Urged for Veterans."

76. Yasuhiro Katagiri, *The Mississippi State Sovereignty Commission: Civil Rights and States' Rights* (Jackson: University Press of Mississippi, 2001), 26–27; "VA Hospital Funds Get Committee OK," *Commercial Appeal*, March 16, 1957; "Mississippians OK Integrated Hospital," *Commercial Appeal*, May 8, 1957.

77. Katagiri, *The Mississippi State Sovereignty Commission*, 26–27; "VA Hospital Funds Get Committee OK"; "Mississippians OK Integrated Hospital."

78. Katagiri, *The Mississippi State Sovereignty Commission*, 27; "Coleman Hits Back

at Editorial Blast," *Commercial Appeal*, May 9, 1957; "An Answer to an Editorial Entitled 'Munich Day in Mississippi,'" May 13, 1957, 1–3, Letter, Robert B. Patterson to Dwight D. Eisenhower, May 27, 1957, John C. Stennis Collection, Series 26, Veterans Administration, Box 2, General Hospitals, 1955–1977, Jackson VA Hospital, Segregation Problem.

79. Katagiri, *The Mississippi State Sovereignty Commission*, 27; "Coleman Hits Back at Editorial Blast"; "An Answer to an Editorial Entitled 'Munich Day in Mississippi,'" 1–3, Letter, Robert B. Patterson to Dwight D. Eisenhower, May 27, 1957.

80. Katagiri, *The Mississippi State Sovereignty Commission*, 27; "Citizens Councils Ask That Hospital Mixing Be Stopped," *Commercial Appeal*, May 22, 1957; "Integration Blamed in Death of Veterans," *Commercial Appeal*, May 25, 1957; John C. Stennis Collection, Series 26, Veterans Administration, Box 2, General Hospitals, 1955–1977, Jackson VA Hospital, Segregation Problem.

81. "Hospital Move Said Yield to 'Blackmail,'" *Commercial Appeal*, May 22, 1957; "Delta Legion Post Attacks Commission," *Jackson State Times*, May 26, 1957; "Negro Legion Head Answers Commander," *Jackson State Times*, May 26, 1957.

82. E. Frederic Morrow, *Black Man in the White House* (New York: Coward-McCann, Inc., 1963), 298–302.

83. News Release, Republican National Committee progress report, August 9, 1955, 2–3, DDE Library, Frederick Morrow Papers, Civil Rights Clippings and Date (3), Box 10.

84. Dwight D. Eisenhower, Annual Message to the Congress on the State of the Union (January 5, 1956), online by Gerhard Peters and John T. Woolley, The American Presidency Project, www.presidency.ucsb.edu/node/233132; Dwight D. Eisenhower, Annual Message to the Congress on the State of the Union (January 12, 1961), online by Gerhard Peters and John T. Woolley, The American Presidency Project, www.preside ncy.ucsb.edu/node/234806.

Chapter 5: From Image to Action

1. January 5, 1960, James Cannon/Ben Bradlee interview with Senator John F. Kennedy, MR2008–18, JFK Library.

2. Richard Reeves, *President Kennedy: Profile of Power* (New York: Simon & Schuster, 1993), 40.

3. Memo, Theodore White to Richard Goodwin, January 25, 1961, JFK Library, WHCSF-E, Box 634, ND 15–2, Coast Guard Academy; Memo, Douglas Dillon to John F. Kennedy, February 8, 1961, JFK Library, WHCSF-E, Box 634, ND 15–2, Coast Guard Academy; Memo, A. C. Richmond to Douglas Dillon, February 7, 1961, JFK Library, WHCSF-E, Box 634, ND 15–2, Coast Guard Academy.

4. Memo, Theodore White to Richard Goodwin, January 25, 1961; Memo, Douglas Dillon to John F. Kennedy, February 8, 1961; Memo, A. C. Richmond to Douglas Dillon, February 7, 1961; Memo, Douglas Dillion to Frederick G. Dutton, March 3, 1961, JFK Library, WHCSF-E, Box 634, ND 15–2; William H. Thiesen, "The Long Blue Line: Merle Smith—The First African American Graduate of the Coast Guard Academy," Coast Guard Academy; Coast Guard: Coast Guard Compass Blog, www.mycg.uscg .mil/News/Article/2937583/the-long-blue-line-a-look-at-the-coast-guard-academy -producing-minority-coast-g.

5. Memo, Frank D. Reeves to John F. Kennedy (Executive), February 7, 1961, JFK Library, WHCSF-E, Box 634, ND 15–2, Coast Guard Academy; Memo, Frederick G. Dutton to Douglas Dillon, February 10, 1961, JFK Library, WHCSF-E, Box 634, ND 15–2, Coast Guard Academy; Memo, Douglas Dillion to Frederick G. Dutton, March 3, 1961, JFK Library, WHCSF-E, Box 634, ND 15–2; Thiesen, "The Long Blue Line: Merle Smith."

6. Memo, Frederick G. Dutton to Douglas Dillion, March 5, 1961, JFK Library, WHCSF-E, Box 634, ND 15–2, Coast Guard Academy; Letter, Frederick G. Dutton to Carlos McCormack, March 7, 1961, JFK Library, WHCSF-G, Box 634, ND 15–2, Coast Guard Academy; Memo, Robert A. Wallace to Fred Dutton, August 7, 1961, JFK Library, WHCSF-E, Box 634, ND 15–2, Coast Guard Academy.

7. Memo, A. Gilmore Flues to Frederick G. Dutton, April 21, 1961, JFK Library, WHCSF-E, Box 634, ND 15–2, Coast Guard Academy (emphasis added); Memo, Frederick G. Dutton to Douglas Dillion, March 5, 1961, JFK Library, WHCSF-E, Box 634, ND 15–2, Coast Guard Academy; Letter, Frederick G. Dutton to Carlos McCormack, March 7, 1961; Memo, Robert A. Wallace to Fred Dutton, August 7, 1961.

8. Memo, Robert A. Wallace to Fred Dutton, August 7, 1961; "W.H. Waller Gets Coast Guard Post," September 5, 1961, *Washington Afro-American*, JFK Library, WHCSF-E, Box 634, ND 15–2, Coast Guard Academy; "C.G. Academy Appoints Chemistry Professor," September 8, 1961, *Washington Afro-American*, JFK Library, WHCSF-E, Box 634, ND 15–2, Coast Guard Academy; "Negro Named to Staff of Coast Guard," *Pittsburgh Courier*, September 9, 1961, JFK Library, WHCSF-E, Box 634, ND 15–2, Coast Guard Academy; Within the holdings of National Archives II are the research papers of Morris J. MacGregor Jr. The papers provide the foundational scholarship of his work *Integration of the Armed Forces, 1940–1965*. Often MacGregor summarized the contents of letters or memos into typed notes. From here on afterword, references that utilize these notes will begin with "Summarization" and a brief description of the document, followed by its location. Summarization of a letter from the Assistant Secretary of the Treasury to Tim Reardon, January 31, 1962, NARA II, RG319, The Integration of the Armed Forces, 1940–1965, Box 8, Chapter XX Limited Response; also see Letter, Assistant Secretary of the Treasury to Tim Reardon, January 31, 1962, JFK Library, WHCSF-E, Box 360; "Coast Guard Academy," *Baltimore Afro-American*, August 21, 1962; Thiesen, "The Long Blue Line: Merle Smith"; "Merle Smith, First Black Graduate of Coast Guard Academy, Dies at 76," *Washington Post*, June 23, 2021, www.washington post.com/local/obituaries/merle-smith-coast-guard-dead/2021/06/23/d135959e-d4 49-11eb-ae54-515e2f63d37d_story.html.

9. Memo, John T. Martin to Frank Reeves, March 27, 1961, JFK Library, WHCSF-E, Box 633, ND 15, Service Schools; Susan D. Hansen, "The Racial History of the U.S. Military Academies," *Journal of Blacks in Higher Education*, no. 26 (Winter 1999–2000): 114.

10. MacGregor, *Integration of the Armed Forces*, 508–510; Philip E. Muehlenbeck, *Betting on the Africans: John F. Kennedy's Courting of African Nationalist Leaders* (New York: Oxford University Press, 2012), 200–201.

11. MacGregor, *Integration of the Armed Forces*, 508–510; Muehlenbeck, *Betting on the Africans*, 200–201.

12. Harris Wofford, *Of Kennedys & Kings: Making Sense of the Sixties* (Pittsburgh:

University of Pittsburgh Press, 1992), 144–147; MacGregor, *Integration of the Armed Forces*, 507.

13. MacGregor, 530; Transcript, Adam Yarmolinsky Oral History Interview, November 11, 1964, by Daniel Ellsberg, 19, JFK Library; aspects of this chapter first appeared in "A Parable of Persisting Failure: Project 100,000," in *Beyond the Quagmire: New Interpretations of the Vietnam War* (Denton: University of North Texas, 2019), ed. Geoffrey W. Jensen and Matthew M. Stith, n.5, 172 (hereinafter Jensen, "A Parable"); Jensen, "It Cut Both Ways," 145–147; Mershon and Schlossman, *Foxholes & Color Lines*, 282–283.

14. MacGregor, *Integration of the Armed Forces*, 530; Transcript, Adam Yarmolinsky Oral History Interview; Jensen "A Parable," n.5, 172; Jensen, "It Cut Both Ways," 145–147; Mershon and Schlossman, *Foxholes & Color Lines*, 282–283.

15. John F. Kennedy, Remarks at the First Meeting of the President's Committee on Equal Employment Opportunity, April 11, 1961, online by Gerhard Peters and John T. Woolley, The American Presidency Project, www.presidency.ucsb.edu/node/234568.

16. MacGregor, *Integration of the Armed Forces*, 505–506.

17. Memo, John F. Kennedy to the Heads of all Executive Departments and Agencies, April 18, 1961, NARA II, RG319, The Integration of the Armed Forces, 1940–1965, Box 8, Chapter XX Limited Response; MacGregor, *Integration of the Armed Forces*, 507, 511–512.

18. Adam Yarmolinsky, *The Military Establishment: Its Impacts on American Society* (New York: Harper & Row, 1971), 324–325.

19. Runge admitted years later that he had always been a conservative Democrat. For more, see Carlisle P. Runge, interview by Donna Hartshorne, August 14, 1982, Oral History Interview # 2, available online at https://minds.wisconsin.edu/bitstream/handle/1793/74461/Runge_249_8_14_1982.mp3?sequence=3&isAllowed=y; Memo and attached Summary Statement, Carlisle P. Runge to Harris Wofford, July 7, 1961, JFK Library, WHSF, Harris Wofford Papers, Box 11, SCGCR—Defense.

20. Memo, Robert McNamara to the Secretaries of the Military Departments et al., March 24, 1961, NARA II, RG319, The Integration of the Armed Forces, 1940–1965, Box 8, Chapter XX Limited Response; Memo, Robert McNamara to the Secretaries of the Military Departments et al., April 28, 1961, NARA II, RG319, The Integration of the Armed Forces, 1940–1965, Box 8, Chapter XX Limited Response; MacGregor, *Integration of the Armed Forces*, 511–512.

21. Memo, Robert McNamara to the Secretaries of the Military Departments et al., March 24, 1961; Memo, Robert McNamara to the Secretaries of the Military Departments et al., April 28, 1961; MacGregor, *Integration of the Armed Forces*, 511–512.

22. MacGregor, 512; Nalty, *Strength for The Fight*, 278–279.

23. Mershon and Schlossman, *Foxholes & Color Lines*, 285; Carl Brauer, *John F. Kennedy and the Second Reconstruction* (New York: Columbia University Press, 1977), 81.

24. Mershon and Schlossman, *Foxholes & Color Lines*, 285; Brauer, *John F. Kennedy and the Second Reconstruction*, 81; Letter, Harold Hunton to Roy Wilkins, January 7, 1963, NAACP, LOC, Group III, Box A326, NAACP Administration files 1956–65, General Office File, United States Air Force, General, 1963–1965; "Purchasing Management Responsibilities Under Executive Order 10925," n.d., NAACP, LOC, Group III,

Box A326, NAACP Administration files 1956–65, General Office File, United States Air Force, General, 1963–1965; "The Nondiscrimination Clause," n.d., 1–2, NAACP, LOC, Group III, Box A326, NAACP Administration files 1956–65, General Office File, United States Air Force, General, 1963–1965; "Nondiscrimination Clause Requirements and Exemptions," n.d., 3–4, NAACP, LOC, Group III, Box A326, NAACP Administration files 1956–65, General Office File, United States Air Force, General, 1963–1965; "Required Activities with First-Tier Subcontractors," n.d., 5–6, NAACP, LOC, Group III, Box A326, NAACP Administration files 1956–65, General Office File, United States Air Force, General, 1963–1965; "Equal Employment Opportunity," n.d., 6, NAACP, LOC, Group III, Box A326, NAACP Administration files 1956–65, General Office File, United States Air Force, General, 1963–1965.

25. Brauer, *John F. Kennedy and the Second Reconstruction*, 81–82; James Giglio, *The Presidency of John F. Kennedy* (Lawrence: University Press of Kansas, 1991), 172–173.

26. Randall Woods, *LBJ: Architect of American Ambition* (New York: Free Press, 2006), 396; Robert Dallek, *An Unfinished Life: John F. Kennedy, 1917–1963* (New York: Little, Brown and Company, 2003), 513.

27. R. Woods, *LBJ*, 396; Papers of John F. Kennedy, JFK Library, Presidential Papers, President's Office Files, Staff Memoranda, Letter, Robert Troutman to John F. Kennedy, June 30, 1962; Dallek, 513; Papers of John F. Kennedy, JFK Library, Presidential Papers, President's Office Files, Staff Memoranda, Letter, John F. Kennedy to Robert Troutman, August 22, 1962.

28. Mershon and Schlossman, *Foxholes & Color Lines*, 285; R. Woods, *LBJ*, 397.

29. Letter, Waddie L. Hall to Mr. (James) Evans, September 27, 1962, LBJ Library, PCEOAF, Box 16, Education-Training-GENERAL.

30. Letter, Waddie L. Hall to Mr. (James) Evans; in *Integration of the Armed Forces*, Morris J. MacGregor, references the laws as 815 and 879, but I believe he mistakenly typed the second as 879, when it was more likely Public Law 874, which had been intertwined with Public Law 815 since World War II; see MacGregor, *Integration of the Armed Forces*, 487–488, 596–599; James C. Evans and John Wiant, "Views of James C. Evans: Integration, Differentiation and Refinement," *Negro History Bulletin* 23, no. 7 (April 1960), 152; "James C. Evans, 1925," MIT Black History, www.blackhistory.mit.edu /archive/james-c-evans-1925.

31. MacGregor, *Integration of the Armed Forces*, 596–599; Mershon and Schlossman, *Foxholes & Color Lines*, 285; Recording of Telephone Conversation between Robert Kennedy and President John F. Kennedy, March 1963, Cassette E (Side 1), 14A.2, Telephone Recordings, Papers of John F. Kennedy President's Office Files Presidential Recordings; "U.S. Suit Attacks School Race Bars," *New York Times*, September 18, 1962; Brauer, *John F. Kennedy and the Second Reconstruction*, 145–146.

32. Recording of Telephone Conversation between Robert Kennedy and President John F. Kennedy, March 1963; MacGregor, *Integration of the Armed Forces*, 596–599.

33. MacGregor, 596–599.

34. Letter, Ira W. Jayne to Roy Wilkins, October 3, 1957, NAACP, LOC, Group III, Box A 327, NAACP Administration files 1956–65, General Office File, U.S. Army General (file), 1956–1965.

35. Letter, Bill Current to Gloster B. Current Director of Branches, NAACP, June

21, 1959, NAACP, LOC, Group III, Box A 328, NAACP Administration files 1956–65, General Office File, U.S. Navy (file), 1958–1963; Letter, Norfolk VA citizen to James O. Eastland, September 19, 1960, James O. Eastland Collection, University of Mississippi, File Series 3, Subseries 1, Box 39, Mershon and Schlossman, *Foxholes & Color Lines*, 275.

36. Mershon and Schlossman, 275.

37. "Remarks of Senator John F. Kennedy at National Conference on Constitutional Rights and American Freedom, New York, New York, October 12, 1960," Papers of John F. Kennedy. JFK Library, Pre-Presidential Papers, Senate Files, Series 12, Speeches and the Press, Box 913, Folder: "National Conference on Constitutional Rights and American Freedoms, New York City, 12 October 1960"; Giglio, *The Presidency of John F. Kennedy*, 104–105, 171–172; Wofford, *Of Kennedys & Kings*, 169–170.

38. Memo, Roy Wilkins to John F. Kennedy, "Racial Discrimination in Federally Assisted Housing in Cocoa, Florida," November 20, 1962, NAACP, LOC, Group III, Box A109, NAACP Administration files 1956–65, General Office File, Discrimination—Housing, 1956–1962; Ira Harrison, "Syracuse the Friendly City and Captain James Anderson," *People's Weekly* (Syracuse), June 1962; for more on Anderson, see also Letter, Ira E. Harrison to JFK Library with attached article from the *People's Weekly* (Syracuse), WHCSF-G, Box 372, HU 2–2: 10/11/1962–11/5/1962.

39. Letter, Paul Mueller to John F. Kennedy, October 8, 1962, JFK Library, WHCSF-G, Box 372, HU 2–2: 10/11/1962–11/5/1962.

40. MacGregor, *Integration of the Armed Forces*, 516–517.

41. "Presidential Decree Worries Builders," *News and Courier*, November 22, 1962; Roulhac Hamilton, "Senators Say New Order May Hurt Building Industry," *News and Courier*, November 22, 1962, 9B.

42. Letter and Progress Report, A. H. Monk to Harris Wofford, June 22, 1961, JFK Library, WHSF, Harris Wofford Papers, Box 14, CRPRF, SCGCR—Veterans Administration.

43. Letter, "Henry W. Poteet, Howard W. Poteet, and Thomas C. Poteet, to Richard B. Russell, June 21, 1962," Richard B. Russell Jr. Papers, RRL, UGA, X. Civil Rights, Box 183; Letter, "James H. Fletcher and Georgia Funeral Directors Association, Inc, to Richard B. Russell, August 15, 1962," Richard B. Russell Jr. Papers, RRL, UGA, X. Civil Rights, Box 183; "Assistance to Survivors of Decedents," VA Circular 10–63–110, May 8, 1963, Richard B. Russell Jr. Papers, RRL, UGA, X, Civil Rights, Box 183.

44. MacGregor, *Integration of the Armed Forces*, 503–504; Papers of John F. Kennedy. Presidential Papers. WHCSF-E. HU: Equality of Races (2), August 1961: 21–31, 48, Digital Identifier: JFKWHCSF-0360-p0050; Undated progress report, JFK Library, WHSF, Harris Wofford Papers, Box 14, CRPRF, SCGCR—Veterans Administration; Letter and Progress Report, A. H. Monk to Harris Wofford, November 9, 1961, JFK Library, WHSF, Harris Wofford Papers, Box 14, CRPRF, SCGCR—Veterans Administration; Letter and Progress Report, A. H. Monk to Harris Wofford, December 7, 1961, JFK Library, WHSF, Harris Wofford Papers, Box 14, CRPRF, SCGCR—Veterans Administration; Ira Katznelson, *When Affirmative-Action was White: An Untold History of Racial Inequality in Twentieth-Century America* (New York: W. W. Norton & Company, 2005), 139–140.

45. MacGregor, *Integration of the Armed Forces*, 503–504; Papers of John F. Kennedy.

Presidential Papers. WHCSF-E. HU: Equality of Races (2), August 1961: 21–31, 48, Digital Identifier: JFKWHCSF-0360-p0050; Undated progress report, JFK Library, WHSF, Harris Wofford Papers, Box 14, CRPRF, SCGCR—Veterans Administration; Letter and Progress Report, A. H. Monk to Harris Wofford, November 9, 1961; Letter and Progress Report, A. H. Monk to Harris Wofford, December 7, 1961, JFK Library, WHSF, Harris Wofford Papers, Box 14, CRPRF, SCGCR—Veterans Administration; Katznelson, 139–140.

46. MacGregor, *Integration of the Armed Forces*, 503–504; Papers of John F. Kennedy. Presidential Papers. WHCSF-E. HU: Equality of Races (2), August 1961: 21–31, 48, Digital Identifier: JFKWHCSF-0360-p0050; Undated progress report, JFK Library, WHSF, Harris Wofford Papers, Box 14, CRPRF, SCGCR—Veterans Administration; Letter and Progress Report, A. H. Monk to Harris Wofford, November 9, 1961; Letter and Progress Report, A. H. Monk to Harris Wofford, December 7, 1961, JFK Library, WHSF, Harris Wofford Papers, Box 14, CRPRF, SCGCR—Veterans Administration.

47. Additionally, of the 35,537 VA employees falling under Classification Act positions, 6,312 African Americans received appointments and earned promotions since 1961. See Letter and Progress Report, A. H. Monk to Harris Wofford, March 2, 1962, JFK Library, WHSF, Harris Wofford Papers, Box 14, CRPRF, SCGCR—Veterans Administration.

48. Letter and Progress Report, A. H. Monk to Harris Wofford, March 2, 1962.

49. Carolyn P. Dubose, *The Untold Story of Charles Diggs: The Public Figure, the Private Man* (Arlington, VA: Barton Publishing House, 1998), 13–15, 30; Interview with Charles Diggs, conducted by Blackside, Inc., on November 6, 1986, for *Eyes on the Prize: America's Civil Rights Years (1954–1965)*, Washington University Libraries, Film and Media Archive, Henry Hampton Collection.

50. Mershon and Schlossman, *Foxholes & Color Lines*, 259–262.

51. Mershon and Schlossman, 259–262.

52. Mershon and Schlossman, 259–262, 291; MacGregor, *Integration of the Armed Forces*, 535–541.

53. Letter, James Lightfoot to Civil Rights Commission, August 18, 1960, LBJ Library, PCEOAF, Box 7, National Guard; "Cops, Papers Agree: It Was a Quiet Riot," *Morning Star Okinawa*, July 6, 1960.

54. Mershon and Schlossman, *Foxholes & Color Lines*, 263; "Chubby Quits Japan Over Racial Incident," *Chicago Daily Defender*, March 18, 1963.

55. MacGregor, *Integration of Armed Forces*, 535–541.

56. MacGregor, 535–541; Matthew D. Lassiter, "Benjamin Muse (1898–1986)," *Encyclopedia Virginia*, Virginia Humanities, February 28, 2014, www.encyclopediavirginia .org/Muse_Benjamin_1898–1986; "The Civic Life of Nathaniel Coley: Husband and Father," The Colley Papers, Center for Sacramento History, Web, https://colley.omeka .net/exhibits/show/theciviclife/husbandandfather; David Asp, "Abe Fortas," *The First Amendment Encyclopedia*, The John Seigenthaler Chair of Excellence in First Amendment Studies, Middle Tennessee State University, www.mtsu.edu/first-amendment/ar ticle/1329/abe-fortas; "Laurence I. Hewes, 86, Dies," *Washington Post*, April 3, 1989, www.washingtonpost.com/archive/local/1989/04/03/laurence-i-hewes-86-dies/cd37 deb9-acef-4f17-83a6-4e2de5d8b7cb.

57. MacGregor, *Integration of the Armed Forces*, 535–541; Mershon and Schlossman, *Foxholes & Color Lines*, 291.

58. MacGregor, *Integration of the Armed Forces*, 535–541; Mershon and Schlossman, *Foxholes & Color Lines*, 291.

59. MacGregor, *Integration of the Armed Forces*, 542–545; Mershon and Schlossman, *Foxholes & Color Lines*, 292–294.

60. MacGregor, *Integration of the Armed Forces*, 542–545; Mershon and Schlossman, *Foxholes & Color Lines*, 292–294.

61. MacGregor, *Integration of the Armed Forces*, 542–545; Mershon and Schlossman, *Foxholes & Color Lines*, 292–294.

62. MacGregor, *Integration of the Armed Forces*, 559–564; Mershon and Schlossman, *Foxholes & Color Lines*, 294–296.

63. Representatives Lucius Mendel Rivers (SC), Felix Edward Hébert (LA), Durward Gorham Hall (MS), and John J. Flynt Jr. (GA), *Congressional Record* (August 7, 1963), 13549–13551, 13553; Geoffrey Gould, "Southerners Rain Fire on McNamara Directive," *Sumter Daily Item*, August 8, 1963; "Biggest Radical BlackJack Yet," *Augusta Herald*, July 30, 1963; "A Case of Planned Blackmail," *Augusta Chronicle*, July 30, 1963.

64. Marjorie Hunter, "M'Namara Is Assailed: Georgia Democrat Declares Pentagon Tries to Impose a New Social Order," *New York Times*, September 18, 1963.

65. Senator John Stennis (MS), "The Gesell Report and Perversion of the Mission of the Military," *Congressional Record* 109:10 (July 31, 1963), 13779.

66. Senator Herman Talmadge (GA), "The Gesell Report and Perversion of the Mission of the Military," *Congressional Record* 109:10 (July 31, 1963), 13780; Senator Herman Talmadge (GA), "Military Dictatorship," *Congressional Record* 109:10 (August 2, 1963), A4946; Letter, J. William Fulbright to Robert S. McNamara, August 22, 1963, 2, NARA II, RG319, The Integration of the Armed Forces, 1940–1965, Box 10, Chapter XXII Equal Opportunity in the Military Community.

67. Senator Stennis (MS), "The Gesell Report and Perversion of the Mission of the Military," 13782; Elizabeth Tandy Shermer, ed., *Barry Goldwater and the Remaking of the American Political Landscape* (Tucson: University of Arizona Press, 2013), 1–5; Robert Alan Goldberg, *Barry Goldwater* (New Haven: Yale University Press, 1995), 184; Senator Barry Goldwater (AZ), "The Gesell Report and Perversion of the Mission of the Military," *Congressional Record* 109:10 (July 31, 1963), 13783; Senator Strom Thurmond (SC), "The Degree of Government by Executive Order," *Congressional Record* 109: reel 419 (September 4, 1963), A5610–A5611.

68. Richard M. Fried, *Nightmare in Red: The McCarthy Era in Perspective* (New York: Oxford University Press, 1990), 159–161; Robert J. Goldstein, *Political Repression in Modern America: From 1870 to 1976* (Urbana: University of Illinois Press, 2001), 374; Fulton Lewis Jr., *Top of the News with Fulton Lewis, Jr.*, vol. 4 (April 1962), 6–7; Fried, *Nightmare in Red*, 159–161.

69. Lewis would claim, with no proof, that Babette Deutsch was "affiliated with at least 10 communist fronts"; see Lewis Jr., *Top of the News*, vol. 4 (April 1962), 6–7.

70. Goldstein, *Political Repression in Modern America*, 374; "Dr. Avrahm Yarmolinsky Dead; Public Library Russian Expert," *New York Times*, September 29, 1975; Natalie Friedman, "Babette Deutsch," *Jewish Women: A Comprehensive Historical Encyclopedia*,

February 27 2009, Jewish Women's Archive, https://jwa.org/encyclopedia/article /deutsch-babette; Lewis Jr., *Top of the News*, vol. 4 (April 1962), 6–7; Ian Frazier, "John Reed's Unblinking Stare," *The American Scholar* 71, no. 3 (Summer 2002): 30; Virginia Hagelstein Marquardt, "'New Masses' and John Reed Club Artists, 1926–1936: Evolution of Ideology, Subject Matter, and Style," *Journal of Decorative and Propaganda Arts*, vol. 12 (Spring 1989): 56; Neil A. Lewis, "Adam Yarmolinsky Dies at 77; Led Revamping of Government," *New York Times*, January 7, 2000.

71. Perhaps the lightest criticism from the conservative right came from Melvin Laird, a Republican representative from Wisconsin. A civil rights advocate throughout the 1960s who championed the removal of racist white officers, helped introduce "human relations" and "racial harmony" groups to the armed forces to bridge the racial divide, and demanded that a portion of basic training in the military included a brief seminar on racial issues, Laird charged that Yarmolinsky's activities tipped the racial balance in favor of African Americans over whites:

It was just 2 years ago that Adam Yarmolinsky made a recommendation to the Chief of the Bureau of Naval Personnel that the procedures for admittance to the service academies, particularly Annapolis, be changed so that the college board exams and the other required examinations for admittance to the Academy be set aside so that special examinations could be given in order to afford preferential entrance treatment. This recommendation went far beyond equal opportunity.

For more, see Dale Van Atta, *With Honor: Melvin Laird in War, Peace, and Politics* (Madison: University of Wisconsin Press, 2008), 332–333; Representative Melvin Laird (WI), *Congressional Record* (August 7, 1963), 13560–13561.

72. Lewis, "Adam Yarmolinsky Dies at 77"; "A resolution petitioning Congress to investigate the Gesell Report and Secretary of Defense Implementation Order, August 29, 1963," University of Mississippi, 77–1 Thomas G. Abernathy Collection, Box 245; Representative Felix Edward Hébert (LA), "The Gesell Report," *Congressional Record* (August 7, 1963), 13598.

73. Carl D. Sutton, "The Military Mission Against Off-Base Racial Discrimination: A Study in Administrative Behavior" (PhD diss., Indiana University, 1973), 63–67.

74. Dudziak, *Cold War Civil Rights*, 179–182; John F. Kennedy, Radio and Television Report to the American People on Civil Rights Online by Gerhard Peters and John T. Woolley, The American Presidency Project, www.presidency.ucsb.edu/node/236675.

75. Edward H. Miller, *Nut Country: Right-Wing Dallas and the Birth of the Southern Strategy* (Chicago: University of Chicago Press, 2015), 1–11.

76. Miller, 1–11.

77. Miller, 1–11; "Soldiers Escort Negroes to School," *Lewiston Morning Tribune*, September 26, 1957; Bob Jones, S. W. Naujocks, and John Dornberg, "Military Channels Used to Push Birch Ideas," *Overseas Weekly*, April 16, 1961; see also "John Birch vs. 24th Info Div," *Overseas Weekly*, April 16, 1961; HQ 24th Inf Div, "Education and Training: 24th Infantry Division Pro Blue Program," January 4, 1961, Billy James Hargis Papers (MC1412), Box 3, File 58, Special Collections, University of Arkansas Libraries, Fayetteville; Jonathan M. Schoenwald, *A Time For Choosing: The Rise of Modern American*

Conservatism (New York: Oxford University Press, 2001), 105–106; "Walker Member of Birch Society," *New York Times*, September 8, 1961.

78. Doris Kearns Goodwin, *Lyndon Johnson and the American Dream* (New York: St. Martin's Press, 1991), 227 and 306; Lyndon B. Johnson, "Address Before a Joint Session of the Congress, November 27, 1963," online by Gerhard Peters and John T. Woolley, The American Presidency Project, www.presidency.ucsb.edu/node/238734.

79. Goodwin, *Lyndon Johnson and the American Dream*, 227 and 306; R. Woods, *LBJ*, 475–476; Dudziak, *Cold War Civil Rights*, 208–209.

80. Reeves, *President Kennedy*, 59–60; Thomas P. Honsa, "Doing the Job: The 1964 Desegregation of the Florida Army National Guard," *Florida Historical Quarterly* 87, no. 1 (Summer 2008): 51.

81. Reeves, *President Kennedy*, 59–60, 185–220.

82. Letter, Roy Wilkins to John F. Kennedy, August 3, 1961, NAACP, LOC, Group III, Box A 328, General Office File, Army, National Guard 1956–1965.

83. NAACP Newsletter, "NAACP Asks President to End Color Bar in National Guard, August 4, 1961," NAACP, LOC, Group III, Box A 328, General Office File, Army National Guard 1956–1965; NAACP Press Release, "Florida Rejects NAACP Pleas to End Military Jim Crow, September 29, 1961," NAACP, LOC, Group III, Box A 328, General Office File, Army National Guard 1956–1965; NAACP News Release, "49th Armored Division Desegregated: NAACP Urges Change of National Guard Policy, September 30, 1961," NAACP, LOC, Group III, Box A 328, General Office File, Army National Guard 1956–1965; NAACP Press Release, "Texas National Guard Accepts First Negro, October 6, 1961," NAACP, LOC, Group III, Box A 328, General Office File, Army National Guard 1956–1965; NAACP Press Release, "NAACP Still Seeks End of Fla. Nat. Guard Bias, October 6, 1961," NAACP, LOC, Group III, Box A 328, General Office File, Army National Guard 1956–1965; NAACP Press Release, "NAACP Seeks End of Jim Crow VA. Nat'l Guard, December 14, 1962," NAACP, LOC, Group III, Box A 328, General Office File, Army National Guard 1956–1965; NAACP Press Release, "Missouri Governor Ends National Guard Jim Crow, December 21, 1962," NAACP, LOC, Group III, Box A 328, General Office File, Army National Guard 1956–1965; NAACP Press Release, "Race Bars to Fall in Missouri Guard, March 25, 1965," NAACP, LOC, Group III, Box A 328, General Office File, Army National Guard 1956–1965; MacGregor, *Integration of the Armed Forces*, 517–519, 552–555, 593–596.

84. Letter, American Veterans Committee to Robert McNamara, December 18, 1962, LBJ Library, PCEOAF, Box 19; Letter, Captain James Johnson Jr. to President John F. Kennedy, December 5, 1961, LBJ Library, PCEOAF, Box 19; MacGregor, *Integration of the Armed Forces*, 517–519, 552–555, 593–596.

85. MacGregor, 517–519, 552–555, 593–596.

86. MacGregor, 517–519, 552–555, 593–596.

87. MacGregor, 517–519, 552–555, 593–596.

88. Memo and attached compendium, Alfred B. Fitt to Lee C. White, May 7, 1964, LBJ Library, Office files of Lee C. White, Box 6, Civil Rights—Miscellaneous 1964.

89. Memo and attached compendium, Alfred B. Fitt to Lee C. White, May 7, 1964; Mershon and Schlossman, *Foxholes & Color Lines*, 295, 300–306.

90. Franklin David Marks, "The Efforts Made to Achieve Equal Opportunity in the Armed Forces, with a Special Emphasis on Development of the Program to Obtain More Off-Base, Open-Housing" (MA thesis, George Washington University, 1970), 87–94; MacGregor, *Integration of the Armed Forces*, 600–601.

91. Lyndon B. Johnson, Special Message to the Congress Proposing Further Legislation to Strengthen Civil Rights (April 28, 1966), online by Gerhard Peters and John T. Woolley, The American Presidency Project, www.presidency.ucsb.edu/node/239224.

92. Shapley, *Promise and Power*, 389.

93. Shapley, 389; MacGregor, *Integration of the Armed Forces*, 583–584, 601–603.

94. MacGregor, 601–605.

95. MacGregor, 601–605.

96. MacGregor, 601–605.

97. MacGregor, 605; "Alfred B. Fitt, Assistant Secretary of Defense (Manpower), October 10, 1967," LBJ Library, Alfred B. Fitt Papers, Box 5, Personal Files: Biographies; Memo, Thomas D. Morris to Robert McNamara, "First Monthly Report on "Off-Base" Housing Program," September 25, 1967, LBJ Library, Alfred B. Fitt Papers, Box 3, Correspondence: Memos for Record (10/6/67–1/13/69); Memo, Alfred Fitt to Robert McNamara, December 22, 1967, LBJ Library, Alfred B. Fitt papers. White, Box 1, Correspondence: General (9/20/67–12/29/67); Memo, Alfred Fitt to Robert McNamara, December 22, 1967, LBJ Library, Alfred B. Fitt Papers, Box 1, Correspondence: General (9/20/67–12/29/67); R. Woods, *The Quest for Identity*, 237–238.

98. United Press International Article, July 26, 1968, LBJ Library, Alfred B. Fitt Papers, Box 2, Correspondence: General (7/1/68–9/13/68); MacGregor, *Integration of the Armed Forces*, 605–606; Memo, Alfred B. Fitt to Clark Clifford, August 24, 1968, LBJ Library, Alfred B. Fitt Papers, Box 2, Correspondence: General (7/1/68–9/13/68).

99. MacGregor, *Integration of the Armed Forces*, 605–606.

100. Equal Employment Opportunity in the U.S. Veterans Administration, NAACP, LOC, Group III, Box A 147, NAACP Administration files, General Office File, Government Federal, Veterans Administration: 1960–1965; The Veterans Administration during the Administration of President Lyndon B. Johnson, November 1963-January 1969, Vol. 1 Administrative History, 52–55, LBJ Library, Administrative History of Veterans Administration, Vol. 1–Narrative History, Chapters I–II.

101. The Veterans Administration during the Administration of President Lyndon B. Johnson, November 1963–January 1969, Vol. 1—Administrative History, 66–67, LBJ Library, Administrative History of Veterans Administration, Vol. 1—Narrative History, Chapters I–II; for an in-depth examination of the Cold War G.I. Bill and the internal and external debates undertaken by the Johnson administration on it, see LBJ Library, Legislative Background Vietnam Veterans Benefits 1967, Box 1.

102. For more, see Glenn C. Altschuler and Stuart M. Blumin, *The GI Bill: A New Deal for Veterans* (New York: Oxford University Press, 2009), 198–203.

103. Deborah Shapley notes that the amount given to Vietnam-era soldiers was less than that of Korean War–era soldiers because of the cost of the Vietnam War; see Shapley, *Promise and Power*, 589–590; Katznelson, *When Affirmative-Action Was White*, 140–141; Westheider, *The African American Experience in Vietnam*, 108; for an in-depth examination of the Cold War GI Bill and the internal and external debates undertaken

by the Johnson administration on it, see LBJ Library, Legislative Background Vietnam Veterans Benefits 1967, Box 1; Lyndon B. Johnson, Remarks Upon Signing the "Cold War GI Bill" (Veterans' Readjustment Benefits Act of 1966) (March 3, 1966), online by Gerhard Peters and John T. Woolley, The American Presidency Project, www.preside ncy.ucsb.edu/node/238508.

104. "Education Assistance for Veteran's Kids," *Chicago Daily Defender*, April 14, 1965, 7; Veterans May Benefit from VA Program," *Chicago Daily Defender*, August 27, 1968, 9; "42,000 War Orphans Get New Education Aid From the VA," *Chicago Daily Defender*, September 7, 1968, 4.

The Veterans Administration during the Administration of President Lyndon B. Johnson, November 1963–January 1969, Vol. 1—Administrative History, 66–67; Shapley, *Promise and Power*, 589–590; Westheider, *The African American Experience in Vietnam*, 108.

105. Doris Kearns Goodwin, *Leadership in Turbulent Times* (New York: Simon and Schuster, 2018), 306–343.

Chapter 6: The Decrescendo of Cold War Racial Reform

1. Representative John Bell Williams (MS), "Integration Cancer Hurting Army Units," *Congressional Record* 112: reel 461 (October 13, 1966), A5310; Ethel L. Payne, "General Hails Negro GIs' Viet Performance," *Chicago Defender*, March 14, 1967, 4.

2. Westheider, *The African American Experience in Vietnam*, 22–23, 27, 34–36.

3. Westheider, 22–3, 27, 34–36.

4. Knauer, *Let Us Fight as Free Men*, 9.

5. Westheider, *The African American Experience in Vietnam*, 22–36; Westheider, *Fighting on Two Fronts*, 13–15; Rodger Streitmatter, *Raising Her Voice: African-American Women Journalists Who Changed History* (Lexington: University Press of Kentucky, 1994), 125–126; Ethel L. Payne, "GIs Tell How They Stand on the Viet War," *Chicago Defender*, April 11, 1967, 2; "The Great Society—In Uniform," *Newsweek*, August 22, 1966, 46; Adam Yarmolinsky, *The Military Establishment*, 324–326, 328, 334–335; Brian Thomas Gallagher, "He Enlisted at 14, Went to Vietnam at 15 and Died a Month Later: Dan Bullock, a boy from Brooklyn, was the youngest American killed in the War," *New York Times*, June 10, 2019, 19.

6. Black service in the Army was 14.8 percent, while it was 8.9 percent in the Marine Corps. See Jack Raymond, "Negro Death Ratio in Vietnam Exceeds Whites." *New York Times*, March 10, 1966, 4; according to Westheider's later findings: "Between 1961 and the end of 1967, African Americans accounted for more than 14 percent of American fatalities in Southeast Asia." See Westheider, *Fighting on Two Fronts*, 13.

7. Westheider, *The African American Experience in Vietnam*; Westheider, *Fighting on Two Fronts*, 13; Raymond, "Negro Death Ratio in Vietnam Exceeds Whites," 4; Thomas A. Johnson, "The U.S. Negro in Vietnam," *New York Times*, April 29, 1968, 16; Gallagher, "He Enlisted at 14."

8. Congressman John Bell Williams (MS), "Integration Cancer Hurting Army Units."

9. Congressman John Bell Williams.

10. Leonard W. Malone, "TAN G.I'S in BERLIN Part One," *Pittsburgh Courier*, November 18, 1961, A16.

11. Leonard W. Malone, "TAN G.I.'S in BERLIN Part Two," *Pittsburgh Courier*, November 25, 1961, A14.

12. Payne, "GIs Tell How They Stand on the Viet War," 2.

13. Westheider, *Fighting on Two Fronts*, 86, see also 85–93.

14. Westheider, 85–93.

15. Westheider, 84–93; Dan T. Carter, *The Politics of Rage: George Wallace, The Origins of the New Conservatism, and the Transformation of American Politics*, 2nd ed. (Baton Rouge: Louisiana State University Press, 2000), 283–284.

16. Westheider, *Fighting on Two Fronts*, 81, 84–93; Carter, *The Politics of Rage*, 283–284.

17. Westheider, *Fighting on Two Fronts*, 81, 84–93; "Random Remarks by Ye Editor," *Cleveland Bolivar Commercial*, January 16, 1969; "Mississippi Marine Ordered to Lower Flag in Vietnam," *Cleveland Bolivar Commercial*, January 16, 1969.

18. Westheider, *Fighting on Two Fronts*, 81, 84–93; "Random Remarks by Ye Editor"; "Mississippi Marine Ordered to Lower Flag in Vietnam"; "Senator Assured Marine's Death Not Related to Flag Incident," *Daily Journal*, February 25, 1969; "Senators Satisfied with Marine Probe," *Jackson Clarion-Ledger*, February 25, 1969.

19. Rosenberg, *How Far the Promised Land?*, 220–221.

20. R. Woods, *LBJ*, 575–576.

21. Goodwin, *Lyndon Johnson and the American Dream*, 251–253.

22. R. Woods, *LBJ*, 575–576; Dr. Martin Luther King Jr., "Beyond Vietnam," April 4, 1967, Stanford University, Martin Luther King Jr. Research and Education Institute, https://kinginstitute.stanford.edu/king-papers/documents/beyond-vietnam; Taylor Branch, *At Canaan's Edge: America in the King Years, 1965–68* (New York: Simon and Schuster, 2006), 591–595.

23. R. Woods, *LBJ*, 575–576; King Jr., "Beyond Vietnam"; Branch, 591–595.

24. Rosenberg, *How Far the Promised Land?*, 220–227; S. J. Unger, "Carmichael Calls for U.S. Defeat in Vietnam War," *Chicago Defender* (national ed.), December 9, 1967, 3; "Stokely Calls for N. Viet Support," *Chicago Defender*, August 31, 1967, 3; R. Woods, *The Quest for Identity*, 253; "Carmichael Joins in Black Antidraft Move," *Chicago Defender*, April 15, 1968, 8.

25. Rosenberg, *How Far the Promised Land?*, 220–227; Unger, "Carmichael Calls for U.S. Defeat in Vietnam War"; "Stokely Calls for N. Viet Support"; R. Woods, *The Quest for Identity*, 253; "Carmichael Joins in Black Antidraft Move."

26. Jensen, "A Parable," 145.

27. Lee Rainwater and William L. Yancey, *The Moynihan Report and the Politics of Controversy* (Cambridge, MA: MIT Press, 1967), 18, 19–20; President's Task Force on Manpower Conservation, *One Third of a Nation: A Report on Young Men Found Unqualified for Military Service*, January 1, 1964, 11, 15; Daniel Patrick Moynihan, *Miles to Go: A Personal History of Social Policy* (Cambridge, MA: Harvard University Press, 1996), 216; three decades later, Moynihan openly questioned his rationale in the early 1960s on the issue, specifically the influence social behavior had on the issue of poverty within the United States. For more, see Moynihan, *Miles to Go*, 218–220; Jensen, "A Parable," 146–147.

28. Goodwin, *Leadership in Turbulent Times*, 311; for more on Johnson's desires as a

social reformer, a good place to begin is by exploring his experiences as a schoolteacher. See Goodwin, *Lyndon Johnson and the American Dream*, 66; Jensen, "A Parable," 147.

29. R. Woods, *LBJ*, 20, 62–65, 670–671; Jensen, "A Parable," 147–148.

30. MacGregor, *Integration of the Armed Forces*, 530; Robert S. McNamara, *The Essence of Security: Reflections in Office* (New York: Harper & Row, 1968), 122–123, 128–131.

31. R. Woods, *LBJ*, 20, 62–65, 670–671; Jensen, "A Parable," 147–148.

32. Frank M. Best, "'Sub-Standard' Men May Join the Ranks," *Journal of the Armed Forces*, 15 (August 1964): 1, 25; Jensen, "A Parable," 148.

33. TeleCon, "Lyndon Johnson and Robert McNamara on 13 August 1964," Conversation WH6408-19-4913, *Presidential Recordings Digital Edition*, ed. David G. Coleman, Kent B. Germany, Ken Hughes, Guian A. McKee, and Marc J. Selverstone (Charlottesville: University of Virginia Press, 2014), http://prde.upress.virginia.edu /conversations/4000757; Edward J. Drea, *McNamara, Clifford, and the Burdens of Vietnam: 1965–1969* (Washington, DC: Historical Office, Office of the Secretary of Defense, 2011), 266; TeleCon, "LBJ and McNamara on November 14, 1964," WH6411.20, LBJ Library; Jensen, "A Parable," 148–149.

34. Michael R. Beschloss, *Reaching for Glory: Lyndon Johnson's Secret White House Tapes, 1964–1965* (New York: Touchstone, 2001), 210–213; Drea, *McNamara, Clifford, and the Burdens of Vietnam*, 266; MacGregor, *Integration of the Armed Forces*, 568; Jensen, "A Parable," 149–510.

35. Beschloss, *Reaching for Glory*, 210–213; Drea, *McNamara, Clifford, and the Burdens of Vietnam*, 266; MacGregor, *Integration of the Armed Forces*, 568; Representative Glenard Paul Lipscomb, *Congressional Record* 111:11 (June 23, 1965), 14475–14476; for the debate between Senators Thurmond, Stennis, and Nelson, see *Congressional Record* 111:16 (August 25, 1965), 21719–21722; Jensen, "A Parable," 149–150.

36. Beschloss, *Reaching for Glory*, 210–213; Drea, *McNamara, Clifford, and the Burdens of Vietnam*, 266; MacGregor, *Integration of the Armed Forces*, 568; Representative Glenard Paul Lipscomb, *Congressional Record* 111:11 (June 23, 1965), 14475–14476; for the debate between Senators Thurmond, Stennis, and Nelson, see *Congressional Record* 111:16 (August 25, 1965), 21719–21722; Jensen, "A Parable," 149–150.

37. Steven Weismen, ed., *Daniel Patrick Moynihan: A Portrait in Letters of An American Visionary* (New York: PublicAffairs, 2010), 90–96; Daniel Patrick Moynihan, "The Negro Family: The Case for National Action" (Washington, DC: Office of Policy Planning and Research, United States Department of Labor, 1965), 42; see also David Sanford, "McNamara's Salvation Army," *The New Republic*, September 10, 1966, 13–14; Jensen, "A Parable," 150–151.

38. Weismen, ed., *Daniel Patrick Moynihan*, 90–96; Daniel Patrick Moynihan, "The Negro Family: The Case for National Action" (Washington, DC: Office of Policy Planning and Research, United States Department of Labor, 1965), 42; see also David Sanford, "McNamara's Salvation Army," *The New Republic*, September 10, 1966, 13–14; Jensen, "A Parable," 150–151.

39. Rainwater and Yancey, *The Moynihan Report*, 172–173, 201, 410, 421–422; "Moynihan Report Racist Tract, Says James Farmer," *Chicago Defender*, December 20, 1965, 6; Jensen, "A Parable," 151.

40. At this time, 2,709,000 men were in the armed forces. See Memo, Daniel

Patrick Moynihan to Harry McPherson, July 16, 1965, LBJ Library, Office Files of Harry McPherson, Box 21, McPherson: Civil Rights-1965 (2).

41. Memo, Daniel Patrick Moynihan to Harry McPherson, July 16, 1965; Jensen, "A Parable," 151–152.

42. R. Woods, *Prisoners of Hope*, 244; Jensen, "A Parable," 152–153.

43. TeleCon, "Lyndon B. Johnson and Richard Russell on June 6, 1966, 8:05 PM," Citation #10204, Recordings and Transcripts of Conversations and Meetings, LBJ Library. For more on Russell's promise to LBJ, see TeleCon, "Lyndon B. Johnson and Robert McNamara on November 24, 1964, 7:20AM," Citation #6471, Recordings and Transcripts of Conversations and Meetings, LBJ Library; R. Woods, *LBJ*, 669–671; Jeff Woods, *Richard B. Russell*, 149; Jensen, "A Parable," 152–153.

44. "Armed Forces to 'Salvage' Draft Rejects," *Chicago Defender*, August 24, 1966, 2; Homar Bigart, "McNamara Plans to 'Salvage' 40,000 Rejected in Draft," *New York Times*, August 24, 1966, 1–2; Deborah Shapley, *Promise and Power: The Life and Times of Robert McNamara* (Boston: Little, Brown and Company, 1993), 385–387; Jensen, "A Parable," 153–154.

45. "Armed Forces to 'Salvage' Draft Rejects"; Bogart, ed., *Project Clear*, 1–2; Shapley, *Promise and Power*, 385–387; Jensen, "A Parable," 153–154.

46. Fred M. Hechinger, "What Mark for Army as Educator?," *New York Times*, August 28, 1966; "About Fred Hechinger," The Hechinger Report," https://hechingerreport .org/about-fred-hechinger; Shapley, *Promise and Power*, 385–387; Jensen, "A Parable," 154.

47. Thomas G. Sticht, William Armstrong, Daniel Hickey, and John Caylor, eds., *Cast-off Youth: Policy and Training Methods from the Military Experience* (New York: Praeger, 1987), 15, 22–23 190; Mershon and Schlossman, *Foxholes & Color Lines*, 20–22; Janice Laurence and Peter F. Ramsberger, *Low-Aptitude Men in the Military: Who Profits, Who Pays?* (New York: Praeger, 1991), 60; Laura Palmer, "The General, at Ease: An Interview with Westmoreland," *MHQ: The Quarterly Journal of Military History* (Autumn 1988): 34; David Anthony Dawson, "The Impact of Project 100,000 on the Marine Corps" (MA thesis, Kansas State University, 1994), 115; Gregory A. Daddis, *No Sure Victory: Measuring U.S. Army Effectiveness and Progress in the Vietnam War* (New York: Oxford University Press, 2011), 185–186; Jensen, "A Parable," 155.

48. Christian G. Appy, *Patriots: The Vietnam War Remembered From All Sides* (New York: Penguin Books, 2003), 445; Transcript, Interviews with Richard Bowen, 2010-03-03 and 2010-03-11, by Mark DePue, Abraham Lincoln Presidential Library *Veterans Remember* Oral History Project, VRC-A-L-2010-009.1, Abraham Lincoln Presidential Library, 29, 32; Transcript, Interview with Lieutenant Colonel Lloyd K. Brown, 1983-4-13, US Army War College and US Army Military History Institute, Company Command in Vietnam Oral History Project, 21, 23; Jensen, "A Parable," 157.

49. Dawson, "The Impact of Project 100,000," 88–93, 99–100.

50. Dawson, 88–93, 99–100.

51. According to Dawson, only 9.5 percent of New Standards Marines throughout the entirety of Project 100,000 were from the medical pool, see Dawson, 90.

52. Dawson, 88–93, 99–100; Office of the Assistant Secretary of Defense (Manpower and Reserve Affairs), Project One Hundred Thousand: Characteristics and

Performance of New Standards Men: Final Report, June 1971 (unpublished), Table A-7 and E-5, HumRRO collection (hereinafter Project One Hundred Thousand: Final Report [unpublished]).

53. Dawson, "The Impact of Project 100,000," 88–93, 99–100; Project One Hundred Thousand: Final Report (unpublished), Tables A-7 and E-5.

54. Dawson, "The Impact of Project 100,000," 88–89–91, 102. For more on the Marines manpower struggles see 102–108.

55. Researcher Janice Laurence notes: "In the early stages of the program, in fact, NSM [New Standards Men] were given service identification numbers beginning with 67, and they became widely known as the 'sixes and sevens.'" Laurence, 59–60; Shapley, *Promise and Power*, 387.

56. In comparison, African American Marines who were not part of Project 100,000 made up 11 percent (10.7 percent) of the Marine Corps. See Dawson, "The Impact of Project 100,000," 144, and Project One Hundred Thousand: Final Report (unpublished), Table B-2.

57. Dawson, "The Impact of Project 100,000," 142, 144–147; Project One Hundred Thousand: Final Report (unpublished), Table B-11; Allan Millett, *Semper Fidelis: The History of the United States Marine Corps*, rev. and expanded ed. (New York: Free Press, 1991), 598–600.

58. Dawson, "The Impact of Project 100,000," 142, 144–147; Project One Hundred Thousand: Characteristics and Performance of "New Standards" Men, Office Secretary of Defense—Assistant Secretary of Defense Manpower and Reserve Affairs, December 1969, xx; William Thomas Allison, *Military Justice in Vietnam: The Rule of Law in an American War* (Lawrence: University Press of Kansas, 2007), 30.

59. According to the final report of the program, 61.8 percent were Caucasian, 36.7 percent were African American, and 1.5 percent were other. The "other" hail largely from Spanish American or Puerto Rican descent; Project One Hundred Thousand: Final Report (unpublished), Table B-2. Consequently, very little has been written on the experiences of Spanish American or Puerto Rican New Standards Men.

60. Project One Hundred Thousand: Final Report (unpublished), Table A-5; George Q. Flynn, *Lewis B. Hersey, Mr. Selective Service* (Chapel Hill: University of North Carolina Press, 1985), 16, 118–121, 228–231, 255–257; Jensen, "A Parable," 163–164.

61. Flynn, *Lewis B. Hersey*, 16, 118–121, 228–231, 255–257; Jensen, "A Parable," 163–164.

62. Flynn, *Lewis B. Hersey*, 235–237, 260, 267; R. Woods, *LBJ*, 676–677.

63. Jon Meacham, *His Truth Is Marching On: John Lewis and the Power of Hope* (New York: Random House, 2020), 180–181.

64. Meacham, *His Truth Is Marching On*, 180–181.

65. Some scholars, such as historian Kimberly Phillips, contend that Hershey used the draft and Project 100,000 to eliminate civil rights criticism by drafting members of that movement and sending them to war. For more, see Kimberly Phillips, *War! What Is It Good For? Black Freedom Struggles and the U.S. Military from World War II to Iraq* (Chapel Hill: University of North Carolina Press, 2012), 204–205; See Paul Starr, *The Discarded Army: Veterans After Vietnam* (New York: Charterhouse, 1973), 191; Westheider, *Fighting on Two Fronts*, 27–29; Jensen, "A Parable," 163–164, n.38.

66. "Rights Leaders Deplore Plan to 'Salvage' Military Rejects," *New York Times,*

August 26, 1966, 3; Benjamin Welles, "Negroes Expected to Make up 30% of Draft 'Salvage,'" *New York Times*, August 25, 1966, 6; Laurence and Peter F. Ramsberger, *Low-Aptitude Men in the Military*, 37; Neil Sheehan, "Military Ready to Absorb Influx of Former 'Rejects,'" *New York Times*, October 16, 1966, 9; Shapley, *Promise and Power*, 386; Jensen, "A Parable," 162–163.

67. Lawrence M. Baskir and William A. Strauss, *Chance and Circumstance: The Draft, The War, and The Vietnam Generation* (New York: Alfred A. Knopf, 1978), 127; Herbert Mitgang, "Vietnam Generation," *New York Times*, July 15, 1978, 15; Jensen, "A Parable," 162–163, n.35.

68. The most comedic example, which still demonstrated a concern over the mental prowess of substandard manpower, came from Barney Cole, an Air Force veteran. Cole recalled an incident involving three alleged New Standards Men who were under his supervision and were painting a shed. At one point, he discovered that the men had stopped working and were throwing rocks at an object. He approached the men. "I said 'aren't you boys supposed to be painting?' Well [they responded,] 'there's a monster out there' and I go out there and there's this poor frightened little horny toad that's had rocks fall all around it." For more, see Transcript, Interview with Barney Cole, Vietnam Center and Archive at Texas Tech University, Vietnam Archive Oral History Project, 2008-8-14, OH0626, 20–21.

69. Myra MacPherson, *Long Time Passing: Vietnam and the Haunted Generation*, new ed. (Bloomington: Indiana University Press, 2001), 561; Transcript, Interviews with Gary B. Roberts, 2005–01–31 and 2005–02–02, Kennesaw State University Oral History Series, Kennesaw State University Oral History Project, 1973–, KSU/45/05/001, Kennesaw State University Archives, 19; Jensen, "A Parable," 156.

70. Remarks by Alfred B. Fitt before the Rotary Club of Wichita, Kansas and the Kansas Chamber of Commerce, April 15, 1968, 4, LBJ Library, Alfred Fitt Papers, Box 5, Personal Files: Speeches; for statistical information on Project 100,000, see Memo, Clark Clifford to Lyndon B. Johnson, July 31, 1968, LBJ Library, Alfred Fitt Papers, Box 2, Correspondence: General 7/1/1968–9/13/1968; Project One Hundred Thousand: Characteristics and Performance of "New Standards" Men, Office Secretary of Defense, xv, xix; R. Woods, *LBJ*, 671.

71. Remarks by Alfred B. Fitt before the Rotary Club of Wichita, Kansas and the Kansas Chamber of Commerce, April 15, 1968; for statistical information on Project 100,000, see Memo, Clark Clifford to Lyndon B. Johnson, July 31, 1968; Project One Hundred Thousand: Characteristics and Performance of "New Standards" Men, Office Secretary of Defense, xv, xix; Dawson, "The Impact of Project 100,000," 92, 99–100, 136–137, 189.

72. "Military Hopes to Help Rejects," *New York Times*, September 4, 1966.

73. "Military Hopes to Help Rejects"; Transcript, Interview with Colonel Walter E. Olson, 1984-4-24, US Army War College and US Army Military History Institute, Company Command in Vietnam Oral History Project, 2–3; Jensen, "A Parable," 156; Transcript, Interview with Colonel Ralph L. Hagler, 1985-4-24, US Army War College and US Army Military History Institute, Company Command in Vietnam Oral History Project, 3–4.

74. Seymour Hersh, *My Lai 4: A Report on the Massacre and Its Aftermath* (New

York: Random House, 1970), 17–19, 20–43; Rick Perlstein, *Nixonland: The Rise of a President and the Fracturing of America* (New York: Scribner, 2008), 481. The lack-of-education narrative carries on in studies involving the My Lai 4 and the subsequent trial that followed. See Louise Barnett, *Atrocity and American Military Justice in Southeast Asia: Trial by Army* (New York: Routledge, 2010), 222; Michal Belknap, *The Vietnam War on Trial: The My Lai Massacre and the Court-Martial of Lieutenant Calley* (Lawrence: University Press of Kansas, 2002), 40; Michael Bilton and Kevin Sim, *Four Hours in My Lai* (New York: Penguin Books, 1992), 51; Jensen, "A Parable," 156.

75. Greg Weiner, *American Burke: The Uncommon Liberalism of Daniel Patrick Moynihan* (Lawrence: University Press of Kansas, 2016), 12–13; R. Woods, *LBJ*, 587–588.

76. R. Woods, *LBJ*, 809–810.

77. R. Woods, 819, 831–832.

78. Robert K. Griffith Jr., *The U.S. Army's Transition to the All-Volunteer Force, 1968–1974* (Washington, DC: Center of Military History, 1997), 158–160; Sticht, Armstrong, Hick, and Caylor, eds., *Cast-off Youth*, 13–16.

79. Westheider, *Fighting on Two Fronts*, 41–45.

80. Westheider, 41–45.

81. Westheider, 45–65.

82. Westheider, 45–65.

83. Westheider, 45–65.

84. Westheider, 74–77.

85. Westheider, 74–77.

86. "750 GIs Riot in 'LBJ' Stockade," *Desert Sun* 42, no. 23 (August 30, 1968); "Race Tensions May Have Caused Riot in Stockade," *Desert Sun* 42, no. 27 (September 4, 1968); "The Forgotten History of a Prison Uprising in Vietnam," August 29, 2018, Radio Diaries, *NPR*, www.npr.org/sections/codeswitch/2018/08/29/642617106/the-forgotten-history-of-a-prison-uprising-in-vietnam.

87. "750 GIs Riot in 'LBJ' Stockade"; "Race Tensions May Have Caused Riot in Stockade"; "The Forgotten History of a Prison Uprising in Vietnam"; Westheider, *The African American Experience in Vietnam*, 75.

88. "Text of Camp Lejeune Committee's Report to Commanding General," *New York Times*, August 10, 1969.

89. Westheider, *Fighting on Two Fronts*, 94–95, 131; "Text of Camp Lejeune Committee's Report to Commanding General"; "Race Riot Quelled at a Marine Prison," *New York Times*, August 27, 1970.

90. John Farrell, *Richard Nixon: The Life* (New York: Doubleday, 2017), 331–333.

91. Farrell, 331–333.

92. Farrell, 331–333.

93. Farrell, 331–333; Justin P. Coffey, *Spiro Agnew and the Rise of the Republican Right* (Santa Barbara, CA: Prager, 2015), 69–70.

94. Melvin Small, *The Presidency of Richard Nixon* (Lawrence: University Press of Kansas, 1999), 162; John D. Weaver, *The Brownsville Raid* (College Station: Texas A&M Press, 1992).

95. Small, *The Presidency of Richard Nixon*, 142, 162; Tim Naftali, "Ronald Reagan's Long-Hidden Racist Conversation with Richard Nixon," *The Atlantic*, July 30, 2019,

www.theatlantic.com/ideas/archive/2019/07/ronald-reagans-racist-conversation-rich ard-nixon/595102.

96. Small, *The Presidency of Richard Nixon*, 142; Tim Naftali, "Ronald Reagan's Long-Hidden Racist Conversation with Richard Nixon."

97. Beth Bailey, *America's Army: Making the All-Volunteer Force* (Cambridge, MA: Belknap Press, 2009), 21–23.

98. Bailey, 21–23.

99. Bailey, 113–114.

100. John Darrell Sherwood, *Black Sailor, White Navy: Racial Unrest in the Fleet during the Vietnam War Era* (New York: New York University Press, 2007), 55–60, 72–102.

101. Sherwood, 55–60, 72–102.

102. Sherwood, 55–60, 72–102.

103. Sherwood, 55–60, 72–102; Earl Caldwell, "Kitty Hawk Back at Home Port; Sailors Describe Racial Conflict," *New York Times*, November 29, 1972.

104. R. Woods, *LBJ*, 786.

105. Richard Nixon, "Address to the Nation on the War in Vietnam, Nov 3, 1969," online by Gerhard Peters and John T. Woolley, The American Presidency Project, www .presidency.ucsb.edu/node/240027.

106. Small, *The Presidency of Richard Nixon*, 28.

107. Small, 161–162, 176–177; Farrell, *Richard Nixon*, 250–251, 259.

108. Small, *The Presidency of Richard Nixon*, 161–162, 176–177; Farrell, *Richard Nixon*, 250–251, 259.

Conclusion

1. Mershon and Schlossman, *Foxholes & Color Lines*, 312–315.

2. Mershon and Schlossman, 312–315.

3. MacGregor, *Integration of the Armed Forces*, 621–622; Maxwell, *Brotherhood in Combat*, 128.

Epilogue

1. Speech of Senator Richard B. Russell, Civil Rights "Dragon" Speech, August 28, 1957, RRL, UGA, Series III, Box 26.

2. Harry S. Truman, "Address of Former President Harry S. Truman Before the Committee on Platform and Resolutions of the Democratic Nation Convention, 1956," 7–13, HST Library, www.trumanlibrary.gov/library/research-files/address-committee -platform-and-resolutions-democratic-national-convention?documentid=NA&page number=1.

3. John Ismay, "The Army Was Open to Replacing Confederate Base Names. Then Trump Said No." *New York Times*, June 10, 2020 (updated July 20, 2020), www.ny times.com/2020/06/10/magazine/army-confederate-base-names.html. Though it succeeded in one fashion, the branch would once again find itself in the crosshairs of reformers as a member of the U.S. Naval Academy's alumni association was forced to resign after he had made derogatory and racists comments on Facebook. For more, see Melissa Alonso and Susannah Cullinane, "Retired Navy Captain Apologies After Racial Slurs Streamed on Facebook," *CNN*, June 8, 2020, www.cnn.com/2020/06/07/us/navy -captain-racial-slurs-facebook/index.html.

4. David Petraeus, "Take the Confederate Names Off Our Army Bases," *The Atlantic*, June 9, 2020, www.theatlantic.com/ideas/archive/2020/06/take-confederate-names-off-our-army-bases/612832; Kyle Rempfer, "Army Won't Follow Marine Corps Lead and Rename Confederate Bases," February 28, 2020, www.armytimes.com/news/your-army/2020/02/28/army-wont-follow-marine-corps-lead-and-rename-confederate-bases.

5. Ismay, "The Army Was Open to Replacing Confederate Base Names. Then Trump Said No."; "US Forces Japan Bans Display of Confederate Flag," July 13, 2020, *Military.com*, www.military.com/daily-news/2020/07/13/us-forces-japan-bans-display-of-confederate-flag.html; ABC News, "'We all have unconscious biases, admitted or not': Gen. David Berger *This Week* Interview with Martha Raddatz," YouTube video, 4:39, July 5, 2020, www.youtube.com/watch?v=Ez87upeutdw; Steve Walsh, "Marine Corps Aims to Tackle Evolving Face of White Supremacy," *NPR*, March 31, 2020, www.npr.org/2020/03/31/824370942/marine-corps-aims-to-tackle-evolving-face-of-white-supremacy.

6. ABC News, "'We all have unconscious biases, admitted or not': Gen. David Berger *This Week* interview with Martha Raddatz"; Steve Walsh, "Marine Corps Aims to Tackle Evolving Face of White Supremacy," *NPR*, March 31, 2020, www.npr.org/2020/03/31/824370942/marine-corps-aims-to-tackle-evolving-face-of-white-supremacy.

7. Ismay, "The Army Was Open to Replacing Confederate Base Names. Then Trump Said No."; Rebecca Shabad, "Trump Threatens to Veto Warren-Backed Defense Bill Removing Confederate Names from Military Bases," *NBC News*, July 1, 2020, www.nbcnews.com/politics/congress/trump-threatens-veto-warren-backed-defense-bill-removing-confederate-names-n1232635; Corey Dickstein, "Austin, Lawmakers Name Eight to Commission for Renaming Military Bases That Honor Confederates," *Stars and Stripes*, February 12, 2021, www.stripes.com/news/us/austin-lawmakers-name-eight-to-commission-for-renaming-military-bases-that-honor-confederates-1.662022.

8. Ismay, "The Army Was Open to Replacing Confederate Base Names. Then Trump Said No."; Shabad, "Trump Threatens to Veto Warren-Backed Defense Bill"; Dickstein, "Austin, Lawmakers Name Eight to Commission."

9. Ismay, "The Army Was Open to Replacing Confederate Base Names. Then Trump Said No."; Shabad, "Trump Threatens to Veto Warren-Backed Defense Bill"; Dickstein, "Austin, Lawmakers Name Eight to Commission."

10. Thomas Gibbons-Neff, Erich Schmitt, and Helene Cooper, "Aggressive Tactics by National Guard, Ordered to Appease Trump, Wounded the Military, Too," *New York Times*, June 10, 2020, www.nytimes.com/2020/06/10/us/politics/national-guard-protests.html; Alex Horton, Andrew Ba Tran, Aaron Steckelberg, and John Muyskens, "A low-flying 'show of force,'" *Washington Post*, June 23, 2020, www.washingtonpost.com/graphics/2020/investigations/helicopter-protests-washington-dc-national-guard; "Police Did Not Clear D.C.'s Lafayette Square of Protesters so Trump Could Hold a Photo Op, New Report Says," NBC News, June 9, 2021, www.nbcnews.com/politics/donald-trump/police-did-not-clear-d-c-s-lafayette-park-protestors-n1270126.

11. Gibbons-Neff, Schmitt, and Cooper, "Aggressive Tactics by National Guard"; Daniel Lippman, "'What I Saw Was Just Absolutely Wrong': National Guardsmen Struggle with Their Role in Controlling Protests," *Politico*, June 9, 2020 (update June 10, 2020), www.politico.com/news/2020/06/09/national-guard-protests-309932.

12. Leo Shane III, "Signs of White Supremacy, Extremism Up Again in Poll of Active-Duty Troops," *MilitaryTimes*, February 6, 2020, www.militarytimes.com/news/pentagon-congress/2020/02/06/signs-of-white-supremacy-extremism-up-again-in-poll-of-active-duty-troops; Bryan Bender, "The Military Has a Hate Group Problem. But It Doesn't Know How Bad It's Gotten," *Politico*, January 11, 2021, www.politico.com/news/2021/01/11/military-right-wing-extremism-457861?utm_source=pocket-newtab; "Pentagon: Active Duty Service Members Participated in Capitol Riots," WUSA9 (CBS affiliate), February 5, 2021, www.wusa9.com/article/news/national/capitol-riots/active-duty-service-members-participated-in-capitol-riots-january-6-insurrection/65-d84d45f5-fe0f-4ff3-8a9f-0cfcab6c0825; Press Release, "Representatives Crow and Trahan Introduce Bill to Include Modern Diversity Training at the Department of Defense," December 17, 2020, official website for Jason Crow Congressman for Colorado's 6th District, https://crow.house.gov/media/press-releases/representatives-crow-and-trahan-introduce-bill-include-modern-diversity.

13. Leo Shane III, "Signs of White Supremacy, Extremism Up Again in Poll of Active-Duty Troops"; Bender, "The Military Has a Hate Group Problem"; "Pentagon: Active Duty Service Members Participated in Capitol Riots."

14. Bailey, *America's Army*, 258–259; James Dao, "First Woman Ascends to Top Drill Sergeant Spot," *New York Times*, September 21, 2009; Roddie Burris, "Former Ft. Jackson Drill School Commander Says Bias Sabotaged Her Job," *Slate*, July 30, 2013, www.thestate.com/news/local/military/article14438579.html; Susanne M. Schafer, "Retired Female Army Drill Sergeant Commander Sues," *Washington Times*, May 20, 2014; Robert Timmons "'Trailblazers' Inducted into Hall of Fame, September 14, 2017," United States Army website, www.army.mil/article/193852/trailblazers _inducted _into_hall_of_fame.

15. Christina Santi, "First Black Woman Graduates from U.S. Army Ranger School," *Ebony*, May 14, 2019, www.ebony.com/news/first-black-woman-graduates-us-army-ranger-school; "DIA Welcomes Lt. Gen. Vincent Stewart as Its 20th Director," DIA Public Affairs, January 23, 2015, www.dia.mil/News/Articles/article/567046/dia-welcomes-lt-gen-vincent-stewart-as-its-20th-director; Lara Seligman, Tyler Pager, Connor O'Brien, and Natasha Bertrand, "Biden Picks Retired General Lloyd Austin to Run Pentagon," *Politico*, December 7, 2020, www.politico.com/news/2020/12/07/lloyd-austin-biden-secretary-defense-frontrunner-contender-443479; Catie Edmondson, "Lloyd Austin Is Confirmed, becoming the First Black Defense Secretary in U.S. history," *New York Times*, January 22, 2021. Of Important note, Austin was only allowed to serve in the position after receiving a waiver. Only a handful have received the waiver: General James Mattis during the Trump administration, and General George Marshall, who was the first to receive it during the Truman administration. For more, see Tom Bowman, "Why Generals Need Congressional Waivers to Become Defense Secretary," *NPR*, January 9, 2017, www.npr.org/2017/01/09/508902893/why-generals-need-congressional-waivers-to-become-defense-secretary.

16. Ian Shapira, "VMI's First Black Superintendent Blasts White Critics of Diversity and Equity Reform," *Washington Post*, January 28, 2022, www.washingtonpost.com/dc-md-va/2022/01/28/vmi-wins-facebook-diversity-battle; Ian Shapira, "VMI Has Toler-

ated 'Racist and Sexist Culture' and Must Change, Investigation Finds," *Washington Post*, June 1, 2021, www.washingtonpost.com/local/vmi-report-investigation-racism/2021 /06/01/380c08c4-c2cb-11eb-93f5-ee9558eecf4b_story.html.

17. Alan Blinder, "Was That Ralph Northam in Blackface? An Inquiry Ends Without Answers," *New York Times*, May 22, 2019, www.nytimes.com/2019/05/22/us/ralph -northam-blackface-photo.html; Astead W. Herndon, "Black Virginians Took Ralph Northam Back. Neither Has Forgotten.," *New York Times*, June 14, 2021, www.nytimes .com/2021/06/14/us/politics/ralph-northam-virginia.html.

18. Shapira, "VMI's First Black Superintendent"; Shapira, "VMI Has Tolerated 'Racist and Sexist Culture.'"

19. Ian Shapira, "VMI Cadets Attack Black Students, Women on Anonymous Chat App as Furor over Racism Grows," *Washington Post*, October 27, 2020, www.wash ingtonpost.com/local/vmi-jodel-racism-cadets/2020/10/27/23d43d34-12f1-11eb -ba42-ec6a580836ed_story.html; Ian Shapira, "VMI Will Change Honor System that Expels Black Cadets at Disproportionate Rates," *Washington Post*, February 5, 2022, www.washingtonpost.com/education/2022/02/05/vmi-honor-court-reforms.

Bibliography

Primary Sources

ABC News. "'We all have unconscious biases, admitted or not': Gen. David Berger *This Week* Interview with Martha Raddatz." YouTube video. 4:39. July 5, 2020. www.you tube.com/watch?v=Ez87upeutdw.

Alonso, Melissa, and Susannah Cullinane. "Retired Navy Captain Apologies After Racial Slurs Streamed on Facebook." *CNN*. June 8, 2020. www.cnn.com/2020/06/07/us /navy-captain-racial-slurs-facebook/index.html.

Bender, Bryan. "The Military Has a Hate Group Problem. But It Doesn't Know How Bad It's Gotten." *Politico*. January 11, 2021. www.politico.com/news/2021/01/11/mili tary-right-wing-extremism-457861?utm_source=pocket-newtab.

Best, Frank M. "'Sub-Standard' Men May Join the Ranks." *Journal of the Armed Forces* 15 (August 1964): 1, 25.

Bowman, Tom. "Why Generals Need Congressional Waivers to Become Defense Secretary." *NPR*. January 9, 2017. www.npr.org/2017/01/09/508902893/why-generals -need-congressional-waivers-to-become-defense-secretary.

Burris, Roddie. "Former Ft. Jackson Drill School Commander Says Bias Sabotaged Her Job." *Slate*. July 30, 2013, www.thestate.com/news/local/military/article14438 579.html.

"Civil Rights and the Election." *Christian Century* (February 18, 1948), 65.

Congressional Record. Various volumes, 1948–1966.

Dickstein, Corey. "Austin, Lawmakers Name Eight to Commission for Renaming Military Bases That Honor Confederates." *Stars and Stripes*, February 12, 2021, www.stripes.com/news/us/austin-lawmakers-name-eight-to-commission-for -renaming-military-bases-that-honor-confederates-1.662022.

Douglass, Frederick. "MEN OF COLOR, TO ARMS!" *Broadside*, Rochester (March 21, 1863).

———. "Should the Negro Enlist in the Union Army?" Address at a Meeting for the Promotion of Colored Enlistments, July 6, 1863, *Douglass' Monthly* (August 1863).

Evans, James C., and John Wiant, "Views of James C. Evans: Integration, Differentiation and Refinement." *Negro History Bulletin* 23, no. 7 (April 1960): 152.

Forrestal, James. *The Forrestal Diaries*. Edited by Walter Millis and E. S. Duffield. New York: Viking Press, 1951.

Frank, Stan. "The Rancorous Mr. Rankin." *Liberty* (October 6, 1945), 19, 64–66, 68.

"A French Directive." *The Crisis* 18, no. 1 (May 1919): 16–18.

"Glancing Back at Certain Remarks." *The Nation* 171, no. 1 (July 1950): 1–2.

Lewis, Fulton. *Top of the News with Fulton Lewis, Jr.* Vol. 4 (April 1962): 6–7.

Library of Congress. "Roosevelt's Hostility to the Colored People of the United States: The Record of the Discharge of the Colored Soldiers at Brownsville." Washington, DC, 1906, Library of Congress. www.loc.gov/item/rbpe.24001000.

Lippman, Daniel. "'What I Saw Was Just Absolutely Wrong': National Guardsmen

Struggle with Their Role in Controlling Protests." *Politico.* June 9, 2020 (updated June 10, 2020). www.politico.com/news/2020/06/09/national-guard-protests-309932.

"Key Cabinet Post for Max Rabb." *American Nationalist* (March 25, 1954).

King Jr., Dr. Martin Luther. "Beyond Vietnam." April 4, 1967. Stanford University. The Martin Luther King, Jr. Research and Education Institute. https://kinginstitute.stan ford.edu/king-papers/documents/beyond-vietnam.

NAACP files, Library of Congress. Various NAACP Administration files, 1956–1965.

"NAACP Leaders with Their Communist-Front Citations!" *Common Sense*, August 1, 1957, 1–4.

National Archives and Records Administration. RG 319, Records of the Army Staff, The Integration of the Armed Forces, 1940–1965. National Archives II, College Park, MD.

Nichols, Lee. *Breakthrough on the Color Front.* New York: Random House, 1954.

"Orson Welles." *NAACP Bulletin* 5 (August–September 1946).

"Pentagon: Active Duty Service Members Participated in Capitol Riots." WUSA9 (CBS affiliate). February 5, 2021. www.wusa9.com/article/news/national/capitol-riots /active-duty-service-members-participated-in-capitol-riots-january-6-insurrec tion/65-d84d45f5-fe0f-4ff3-8a9f-0cfcab6c0825.

Petraeus, David. "Take the Confederate Names Off Our Army Bases." *The Atlantic*, June 9, 2020. www.theatlantic.com/ideas/archive/2020/06/take-confederate-names -off-our-army-bases/612832.

"Police Did Not Clear D.C.'s Lafayette Square of Protesters so Trump Could Hold a Photo Op, New Report Says." NBC News, June 9, 2021. www.nbcnews.com/poli tics/donald-trump/police-did-not-clear-d-c-s-lafayette-park-protestors-n1270126.

Quarles, Benjamin. "Will a Long War Aid the Negro?" *The Crisis* 50, no. 9 (September 1943), 268, 286.

Reddick, L. D. "The Negro in the United States Navy During World War II." *Journal of Negro History* 32, no. 2 (April 1947).

Reinhardt, George C. "No Segregation in Foxholes." *The Crisis* 60, no. 8 (October 1953): 457.

Rempfer, Kyle. "Army Won't Follow Marine Corps Lead and Rename Confederate Bases." *Army Times.* February 28, 2020, www.armytimes.com/news/your-army/20 20/02/28/army-wont-follow-marine-corps-lead-and-rename-confederate-bases.

Sanford, David. "McNamara's Salvation Army." *New Republic*, September 10, 1966, 13–14.

Santi, Christiania. "First Black Woman Graduates from U.S. Army Ranger School." *Ebony*, May 14, 2019. www.ebony.com/news/first-black-woman-graduates-us-army -ranger-school.

Seligman, Lara, Tyler Pager, Connor O'Brien, and Natasha Bertrand. "Biden Picks Retired General Lloyd Austin to Run Pentagon." *Politico*, December 7, 2020. www.politico.com/news/2020/12/07/lloyd-austin-biden-secretary-defense-frontrunner -contender-443479.

Shabad, Rebecca. "Trump Threatens to Veto Warren-Backed Defense Bill Removing Confederate Names from Military Bases." NBC News, July 1, 2020. www.nbcnews

.com/politics/congress/trump-threatens-veto-warren-backed-defense-bill-removi
ng-confederate-names-n1232635.

Shane III, Leo. "Signs of White Supremacy, Extremism Up Again in Poll of Active-Duty
Troops." *MilitaryTimes*, February 6, 2020. www.militarytimes.com/news/pentagon
-congress/2020/02/06/signs-of-white-supremacy-extremism-up-again-in-poll-of
-active-duty-troops.

"The Great Society—In Uniform." *Newsweek*, August 22, 1966, 46.

Stimson, Henry L., and McGeorge Bundy. *On Active Services in Peace and War*. New
York: Harper and Brothers, 1947.

"The Supreme Court—Communism's Trojan Horse in the U.S." *Common Sense*, July
15, 1957, 1.

Twain, Mark. *Mark Twain in Eruption: Hitherto Unpublished Pages About Men and
Events*. Edited by Bernard Devoto. New York: Harper & Brothers, 1940.

"US Forces Japan Bans Display of Confederate Flag." *Military.com*, July 13, 2020. www
.military.com/daily-news/2020/07/13/us-forces-japan-bans-display-of-confed
erate-flag.html.

Walsh, Steve. "Marine Corps Aims to Tackle Evolving Face of White Supremacy." *NPR*,
March 31, 2020. www.npr.org/2020/03/31/824370942/marine-corps-aims-to-tackle
-evolving-face-of-white-supremacy.

Wilkins, Roy. "Defending Democracy." *The Crisis* 46, no. 10 (October 1939): 305.

———. "Now Is the Time Not to Be Silent." *The Crisis* 49, no. 1 (January 1942): 7.

Woodard, Isaac. Affidavit, April 23, 1946, NAACP Papers, Reel 28. Library of Congress,
Washington, DC.

Newspapers

Afro-American
Augusta Chronicle
Augusta Herald
Baltimore Afro-American
Chicago Defender
Cleveland Bolivar Commercial
Commercial Appeal
Daily Journal
Desert Sun
Fort Worth Star Telegram
Jackson Clarion-Ledger
Jackson State Times
Lewiston Morning Tribune
Minneapolis Spokesman
Morning Star Okinawa
News and Courier
New York Herald Tribune
New York Post
New York Times

Overseas Weekly
People's Weekly (Syracuse)
Philadelphia Bulletin
Pittsburgh Courier
Shreveport Journal
St. Petersburg Times
Sumter Daily Item
Washington Afro-American
Washington Post

Official Documents

Adkins, Robert E. *Medical Care of Veterans.* Washington, DC: US Government Printing Office, 1967. Printed for the use of the Committee on Veterans Affairs, 90th Cong., 1st sess., House Committee Print No. 4.

Army Talk #70, May 5, 1945.

"DIA Welcomes Lt. Gen. Vincent Stewart as Its 20th Director." DIA Public Affairs. January 23, 2015. www.dia.mil/News/Articles/article/567046/dia-welcomes-lt-gen -vincent-stewart-as-its-20th-director.

Federal Records of World War II: Military Agencies, United States, National Achieves and Records Service, January 1, 1951, US Government Printing Office, 274.

Griffith Jr., Robert K. *The U.S. Army's Transition to the All-Volunteer Force, 1968–1974.* Washington, DC: Center of Military History, 1997.

Moynihan, Daniel Patrick. "The Negro Family: The Case for National Action." Washington, DC: Office of Policy Planning and Research, United States Department of Labor, 1965.

Office of the Assistant Secretary of Defense (Manpower and Reserve Affairs). Project One Hundred Thousand: Characteristics and Performance of New Standards Men: Final Report, June 1971 (unpublished), Table A-7 and E-5, HumRRO collection.

The President's Committee on Civil Rights. *To Secure These Rights: The Report of the President's Committee on Civil Rights.* Washington, DC: U.S. Government Printing Office, 1947.

The President's Task Force on Manpower Conservation. *One Third of a Nation: A Report on Young Men Found Unqualified for Military Service.* January 1, 1964.

Press Release. Representatives Crow and Trahan Introduce Bill to Include Modern Diversity Training at the Department of Defense, December 17, 2020. Official website for Jason Crow Congressman for Colorado's 6th District. https://crow.house.gov /media/press-releases/representatives-crow-and-trahan-introduce-bill-include -modern-diversity.

Project One Hundred Thousand: Characteristics and Performance of "New Standards" Men. Office Secretary of Defense—Assistant Secretary of Defense Manpower and Reserve Affairs. December 1969.

The Utilization of Negro Manpower in the Army: A 1951 Study. McLean, VA: Research Analysis Corporation, 1967.

Oral Histories

Abraham Lincoln Presidential Library, Springfield, Illinois
Transcript, Interviews with Richard Bowen, 2010-03-03 and 2010-03-11. Interviewed by Mark DePue, Abraham Lincoln Presidential Library. Veterans Remember Oral History Project, VRC-A-L-2010-009.1.

Harry S. Truman Presidential Library and Museum, Independence, Missouri
Stuart R. Symington Oral History Interview. May 29, 1981. Interviewed by James R. Fuchs.

John F. Kennedy Presidential Library and Museum, Boston, Massachusetts
Adam Yarmolinsky Oral History Interview. November 11, 1964. Interviewed by Daniel Ellsberg.

Kennesaw State University Archives, Kennesaw, Georgia
Transcript, Interviews with Gary B. Roberts, 2005-01-31 and 2005-02-02, Kennesaw State University Oral History Project, 1973–. KSU/45/05/001.

Texas Tech University Vietnam Center and Archive, Lubbock, Texas
Transcript, Interview with Barney Cole, Vietnam Center and Archive at Texas Tech University, Vietnam Archive Oral History Project, 2008-8-14, OH0626.

US Army War College and US Army Military History Institute, Carlisle Barracks, Pennsylvania
Transcript, Interview with LTC Lloyd K. Brown, 1983-4-13, US Army War College and US Army Military History Institute, Company Command in Vietnam Oral History Project.
Transcript, Interview with Col. Ralph L. Hagler, 1985-4-24, US Army War College and US Army Military History Institute, Company Command in Vietnam Oral History Project.
Transcript, Interview with Col. Walter E. Olson, 1984-4-24, US Army War College and US Army Military History Institute, Company Command in Vietnam Oral History Project.

University of Wisconsin Oral History Program, Madison, Wisconsin
Carlisle P. Runge, interview by Donna Hartshorne, August 14, 1982, Oral History Interview # 2. University of Wisconsin Oral History Program. https://minds.wisconsin.edu/bitstream/handle/1793/74461/Runge_249_8_14_1982.mp3?sequence=3&isAllowed=y.

Washington University, St. Louis, Missouri
Interview with Charles Diggs, conducted by Blackside, Inc. on November 6, 1986, for *Eyes on the Prize: America's Civil Rights Years (1954–1965)*. Washington University Libraries, Film and Media Archive, Henry Hampton Collection.

Presidential Addresses, Executive Orders, and News Conferences (in Chronological Order)

Eisenhower, Dwight D.

Annual Message to the Congress on the State of the Union, February 2, 1953. Online by Gerhard Peters and John T. Woolley. The American Presidency Project. www.presidency.ucsb.edu/node/231684.

The President's News Conference, March 19, 1953. Online by Gerhard Peters and John T. Woolley. The American Presidency Project. www.presidency.ucsb.edu/node/231547.

Annual Message to the Congress on the State of the Union, January 5, 1956. Online by Gerhard Peters and John T. Woolley. The American Presidency Project. www.presidency.ucsb.edu/node/233132.

Radio and Television Address to the American People on the Situation in Little Rock, September 24, 1957. Online by Gerhard Peters and John T. Woolley. The American Presidency Project. www.presidency.ucsb.edu/node/233623.

The President's News Conference, October 30, 1957. Online by Gerhard Peters and John T. Woolley. The American Presidency Project. www.presidency.ucsb.edu/node/233887.

Annual Message to the Congress on the State of the Union, January 12, 1961. Online by Gerhard Peters and John T. Woolley. The American Presidency Project. www.presidency.ucsb.edu/node/234806.

Johnson, Lyndon B.

Address Before a Joint Session of the Congress, November 27, 1963. Online by Gerhard Peters and John T. Woolley. The American Presidency Project. www.presidency.ucsb.edu/node/238734.

Lyndon B. Johnson, Remarks Upon Signing the "Cold War GI Bill" (Veterans' Readjustment Benefits Act of 1966), March 3, 1966. Online by Gerhard Peters and John T. Woolley. The American Presidency Project. www.presidency.ucsb.edu/node/238508.

Special Message to the Congress Proposing Further Legislation to Strengthen Civil Rights, April 28, 1966. Online by Gerhard Peters and John T. Woolley. The American Presidency Project. www.presidency.ucsb.edu/node/239224.

Kennedy, John F.

Remarks at the First Meeting of the President's Committee on Equal Employment Opportunity, April 11, 1961. Online by Gerhard Peters and John T. Woolley. The American Presidency Project. www.presidency.ucsb.edu/node/234568.

Radio and Television Report to the American People on Civil Rights, June 11, 1963. Online by Gerhard Peters and John T. Woolley. The American Presidency Project. www.presidency.ucsb.edu/node/236675.

Nixon, Richard M.

Address to the Nation on the War in Vietnam, November 3, 1969. Online by Gerhard

Peters and John T. Woolley. The American Presidency Project. www.presidency.uc
sb.edu/node/240027.

Truman, Harry S.

Address Before the National Association for the Advancement of Colored People, June 29, 1947. Online by Gerhard Peters and John T. Woolley. The American Presidency Project. www.presidency.ucsb.edu/node/231974.

Special Message to the Congress on Civil Rights, February 2, 1948. Online by Gerhard Peters and John T. Woolley. The American Presidency Project. www.presidency.uc sb.edu/node/232898.

Executive Order 9981—Establishing the President's Committee on Equality of Treatment and Opportunity in the Armed Services, July 26, 1948. Online by Gerhard Peters and John T. Woolley. The American Presidency Project. www.presidency.uc sb.edu/node/231614.

The President's News Conference of July 29, 1948. Online by Gerhard Peters and John T. Woolley. The American Presidency Project. www.presidency.ucsb.edu/node/23 2710.

Address in Harlem, New York, Upon Receiving the Franklin Roosevelt Award, October 29, 1948. Online by Gerhard Peters and John T. Woolley. The American Presidency Project. www.presidency.ucsb.edu/node/233997.

Address of Former President Harry S. Truman Before the Committee on Platform and Resolutions of the Democratic Nation Convention, 1956." Harry S. Truman Library and Museum. www.trumanlibrary.gov/library/research-files/address-committee -platform-and-resolutions-democratic-national-convention?documentid=NA& pagenumber=1.

Archival and Collected Material

Presidential Papers

Dwight D. Eisenhower Presidential Library and Museum,
Abilene, Kansas
Eisenhower, Dwight D. *The Papers of Dwight David Eisenhower.* Vol. 14, *The Presidency: The Middle Way.* Baltimore: Johns Hopkins University Press, 1970.
Ann Whitman File, Administration Series
Frederic Morrow Papers
Maxwell Rabb Papers

Harry S. Truman Presidential Library and Museum,
Independence, Missouri
General File, Negro File
Papers of George M. Elsey
Papers of Philleo Nash
President's Committee on Civil Rights (PCCR) General Correspondence
President's Secretary's Files
Robert L. Dennison Files
White House Central File: Official File (OF)

JOHN F. KENNEDY PRESIDENTIAL LIBRARY AND MUSEUM,
BOSTON, MASSACHUSETTS
Harris Wofford Papers
Pre-Presidential Papers. Senate Files
President's Office Files
White House Central Subject File, Executive (WHCSF-E)
White House Central Subject File, General (WHCSF-G)

LYNDON BAINES JOHNSON PRESIDENTIAL LIBRARY AND MUSEUM, AUSTIN, TEXAS
Administrative History of Veterans Administration
Alfred B. Fitt Papers
Office Files of Harry McPherson
Office Files of Lee C. White
President's Committee on Equal Opportunity in the Armed Forces (PCEOAF)

Recordings
James Cannon/Ben Bradlee interview with Senator John F. Kennedy, January 5, 1960.
    MR2008-18, John F. Kennedy Presidential Library and Museum, University of Massachusetts Boston, Boston, MA. www.jfklibrary.org.
Recording of Telephone Conversation between Lyndon B. Johnson and Richard Russell, June 6, 1966, 8:05 PM, Citation #10204, Recordings and Transcripts of Conversations and Meetings, Lyndon Baines Johnson Library and Museum, The University of Texas at Austin, Austin, TX. lbjlibrary.org.
Recording of Telephone Conversation between Lyndon Johnson and Robert McNamara, 13 August 1964, Conversation WH6408-19-4913, *Presidential Recordings Digital Edition*. Edited by David G. Coleman, Kent B. Germany, Ken Hughes, Guian A. McKee, and Marc J. Selverstone. Charlottesville: University of Virginia Press, 2014. http://prde.upress.virginia.edu/conversations/4000757.
Recording of Telephone Conversation between Lyndon Johnson and Robert McNamara, November 14, 1964. WH6411.20, LBJ Library.
Recording of Telephone Conversation between Lyndon B. Johnson and Robert McNamara, November 24, 1964, 7:20AM." Citation #6471, Recordings and Transcripts of Conversations and Meetings, LBJ Library.
Recording of Telephone Conversation between Robert Kennedy and President John F. Kennedy, March 1963, Cassette E (Side 1), 14A.2, Telephone Recordings, Papers of John F. Kennedy President's Office Files Presidential Recordings.
Welles, Orson. *Orson Welles Commentaries*, Lilly Library, Indiana University, Bloomington, Indiana.
    July 28, 1946, Welles mss, LMC 2009.
    August 4, 1946, Welles mss, LMC 2009.
    August 11, 1946, Welles mss, LMC 2009.
    August 18, 1946, Welles mss, LMC 2009.
    August 25, 1946, Welles mss, LMC 2009.

University Archives: Other Papers and Collections

CLEMSON UNIVERSITY LIBRARIES, CLEMSON, SOUTH CAROLINA
Strom Thurmond Collection

MISSISSIPPI STATE UNIVERSITY LIBRARIES, STARKVILLE, MISSISSIPPI
John C. Stennis Collection

UNIVERSITY OF ARKANSAS LIBRARIES, FAYETTEVILLE, ARKANSAS
Billy James Hargis Papers
J. William Fulbright Papers

UNIVERSITY OF GEORGIA LIBRARIES, ATHENS, GEORGIA
Richard B. Russell Papers

UNIVERSITY OF MISSISSIPPI LIBRARIES, OXFORD, MISSISSIPPI
James O. Eastland Collection
Thomas G. Abernathy Collection

Secondary Sources

"About Fred Hechinger." The Hechinger Report. https://hechingerreport.org/about
-fred-hechinger.

Abrams, Elliot, and Andrew J. Bacevich. "A Symposium on Citizenship and Military
Service." *Parameters* 31, no. 2 (Summer 2001): 18–22.

Allison, William Thomas. *Military Justice in Vietnam: The Rule of Law in an American
War.* Lawrence: University Press of Kansas, 2007.

Altschuler, Glenn C., and Stuart M. Blumin. *The GI Bill: A New Deal for Veterans.* New
York: Oxford University Press, 2009.

Ambrose, Hugh. "Eisenhower and My Father, Stephen Ambrose." History News Network. George Washington University. https://historynewsnetwork.org/article/12
6907.

Ambrose, Stephen. *Duty, Honor, Country: A History of West Point.* Baltimore: Johns
Hopkins University Press, 1966.

———. *Eisenhower: Soldier and President.* New York: Simon & Schuster, 1990.

Anderson, Carol. *Eyes off the Prize: The United Nations and the African American
Struggle for Human Rights, 1944–1955.* New York: Cambridge University Press, 2011.

Appy, Christian G. *Patriots: The Vietnam War Remembered from All Sides.* New York:
Penguin Books, 2003.

Asp, David. "Abe Fortas." *The First Amendment Encyclopedia.* The John Seigenthaler
Chair of Excellence in First Amendment Studies, Middle Tennessee State University. www.mtsu.edu/first-amendment/article/1329/abe-fortas.

Ayers, Edward. *What Caused the Civil War? Reflections on the South and Southern History.* New York: Norton Books, 2005.

Bailey, Beth. *America's Army: Making the All-Volunteer Force.* Cambridge, MA: Belknap
Press, 2009.

Barnett, Louise. *Atrocity and American Military Justice in Southeast Asia: Trial by Army.*
New York: Routledge, 2010.

Baskir, Lawrence M., and William A. Strauss. *Chance and Circumstance: The Draft, The War, and The Vietnam Generation.* New York: Alfred A. Knopf, 1978.

Belknap, Michal. *The Vietnam War on Trial: The My Lai Massacre and the Court-Martial of Lieutenant Calley.* Lawrence: University Press of Kansas, 2002.

Beschloss, Michael R. *Reaching for Glory: Lyndon Johnson's Secret White House Tapes, 1964–1965.* New York: Touchstone, 2001.

Bilton, Michael, and Kevin Sim. *Four Hours in My Lai.* New York: Penguin Books, 1992.

Bogart, Leo. ed. *Project Clear: Social Research and the Desegregation of the United States Army.* New Brunswick, NJ: Transaction Books, 1991.

Bowers, William T., William M. Hammond, and George L. MacGarrigle. *Black Soldier, White Army: The 24th Infantry Regiment in Korea.* Washington, DC: Center of Military History, United States Army, 1996.

Bradley, Omar, and Clay Blair. *A General's Life.* New York: Simon and Schuster, 1983.

Branch, Taylor. *At Canaan's Edge: America in the King Years, 1965–68.* New York: Simon and Schuster, 2006.

Brauer, Carl. *John F. Kennedy and the Second Reconstruction.* New York: Columbia University Press, 1977.

Brownell, Herbert, and John P. Burke. *Advising Ike: The Memoirs of Attorney General Herbert Brownell.* Lawrence: University Press of Kansas, 1993.

Buckley, Gail. *American Patriots: The Story of Blacks in the Military from the Revolution to Desert Storm.* New York: Random House, 2001.

Buchanan, Scott. "Three Governors Controversy." New Georgia Encyclopedia, last modified October 5, 2021. www.georgiaencyclopedia.org/articles/government-politics/three-governors-controversy.

Byrd, W. Michael, and Linda A. Clayton. *An American Health Dilemma.* Vol. 2, *Race, Medicine, and Health Care in the United States, 1900–2000.* New York and London: Routledge, 2000.

Carter, Dan T. *The Politics of Rage: George Wallace, The Origins of the New Conservatism, and the Transformation of American Politics.* 2nd ed. Baton Rouge: Louisiana State Univeristy Press, 2000.

Cash, W. J. *The Mind of the South.* New York: Vintage Books, 1991.

"The Civic Life of Nathaniel Coley: Husband and Father." The Colley Papers, Center for Sacramento History. https://colley.omeka.net/exhibits/show/theciviclife/husbandandfather.

Child, Robert. *Immortal Valor: The Black Medal of Honor Winners of World War II.* New York: Osprey, 2022.

Clifford, Clark. *Counsel to the President: A Memoir.* New York: Random House, 1991.

Coffey, Justin P. *Spiro-Agnew and the Rise of the Republican Right.* Santa Barbara, CA: Prager, 2015.

Collins, Elizabeth A. "Red-Baiting Public Women: Gender, Loyalty, and Red Scare Politics." PhD diss., University of Illinois at Chicago, 2008 (Ann Arbor, MI: ProQuest LLC, 2011).

Collins, J. Lawton. *Lightning Joe: An Autobiography.* Novato, CA: Presidio Press, 1994.

Cook, James. *Carl Vinson: Patriarch of the Armed* Forces. Macon, GA: Mercer University Press, 2004.

Cutrer, Thomas W., and T. Michael Parrish, *Doris Miller, Pearl Harbor, and The Birth of the Civil Rights Movement*. College Station: Texas A&M University Press, 2018.

Daddis, Gregory A. *No Sure Victory: Measuring U.S. Army Effectiveness and Progress in the Vietnam War*. New York: Oxford University Press, 2011.

Dalfiume, Richard M. *Desegregation of the U.S. Armed Forces: Fighting on Two Fronts: 1939–1953*. Columbia: University of Missouri Press, 1975.

Dallek, Robert. *An Unfinished Life: John F, Kennedy, 1917–1963*. New York: Little, Brown and Company, 2003.

Daniels, Jonathan. *The Man of Independence*. Columbia: University of Missouri Press, 1998.

Davis, Deborah. *Guest of Honor: Booker T. Washington, Theodore Roosevelt, and the White House Dinner That Shocked a Nation*. New York: Atria Books, 2012.

Dawson, David Anthony. "The Impact of Project 100,000 on the Marine Corps." MA thesis, Kansas State University, 1994.

DiNicolo, Gina M. *The Black Panthers: A Story of Race, War, and Courage—the 761st Tank Battalion in World War II*. Yardley, PA: Westholme Publishing, 2014.

Dixon, Chris. *African Americans and the Pacific War, 1941–1945*. New York: Cambridge University Press, 2018.

Dolinar, Brian. *The Black Cultural Front: Black Writers and Artists of the Depression Generation*. Jackson: University Press of Mississippi, 2012.

Drea, Edward J. *McNamara, Clifford, and the Burdens of Vietnam: 1965–1969*. Washington, DC: Historical Office, Office of the Secretary of Defense, 2011.

Dubose, Carolyn P. *The Untold Story of Charles Diggs: The Public Figure, the Private Man*. Arlington, VA: Barton Publishing House, 1998.

Dudziak, Mary. *Cold War Civil Rights: Race and the Image of American Democracy*. Princeton, NJ: Princeton University Press, 2000.

Dyer, Thomas G. *Theodore Roosevelt and the Idea of Race*. Baton Rouge: Louisiana State University Press, 1980.

The Editors of *Encyclopedia Britannica*. "Bougainville Island." *Encyclopedia Britannica*. https://www.britannica.com/place/Bougainville-Island.

Eisenhower, Dwight D. *The White House Years: Mandate for Change, 1953–1956*. New York: Doubleday, 1963.

Equal Justice Initiative. "Lynching in America: Targeting Black Veterans." 2017. https://eji.org/reports/targeting-black-veterans.

"Eustace Mullins, Anti-Semitic Conspiracy Theorists, Dies at Age 86." *ADL*. February 4, 2010. www.adl.org/news/article/eustace-mullins-anti-semitic-conspiracy-theorist-dies-at-age-86.

Farrell, John. *Richard Nixon: The Life*. New York: Doubleday, 2017.

Ferrell, Robert H. *Off the Record: The Private Papers of Harry S. Truman*. Columbia: University of Missouri Press, 1997.

———. *Unjustly Dishonored: An African American Division in World War I*. Columbia: University of Missouri Press, 2011.

Flynn, George Q. *Lewis B. Hersey, Mr. Selective Service*. Chapel Hill: University of North Carolina Press, 1985.

Foner, Eric. *The Fiery Trial: Abraham Lincoln and American Slavery.* New York: Norton, 2010.

Foner, Jack D. *Blacks and the Military in American History.* New York: Prager, 1974.

"The Forgotten History of a Prison Uprising in Vietnam." *NPR*, August 29, 2018, Radio Diaries. www.npr.org/sections/codeswitch/2018/08/29/642617106/the-forgotten-history-of-a-prison-uprising-in-vietnam.

Franklin, John Hope. *The Militant South, 1860–1861.* Urbana: University of Illinois Press, 2002.

Frazier, Ian. "John Reed's Unblinking Stare." *American Scholar* 71, no. 3 (Summer 2002): 29–39.

Fredrickson, Kari. *The Dixiecrat Revolt and the end of the Solid South, 1932–1968.* Chapel Hill: University of North Carolina Press, 2001.

Fried, Richard M. *Nightmare in Red: The McCarthy Era in Perspective.* New York: Oxford University Press, 1990.

Friedman, Natalie. "Babette Deutsch." *Jewish Women: A Comprehensive Historical Encyclopedia.* February 27, 2009. Jewish Women's Archive. https://jwa.org/encyclopedia/article/deutsch-babette.

Gallagher, Gary W., and Alan T. Nolan. eds. *The Myth of the Lost Cause and Civil War History.* Bloomington: Indiana University Press, 2000.

Gamble, Vanessa Northington. *Making a Place for Ourselves: The Black Hospital Movement 1920–1945.* New York: Oxford University Press, 1995.

Gardner, Mark Lee. *Rough Riders: Theodore Roosevelt, His Cowboy Regiment, and the Immortal Charge Up San Juan Hill.* New York: William Morrow, 2016.

Gardner, Michael. *Harry Truman and Civil Rights: Moral Courage and Political Risks.* Carbondale: Southern Illinois University Press, 2002.

Gates Jr., Henry Louis. "Was Jackie Robinson Court-Martialed?" *The African Americans: Many Rivers to Cross with Henry Louis Gates, Jr.* PBS. www.pbs.org/wnet/african-americans-many-rivers-to-cross/history/was-jackie-robinson-court-martialed.

Gatewood Jr., Willard B. *Black Americans and the White Man's Burden: 1898–1903.* Urbana: University of Illinois Press, 1975.

———. *"SMOKED YANKEES" and the Struggle for Empire: Letters from Negro Soldiers, 1898–1902.* Fayetteville: University of Arkansas Press, 1987.

The Georgia Civil Rights Cold Cases Project. "Maceo Snipes." https://coldcases.emory.edu/maceo-snipes/#f2.

Gergel, Richard. *Unexampled Courage: The Blinding of Isaac Woodard and the Awakening of President Harry S. Truman and Judge J. Waties Waring.* New York: Sarah Crichton Books, 2019.

Geselbracht, Raymond H., ed. *The Civil Rights Legacy of Harry S. Truman.* Kirksville: Truman State University Press, 2007.

Gibran, Daniel K. *The 92nd Infantry Division and the Italian Campaign in World War II.* Jefferson, NC: McFarland, 2001.

Giglio, James. *The Presidency of John F. Kennedy.* Lawrence: University Press of Kansas, 1991.

Goldberg, Robert Alan. *Barry Goldwater.* New Haven, CT: Yale University Press, 1995.

Goldstein, Robert J. *Political Repression in Modern America: From 1870 to 1976*. Urbana: University of Illinois Press, 2001.

Goodwin, Doris Kearns. *The Bully Pulpit: Theodore Roosevelt, William Howard Taft, and the Golden Age of Journalism*. New York: Simon & Schuster, 2013.

———. *Leadership in Turbulent Times*. New York: Simon and Schuster, 2018.

———. *Lyndon Johnson and the American Dream*. New York: St. Martin's Press, 1991.

———. *No Ordinary Time: Franklin and Eleanor Roosevelt: The Home Front in World War II*. New York: Simon & Schuster, 1994.

Greenstein, Fred I. *The Hidden-Hand Presidency: Eisenhower as Leader*. New York: Basic Books, 1982.

Guglielmo, Thomas A. *Divisions: A New History of Racism and Resistance in America's World War II Military*. New York: Oxford University Press, 2021.

Halberstam, David. *The Coldest Winter: America and the Korean War*. New York: Hyperion Books, 2007.

Hamby, Alonzo. *Man of the People: A Life of Harry S. Truman*. New York: Oxford University Press, 1998.

Hamilton, Charles V. *Adam Clayton Powell Jr.: The Political Biography of an American Dilemma*. New York: Cooper Square Press, 2002.

Hansen, Susan D. "The Racial History of the U.S. Military Academies." *Journal of Blacks in Higher Education*, no. 26 (Winter 1999–2000): 111–116.

Hersh, Seymour. *My Lai 4: A Report on the Massacre and Its Aftermath*. New York: Random House, 1970.

Hervieux, Linda. *Forgotten: The Untold Story of D-Day's Black Heroes, at Home and at War*. New York: HarperCollins, 2016.

Hobbs, Allyson, Amy Davidson Sorkin, and Evan Osnos. "A Hundred Years Later, 'The Birth of a Nation' Hasn't Gone Away." *The New Yorker*, December 13, 2015. www.newyorker.com/culture/culture-desk/hundred-years-later-birth-nation-hasnt-gone-away.

Hoffman, Timothy J. "The Civil Rights Realignment: How Race Dominates Presidential Elections." *Political Analysis* 17, article 1 (2015): 1–22.

Hofstadter, Richard. *The Paranoid Style in American Politics and Other Essays*. With a new foreword by Sean Wilentz. New York: Vintage Books, 2008.

Honsa, Thomas P. "Doing the Job: The 1964 Desegregation of the Florida Army National Guard." *Florida Historical Quarterly* 87, no. 1 (Summer 2008): 50–70.

Humphrey, Hubert H. *The Education of a Public Man: My Life and Politics*. Minneapolis: University of Minnesota Press, 1991.

Inbolden, William. *Religion and American Foreign Policy, 1945–1960: The Soul of Containment*. Cambridge: Cambridge University Press, 2008.

Jager, Sheila Miyoshi. *Brothers at War: The Unending Conflict in Korea*. New York: Norton, 2013.

"James C. Evans, 1925." MIT Black History website. 1925. www.blackhistory.mit.edu/archive/james-c-evans-.

Jefferson, Robert F. *93rd Infantry Division (1942–1946)*. BlackPast.org. https://www.blackpast.org/african-american-history/u-s-ninety-third-infantry-division-1942-1946.

———. *Fighting for Hope: African American Troops of the 93rd Infantry Division in World War II and Postwar America*. Baltimore: John Hopkins University Press, 2008.

Jensen, Geoffrey W. "It Cut Both Ways: The Cold War and Civil Rights Reform Within the Military, 1945–1968." PhD diss., University of Arkansas, 2009.

———, ed. *The Routledge Handbook of the History of Race and the American Military*. New York: Routledge, 2016.

Jensen, Geoffrey W., and Matthew M. Stith, eds. *Beyond the Quagmire: New Interpretations of the Vietnam War*. Denton: University of North Texas Press, 2019.

Jian, Chen. *China's Road to the Korean War*. New York: Columbia University Press, 1994.

Jones, Jeffrey M. "The Short Answer: Who Had the Lowest Gallup Presidential Job Approval Rating." Gallup. https://news.gallup.com/poll/272765/lowest-gallup-presidential-job-approval-rating.aspx.

Katagiri, Yasuhiro. *The Mississippi State Sovereignty Commission: Civil Rights and States' Rights*. Jackson: University of Mississippi Press, 2001.

Katznelson, Ira. *Fear Itself*. New York: Norton, 2013.

———. *When Affirmative-Action Was White: An Untold History of Racial Inequality in Twentieth-Century America*. New York: Norton, 2005.

Kestnbaum, Meyer. "Citizenship and Compulsory Military Service: The Revolutionary Origins of Conscription in the United States." *Armed Forces & Society* 27, no. 1 (Fall 2000): 7–36.

Kickler, Troy. "Albion Tourgee (1838–1905)." *NorthCarolinahistory.org: An Online Encyclopedia*. North Carolina History Project. https://northcarolinahistory.org/encyclopedia/albion-tourgee-1838–1905

Kipling, Rudyard. "The White Man's Burden." Modern History Sourcebook, Fordham University. https://sourcebooks.fordham.edu/mod/kipling.asp.

Knauer. Christine. *Let Us Fight as Free Men: Black Soldiers and Civil Rights*. Philadelphia: University of Pennsylvania Press, 2014.

Korda, Michael. *Ike: An American Hero*. New York: HarperCollins, 2008.

Kryder, Daniel. *Divided Arsenal: Race and the American State During World War II*. New York: Cambridge University Press, 2000.

Laurence, Janice, and Peter F. Ramsberger. *Low-Aptitude Men in the Military: Who Profits, Who Pays?* New York: Praeger, 1991.

Lassiter, Matthew D. "Benjamin Muse (1898–1986)." *Encyclopedia Virginia*. Virginia Humanities, 28 February 2014. www.encyclopediavirginia.org/Muse_Benjamin_1898–1986.

Lee, Ulysses. *The Employment of Negro Troops*. Honolulu: University Press of the Pacific, 2004 [Washington, DC: Government Printing Office, 1966].

Lentz-Smith, Adriane. *Freedom Struggles: African Americans and World War I*. Cambridge, MA: Harvard University Press, 2009.

Leuchtenburg, William E. *The White House Looks South: Franklin D. Roosevelt, Harry S. Truman, Lyndon B. Johnson*. Baton Rouge: Louisiana State University Press, 2005.

Lewis, Adrian. *The American Culture of War*. 3rd ed. New York: Routledge, 2018.

Love, Spencie. *One Blood: The Death and Resurrection of Charles R. Drew*. Chapel Hill: University of North Carolina Press, 1996.

Lynch, Michael E. *Edward M. Almond and the US Army: From the 92nd Infantry Division to the X Corps.* Lexington: University Press of Kentucky, 2019.

MacGregor Jr., Morris J. *Integration of the Armed Forces, 1940–1965.* Washington, DC: Center of Military History, United States Army, 1981.

MacGregor Jr., Morris J., and Bernard C. Nalty, eds. *Blacks in the United States Armed Forces: Basic Documents.* 13 vols. Wilmington, DE: Scholarly Resources, 1977.

MacLean, Nancy. *Behind The Mask of Chivalry: The Making of the Second Ku Klux Klan.* New York: Oxford University Press, 1994.

MacPherson, Myra. *Long Time Passing: Vietnam and the Haunted Generation.* New ed. Bloomington: Indiana University Press, 2001.

Manchester, William. *American Caesar: Douglas MacArthur: 1880–1964.* New York: Back Bay Books, 2008.

Marks, Franklin David. "The Efforts Made to Achieve Equal Opportunity in the Armed Forces, with a Special Emphasis on Development of the Program to Obtain More Off-Base, Open-Housing." MA thesis, George Washington University, 1970.

Marquardt, Virginia Hagelstein. "'New Masses' and John Reed Club Artists, 1926–1936: Evolution of Ideology, Subject Matter, and Style." *Journal of Decorative and Propaganda Arts* 12 (Spring 1989): 56–75.

Martin, Harold H., and Matthew B. Ridgway. *Soldier: The Memoirs of Matthew B. Ridgway.* New York: Harper & Brothers, 1956.

Maxwell, Jeremy P. *Brotherhood in Combat: How African Americans Found Equality in Korea and Vietnam.* Norman: University of Oklahoma Press, 2018.

McCullough, David. *Truman.* New York: Simon and Schuster, 1992.

McGee Smith, Charlene E. *Tuskegee Airman: The Biography of Charles E. McGee: Air Force Fighter Combat Record Holder.* Boston: Branden Publishing Company, 2000.

McLaurin, Melton A. *The Marines of Montford Point: America's First Black Marines.* Chapel Hill: University of North Carolina Press, 2007.

McMillen, Neil R. *The Citizens' Council: Organized Resistance to the Second Reconstruction, 1954–1964.* Champaign–Urbana: University of Illinois Press, 1994.

McNamara, Robert S. *The Essence of Security: Reflections in Office.* New York: Harper & Row, 1968.

McPherson, James M. *Tried by War: Abraham Lincoln as Commander in Chief.* New York: Penguin Press, 2008.

Meacham, Jon. *His Truth Is Marching On: John Lewis and the Power of Hope.* New York: Random House, 2020.

———. *The Soul of America: The Battle for Our Better Angels.* New York: Random House, 2018.

"Medal of Honor: Sergeant Henry Johnson." Army.MIL Features. www.army.mil /medalofhonor/johnson.

Mershon, Sherie, and Steven Schlossman. *Foxholes & Color Lines: Desegregating the U.S. Armed Forces.* Baltimore: Johns Hopkins University Press, 1998.

Miller, Edward H. *Nut Country: Right-Wing Dallas and the Birth of the Southern Strategy.* Chicago: University of Chicago Press, 2015.

Millett, Allan. *Semper Fidelis: The History of the United States Marine Corps.* Rev. and expanded ed. New York: Free Press, 1991.

Moore, Brenda L. *To Serve My Country, To Serve My Race*. New York: New York University Press, 1996.

Morris, Edmund. *Theodore Rex*. New York: Random House, Revised Edition, 2002.

Morrow, Curtis James. *What's a Commie Ever Done to Black People: A Korean War Memoir of Fighting in the U.S. Army's Last All Negro Unit*. Jefferson, NC: McFarland, 1997.

Morrow, E. Frederic. *Black Man in the White House*. New York: Coward-McCann, Inc., 1963.

Moye, J. Todd. *Freedom Flyers: The Tuskegee Airmen of World War II*. New York: Oxford University Press, 2010.

Moynihan, Daniel Patrick. *Miles to Go: A Personal History of Social Policy*. Cambridge, MA: Harvard University Press, 1996.

Muehlenbeck, Philip E. *Betting on the Africans: John F. Kennedy's Courting of African Nationalist Leaders*. New York: Oxford University Press, 2012.

Myers, Andrew H. *Black, White & Olive Drab*. Charlottesville: University of Virginia Press, 2006.

Myrdal, Karl Gunnar. *An American Dilemma: The Negro Problem and Modern Democracy*. Vol. 1. New Brunswick, NJ: Transaction Publishers, 1996.

Naftali, Tim. "Ronald Reagan's Long-Hidden Racist Conversation with Richard Nixon." *The Atlantic*, July 30, 2019. www.theatlantic.com/ideas/archive/2019/07/ronald -reagans-racist-conversation-richard-nixon/595102.

Nalty, Bernard C. *Strength for the Fight*. New York: Free Press, 1986.

Nelson, Anna Kasten. "Anna Rosenberg, an 'Honorary Man.'" *Journal of Military History* 68 (January 2004): 133–161.

Nichols, David A. *A Matter of Justice: Eisenhower and the Beginning of the Civil Rights Revolution*. New York: Simon & Schuster, 2007.

Nichols, Lee. *Breakthrough on the Color Front*. New York: Random House, 1954.

Olson, James C. *Stuart Symington: A Life*. Columbia: University of Missouri Press, 2003.

Ossad, Steven L. *Omar Nelson Bradley: America's GI General: 1893–1981*. Columbia: University of Missouri Press, 2017.

Pach, Chester, and Elmo Richardson. *The Presidency of Dwight D. Eisenhower*. Rev. ed. Lawrence: University Press of Kansas, 1991.

Palmer, Laura. "The General, at Ease: An Interview with Westmoreland." *MHQ: The Quarterly Journal of Military History* (Autumn 1988): 31–35.

Paradis, Michel. "The Lost Cause's Long Legacy." *The Atlantic*, June 26, 2020. www.the atlantic.com/ideas/archive/2020/06/the-lost-causes-long-legacy/613288.

Perlstein, Rick. *Nixonland: The Rise of a President and the Fracturing of America*. New York: Scribner, 2008.

Perret, Geoffrey. *Old Soldiers Never Die: The Life of Douglas MacArthur*. Holbrook, MA: Adams Media Corporation, 1996.

Perry, Barbara A. "How John F. Kennedy and Eleanor Roosevelt Went from Rivals to Allies." *Dallas Morning News*, August 30, 2020. https://www.dallasnews.com/opin ion/commentary/2020/08/30/how-john-kennedy-and-eleanor-roosevelt-went -from-rivals-to-allies.

Pfeffer, Paula P. *A. Phillip Randolph, Pioneer of the Civil Rights Movement*. Baton Rouge: Louisiana State University Press, 1990.

Phillips, Kimberly. *War! What Is It Good For? Black Freedom Struggles and the U.S. Military from World War II to Iraq*. Chapel Hill: University of North Carolina Press, 2012.

Pitch, Anthony. *The Last Lynching: How a Gruesome Mass Murder Rocked a Small Georgia Town*. New York: Skyhorse, 2016.

Powell Jr., Adam Clayton. *Adam by Adam: The Autobiography of Adam Clayton Powell Jr*. New York: Kensington Books, 2002.

Quarles, Benjamin. *The Negro in the American Revolution*. New York: Norton, 1961.

Rainwater, Lee, and William L. Yancey. *The Moynihan Report and the Politics of Controversy*. Cambridge, MA: MIT Press, 1967.

Reeves, Richard. *President Kennedy: Profile of Power*. New York: Simon & Schuster, 1993.

Rice, Alan. "Black Troops Were Welcome in Britain, but Jim Crow Wasn't: The Race Riot of One Night in June 1943." *The Conversation* (June 21, 2018). https://getpocket.com/explore/item/black-troops-were-welcome-in-britain-but-jim-crow-wasn-t-the-race-riot-of-one-night-in-june-1943?utm_source=pocket-newtab.

Ridgway, Matthew. *The Korean War*. New York: Doubleday, 1967.

Robinson, Jackie. *First Class Citizenship: The Civil Rights Letters of Jackie Robinson*. Edited by Michael G. Long. New York: Holt and Company, 2007.

Rolph, Stephanie R. *Resisting Equality: The Citizens' Council, 1954–1968*. Baton Rouge: Louisiana State University Press, 2018.

Roosevelt, Theodore. *The Rough Riders*. New York: Charles Scribner's Sons, 1899.

Rosenberg, Jonathan. *How Far the Promised Land? World Affairs and the American Civil Rights Movement from the First World War to Vietnam*. Princeton, NJ: Princeton University Press, 2005.

Rozek, Stacy A. "'The First Daughter of the Land': Alice Roosevelt as Presidential Celebrity, 1902–1906." *Presidential Studies Quarterly* 19, no. 1, Part I: American Foreign Policy for the 1990s; and Part II: T. R., Wilson, and the Progressive Era, 1901–1919 (Winter 1989): 51–70.

Rushay Jr., Samuel W. "Harry Truman's History Lessons." *Prologue Magazine* 41, no. 1 (Spring 2009). www.archives.gov/publications/prologue/2009/spring/truman-history.html.

Russell, Sir William Howard. *Pictures of Southern Life, Social, Political, and Military*. New York: James A. Gregory. 1861.

Salazar, Jaime. *Mutiny of Rage: The 1917 Camp Logan Riots and Buffalo Soldiers in Houston*. Lanham, MD: Prometheus Books, 2021.

Sammons, Jeffrey T., and John H. Morrow Jr. *Harlem's Rattlers and the Great War: The Undaunted 369th Regiment and the African American Quest for Equality*. Lawrence: University Press of Kansas, 2015.

Schneller Jr., Robert J. *Blue & Gold and Black: Racial Integration of the U.S. Naval Academy*. College Station: Texas A&M University Press, 2008.

Schoenwald, Jonathan M. *A Time for Choosing: The Rise of Modern American Conservatism*. New York: Oxford University Press, 2001.

Shakespeare, William. *Henry IV, Part 2*. Edited by Barbara A. Mowat and Paul Werstine. New York: Simon & Schuster, 2020.

Shapley, Deborah. *Promise and Power: The Life and Times of Robert McNamara*. Boston: Little Brown and Company, 1993.

Shermer, Elizabeth Tandy. ed. *Barry Goldwater and the Remaking of the American Political Landscape*. Tucson: University of Arizona Press, 2013.

Sherwood, John Darrell. *Black Sailor, White Navy: Racial Unrest in the Fleet during the Vietnam War Era*. New York: New York University Press, 2007.

Small, Melvin. *The Presidency of Richard Nixon*. Lawrence: University Press of Kansas, 1999.

Smith, Jean Edward. *Eisenhower in War and Peace*. New York: Random House, 2012.

Starr, Paul. *The Discarded Army: Veterans After Vietnam*. New York: Charterhouse, 1973.

Steil, Benn. *The Marshall Plan: Dawn of the Cold War*. Oxford University Press, 2018.

Sticht, Thomas G., William Armstrong, Daniel Hickey, and John Caylor. eds. *Cast-Off Youth: Policy and Training Methods from the Military Experience*. New York: Praeger, 1987.

Streitmatter, Rodger. *Raising Her Voice: African-American Women Journalists Who Changed History*. Lexington: University Press of Kentucky, 1994.

Sutton, Carl D. "The Military Mission Against Off-Base Racial Discrimination: A Study in Administrative Behavior." PhD diss., Indiana University, 1973.

Taylor, Jon E. *Freedom to Serve: Truman, Civil Rights, and Executive Order 9981*. New York: Routledge, 2013.

Taylor, William A. *Every Citizen a Soldier: The Campaign for Universal Military Training After World War II*. College Station: Texas A&M University Press, 2014.

———. *Military Service and American Democracy: From World War II to the Iraq and Afghanistan Wars*. Lawrence: University Press of Kansas, 2016.

Thiesen, William H. "The Long Blue Line: Merle Smith—The First African American Graduate of the Coast Guard Academy." Coast Guard Academy. Coast Guard: Coast Guard Compass Blog. www.mycg.uscg.mil/News/Article/2937583/the-long-blue-line-a-look-at-the-coast-guard-academy-producing-minority-coast-g.

Timmons, Robert. "'Trailblazers' Inducted into Hall of Fame, September 14, 2017." United States Army website. www.army.mil/article/193852/trailblazers_inducted_into_hall_of_fame.

Toll, Ian W. *Pacific Crucible: War at Sea in the Pacific, 1941–1942*. New York: Norton & Company, 2011.

———. *Six Frigates: The Epic History of the Founding of the U.S. Navy*. New York: Norton, 2006.

Truman, Harry S. *The Memoirs of Harry S. Truman*. Vol. 2, *Years of Trial and Hope, 1946–1953*. London: Hodder & Stoughton, 1956.

Tyson, Timothy B. *The Blood of Emmett Till*. New York: Simon & Schuster, 2017.

Van Atta, Dale. *With Honor: Melvin Laird in War, Peace, and Politics*. Madison: University of Wisconsin Press, 2008.

Van Buskirk, Judith L. *Standing in Their Own Light: African American Patriots in the American Revolution*. Norman: University of Oklahoma Press, 2017.

Walter, John C. "Congressman Carl Vinson and Franklin D. Roosevelt: Naval Preparedness and the Coming of World War II, 1932–1940." *Georgia Historical Quarterly* 64, no. 3 (Fall 1980): 294–305.

Weaver, John D. *The Brownsville Raid*. College Station: Texas A&M University Press, 1992.

Weiner, Greg. *American Burke: The Uncommon Liberalism of Daniel Patrick Moynihan*. Lawrence: University Press of Kansas, 2016.

Weismen, Steven. ed. *Daniel Patrick Moynihan: A Portrait in Letters of An American Visionary*. New York: PublicAffairs, 2010.

Westheider, James E. *The African American Experience in Vietnam: Brothers in Arms*. Lanham, MD: Rowman & Littlefield, 2008.

———. *Fighting on Two Fronts: African Americans and the Vietnam War*. New York: New York University Press, 1997.

Wexler, Laura. *Fire in a Canebrake: The Last Mass Lynching in America*. New York: Scribner, 2003.

White, Walter. *A Man Called White: The Autobiography of Walter White*. Athens: University of Georgia Press, 1995.

Williams, Chad. *Torchbearers of Democracy: African American Soldiers in the World War I Era*. Chapel Hill: University of North Carolina Press.

Williams, Juan. *Thurgood Marshall: American Revolutionary*. New York: Three Rivers Press, 1998.

Wilson, Woodrow. *The Messages and Papers of Woodrow Wilson*. Vol. 1. Edited by Albert Shaw. New York: The Review of Reviews Corporation, 1924.

Wofford, Harris. *Of Kennedys & Kings: Making Sense of the Sixties*. Pittsburgh: University of Pittsburgh Press, 1992.

Wood, Graeme. "Into the Psyche of Eustace Mullins." *The Atlantic*, September 23, 2010. www.theatlantic.com/entertainment/archive/2010/09/into-the-psyche-of-eustace -mullins/63457.

Woods, Jeff. *Black Struggle, Red Scare: Segregation and Anti-Communism in the South, 1948–1968*. Baton Rouge: Louisiana State University Press, 2004.

———. *Richard B. Russell: Southern Nationalism and American Foreign Policy*. New York: Rowman & Littlefield, 2007.

Woods, Randall B. *LBJ: Architect of American Ambition*. New York: Free Press, 2006.

———. *Prisoners of Hope: Lyndon B. Johnson, the Great Society, and the Limits of Liberalism*. New York: Basic Books.

———. *The Quest for Identity*. New York: Cambridge University Press, 2005.

Wynn, Neil A. *The African American Experience During World War II*. New York: Rowman & Littlefield, 2011.

Yared, Ephrem. *92nd Infantry Division (1917–1919, 1942–1945)*. BlackPast.org. https:// www.blackpast.org/african-american-history/92nd-infantry-division-1917-1919 -1942-1945-0.

Yarmolinsky, Adam. *The Military Establishment: Its Impacts on American Society*. New York: Harper & Row, 1971.

Yockelson, Mitchell. *The Paratrooper Generals: Matthew Ridgway, Maxwell Taylor, and the American Airborne from D-Day Through Normandy*. Lanham, MD: Stackpole Books, 2020.

Index